James Baldwin Now

James Baldwin Now

EDITED BY

Dwight A. McBride

New York University Press

NEW YORK AND LONDON

NEW YORK UNIVERSITY PRESS
New York and London

Library of Congress Cataloging-in-Publication Data
James Baldwin now / edited by Dwight A. McBride.
p.   cm.
Includes bibliographical references (p.   ) and index.
ISBN 0-8147-5617-4 (alk. paper)
ISBN 0-8147-5618-2 (pbk. : alk. paper)
1. Baldwin, James, 1924–   —Criticism and interpretation.
2. Modernism (Literature)—United States. 3. Afro-Americans in
literature. 4. Gay men in literature. 5. Exiles in literature.
6. Race in literature. 7. Sex in literature.   I. McBride, Dwight A.
PS3552.A45 Z74 1999
818'.5409—dc21   99-6546
[B]   CIP

New York University Press books are printed on acid-free paper,
and their binding materials are chosen for strength and durability.

Manufactured in the United States of America

10 9 8 7 6 5 4 3 2 1

Contents

     James Baldwin   393
         Jeffrey W. Hole

     Contributors   *411*
     Index   *415*

Acknowledgments

Authors of any scholarly endeavor, no matter how modest, inevitably incur many debts during the production of their work. This collection of essays certainly represents no exception in this regard.

James Baldwin Now would never have been possible without the support, advice, and encouragement of many people who proved in so many ways that they believed in me and in the importance of this work. For all of their help, understanding, kindness, and a place to lay my head when I was in town, I thank the following friends: Darrell Darrisaw and Fred Haug in Los Angeles; Lisa B. Thompson, Jay Louser, and Allen Nielsen in the San Francisco Bay area; Bob E. Myers and David Blackmore in New York; Andrew Dechet in London; and Olivier Leymarie in Paris.

I also owe a great debt of gratitude to the following friends and colleagues, who constitute a scholarly community for me: Jennifer Devere Brody (George Washington University), whose expert reading of this manuscript helped me clarify the value of this undertaking; Chris Cunningham (Drew University); Karen Lang (University of Southern California); Jonathan Holloway (Yale University); Jeffrey Shoulson (University of Miami); William R. Handley (University of Southern California); Charles Rowell (University of Virginia); Lindon Barrett (University of California, Irvine); Michelle M. Wright (Carnegie Mellon University); Devon Carbado (University of California, Los Angeles [UCLA] Law); Rachel Lee, Anne K. Mellor, Valerie Smith, Emily Apter, and Barbara Packer (UCLA); and the entire administrative staff of the UCLA English Department, especially Jeanette Gilkerson and Doris Wang.

I also thank the following colleagues and institutions that have supported and sustained me during the time in which this work was accomplished: the University of California Office of the President, for a year of postdoctoral study; the UCLA English Department; the National Endowment for the Humanities, for a summer stipend; Raymond Paredes, UCLA associate vice-chancellor for academic development, for providing funds for research assistance; the University of Pittsburgh Department of English; the University of Pittsburgh Office of the Dean of the Faculty of Arts and Sciences; and Jack Daniel, vice-provost at University of Pittsburgh, for providing funds for research assistance.

As always, I owe a great debt of gratitude to my sister and brother-in-law, Makelia McBride-Hampton and Willie Hampton, for their love and support, which has always been unfailing. And to my parents, James and Bettye McBride, my debt is too deep to be repaid.

The bulk of this work was completed while I was on the faculty of the University of Pittsburgh's Department of English. Many thanks to all my colleagues there who provided such an intellectually fecund and collegial community in which to work. Among them, I especially thank the following for their time, friendship, and support of me and of my work: David Bartholomae (my department chair), Jonathan Arac, Toi Derricotte, Ronald Judy, Eric Clarke, Paul Bové, Marcia Landy, Jane Feuer, Brenda Berrian, Fiona Cheong, Lynn Emmanuel, Catherine Gammon, the late Carol Kay, Colin MacCabe, Donald Petesch, Shalani Puri, Nancy Glazener, and Richard Tobias. The staff of the University of Pittsburgh English department has also been extraordinary and unflagging in its support. Many thanks to Annette, Gerri, Maria, Connie, Peg, Pat, Sue, and Sandy. I am also deeply grateful to my editor at New York University Press, Eric Zinner. His support and guidance have been remarkable!

Finally, it remains to thank five people who helped give life to this project before it was ever articulated *as* a project. Among the first people to recognize the importance of undertaking this work at this particular time were Wahneema Lubiano (Duke University), Hortense Spillers (Cornell University), and Toni Morrison (Princeton University). I am thankful to them for their support and encouragement. And finally, none of this would have been possible without the very able research assistance of Neina Chambers at UCLA and Jeffrey W. Hole at the University of Pittsburgh. Their work was absolutely invaluable to this project.

Introduction

"How Much Time Do You Want for Your Progress?" New Approaches to James Baldwin

Dwight A. McBride

The essays collected here explore not only new ways of thinking about the life and work of James Baldwin, one of the most prolific and influential African American writers ever to live, but also open up new ways in which his work helps us understand many of our contemporary societal problems. Baldwin's life was committed to struggle. He resisted hegemonies in their myriad forms by fighting for racial equality, against elitism both in the United States and abroad, and against the forces of heterosexism both inside and outside the black community. Following the logic of the old Negro spiritual, he once said, "If trouble don't last always, neither does power." And he was unrelenting in his critique of power, as many of the essays here demonstrate. Written as they are by students and scholars who are still in the early stages of their careers, and who either were trained or are being trained in the academy during a time when interdisciplinary work and cultural studies are at what seems their nadir, these essays offer perspectives which are unique, in that they are not shackled by the traditional modes of conducting scholarship but rather are informed by a host of approaches that provide fresh, innovative analyses, distinguishing themselves from much of the earlier work on Baldwin. The company of critics assembled here, composed of a political scientist, sociologists, literary critics, and communicationists, come to Baldwin with different concerns, to be sure. But whatever their critical orientations or questions, all demonstrate that their thinking has been altered by the challenges that Baldwin's work poses.

Given the advent of cultural studies in the academy—with its focus on interdisciplinarity or transdisciplinarity, critical theory, and an ever-broadening notion of "culture"—it seems more possible today than ever before to engage Baldwin in all of the complexity he represents to critical inquiry, considering the various roles he has occupied. Baldwin was no more content to be simply a black writer, a gay writer, or an activist than he was to write exclusively in the genre of the novel, drama, poetry, or the essay. Baldwin was, and continues to be, many things to many people. To paraphrase Walt Whitman (in another context), Baldwin is large; he contains multitudes! And Baldwin has spoken to most every issue of great importance in our time. Scholarship, however, has often tended to relegate Baldwin to one or the other of these identity categories. This collection, by design, encourages us to move our thinking, not only of Baldwin but of African American cultural studies generally, in a direction that speaks to the intricate social positions African Americans occupy. Cultural studies work has proven it is possible to think critically about African Americans and African American culture without simply essentializing the category of blackness or appealing to outmoded and problematic notions of black authenticity.

Baldwin himself knew all too well the pitfalls of being at the margins of many identities that were thought to be exclusive (gay and black and American, for example). Sometimes he did the dance of the margins elegantly, but at other times his grace was not adequate to the task. Those times he faltered were emblematic of the dangers of privileging—in our thinking about African Americans—the category of race over all other forms of difference. Baldwin knew all too well this was precisely the move that black antiracist discourse required of him if he was to have the kind of political efficacy with and for African Americans that he ultimately did have in his lifetime.[1]

With the advent of cultural studies, it is finally possible to understand Baldwin's vision of and for humanity in its complexity, locating him not as exclusively gay, black, expatriate, activist, or the like but as an intricately negotiated amalgam of all of those things, which had to be constantly tailored to fit the circumstances in which he was compelled to articulate himself. That is one of the chief goals of this volume of essays. And though the collection is divided into similar categories for the sake of convenience in organization, the diligent reader will soon find that each of the essays in this volume moves to problematize the very category under which I have placed it. This quality of working within a category of analysis to explode it and to integrate it with other ways of seeing, reading, and analyzing will, I trust, serve as a road map for future critical practice in Baldwin scholarship and in African American cultural studies generally.

Part I of this book, "Baldwin and Race," begins with Marlon B. Ross's masterful essay "White Fantasies of Desire: Baldwin and the Racial Identities of Sexuality," which he opens by discussing the deceptively simple problem of whiteness in *Giovanni's Room*. While everybody assumed Baldwin's homosexuality when he wrote *Giovanni's Room*, the fact that it is also a novel about white characters seems to have presented no challenge to Baldwin's racial identity. This foregrounds Ross's discussion of whiteness and sexuality in Baldwin and in the responses of his critics to this work. Ross's analysis is conducted with a degree of subtlety rarely found in critical work on this topic.

Ross's essay transitions nicely to Rebecca Aanerud's piece, "Now More than Ever: James Baldwin and the Critique of White Liberalism," which explores Baldwin's complicated relationship to and critiques of white liberalism. The essay begins with a discussion of the contradictory role of white liberalism as an "antiracist" social category and then positions Baldwin's work in light of that category. Aanerud maintains that Baldwin's critique of white liberalism and white liberals, as well as his use of concepts such as "personal incoherence," "missionary complex," "white liberal as an affliction," and "white guilt," offers an ideal opportunity to evaluate structural and individual responses to racism within a liberal state.

Concluding Part I of the book is Lawrie Balfour's "Finding the Words: Baldwin, Race Consciousness, and Democratic Theory." While much of the critical attention generated by Baldwin's essay "Everybody's Protest Novel" has focused on the question of whether Baldwin's own novels escape his complaints about protest fiction, Balfour revisits the essay to demonstrate that at the same time that Baldwin demolishes the literary value of the protest novel, he also demands an alternative standard for moral and political critique. Baldwin's search, Balfour observes, is for a language to express the wrongs of racial injustice without losing sight of the complicated

4 DWIGHT A. MCBRIDE

workings of race consciousness in American society. Balfour contends that "the ease with which the formal equality guaranteed by the civil rights legislation of the 1960s has been deployed against the purposes of the Civil Rights movement indicates the urgency of Baldwin's warnings about the dangers of disconnecting democratic principles from the lives of the women and men who are expected to abide by them."

Part II, "Baldwin and Sexuality," opens with William J. Spurlin's essay "Culture, Rhetoric, and Queer Identity: James Baldwin and the Identity Politics of Race and Sexuality." Spurlin reexamines Baldwin's literary and cultural reception in the early 1960s in the dominant culture and his reception later in the decade in the U.S. Black Power movement, marking both receptions as themselves interpretive acts. Spurlin focuses on a specific, historicized representation of homosexuality by reading what he calls the "cultural lenses" and "rhetorical practices" that informed interpretations of queer and African American identity in Baldwin and in his work in the 1960s. He sets these in the context of broader social and cultural discourses on homosexuality and race at the time and explores their contemporary social and political implications.

Following Spurlin's essay is Nicholas Boggs's treatment of a rarely discussed text by Baldwin, his children's book *Little Man Little Man: A Story of Childhood*, on an even more rarely discussed topic—a queer, African Americanist exploration of childhood subjectivity. Boggs instructs us that the queer trajectory of Baldwin's text, which is accompanied by the illustrations of Baldwin's close friend Yoran Cazac, can be located in its veiled attention to the lives of black children whose identifications and desires fall outside of the heavily policed boundaries of white hetero-normativity. Yet throughout the text of *Little Man Little Man*, Baldwin and Cazac complicate W. E. B. Du Bois's famous formulation of double consciousness by queering the "twoness" of the black American experience into the triple consciousness of being black, American, and queer.

In a return to one of Baldwin's canonical texts, James A. Dievler's essay "Sexual Exiles: James Baldwin and *Another Country*," concluding Part II of this book, contends that the novel portrays the devastation wrought in a country dominated by a categorically impoverished sexual culture and offers both a view of and the means of transport to "another country," beyond the confines of the narrow identity categories that imprisoned Americans in the immediate postwar period. According to Dievler, Baldwin asserts in *Another Country* that all these categories are intertwined and are most effectively transcended through love-based sex—sex that is itself taking place beyond the socially constructed senses of sexuality that have dominated the twentieth century. Dievler writes that Baldwin is "advocating a postcategorical, poststructural concept of sexuality that we might call 'postsexuality.' And he [Baldwin] believes it is only in such a 'country' that the other categories (race, gender) will cease to exist as well."

Beginning Part III on "Baldwin and the Transatlantic" is James Darsey's essay "Baldwin's Cosmopolitan Loneliness." Darsey takes seriously Baldwin's claim that he was a "transatlantic commuter" and the implications that term has for reading Baldwin's work. This is the sensibility that Darsey brings to Baldwin's nuanced analysis of oppression in his famous essay "Everybody's Protest Novel."

Continuing with this transatlantic theme and furthering the analysis of "Everybody's Protest Novel" is Michelle M. Wright's essay "'Alas, Poor Richard!': Transatlantic Baldwin, the Politics of Forgetting, and the Project of Modernity." Why, Wright queries at the beginning of her essay, was "Everybody's Protest Novel" the first essay that Baldwin finished and published while in Paris? She contends that by leaving New York, Baldwin was already expanding his understanding of the African American Subject beyond the mere geographical confines of the "Negro question." "By emphasizing his move to Paris as a move *from* New York, and by splitting with [Richard] Wright publicly, Baldwin suggests that his own understanding of the African American Subject moves beyond national borders," Wright argues. She also warns her reader against oversimplifying the matter, suggesting that Baldwin's understanding of the Subject does fully transcend geographical boundaries but that his understanding also is partially located in the in-between transit itself. In this sense, she concludes, the African American Subject is a transatlantic Subject.

Concluding Part III is Roderick A. Ferguson's essay "The Parvenu Baldwin and the Other Side of Redemption: Modernity, Race, Sexuality, and the Cold War." This chapter historicizes Baldwin's dual interest in race and sexuality within the racial and sexual anxieties of post–World War II America and attempts to address Baldwin's interest in the United States' preoccupation with "color and sex" by situating that preoccupation in the cold war—that is, in the rise of the

United States as a world power and the emergence of the Soviet state as a threat to that power. Ferguson contends that Baldwin's essay "Preservation of Innocence" symbolized "the social contradictions operating in and reconstituted by the post–World War II era. These contradictions included the constitution of an American gay subculture during World War II and the denial/negation of that subculture by the American state immediately after the war. This negation was part of the state's efforts to universalize heterosexual culture and thereby to construct the liberal citizen-subject of the United States as implicitly masculine and heterosexual."

Leading off Part IV, "Baldwin and Intertextuality," is Sharon Patricia Holland's "(Pro)Creating Imaginative Spaces and Other Queer Acts: Randall Kenan's *A Visitation of Spirits* and Its Revival of James Baldwin's Absent Black Gay Man in *Giovanni's Room*." Holland begins her essay, echoing the concerns of Marlon Ross in Chapter 1, with the express task of devising a means by which "black" and "queer" can speak to each other. This is most effectively achieved in this chapter by engaging and, indeed, by queering the idea of the African American literary tradition through an intertextual reading of Baldwin's *Giovanni's Room* with Randall Kenan's *A Visitation of Spirits*. The result is an elucidation of the "particular imaginative place/space that black gay men occupy in the literary 'tradition'" and specifically in Kenan's *A Visitation of Spirits*, which signifies on Baldwin's earlier text and attempts to re-create an imaginative place for black gay experience in the African American tradition.

In his essay "'I'm Not Entirely What I Look Like': Richard Wright, James Baldwin, and the Hegemony of Vision; Or, Jimmy's FBEye Blues," Maurice Wallace marshals an impressive range of cultural evidence to revisit the relationship between Baldwin and Wright in a markedly different way than that taken by others who have addressed it, in this book and elsewhere in the past. Wallace's chapter looks backward to the unfulfilled criminographic, that is, the examination of black case studies, ambitions of *American Pages* (a magazine that Wright and company were never able to start, which was to address contemporary Negro concerns) and to Wright's implicit panoptic critique of his unfulfilled intended exhibition on black criminal subjects, in order to examine their influence on the fictional designs of book 3 of *Native Son*. This allows Wallace to look forward, later—by way of a reading of the FBI's files on Baldwin—at the scopic exercises of the criminographic imagination upon Baldwin's queer black body.

Josh Kun's essay "Life according to the Beat: James Baldwin, Bessie Smith, and the Perilous Sounds of Love," appropriately concludes this section on intertextuality with attention to one of the influences on Baldwin's work that Baldwin himself was quick to recognize but which his critics have largely ignored: music. Kun's chapter helps fill that critical gap. Returning to the time Baldwin spent in Switzerland in his mountain retreat, where he completed his first novel, *Go Tell It on the Mountain*, and two essays of note, "A Stranger in the Village" and "The Discovery of What It Means to Be an American," Kun troubles over the significance of the music of Bessie Smith that Baldwin took with him to that retreat. "We know of James Baldwin the writer," he writes, "but what do we know of James Baldwin the listener?" This essay intervenes in the technological gaps between typewriter and phonograph and provides some illuminating insights.

Part V, explicitly devoted to "Baldwin and the Literary," consists of two essays and a thorough select bibliography, compiled and introduced by Jeffrey W. Hole, that is sure to be useful to Baldwin scholars for some time to come. This section opens with Joshua L. Miller's "The Discovery of What It Means to Be a Witness: James Baldwin's Dialectics of Difference," which gives as much attention to the influence of the visual on Baldwin's work as Kun's chapter does to the musical. By centering on an examination of *Nothing Personal*, Baldwin's collaborative project with his friend Richard Avedon, Miller carefully unravels and illuminates the intricacies of the term *witness* for and in the work and life of Baldwin.

Finally, Lauren Rusk's "Selfhood and Strategy in *Notes of a Native Son*" speaks to how James Baldwin's first collection of essays portrays his personal experience of the ill-fitting, anonymous role inflicted on African Americans by white society. Rusk shows how *Notes of a Native Son*, a work of rhetorical life writing, speaks to an audience divided by racial difference: "In it, Baldwin pulls out all the stops to demonstrate, especially to white readers, the pathological relations between and essential kinship of black and white Americans."

The title of my introduction, taken as it is from a comment Baldwin made in a televised interview, responds to an old sentiment often attributed to well-meaning white liberals: that is, racial progress takes time.[2] A younger Baldwin might have had more patience with such an assertion, but an exasperated older Baldwin, near the end of his life, did not. It is in this context that Baldwin replies to the reporter, "It has taken my mother's time, my father's time, my brothers and my sisters' time, my nieces and my nephews' time. . . . How much time do you want for your progress?" With a slight shift in focus, one could ask the same pointed question of much of the secondary criticism of Baldwin's work to date. What strikes one most on excursions into the secondary works on Baldwin is the critics' and commentators' fascination with not just Baldwin's work but with Baldwin the man, Baldwin the thinker, Baldwin the activist. No fewer than four full-length biographical works on Baldwin exist, from Fern Marja Eckman's *The Furious Passage of James Baldwin* (New York: M. Evans, 1966), to W. J. Weatherby's *James Baldwin: Artist on Fire* (1989), James Campbell's *Talking at the Gates: A Life of James Baldwin* (1992), and finally David Leeming's *James Baldwin: A Biography* (1994). In addition to these are numerous interviews with and personal recollections about Baldwin, some of which have been collected and published. Quincy Troupe edited such a collection of recollections by writers, critics, and other artists in *James Baldwin: The Legacy* (1989). And Fred L. Standley and Louis H. Pratt edited a collection of interviews that appeared in 1989 in *Conversations with James Baldwin*.

These, along with the 1989 documentary *James Baldwin: The Price of the Ticket*; countless other interviews; the number of appearances Baldwin's words make as an epigraph in films, by directors ranging from Marlon Riggs to Spike Lee; the allusions to Baldwin in contemporary black gay fiction, as in James Earl Hardy's *B-Boy Blues*; the number of times that Baldwin has been quoted in African American literary and cultural criticism from Henry Louis Gates, Jr., to Cornel West, all suggest not only Baldwin's centrality but that he was of interest to an entire generation and continues to be of interest to a new generation of scholars, readers, and culture producers for reasons that exceed his mere textual acumen and dexterity. The fascination is with Baldwin's life, his presence, his political thought, as well as his work. This is evidenced by the paucity of real critical treatment of Baldwin's work in favor of the more biographical portraitures of the man.

This book of essays represents a Baldwin revival of sorts. Since 1990, some fifteen dissertations have been written on Baldwin, either in whole or in part, from a variety of disciplines. Some of the writers of those dissertations are among the authors in this collection. This critical mass may point to a return to Baldwin in a way that might not have been possible ten, fifteen, or twenty years ago. It is common fare in critical discourse today to talk of transnationality and the new ways in which that category requires us to understand other categories, such as identity. The fact that we can today think about the complicated relationships that not only obtain but are inevitable between race, gender, class, and sexuality makes possible a reassessment and a critical treatment of Baldwin that perhaps was not before imaginable. And who better to make those reevaluations and interventions than a group of younger scholars, represented by those collected here, who were trained in the academy just as it was realizing the impact of cultural studies on critical thought. The chapters that follow signal not only a new direction for Baldwin scholarship but a new day for African American cultural critique. As new scholarship continues to emerge, the centrality and exemplarity of Baldwin to this new critical terrain will, no doubt, continue to come into sharper focus.

NOTES

1. For a fuller discussion of this idea of the primacy of the category of race over all other categories of difference, see Dwight A. McBride, "Can the Queen Speak?: Racial Essentialism, Sexuality and the Problem of Authority," *Callaloo* 21, 2 (1998): 363–379.

2. For a textual discussion of this idea, see "Preface to the 1984 edition of *Notes of a Native Son*, by James Baldwin (Boston: Beacon Press, 1984).

Part I

Baldwin and Race

Chapter 1

White Fantasies of Desire
Baldwin and the Racial Identities of Sexuality

Marlon B. Ross

> Both clung to a fantasy rather than to each other, tried
> to suck pleasure from the crannies of the mind, rather
> than surrender the secrets of the body.
> —Baldwin, *Another Country*[1]

> It is quite possible to say that the price a Negro pays
> for becoming articulate is to find himself, at length,
> with nothing to be articulate about.
> —Baldwin, *Notes of a Native Son*[2]

The only way to claim the legitimacy of your desire when the dominant culture fears it is to pretend desire can be exposed to light, can be discussed, analyzed, categorized, mapped, recorded—to pretend it is a surface phenomenon. This act of exposure not only distorts the course of desire; it also has no choice but to express desire in terms the culture has already provided. Your desire and its articulation will resist those terms, just as homosexuals took the trivializing epithet *gay* and transformed it into a term indicating a legitimate cultural group with a powerful political base, seeking to overturn their sexual oppression. Always residual in the term *gay*, however, will be mainstream society's terrified projection of intragender bonding; it is a term always on the verge of suggesting a decadent individual who trivializes society's grandest natural and moral directive to reproduce: pansy, punk, sissy, fag.

No matter how articulate an oppressed group may be, they cannot fully explain what it feels like to inhabit a society that represses their desire, not only because feelings are notoriously internal but also because expression is notoriously decided. What Baldwin has said about African American experience can also be applied to intragender desire: "No true account really of black life can be held, can be contained in the American vocabulary. As it is, the only way that you can deal with it is by doing great violence to the assumptions on which the vocabulary is based."[3] We have to communicate in the very language that has articulated oppression as a viable existence, but by doing so, we reveal how that language and that culture belong to us in ways that put the secure grasp of dominant culture at risk. The only option is to divert language toward in-group cultural expression, which dominant society will have a hard time deciphering but nevertheless will endlessly decipher and exploit for its own ends. The desire of the oppressed is put on the defensive even as it finds its borrowed language. The question is always "What do you want?" It is easy for a group whose desire is suppressed to spend a lot of energy trying to answer that question, not only because an answer is vital to sustaining the myth of collective desire, strength in solidarity, but also because *not* to answer the question leaves you in an even more vulnerable position. Needless to say, as you field the question and invent answers, the oppressors are busy making those answers fit the straitjacket of their projected fear. "We want exactly what you want" is never a good enough answer.

When desire is involved, sometimes the most direct route to a solution is a detour. In this case, we advance to the topic of African American intragender desire by way of the detour of two stories written by black men about (white) homosexuality. In 1956, James Baldwin took a great risk in publishing one of the earliest affirmative American novels on an overtly homosexual topic, a novel that has become a foundational text for gay culture and for gay and lesbian studies; although in canonizing this text, the field has done so at the expense of the novel's racial implications. Adding to this risk was the fact that all the characters in his novel were "white," though we shall see how relative a notion whiteness can be. According to Fern Marja Eckman, Baldwin went into a deep depression upon completing *Giovanni's Room*.[4]

The homosexual theme had initially frightened Baldwin; now it made the publishers draw back. But they issued paternalistic warnings to Baldwin that they were rejecting the book for his own good, really, since publication would surely "wreck" his career.

"They said I would—I was a *Negro* writer and I would reach a very special audience," Baldwin says now. "And I would be *dead* if I alienated that audience. That, in effect, nobody would accept that book–coming from *me.*" His eyes smolder. "My agent told me to *burn* it."[5]

Baldwin's fear and the publishers' predictions, though inauspicious, contained a kernel of truth. The immediate critical reception to *Giovanni's Room* in the mainstream media was cautiously positive. After all, the novel seemed like a curious little detour, which is how it is still frequently treated. What did white men have to lose from mildly praising such a novel? In fact, much of that praise seems predicated on the unstated element of surprise that a black author would attempt such a project and astonishment that he could succeed in constructing white characters. In *The Gay Novel in America*, James Levin sums up the attitude of these first white reviewers: "Baldwin could write about homosexuality because his literary reputation had been confirmed and because those who wished to support him as a black writer refrained from attacking him on what seemed to be an extraneous or possibly detrimental issue [homosexuality]."[6] The longer critical history of *Giovanni's Room* reveals the deeper discomfort entailed in the reception to Baldwin's treatment of this "extraneous or possibly detrimental issue."

From its publication to the present, *Giovanni's Room* has been read as a homosexual novel, exposing the fact that desire between men can be mapped without making desire itself a scandal. Baldwin's first book, *Go Tell It on the Mountain* (which depicts the emotional, economic, racial, and spiritual struggles of a first-generation Harlem family), published in 1953, is considered one of the most powerful novels depicting the African American experience.[7] In his first novel, the black man speaks; in his second, the homosexual. Only with the emergence of a more autonomous gay black sociopolitical consciousness in the early 1980s did a public discourse arise that began to integrate Baldwin's "gay" novel into an African American context. It is as if only an openly gay black readership could give a valid racial identity to a novel otherwise cut off from black experience, and it is no surprise that Baldwin's work as a whole has been a major cultural resource for people who identify as black and gay. Nonetheless, the easy categorization of the first novels projects onto them the very denials that Baldwin was attempting to bring to the surface, and the potential ghettoization of Baldwin as an author "for" black gay people also contains assumptions against which his work struggles. Everyone assumed that Baldwin was homosexual because he had chosen to write a novel about same-gender love. This is ironic, considering that as a black man, he was also writing a novel about "white" characters in which whiteness itself—or Baldwin's own blackness—was apparently not an issue. Fortunately, no one could accuse Baldwin of secretly being white simply because he had written a novel with all European characters. Of course, *a secret desire to be white* is another matter, another sort of accusation, and one implied or made outright in much of the criticism until quite recently. While the novel has gained a central place in (white) gay culture and is often a focus of attention in (white) gay studies, in the context of African American literary and cultural studies, historically it has been alternately dismissed or ignored altogether, stumblingly acknowledged or viciously attacked.

Apologetics and abuse sometimes have characterized the same discussion, whereby the critic justifies Baldwin's right to publish such a novel but then chastises him for having done so. Nathan A. Scott, Jr., for instance, writes about *Giovanni's Room* that it "is a book that strikes us as a deflection, as a kind of detour," whereas *Go Tell It on the Mountain* is "a passionate gesture of identification with his people."[8] The clear implication is that *Giovanni's Room* is *not* "a passionate gesture of identification" with African American culture, that in fact it is a deviation from such identification. In *The Negro Novel in America,* Robert Bone, a white critic who has been influential in black literary studies, classifies *Giovanni's Room* and *Another Country* (Baldwin's third novel) with a genre of "raceless novels" written by African Americans during the 1940s and 1950s.[9] Bone argues that Baldwin equates spiritual salvation with interracial homosexuality: "The stranger the sex partner, the better the orgasm, for it violates a stronger taboo. Partners of a different race, or the same sex, or preferably both, afford the maximum spiritual opportunities" (238).

In *White Papers for White Americans,* Calvin C. Hernton takes Bone's logic of racial estrangement a step further: "Psychologically, [Baldwin] embraced the white world and especially identified with young, handsome, blond males. Realizing, however, that this was no solution to his agony, he confessed that one day he could hate white people as much as he did Negroes, that is, if God did not change his life."[10] Baldwin almost redeems himself for Hernton after writing the play *Blues for Mister Charlie*:[11] "This Baldwin—the *Blues for Mister Charlie* Baldwin—is an aggressive, a masculine Baldwin. Add to this the fact that the sexuality of the Negroes in the play is earthy, rich, full of power and human animalism, all of which Baldwin does not apologize for, but which he affirms with dignity and prowess" (131). Splitting Baldwin in two in order to salvage his legitimacy as a racial spokesman, Hernton suggests that *Blues* is a better work than *Giovanni's Room* and *Another Country*, because it does not harbor any tincture of same-sex desire, which by implication here becomes concern with nonblack desire.[12]

In a now infamous passage of *Soul on Ice,* where homosexuality is compared with "baby-rape or wanting to become the head of General Motors," Eldridge Cleaver achieves the nadir of homophobic ranting against Baldwin's sexual, and therefore racial, perversion:

> Many Negro homosexuals, acquiescing in this racial death-wish, are outraged and frustrated because in their sickness they are unable to have a baby by a white man. The cross they have to bear is that, already bending over and touching their toes for the white man, the fruit of their miscegenation is not the little half-white offspring of their dreams but an increase in the unwinding of their nerves—though they redouble their efforts and intake of the white man's sperm.[13]

In Cleaver's vision of Baldwin's desire for blond homosexuals, he curiously assumes a rigid bifurcation of sexual roles in male-male intercourse and, further, that the black man must take the "feminine" position of the "bottom," while the white man automatically takes the "masculine" role of the "top." According to Cleaver's racial logic—or more precisely, illogic—black homosexual desire is ultimately desire for whiteness, desire to vacate black manhood for an abject position appropriate only to the white female. By castigating Baldwin and praising Norman Mailer and his idea of black masculine sexual superiority, however, Cleaver casts aside an opportunity for racial solidarity with a black man in favor of putatively "straight" male bonding with a white man. The irony is painfully apparent, suggesting that it is Cleaver, not Baldwin, who desires to be inseminated by the white father.

The complexities of Cleaver's cross-identifications are too entangled to unravel here, but it must be remembered that Baldwin (especially his *The Fire Next Time*) was the writer who most influenced the young male generation of 1960s militant writers, including Cleaver himself.[14] Even as Cleaver writes under the palpable influence of Baldwin's distinctive blend of the personal, philosophical, and political, and even as the younger writer borrows from his elder the tactic of sexual exposure in order to understand racial entanglements, he attempts to distance himself from Baldwin's sexual stance by creating a posture of conventionally coded aggressive manliness, ironically bolstered by his bonding with Baldwin's white rival, Mailer.[15]

Houston A. Baker, Jr.'s "The Embattled Craftsman" is an especially instructive essay in this context, for in it Baker attempts to undo some of the damage done to Baldwin's racial image as a result of homophobic attacks on the part of some advocates of Black Power.[16] Baker wants to rescue Baldwin's seminal place in the canon of African American literature and culture, as opposed to the inseminated position in a miscegenated relation to white culture given him by some of the late 1960s militants. Instead of claiming a place for sexual variation in the African American canon, and thus in black culture, Baker opts to celebrate Baldwin's concern with race by diminishing the writer's interest in the relation between sexual variation and racial identity. Although the essay seeks to reinstate Baldwin as a worthy black father by focusing on his craft, it does so by establishing African American culture as the exclusive center of Baldwin's work. Baker leaves *Giovanni's Room* out of his analysis except for asides in the discussion of other works, and he glosses over the significance of intragender desire in Baldwin's other writings. The dis/stress in logic found in Baker's transition from *Another Country* to *The Fire Next Time* is emblematic of this tactical reconstruction of racial identity and tradition at the expense of same-sex desire: "It hardly seems overstatement to say *Another Country* is *not* a prolegomenon for a homosexual revolution. And when one turns to *The Fire Next Time*, one can see how the novel fits into a total corpus" (69). Because the homosexual theme is not *overtly* continued in *The Fire Next Time* (though it *is* there subtly and circuitously), Baker assumes we need not consider the issue of same-gender desire in light of Baldwin's further development and his politics of race. It could be easily argued that *Another Country* is exactly a prolegomenon for a revolution that is (homo)sexual and racial simultaneously, that the fire next time cannot merely be a fire that sears the racial existence of Americans but also must be one that disrupts their sexual psychology. As Baldwin asserts consistently throughout his work, the reform of racial relations must be total if it is to happen at all, and it cannot happen at all without a concomitant revolution in Americans' psycho-erotica. Baker constructs a "total corpus" *as* total and enlists Baldwin as a genuine son of the African American tradition by excising Baldwin's black faggotry from that corpus and thus from that tradition. This need not be the case, and given Baldwin's belief that sexual knowledge and exposure are crucial to racial understanding and progress, it should not be the case.[17]

Because Baldwin himself links the most explicit, open, and socially autonomous form of homosexuality to white characters in his early novels, it could be argued that these critics are simply taking Baldwin at his word. In contrast to the cross-racial same-gender relationships engaged in by Rufus Scott in *Another Country,* it is not until 1968, with the publication of *Tell Me How Long the Train's Been Gone,* that Baldwin emplots overt sexual relations between two black men in a novel, and not until 1979 with *Just Above My Head,* his last novel, that he explores love between two black men, both of whom express their sexuality in an "exclusively" same-gender bond (as opposed to being "bisexual" like Rufus of *Another Country* or like Leo Proudhammer in *Tell Me How Long*).[18] From Baldwin's early work, in which "out" homosexuality is mostly associated with whiteness, a reader already uncomfortable with sexual variance may lessen that level of discomfort by segregating blackness from intragender desire. We could say, then, that important critics such as Scott and Baker picked up on Baldwin's own discomfort with representing sexual variance as integral to African American experience in the earlier novels. At the least, however, we must recognize that Baldwin's engagement with this relationship between same-sexuality and race takes the form of a progressive, consistent thinking through, rather than something quixotic, sporadic, regressive, or exculpatory—an intentionally politicized engagement rather than a whimsical detour.

Baldwin was not the first black male writer to choose the apparently curious option of treating male homosexuality through the fictional experience of white characters, if not from a white point of view. In 1952, Chester Himes published *Cast the First Stone,* a novel depicting intragender romance in a prison setting and pleading for understanding of sexual variation.[19] Like Baldwin's, Himes's "handsome" white hero at first resists same-sex desire, then falls in love with a darker, younger man, who identifies himself more comfortably with the capacity for intragender intercourse. As in Baldwin's novel, the white hero leaves the younger, darker, more sexually articulated male just when the younger man needs him most. Like Baldwin, Himes uses first-person narration, putting us inside the head of the resistant hero and bringing our sympathies in line with his, teaching us as readers as he learns for himself through his firsthand experience of homoerotic love. Himes also provides an "exotic" setting for his story of same-sex love, and in the work of both Baldwin and Himes, the love is simultaneously articulated and cramped by the couple's literal or symbolic imprisonment in a claustrophobic space: in Baldwin, by Giovanni's room; in Himes, by the prison. Like Baldwin's Paris, Himes's prison is another country, where sexual bonding between men is much more part of the surface of life than in respectable (white, middle-class) American society.

Both authors end their homosexual fantasies tragically. In both novels we must question the heroes' culpability in not being able to fulfill their lovers' emotional needs. In each novel the more sexually self-accepting character comes to a fatal end—Baldwin's through execution, Himes's through suicide. Unable to integrate his love into a society that condemns it and turns it into prostitution, Baldwin's Giovanni becomes a hunted criminal and then a broken prisoner, awaiting execution. Himes's association of homosexuality and imprisonment is the other side of the coin: when the hero is released from prison, his lover is left alone and broken. The hero's initial criminal behavior in the "outside" (i.e., "normal") world ironically has given him access to a room, a prison cell, where he can discover his passion for another man (without actual contamination of sexual intercourse), and he is able to leave this "inside" world behind after he has learned—or in Baldwin's novel, has *not* learned—from its deviance. As in Baldwin's, in Himes's novel society's rules demand punishment, as the bereft younger man takes his own life.

Finally, there is evidence for autobiographical elements in both novels, and both writers rewrite their white fantasies in other versions—Baldwin incorporating his into *Another Country,* with a black

hero who has an affair with a white homosexual from another country (France); Himes changing the color of his characters from black to
white in the final version.

If Baldwin's critical history is shaped by an attempt to segregate
race from sexuality, Himes's reception has an analogous history—but
with major differences. *Cast the First Stone* was greeted negatively by
the critical establishment; then it was generally forgotten, unlike *Giovanni's Room*.[20] As H. Bruce Franklin has pointed out, recent reassess-
ments of Himes's work have focused on the later hard-boiled detective fiction rather than the early prison fiction.[21] Just as for Baldwin,
the tide turned against Himes's early work, especially during the
Black Power period, because of the prevalence of cross-racial sexuality in those largely autobiographical protest novels. Intimately related to this crossover dynamic in their fiction is the protest tradition
in which both Himes and Baldwin wrote but which both were constantly trying to write themselves out of in the early novels. It is no
coincidence that some of the black nationalists, in turning against the
fictional representation of crossover sexuality, also turned against the
protest tradition itself—a tradition that takes racial integration as a
fundamental solution to the problem of racism and focuses on the
need to improve race *relations,* the struggle to reconcile black and
white into a single egalitarian national culture. The slippage that ties
interracial relations with interracial sexual relations has operated in
American culture since before emancipation, and it has been an important theme among African American writers across the political
spectrum and throughout the literary tradition. This slippage has
been figured as a sign for the im/possibility of racial reconciliation.
When Himes resorts to writing detective novels, he is giving up on
revising the form of the protest novel altogether; but this does not
mean he gives up on the searching themes contained in the earlier fiction, as can be seen from the presence of black faggotry in some of the
detective fiction.

Given the uncanny similarity between *Cast the First Stone* and *Giovanni's Room* (suggesting that Baldwin may have known the earlier
novel), the different reception—or lack thereof—of Himes in sexuality and gay-lesbian studies helps us grasp the racial implications of
how Baldwin's work has been exploited in these fields. Most of
Himes's crime novels take place in Harlem, giving us the justly celebrated black detectives Coffin Ed Johnson and Grave Digger Jones,

with their hard, quiet, relentless, masculine, understated charm. For the later Himes, visibly black and traditionally masculine, to gain the upper hand, the early Himes, preoccupied with interracial relations and sexual variance, must be disciplined through a formulaic genre whose gender and sexuality are highly conventional. Whereas Baldwin's articulation of same-gender desire becomes more comprehensive and integrated into his vision of African American tradition and community, so that "deviance"—a refusal to accept the unloving inhumanities of the norm—comes to represent the most sacred values of that tradition, Himes goes in the other direction. His concern with same-gender desire becomes—not silenced, exactly—whisperingly voiced through the apparently conventional bonding of two apparently "straight" detectives and their occasional policing of others' deviant sexuality. In his detective novels, Himes continues to explore variant sexuality through the frame of this formulaic coupling of Coffin Ed Johnson and Grave Digger Jones. Just as the formula of male bonding is rerouted and exploded through the eyes of this passionately, quietly bonded black male couple, however, so the sexual crimes that these detectives must solve are reoriented by a landscape of variant sexual practices depicted as so routine in Harlem that dealing with their expression is second nature to the detectives.[22]

Despite the vigilance of gay and lesbian studies scholars when it comes to resurrecting homosexual works, *Cast the First Stone* remains unexamined in the scholarship. Because Himes was reputedly straight, his novel was not prone to canonization under the cult of gay personality, which identifies gay literature as the production of writers who must themselves be identifiably (or arguably) gay—a tendency that has been hard to overcome, despite some excellent theoretical work on why it is problematic.[23] Himes's writing does not possess the odd double life (a queer version for gay and sexuality studies, a black version for African American and race studies) that Baldwin's has been subjected to, despite the fact that homosexuality is a theme that shows up repeatedly in Himes's work.

Perhaps even more important, *Cast the First Stone* is unknown in the gay community and in the scholarship because of its class position. Homosexuality has been coded in mainstream discourses since the 1960s not only as a largely white, male phenomenon but also as a white, middle-class phenomenon. Prison homosexuality is still seen by many as a different animal from authentic gay desire, because it is scripted in dominant literary and popular culture largely as behavior forced out as a result of circumstance, coercion, or confusion of gender roles where there are no women to play the passive part.[24] "The novel is a highly detailed account of one man's prison term," Stephen F. Milliken writes. "Prison is its one and only subject, its unique and exclusive concern."[25] What Milliken means here is that racism has been curiously cordoned off, though race exists in the novel in the form of black "background" characters. Similar to Baker's approach to Baldwin, however, Milliken's rush to explain the centrality of race—or in this case, to blast its central absence—causes him to erase the novel's interest in sexual variance among men. In other words, there is no one, central concern in the novel but a myriad of concerns matrixed through the characteristics of race, sexuality, class, and criminality. As long as these characteristics are viewed as single aspects of identity and difference, however, they will always be viewed as competing, rather than as messily intertwined concerns which can be isolated neither in experience nor in its representation. Not only does the prison experience overshadow the role of variant sexuality in Milliken's reading; it also overshadows the symbolic and literal interconnections between the prison experience and racial oppression, so that Milliken is unable to see the novel's racial implications:

> And in making Jimmy Monroe white, Himes effected an even more drastic narrowing of scope. He eliminated the entire subject of racism, the central theme of his first two novels. It is the most radical change imaginable, a basic alteration in the nature of the reality portrayed. But racism is not an easy truth for an artist to handle. . . . It distorts and obscures all lesser or subtler truths. . . .
>
> To remove racism from consideration, in any story of modern society that aims at completeness, is, of course, much like taking the sun out of the firmament. It is a massive distortion, leaving a gaping hole. It does, however, throw into sharper relief myriad points of detail that are normally blurred. (160, 161)

Unable to see the connections between class, racial, sexual, and penal oppressions, Milliken overlooks the very plausible possibility that, rather than Himes's having totally purged the question of racial oppression from the novel, what he has done is emplot both the issue of color and the question of same-sex desire as notions isolated in discourse but not in experience. If this only book-length critical study of

Himes is an indication, the response to *Cast the First Stone*, once the novel becomes better known, might suffer from the same double blindness that has characterized so much of the criticism on *Giovanni's Room*. Rather than seeing *Giovanni's Room* and *Cast the First Stone* as unfortunate detours that take the authors away from their only legitimate concern, readers should approach both novels attuned to the ways in which intragender desire has been historically situated within African American culture and to the kinds of cultural knowledge that enable Baldwin and Himes to write these texts as fantasies of white male desire. To do otherwise is to miss both the historical complexity of forms of erotic desire and the cultural complexity of African American desire itself.

Although the dual existence of Baldwin's works and the oblivion of Himes's in queer studies many stem from a complex network of reasons, their different receptions indicate to what extent identity has been formulated as a base of singular experience, determining how a writer is identified and critiqued.[26] The recent rash of rhetoric concerning dual and triple identities, interrelated, combined, and performed identities, has not uprooted the base paradigm of singularity, one in which the logic is curiously additive, and in which race dominates self-consciously when blackness is at stake and silently when white people take their own sexuality—homo or hetero—as an unarticulated norm for everyone else's. Baldwin may be seen to have a dual identity, but in this paradigm the characteristics of race and sexuality always compete for dominance. When it comes to identity, only one, master characteristic is possible; all others search for a place to settle within the framework of that master characteristic.[27] Both Baldwin and Himes were attempting to uncover this scandal of "identity." Through their fiction, they were suggesting that identification occurs through the pressure of circumstance on impulse; that the most uptight Puritan blue blood (Baldwin's hero) and the most reckless Southern redneck (Himes's hero) can, under the right circumstances, find their desire reconstructed by their erotic passion for another man. That both writers felt compelled to darken this other man, to make him ethnically other, so to speak, indicates to what extent they understood the insufficiency of identity to account for the (im)balancing acts of desire's unpredictable attractions and identifications. Both the heroes and the men they come to desire represent not necessarily the authors themselves but the capacity for these writers to fantasize, to identify with another through the axis of desire. Does sexual difference look more like racial difference than we'd suppose, they ask, not so much in its historical formation as in its structure of felt experience?

The reception to *Giovanni's Room*, then, has disallowed Baldwin's attempt to bracket the question "What does Baldwin want?" One obvious answer is that Baldwin wanted to prove that once the black man becomes articulate, he does have something to say, and he can say it in whatever color he chooses. If the characters had been black, the novel would have been read as being "about" blackness, whatever else it happened actually to be about. The whiteness of the characters seems to make invisible the question of how race or color has, in fact, shaped the characters—at least as far as most readers have dealt with the novel. Nobody asks, What does the white man want?—even though a large chunk of the novel shows us a specific fictional white man asking himself relentlessly, What is it exactly that I want? In other words, Baldwin revises W. E. B. Du Bois's question "How does it feel to be a problem?" For Baldwin, it is not "the strange meaning of being black" that is the "problem of the Twentieth Century," nor even "the problem of the color-line."[28] Baldwin makes the central problem of the twentieth century the strange meaning of being white, as a structure of feeling within the self and within history—a structure of felt experience that motivates and is motivated by other denials. In *Giovanni's Room* he posits the white man as a problem and then fantasizes what it might mean for a particular upper-class white man to become aware of the problematic nature of his desire—color not as a "line" of demarcation but instead as a point of departure. Given the invisibility of whiteness as a racially constricted burden of desire, however, Baldwin also shows how even the most deeply taboo and widely outlawed desire can be cushioned by the privileged invisibility of whiteness.[29]

Color is usually taken as merely a surface matter in *Giovanni's Room* meaning that it is a matter of mere description rather than identity—the instance of a characteristic rather than the essence of character. The two lovers, David and Giovanni, are specific instances of individuals with representative (white?) problems that need human (white?) solutions. Their race signifies nothing beyond itself. It is merely a way of observing what they look like, not why it is that they want whatever it is they want. Baldwin, however, refers to color and racial characteristics constantly as a way of locating the cultural situation of the characters.[30] But by taking these racial cues seriously rather than merely as uncritical, descriptive details for establishing the "look" of his characters, we might argue that in *Giovanni's Room*, Baldwin examines how desire becomes coded and enacted among a particular group of men whose racial heritage shapes attitudes toward sex, romance, love, and friendship. This reading of the novel gives depth to what otherwise must remain on the surface: the color casting (stereotyping even) of the characters' personalities. In this reading, it is not only each character's sexual identity that makes him representative or unique but also/instead his racial difference, coded as ethnic and sexual identity. Without the ethnic difference between Giovanni, the impulsive Italian, and David, the methodical Teuton, it would be impossible for the novel to script its story of tortured same-sex desire. The whiteness of Baldwin's characters splits the author's identity from the author's fantasy, the author's authority from the author's projected desire. That Baldwin could succeed with such a novel necessarily provokes a crisis of identity and authority for the author and for his readers in a race-coded environment.

Actually, Baldwin's writing of the novel is a way of answering this crisis. But for his readers—black, white, and otherwise—the success of *Giovanni's Room* may raise a question in their minds. For many whites, as we have seen, the question is whether Baldwin's identity is too miscegenated, impure, for him to serve reliably as a mediator, a spokesman, between dominant America and the black experience of America. For some African Americans, as we have seen, the question is whether Baldwin's fascination with (white) homosexuality distracts him from articulating an authentic and respectable vision of African American experience. Both groups project their particular fears onto the author's desire. As Baldwin constantly pointed out, to be black in America is to become the target of fantastic racial-sexual projections and denials. In *Giovanni's Room*, he gets to turn the tables.

Exploding Identity, Exposing Secrecy

> If you're a Negro, you're in the center of that *peculiar* affliction because *anybody* can touch *you*—when the sun goes down. You know, you're the target for everybody's fantasies.
>
> —James Baldwin[31]

The sexual question and the racial question have always been entwined, you know. If Americans can mature on the level of racism, then
they have to mature on the level of sexuality.

—James Baldwin[32]

These misgivings about Baldwin—in fact, misgivings that Baldwin
had about himself—are epitomized in Baldwin's relation to the two
most influential African American writers of the previous generation,
Richard Wright and Langston Hughes. In his first volume of essays,
Notes of a Native Son, Baldwin made it clear that he did not intend to
become a protest novelist (represented by Wright), limited to and by
the rhetoric of advocacy. "By the time I was twenty-four," Baldwin
wrote, "I had decided to stop reviewing books about the Negro problem—which, by this time, was only slightly less horrible in print than
it was in life" (4). Toward the end of the essay "Autobiographical
Notes," which prefaces the 1955 collection, Baldwin says, "I have not
written about being a Negro at such length because I expect that to be
my only subject, but only because it was the gate I had to unlock before I could hope to write about anything else" (8). The critical success of *Go Tell It on the Mountain* was the gate that unlocked "anything
else."

Baldwin did not so much fear repeating what Wright had already
done as a novelist; however much Wright had influenced Baldwin,
the stylistic differences between the two writers were tremendous.
What Baldwin feared more was repeating himself, the way he felt
Wright had done. By defining one's identity so narrowly, one also
risked defining narrowly the authority deriving from that identity. To
define identity solely through what is most characteristic on the surface is to limit identity to that surface. According to the logic of cultural projection, most blacks are apparently heterosexual; therefore,
homosexuality cannot be a synecdochic characteristic defining one's
blackness, that is, it cannot be a part that authentically represents the
notion of a black race as a whole. Such accepted synecdochic factors,
such as skin color or geographic origin of one's foreparents in Africa,
in addition to being projected as unifying the race, must not be seen
as differentiating too much among the people imagined as belonging
to the racial whole—as sexual variation threatens to do in certain contexts. Too much variety within the group threatens the convenient
idea that what hold the group together are obvious characteristics,

shared by all members of the group, which can be easily read by any teenager on the street.

According to this logic, there may be some blacks who are homosexual, but their homosexuality is not a black matter. For it to be a black matter would mean that it would have to be shared equally by all members of the race. If it is a black matter, then all blacks must be homosexual. For the racist, this fits the idea of black sexual degeneracy. For some black nationalists, it is the threat of contamination posed by any characteristic seen as not ideally shareable by all members of the race, as well as the threat of sexual unproductivity usually associated with homosexuality and usually feared by nationalists of any stripe. When a black writer becomes an "authority" on homosexuality, when a black man authors queer desire, he necessarily steps outside black desire, relinquishing some of his "authority" on black culture. Everybody knows what a real black man wants.

In Baldwin's preface to the 1984 edition of *Notes of a Native Son*, he clarifies the significance of identity for his development as a writer. The ulterior motive of all the essays in *Notes* is to enlarge Baldwin's authorial identity, and thus authority, from the burden of race to the burden of human insight. "If I was trying to discover myself," Baldwin wrote in 1984, "on the whole, when examined, a somewhat dubious notion, since I was also trying to avoid myself—there was, certainly, between that self and me, the accumulated rock of ages. This rock scarred the hand, and all tools broke against it. . . . The hope of salvation—identity—depended on whether or not one would be able to decipher and describe the rock" (xxxi). Baldwin's reference here is to a hymn popular in the black church: "Rock of ages, cleft for me, / let me hide myself in thee." In the hymn the rock is the salvation freely offered by Christ to the lost sinner. In African American tradition, the religious connotation of "rock" takes on political and cultural meanings, indicating the relations among faith, obligation, suffering, and eventual overcoming for those tested by the injustices of the white world, along with an appropriate judgment of the white world for its sins. It is the rock of refuge, as heard in the pleas of the psalmist: "O Lord, my rock and my redeemer" (Psalms 19:14) or "Be thou a rock of refuge for me, a strong fortress to save me!" (Psalms 31:2; Revised Standard Version). But it is also the rock of resistance, a testing place for a people whom God has given a special task, and an assurance that those who practice evil shall eventually be cast down: the Lord "will become a sanctuary, and a stone of offense, and a rock of stumbling to both houses of Israel, a trap and a snare to the inhabitants of Jerusalem. And many shall stumble thereon; they shall fall and be broken; they shall be snared and taken" (Isaiah 8:14–15). Perhaps most important, it is a rock of responsibility, a charge given to the strong of heart, as Christ uses the pun in his anointing of the disciple Peter (whose name means rock): "On this rock I will build my church, and the powers of death shall not prevail against it" (Matthew 16:18). All these meanings resonate in Baldwin's metaphor—indicating the way in which the black writer relies on the uniqueness of African American experience as refuge, as a site of self-testing, as an offensive weapon of resistance, and as an obligatory charge to become a herald or witness on which the people can depend.

In sum, the rock is the author's inheritance, one that is both a strength, enabling identity and survival, and a stumbling block, obstructing the way toward uninterrupted human desire by giving the individual a secure place to hide from the nakedness of desire (i.e., an identity). As a mode of false security, identity can easily become "avoidance." "This rock scarred the hand," Baldwin writes. Every African American must struggle with this rock, using whatever tools are available; but ultimately, it will be the bare hands that succeed. The hands are scarred due to the history of hard labor and struggle for achievement under pressing circumstances. "My inheritance was particular, specifically limited and limiting: my birthright was vast, connecting me to all that lives, and to everyone, forever. But one cannot claim the birthright without accepting the inheritance" (xxxii). Baldwin found himself struggling to forge an authorial identity that would allow him to speak through his inheritance as a black man without forfeiting his authority on all human experience, his birthright as a writer.[33] In other words, Baldwin needed to expand the repertoire of characteristics identified with blackness, not by questioning the integrity of black culture (the rock of identity) but by questioning the uniformity of black identity (the stumbling block of the projected stereotype). "I was trying to locate myself within a specific inheritance and to use that inheritance, precisely, to claim the birthright from which that inheritance had so brutally and specifically excluded me" (xxxii).

Norman Podhoretz is one of the early reviewers of Baldwin's work who seems to have understood the implications of this dilemma. He correctly suggests that in *Another Country*, Baldwin

> is saying that the terms white and Negro refer to two different conditions under which individuals live, but they are still individuals and their lives are still governed by the same fundamental laws of being. And he is saying, similarly, that the terms homosexuality and heterosexuality refer to two different conditions under which individuals pursue love, but they are still individuals and their pursuit of love is still governed by the same fundamental laws of being. Putting the two propositions together, he is saying finally, that the only significant realities are individuals and love, and that anything which is permitted to interfere with the free operation of this fact is evil and should be done away with.[34]

This strain of radical individualism can make it feel as though Baldwin wants to toss out his African American inheritance along with the concept of race itself, given that that inheritance exists so squarely because of racial domination.

Amiri Baraka also puts his finger on this individualist ethos in Baldwin and uses it to attack him, as a writer representing an outmoded integrationist ethic and aesthetic, in need of being replaced by a black nationalist aesthetic.[35] Part of what the young nationalists were reacting against in Baldwin, then, is exactly the danger of one who betrays the race by placing what appears to be an individual whim (desire) over racial consolidation. In this line or reasoning, same-sex desire becomes a metonym for this danger, because focusing on it seems to set the individual apart from the racial whole, and because homosexuality traditionally in U.S. culture has been allied to notions of national decadence, unreproductivity, waywardness, and, especially during the cold war, betrayal. Black nationalists did not want to sacrifice the charge of (white) homosexuality—which had become highly visible in major cities during the 1960s—as a powerful weapon that could be lodged against white America, a charge that could easily link homosexual decadence with the irreversible decline of the (white) nation-state at the same time that it could be used as a symbol of the reproductive power and consolidation of the emerging black national family. In other words, the black nationalists took the charge that powerful white men had invented to create so much fear and anxiety among themselves during the cold war—that of an insidious, pervasive homosexual decadence and betrayal lurking within America's seats of greatest power—and aimed it back at those seats of power.

To be set apart, for a nationalist, is to be set against. The irony is that Baldwin, too, recognizes this danger; and so we must add to Podhoretz's statement almost its opposite: Baldwin's work poses the danger in denying or forgetting that one can never escape the inherited conditions that define one's being. In *The Fire Next Time* he calls this state "innocence," and he identifies it with a destructive arrogance embedded in white privilege as a condition that encourages a person to deny the historical, political, bodily, and natural limitations of human mortality. In a sense, we are all too secure in our identities and yet, at the same time, so insecure in them that we always seek to avoid the limits they announce and impose.

It is not surprising, then, that the final section of *Notes* revolves around the figure of the black man in Europe, a stranger in a strange land, attempting to escape or avoid the brutality of his inheritance, only to find that his birthright *is* that inheritance. The common figure of the African American artist in Europe raises a range of issues concerning crossover, betrayal, and cultural allegiance. Like many African American artists, Baldwin understood that the expatriate African American had substantially and necessarily different motives from the expatriate European American. Whereas the white American could see his trek to Europe as a return to the origins, as a continuity, as a quest for clarification of U.S. culture by seeking out the touchstones of the parent culture, the black American could find there only another site of alienation; but a useful site nonetheless. For the black American, Africa always looms as the backdrop of Europe, calling into question the authenticity of the artist's relation to those European touchstones and reminding the artist that the American myth of color was born not in America but in the struggle between Europe and Africa. "I must accept the status which myth, if nothing else, gives me in the West before I can hope to change the myth," Baldwin says (174). The struggle between Europe and Africa takes on a greater intensity, a more intense intimacy in the "New" World—an intimacy enabling greater insight into the human history of struggle. The revelation that comes at the end of *Notes* is not merely that American blacks have more in common with American whites than either have in common with either Europeans or Africans.[36] For Baldwin, the greater revelation is that the history binding blacks to whites, and vice versa, in the "New" World has changed both blacks and whites so radically that neither can abandon that history to the other:

> This fact faced, with all its implications, it can be seen that the history of the American Negro problem is not merely shameful, it is also something of an achievement. For even when the worst has been said, it must also be added that the perpetual challenge posed by this problem was always, somehow, perpetually met. (Notes, 175)

The real problem of color becomes, for Baldwin, a larger and more fundamental problem of denial. The mechanisms of denial (synecdoche, metonymy, and projection) are, in addition to being instruments of oppression, inevitably the weapons of (self-)destruction. "The American vision of the world," he writes in the conclusion of Notes, "allows so little reality, generally speaking, for any of the darker forces in human life" and "tends until today to paint moral issues in glaring black and white" (174). The black-white polarity enables Americans to continue to deny the polymorphous course of all human desire. Giving Americans a screen for projecting fear, this polarity prevents them from dealing directly with the unclassifiable, uncolored course of desire itself:

> It is only now beginning to be borne in on us—very faintly, it must be admitted, very slowly, and very much against our will—that this vision of the world is dangerously inaccurate, and perfectly useless. For it protects our moral high-mindedness at the terrible expense of weakening our grasp of reality. People who shut their eyes to reality simply invite their own destruction, and anyone who insists on remaining in a state of innocence long after that innocence is dead turns himself into a monster. (175)

The lie of "glaring black and white" denies, for Baldwin, the reality of a common desire, forged under the conditions of history and underlying and shaping that very history. The polarity of black and white provides a strict code for moral standards: for whites, "black" means all that is inferior, darkly mysterious, and evil; for blacks, white is the color of injustice, giving African Americans the moral upper hand in a long contest between good and evil. The black-white dilemma is not only a way of attempting to escape the consequences of history; it is, more disastrously, an attempt to escape the natural

course of desire, which knows no bounds and fulfills itself by desiring whatever it wants.[37] In *Notes of a Native Son*, Baldwin expresses
this very pointed moral in terms of the American race problem; but it
is exactly the point of *Giovanni's Room*, where the color dilemma is
mapped onto the question of same-sex desire. People like David, who
shut their eyes to the reality of their desire, simply invite their own
destruction. David's moral high-mindedness comes at a terrible expense. By insisting on remaining in a state of innocence, which is really an illusion, he turns himself into the monster he hopes to escape.
Who David is, a white American running away from the consequences
of his own history and biography, equals *what David is*, a homosexual
American running away from the course of his desire. David's fear of
himself derives as much from his inheritance as a white, Protestant,
upper-class American, deserving of the reins of power, as it derives
from his fear of his own desire. The "white" homosexual desire depicted in *Giovanni's Room*, then, is also Baldwin's inheritance, for it is
the further thinking through of the fundamental moral dilemma
foisted on him by the history of denial he shares with all the Davids
of the world.

Baldwin's freedom to write *Giovanni's Room* is encapsulated in the
final two sentences of *Notes*: "It is precisely this black- white experience which may prove of indispensable value to us in the world we
face today. This world is white no longer, and it will never be white
again" (175). In working through the problem of identity, Baldwin becomes aware to what extent the world is not really white, though so
much of it is imperialistically controlled by people of European descent. The essential problems of humanity—problems of repressed
and oppressed desire—can be worked through only by those who are
in touch with the realities of denial. White control does not make the
world white, because total control itself is not a genuine expression of
desire, and because the nonwhites of the world constantly interrupt
and disrupt any aspiration toward controlled purity. Just as one cannot reach for the illusion of control without stumbling on the stone of
denial, so one cannot expose denial without giving up the illusion of
control. Such control is, instead, an expression of fear, a denial of desire. Rather than seeing Baldwin's movement from this coloring statement ("this world is white no longer, and it will never be white
again") to an all-white novel (*Giovanni's Room*) as some sort of desperate irony or puzzling detour, it makes more sense to see the sequence

as a culmination. Since Baldwin no longer saw himself as a stranger lost in a white world that he could neither know nor claim, he was free to write inside whiteness without being trapped in it or by it, and without being afraid of losing the inheritance given him by historical blackness. The uncloseting of desire—sexual desire—would be a necessary step if Americans hoped to unwarp their imaginations from the destructive bent of racism.

Uncloseting Sexual Desire, Exhibiting the Promiscuous Self

Ironically, this project of unwarping desire put Baldwin at odds with both the older generations of race-conscious, black-uplift Negroes early on and the younger generations of Black Power nationalists later in his career. In both cases, Baldwin raised doubts about the role of respectability and authenticity, the twin moral principles undergirding historical concepts of black cultural wholeness. Though Baldwin's argument with Wright over the author's authority and identity was the more visible as a public skirmish, his controversy with Langston Hughes was more visceral. In his definitive biography *The Life of Langston Hughes*, Arnold Rampersad explains how Hughes linked Baldwin's sexually explicit fiction with integration and integration with the loss of traditional black values:

> To Langston, there was little that was truly creative, much less visionary about *Another Country*. Privately to Arna Bontemps, he described Baldwin as aiming for a best-seller in "trying to out-Henry Miller Henry Miller in the use of bad BAD bad words, or run [Harold Robbins's] *The Carpetbaggers* one better on sex in bed and out, left and right, plus a description of a latrine with all the little-boy words reproduced in the telling." In the same letter, Langston linked what he saw as Baldwin's excesses to the trend of integration sapping the strength of black youth. Paying a stiff price for the modicum of integration allowed them, young blacks were abandoning the old values and practices in the rush to be like whites. "Cullud is doing everything white folks are doing these days!" Langston mocked.[38]

Like recent Afrocentrists, Hughes understood well what integration meant for the integrity of African American neighborhoods and thus the vision of an empowered political and economic group (a matter about which Baldwin was much less perceptive). Rampersad clarifies Hughes's view of the matter: "Flocking now to white barber-shops, blacks were beginning to ignore parlors owned by members of their own race. Some blacks were seeking to bury their dead with Park Avenue undertakers and were even insisting on white pallbear-ers. 'Integration is going to RUIN Negro business,' he predicted—as it apparently threatened to ruin the finest young writer of fiction [Bald-win] in the race" (*Life of Langston Hughes*, 2:335). The traditional con-cept of racial uplift, adhered to by Hughes, meant that African Amer-ican progress relied on the flourishing of African American culture. Du Bois's "talented tenth" had a special obligation to represent the culture in the best light, to itself and to the white world (the principle of respectability), as well as an obligation to record and celebrate the achievements of the culture with objectivity and sensitivity for all members of the group, past, present, and future (the principle of au-thenticity).[39] On the publication of Baldwin's first novel, Hughes ex-pressed his reservations, evidently picking up on some strain in the novel that touched a nerve. Rampersad writes:

> Criticizing Baldwin's sometimes unstable blending of gritty realism and refined rhetoric in the novel, Hughes judged that if Zora Neale Hurston, "with her feeling for the folk idiom," had been its author, "it would probably be a *quite* wonderful book." Baldwin, however, "over-writes and over-poeticizes in images way over the heads of the folks supposedly thinking them," in what finally was "an 'art' book about folks who aren't 'art' folks." *Go Tell It on the Mountain*, he concluded, was "a low-down story in a velvet bag—and a Knopf binding." (*Life of Langston Hughes*, 2:205)

As the final jab at his former publisher, Alfred A. Knopf, indicates, Hughes's reaction to the rising young writer contains a note of envy, no doubt heightened by the quickly changing opportunities available to a black writer of Baldwin's caliber in the new age of civil rights—opportunities too late for Hughes to grab. Hughes expresses his dis-content with Baldwin's writing as a tendency toward excess: "over-writes," "over-poeticizes," "over the heads." Baldwin's materials may be authentic enough; he is, after all, dealing with a central char-acter of black cultural experience: the church. But it is Baldwin's inau-thentic treatment of this authentic material that Hughes seems to crit-icize. Baldwin's writing—more precisely, his style (images and dic-tion)—comes from outside the culture. If the characters in Baldwin's first novel led Hughes to question the novelist's authenticity, how much more disturbing must Baldwin's second and third novels have been? The age-old conundrum of exactly what defines an authentic treatment of blackness is really secondary here. In Hughes's mind, integration threatened not only the integrity of the black community, from which alone that wellspring of authentic expression could flow, but also the integrity of the black writer's motives, tempting him toward an exhibitionist desire that, even if enacted in private life, should never be exemplified for the whole world to see.

Baldwin's alleged excesses (overly poetic images, gutter language, too much sex) are mere covers for this deeper issue of exhibitionism or promiscuity, racial and sexual. The image of Baldwin that Hughes suggests, with his characteristic circumspection, and that black nationalists would more openly and harshly put forward is the image of the black writer as irresponsible exhibitionist: the writer more concerned with exhibiting his talents to the white world for profit and prestige than with employing that talent for the purposes of racial uplift. Again, this exhibitionist impulse has a complicated relation to the protest tradition. When Baldwin rejects this tradition, he is rejecting the equation of surface characteristics (e.g., race) with cultural knowledge (e.g., the African American heritage). According to Baldwin, protest fiction plays up the illusion that we can understand injustice by fictionally *representing* the categories on which that injustice is based. Instead, Baldwin wants to *explode* those categories, offering not a protest but rather a critique that disables the categories from retaining their oppressive power. Ironically, Baldwin's project of exposure and explosion could look a lot like exhibitionism, if not like the exhibition of racial anger and violence that had become a marker of black protest. The moment Baldwin begins to expose/explode the vagaries and slippages of desire, he seems to be writing a titillating project that places sexual revelations, confessions even, at the heart of cultural identity. When younger writers such as Baraka took Baldwin to task for his individualism and his exhibition of his talents, they were speaking from motives similar to Hughes's but from an altered historical-political position. Their concern was much less a desire for black respectability and integrity (Hughes's major drive) than a signal to black cultural integrity, much more a desire for black disrespectability, the capacity for blacks to purge the cultural habit of basing black integrity on the relationship between black and white.

How does fear of this exhibitionist figure get imagined and im-
aged? It gets projected, not surprisingly, onto the experience of same-
sex desire. It expresses itself blatantly as a fear of cross-racial same-
sex desire, but as we shall see, this serves to hide a deeper, unspoken
fear. Exhibitionist behavior finds its perfect image in the articulate
homosexual who writes articulately about same-sex desire. There is
no mistaking that same-sex desire is the charged and unspoken subtext in Hughes's unease with Baldwin's writing. Baldwin's depiction
of polymorphous, promiscuous desire, desire that respects no cultural boundaries, may logically begin with interracial sex (integrationist love), but it must logically end up with something even more
frightening and damaging to those concerned with the respectable
image of the race as a whole: intraracial homosexuality. The love between black men that some Harlem Renaissance writers of the 1920s
and 1930s represented in their writing—including Hughes himself,
coyly, in his novel *Not without Laughter* and in some of his poetry—by
the late 1960s had become overshadowed by the controversy over interracial homosexuality, as aided by some leading young black male
writers of the period.[40]

It is difficult to say whether the public representation of interracial
or of intraracial love between men creates more controversy in the abstract, for these controversies are so interwoven with the historical
moment in which they are made public and with the particular racial-
sexual politics out of which they frequently derive.[41] Either of these
modes of intragender sexuality certainly creates more scandal than
the interracial heterosexual couple, which is the way in which the
anxiety over the racial boundaries of sexual desire normally expresses itself as a fetish in U.S. society. Whereas the exhibition, in literary and mass media, of interracial bonding between men can be ra-
tionalized, as it almost always is, as a commentary on the relations
between the races, the exhibition of same-sex love within the race
cannot be so easily projected as an external or purely racial matter. A
black man holding a white man in his arms—the immortal image cat-
apulted into Hollywood film when Sidney Poitier holds Tony Curtis
in his arms in the 1958 movie *The Defiant Ones*—can easily be translated as the brotherly love of buddies in the constitution of a potent
U.S. national manhood, developing out of and across the color line.[42]
The difference of race, the overcoming of racial difference, decenters
and defers the more disturbing possibility of physical attraction. Just

as the arena of manly sports (so riddled with white men admiring black bodies) enables men to pat each other on the butt without this gesture being read sexually, so the larger arena of manly interracial politics enables black-white male bonding, with its potential erotic implications, to be read nonsexually. But with the image of a black man holding another black man, racial difference no longer operates effectively as a screen of potential sexual attraction. The way in which black men are projected as overly sexualized by white culture heightens the opportunities for sexual implications. Likewise, black men are projected by mainstream culture, and to some extent, self-projected by black culture in its most public guises, as bonding with other black men only in the arena of sports, in the contest for a female, or in competition for a prize. The kind of aggressive tension depicted between two white male-bonding partners tends to be more greatly exaggerated when two black men are shown.

In fact, images of black male partners were very rare in dominant U.S. cultural media between World War II and the 1970s, despite the popularity of such images in Harlem Renaissance narratives.[43] The white partner in the interracial couple helps diminish the fear of what two strong black men together might do. In addition to stirring up anxieties in a white audience, the representation of erotically tinged devotion between two black men can be troubling to some African Americans concerned with respectability or reproductivity of the race as principles of black cultural integrity or nationalism. Thus, in some black nationalist and Afrocentrist literature, such images have been conveniently policed by overstressing the natural whiteness of homosexuality, its intrinsic alienation from original African and historical African American culture. Erotic bonding between black men becomes, in some of this literature, a disease imported into black culture from decadent European culture.[44] If homosexual desire is represented as an integral part of African American experience, will it become too closely associated—perhaps equated—with blackness in dominant culture, considering the way in which that culture has projected other social deviances uniformly onto black culture? Such racial anxieties operate variously in African American culture and its representation in the 1960s and 1970s sexual controversies. Baldwin exhibits all three modes of scandalous sexual attraction—interracial heterosexuality, interracial homosexuality, and intraracial homosexuality—in his two novels of the 1960s, *Another Country* and *Tell Me How*

Long the Train's Been Gone, a fact that makes him an especially visible target of such fears and projections.[45]

The best way to police feared desire is to get the individual to become his own policeman—a strategy that can work as well in an ideology of racial uplift as in nationalist ideology, in an oppressed group as in a dominating group. This strategy shaped Langston Hughes's outlook and style. According to Rampersad, "For the greater part of his life, Hughes made almost a fetish of the secrecy about his sexual interests, so that from the start of his adulthood even close friends of liberated sexuality . . . vouched privately not for the nature or relative strength of his sexuality but for its maddening elusiveness" (*Life of Langston Hughes,* 2:336). Rampersad suggests that Hughes's secrecy is connected to his role as poetic spokesman for the race. Although Rampersad speaks as though Hughes's obsession with hiding his sexual predilection is highly unusual, as Baldwin points out through *Giovanni's Room,* such "fanatical discretion" has been the norm in dominant U.S. society and, because the African American middle class has often been obsessed with the public integrity of the race, has become an ambivalent value in middle-class black society. This was true especially for someone like Hughes, who was seen as a spokesman of the race.

In American society, especially before the late 1960s, the scandal was for desire to be exposed. That we have no documentary record of Hughes's desire should not surprise us.[46] Even when desire is expressed in the form of a sexual act, it is intensely ephemeral, resisting every form of documentation and verification. We cannot tell what a person desires by noting the characteristics (age, gender, color, class) of those he did or did not have intercourse with. The writer who hopes to bring desire to the surface, to map it, must be willing to brook the kind of criticism that Hughes levels at Baldwin. The irony is that Hughes's obsessive attempts to hide his desire only make us more fascinated with what is hidden. Rather than containing or controlling desire they foster rumors, speculation, and more intense projection. The more desire is unarticulated, the more motivation there is for talking about it, the more there is to say about it. Baldwin wanted to make desire articulate by bringing it to the surface, so that it would no longer have anything to say, so that it could become an unpoliced, ordinary act of physical love. Hughes, in contrast, believed the only way to protect the rock of his inheritance was to sublimate desire, to sacrifice intimacy for the sake of racial harmony and wholeness.

Although Hughes was closer to the mark in his understanding of the potential damage that could be done to African American culture by integration, Baldwin was closer to the mark concerning the sinister role that policing desire plays in perpetuating an oppressor-oppressed mentality, the instrument and site of racist ideology. The consequence of Hughes's attempt to police his own desire is not necessarily greater racial harmony but instead a greater confusion about the role that "deviant" desire plays in the institution and sustenance of racial oppression. On the surface, sacrificing individual sexual orientation for a transparent unity of racial desire sounds admirable, but in terms of political reality, it is a disastrous project. This means Hughes's policed desire becomes not a rock of racial responsibility but instead a stumbling block to clarifying African American experience. In simple terms, this means we will always be distracted by what we fear we do not know. When desire is well hidden from view, speculation is not only appropriate but necessary. What is it that Hughes really wants?

Despite Rampersad's ultra cautious approach to Hughes's sexuality, for instance, he still feels confident in speculating about the surface of Hughes's desire. Note the certainty of this claim, based as it is, on necessarily external documentation:

> *What also seems clear,* however, is that Hughes found some young men, especially dark-skinned men, appealing and sexually fascinating. (Both in his various artistic representations, in fiction especially, and in his life, he appears to have found young white men of little sexual appeal.) Virile young men of very dark complexion fascinated him. (*Life of Langston Hughes,* 2:336; emphasis added)

In accord with Rampersad's theory that Hughes's greatest legacy is his commitment to racial uplift and to an African-focused solution to the racial problem, he decides that *if* Hughes desired men, it could only have been "dark-skinned" black men that he desired. How is it that Rampersad can be so willing to leave the nature of Hughes's sexual orientation totally hypothetical while claiming so confidently that Hughes could have found only particular kinds of men "appealing and sexually fascinating"? How can we know for certain what a person's object choice is, where there is supposedly so much doubt about the direction of his desire? If we can never know for sure whether Hughes was a homosexual, then logically, we also can never know whether he desired women or men, much less whether he desired black men or white men or both equally.

This speculation about Hughes's object choices grows out of the contrast that Rampersad makes between Hughes and Baldwin. The comparison is more than implicit; it is clearly enunciated in this telling paragraph of Rampersad's biography:

> Between Hughes, on the one hand, and Baldwin and Ellison, on the other, was one difference far greater than any between the latter writers. While Langston psychologically needed the race in order to survive and flourish, their deepest needs as artists and human beings were evidently elsewhere. He wanted young black writers to be objective about the race, but not to scorn or to flee it. . . . Baldwin's second novel had contained no black characters; his third would include blacks, but as characters secondary to his hero, a white American writer. To some extent, Baldwin was much more concerned with the mighty and dangerous challenge of illuminating—as a virtual pioneer in modern American fiction—the homosexual condition than with the challenge of writing about race, which by contrast had been exhaustively treated. (2:297)

Rampersad's contrast between Hughes, the black writer genuinely concerned about his race, and Baldwin, the black writer whose concerns are "elsewhere," relies on the identity logic that we have seen with the earlier critics and that Baldwin was combating. Just as Rampersad uses the dark-skinned young men in Hughes's fiction and life as evidence for the apparency of Hughes's desire for only very black young men—in the sense of color and culture—so he uses the fact that Baldwin includes very white young men in his fiction as evidence that Baldwin's interests were "elsewhere." Hughes's apparent attraction (sexually exciting but nonsexual?) to dark-skinned young men becomes an emblem for his deep-seated and unquestionable desire for advancing the race. His many actual acts of kindness toward these young men embody and symbolize not merely his desire for these men but, even more, his desire for his race. In contrast, Baldwin's surface interest in sexuality necessarily precludes his genuine interest in his own race.

What an amazing condition, not to be able to desire more than one thing at a time! Rampersad cannot see the relevance of Baldwin's interest in same-sex desire in relation to his interest in black desire. This miscalculation encourages Rampersad to go so far as to suggest that Vivaldo, "a white American writer," is the hero of *Another Country*. According to this logic, Baldwin displaces himself, a real-life black writer, with a fictional white writer. Vivaldo, a lower-class Italian American who struggles with the American system of color, class, and sexuality in a way analogous to the hero, Rufus Scott, has an affair with an Anglo-Saxon homosexual from the Southern United States, Eric, and begins to work through his identity as a man through this relationship. Accordingly, this should mean that Baldwin displaces his own color for a (secret?) fantasy of whiteness, whereby he becomes a white (Italian American?) writer who desires to know himself through his love for a (another?) white man.

Despite Hughes's circumspection (mimicked here by Hughes's great biographer, Rampersad), or perhaps because of it, his fate has been and always will be identified as much with same-sex desire as with racial uplift. This is not because there is some natural division between same-sexuality and blackness but rather because such division will never succeed. Hughes's own work and life give testimony to the nexus, the often bewildering interfusion, that inescapably intertwines sexual desire and racial orientation with cultural knowledge and self-knowledge. If we could get beyond identity (which grounds cultural knowledge in a singularity of sameness), the plight of a writer such as Hughes would be clarified. We would begin to see that variables within a cultural frame compete with one another only to the extent that we conceptualize them as differences, rather than as variables, variations, or variances.

One of Hughes's poems that has become famous in queer culture exemplifies this bewildering interfusion, indicating that despite his circumspection, Hughes, like Baldwin, leads multiple lives, with at least one version of the author being celebrated in one part of African American culture, another in one part of gay-lesbian culture, and yet another—though *not* a *different*—in gay-identified African American culture. As Charles I. Nero points out, this poem, "Café: 3 A.M.," is, significantly, nowhere discussed in Rampersad's comprehensive two-volume biography. In "Café: 3 A.M.," Hughes places us as readers in the position of cop watchers. The vice squad, the traditional enemy of homosexuals during the pre-Stonewall era, goes in search of degenerates, not realizing that their policing eyes reflect their own projected degeneracy:

> Detectives from the vice squad
> with weary sadistic eyes
> spotting fairies.
> *Degenerates,*
> some folks say.
>
> But God, Nature,
> or somebody
> made them that way.
>
> Police lady or Lesbian
> over there?
> *Where?*[47]

The weary, overworked eyes of the vice detectives signal not only how difficult it can be to spot fairies, to distinguish gays from "normal" citizens, but also how futile their task is, since their surveillance seems not to stem but to swell the tide of "deviant" sexuality. The final lines of the poem satirize the activity of "spotting fairies." We liberal readers do it, too, even though we feel that they (or we) should be left alone ("God, Nature, / or somebody / made them that way"). The activity of policing is contagious; it is also duplicitous. The "Police lady," the stereotype of the butch female cop, cannot be distinguished from the stereotype of a "Lesbian," just as the detectives' weary, sadistic eyes seem to mirror the "degenerate" desire of fairies, whom the detectives are supposed to be entrapping. The cops' cruising stares are the same as the cruisy sexual stares of the fairies.

In this poem, Hughes indicates his understanding of what it feels like to exist in the opaque glass house of observed desire, where banal café gossip about who is or is not "that way" entangles everyone in the cycle of degenerate, voyeuristic, repressed desire. Repression gives rise to speculation, and speculation always reveals our own anxieties rather than the realities of other people's desire. To suggest that this poem has nothing to do with the African American experience because it focuses on queer-baiting would be to deny the inescapable relation between how police have traditionally treated homosexuals and how they have treated black people. Whatever variances exist between the policing of these two populations—the fact that homosexual desire sometimes hides itself more easily, for instance—Hughes is drawing also on his African American experience of being watched suspiciously by cops' sadistic eyes.[48] In writing this poem, Hughes is writing out of his African American experience in terms not only of his cultural knowledge of what it feels like to be surveyed by hostile cop eyes but also of his take on same-sex behavior as a form of resistance to intrusive authorities. As Nero remarks, "In light of this homophobic climate, Hughes's sympathetic treatment of gays and lesbians amounts to remarkably radical support for gays and lesbians, as well as an indictment of the state."[49] For the purposes of this poem, regardless of whether he ever had sexual intercourse with another man or not, Hughes is not merely black but gay at the same time. Also, more significantly, his cognition of what it means to be black constitutes his understanding of what it feels like to be homosexual; the structure of what it means to be openly or secretly homosexual structures his understanding of what it feels like to be an African American.

Under these circumstances, Hughes's obsession with keeping his desire a private matter is understandable. As some leading uplifters, black nationalists, and Afrocentrists have argued in different ways, African Americans must be willing to sacrifice mere personal desires for the greater cause of African American community. The question is whether homosexual desire constitutes such mereness. Baldwin's exhibitionism threatened the integrity of Hughes's circumspection. If Baldwin can speak deeply to the African American experience while keeping his same-sex desire intact, then there is no basis for policing and purging homosexuality from black culture. More to the point, since policing and purging are doomed to fail, the more pertinent question is how to make the contribution offered by the black cultural expression of same-sex desire succeed. Baldwin's contribution to African American culture lies in his ability to imbalance the cultural conception of normalcy and in his linking of normalcy to racist ideology. The concept of normalcy, according to Baldwin, is the legacy of a European American system of racism. White supremacist culture needs a norm in order to trust its own illusion of black inferiority and white supremacy. More precisely, it needs a sexual norm in order to perpetuate the myth of whiteness as a racial norm. If African Americans are to think clearly about the behavior of racism, we must be able to disentangle the image of sexual desire projected onto us by white society from our own dread of sexual desire fostered by this projection. If we search our own communities, articulate our desires, so that we have nothing to hide and nothing to purge (insofar as this is possible), we shall be better able to dismiss and disregard the white obsession with policing our sexualities—a policing that we ourselves have unfortunately, on occasion, internalized as a self-project, in effect attempting to do their dirty work for them.

We might go so far as to say that Hughes, despite his obsession with protecting his erotic tendencies, understood as well as Baldwin, who scripted his characters' sexual fantasies for everyone to project onto his own, that the criminalization of same-sexuality is not in its enactment but in its exposure.

NOTES

1. James Baldwin, *Another Country* (New York: Dell Publishing, 1960), 115.

2. James Baldwin, *Notes of a Native Son* (Boston: Beacon, 1955), 6.

3. See Quincy Troupe, "The Last Interview," in *James Baldwin: The Legacy,* ed. Quincy Troupe (New York: Simon & Schuster, 1989), 204.

4. See James Baldwin, *Giovanni's Room* (New York: Dell Publishing, 1956).

5. Fern Marja Eckman, *The Furious Passage of James Baldwin* (New York: M. Evans & Co., 1966), 137.

6. James Levin, *The Gay Novel in America* (New York: Garland Publishing, 1991), 143.

7. James Baldwin, *Go Tell It on the Mountain* (New York: Dell Publishing, 1953).

8. Nathan A. Scott, Jr., "Judgment Marked by a Cellar: The American Negro Writer and the Dialectic of Despair," *Denver Quarterly* 2, 2 (Summer 1967): 27–28.

9. Robert Bone, *The Negro Novel in America,* rev. ed. (New Haven: Yale University Press, 1965), 175–85.

10. Calvin C. Hernton, *White Papers for White Americans* (New York: Doubleday, 1966), 114.

11. James Baldwin, *Blues for Mister Charlie* (New York: Dell Publishing, 1964).

12. Hernton must overlook the implicit homoeroticism in Baldwin's first novel to stick to such logic, or he accepts the portrayal of such desire as long it is buried and does not speak its name too loudly.

13. Eldridge Cleaver, *Soul on Ice* (New York: Dell Publishing, 1968), 106

and 100. It is important to note, however, that Cleaver castigates Baldwin, ironically, in order to join arms (speaking metaphorically in terms of weaponry but not discounting the erotic pun) with Norman Mailer. Mailer portrays black men as the source of unbridled, primal sexuality and white men as desiccated by bureaucratic culture (especially in "The White Negro," in *Advertisements for Myself* [1959; reprint Cambridge: Harvard University Press, 1992], 337–58). Therefore, Cleaver feels more comfortable embracing Mailer than Baldwin, not only because this is Cleaver's own take in *Soul on Ice* but also because it seems to put the black man in the dominant position of giving (semen) to the envious white man, rather than the other way around, by suggesting that black men are the standard for masculinity. The confusions in the sexual politics of *Soul on Ice* are multiplied when Cleaver climaxes the text with love letters to his white female lawyer alongside essays celebrating the beauty of black women. As Jennifer Jordan has cogently pointed out, by siding with Mailer over Baldwin, Cleaver makes white men (D. H. Lawrence, Norman Mailer, Wilhelm Reich) the intellectual fathers of hip, limiting black men to the "physical model for the life of the hipster"; see her "Cleaver vs. Baldwin: Icing the White Negro," *Black Books Bulletin* 1 (Winter 1992): 13. More generally on the role of homophobia and sexism in black nationalism, see Phillip Brian Harper, *Are We Not Men? Masculine Anxiety and the Problem of African-American Identity* (New York: Oxford University Press, 1996), 49–51; and Joyce Hope Scott, "From Foreground to Margin: Female Configurations and Masculine Self-Representation in Black Nationalist Fiction," in *Nationalisms and Sexualities,* ed. Andrew Parker, Mary Russo, Doris Sommer, and Patricia Yaeger (New York: Routledge, 1992), 296–312. As David L. Dudley has pointed out, Cleaver here is engaging in a kind of Oedipal conflict, similar to the way in which Baldwin earlier attacked Richard Wright as the reigning great (male) writer of black America; see Dudley's *My Father's Shadow: Intergenerational Conflict in African American Men's Autobiography* (Philadelphia: University of Pennsylvania Press, 1991), 137–65.

14. See James Baldwin, *The Fire Next Time* (New York: Random House/Vintage Books, 1962). In terms of tone, style, and structure of ideas, *Soul on Ice* especially mimics Baldwin's *Notes of a Native Son,* as well as *The Fire Next Time.*

15. The rivalry between Baldwin and Mailer was professional, spilling over into the personal through the public arena. Their love-hate relationship was publicly played out not only in their competing journalistic stories on the same events, such as the Patterson-Liston boxing match, but also in their writing about each other. Characteristically, the latter, Mailer hides what in Baldwin becomes the exposure of an erotic undercurrent. See, for instance, Baldwin's "The Black Boy Looks at the White Boy," a 1961 *Esquire* essay he labels a "love letter" to Mailer (reprinted in *The Price of the Ticket* [New York: St.

Martin's, 1985], 289–303); also see Mailer's "Evaluations—Quick and Expensive Comments on the Talent in the Room," in *Advertisements for Myself,* in which Mailer's anxiety over and fascination with Baldwin's sexuality, and black male sexuality in general, is screened by his dismissive comments on Baldwin's style as "noble toilet water" (472) and "sprayed with perfume" (471); and about *Giovanni's Room,* Mailer writes that it "was a bad book but mostly a brave one" (471). On the Baldwin-Mailer relationship, see James Campbell, *Talking at the Gates: A Life of James Baldwin* (New York: Penguin Books, 1991), 137–44. On their divergent coverage of the 1962 Patterson-Liston fight, see W. J. Weatherby, *Squaring Off: Mailer vs. Baldwin* (New York: Mason/Charter, 1977), 79; and David Leeming, *James Baldwin: A Biography* (New York: Knopf, 1994), 183–86. The most interesting treatment of this topic can be found in Gerald Early, *Tuxedo Junction: Essays on American Culture* (Hopewell, N.J.: Ecco Press, 1989), 183–95.

16. Baker's essay was an important intervention, but even so astute a critic as Baker found it difficult to articulate a fusion between variant sexuality and African American experiences in 1977, the year the essay appeared (reprinted in *Critical Essays on James Baldwin,* ed. Fred L. Standley and Nancy V. Burt [Boston: G. K. Hall & Co., 1988], 62–77. It must be noted that Baker, as well as many of these other critics, was writing out of and in response to a climate of heightened anxiety about the prominence of same-sexuality in African American culture, at a point when the gay liberation movement, figured as largely white in the media, had begun to mimic the political strategies of the Black Power movement. The attack against Baldwin is part of a larger trend that occurred during the late 1960s and early 1970s, in which homosexuality became a convenient scapegoat in the discourse of black nationalism. However it would be a mistake to equate African American attitudes toward same-gender desire with this generally homophobic black nationalist stance. African American articulations of same-sexuality among men vary historically, but frequently the African American literary record suggests a great deal more acknowledgment and integration of same-sexuality into community life than in American culture at large. Likewise, it would be a mistake to suggest that all black nationalists have been homophobic or that Black Power ideology is inherently heterosexist, as many scholars have begun to claim, based on the most salient statements made by individuals such as Cleaver; see, for instance, the otherwise excellent studies by Harper, *Are We Not Men?*, 49–53; bell hooks, *Black Looks: Race and Representation* (Toronto: Between the Lines, 1992), 96–113; and Lee Edelman, *Homographesis: Essays in Gay Literary and Cultural Theory* (New York: Routledge, 1994), 53–59.

The homophobic scapegoating that occurs in black nationalist literature emerged in the mid-1960s in the context of an ideological struggle within and between Black Power movements. The history of this struggle, and why homosexuality is crucial to it, is far too complicated to summarize here. Suffice it to say that Cleaver's homophobic posturing, though highly influential, staged an extreme reaction to this struggle over how to understand the role of black sexuality within black liberation. The Black Panther leader Huey P. Newton voiced another commonly held approach to gender roles and sexuality within African American communities when he attacked Cleaver, once his fellow Panther, for using guns, uniforms, and other conventionally masculine symbols to prop up his insecure gender identity; see Newton (with the assistance of J. Herman Blake), *Revolutionary Suicide* (1973; reprint New York: Writers and Readers Publishing, 1995), 133. In one of the most eloquent and insightful pro-gay statements from the period, on the relation between the women's, gay, and black liberation movements, see Newton's collection of speeches *To Die for the People: The Writings of Huey P. Newton,* ed. Toni Morrison (1972; reprint, New York: Writers and Readers Publishing, 1995), 152–55. We have to ask why, in current debates about attitudes toward same-sexuality in Black Power discourse, Cleaver is repeatedly quoted as exemplary while Newton's critiques are wholly forgotten. As I suggest elsewhere, this pattern in the scholarship falls in line with mass media representations of black men's relation to homosexuality: black men are projected as either the ultimate embodiment of other Americans' extreme homophobia or as the ultimate embodiment of stereotyped, highly effeminate homosexuality. The complicated reality of diverse and conflicting points of view among African American men across history and at present gets silenced.

17. The idea that Baldwin is too comfortable with whites and uncomfortable with blacks is widespread, especially in the earlier criticism. This attitude is closely tied to the role of homosexuality and cross-racial sexuality in Baldwin's novels. For example, see Marion Berghahn's essay "Images of Africa in the Writings of James Baldwin," in *James Baldwin: Modern Critical Views,* ed. Harold Bloom (New York: Chelsea House, 1986), 97–108. Heterosexually panicky readings of Baldwin's work, especially of *Giovanni's Room* and *Another Country,* are too pervasive and too numerous to mention. For a sampling, see Donald B. Gibson, "James Baldwin: The Political Anatomy of Space," in *James Baldwin: A Critical Evaluation,* ed. Therman B. O'Daniel (Washington, D.C.: Howard University Press, 1977), 3–18; Fred L. Standley, "James Baldwin: The Crucial Situation," *South Atlantic Quarterly* 65, 3 (Summer 1966): 371–81, especially 378; and the early reviews and essays collected in *James Baldwin: A Collection of Critical Essays,* ed. Keneth Kinnamon (Englewood Cliffs, N.J.: Prentice- Hall, 1974).

Some readers tend to equate Baldwin's exploration of homosexuality with "propaganda for homosexualism" (Hernton, *White Papers,* 139). John S. Lash tries to make Baldwin into an advocate of "phallicism," the celebration of male-male sex as "self-fulfillment beyond the necessity for proof and measurement, peace and security reuniting the male and masculine flesh and spirit" "Baldwin Beside Himself: A Study in Modern Phallicism," in O'-Daniel, 48). In *Playing the Game: The Homosexual Novel in America* (Indianapolis: Bobbs-Merrill Co., 1977), Roger Austen's cursory and token treatment of Baldwin's first two novels and of Charles Wright's *The Messenger* is a good example of how a failure to take racial variance into account when discussing sexual variance can lead to misreading (see the section "To Be Young, Bisexual, and Black" [201–4]).

As indicated by this brief list, even some of the most insightful readers can occasionally lapse into this kind of logic, either protesting the existence of homosexuality in the works as a diminishment of the racial focus or viewing homosexuality as Baldwin's solution to all life's problems. Another class of readers makes curious assumptions about the validity of homosexual desire. Falling into the last category are Stanley Macebuh, *James Baldwin: A Critical Study* (New York: Joseph Okpakn, 1973), 62; Louis H. Pratt, *James Baldwin* (Boston: Twayne, 1978), 57–59, 80; Trudier Harris, *Black Women in the Fiction of James Baldwin* (Knoxville: University of Tennessee Press, 1985), 189; and idem, *Exorcising Blackness: Historical and Literary Lynching and Burning Rituals* (Bloomington: Indiana University Press, 1984), 62–68. They occasionally view homosexuality not as a failure to be fully black but rather as a failure to be heterosexual. No doubt some of these critics, if writing about these issues today, would alter their phrasing, if not their personal opinions, in light of the consciousness-raising performed by queer studies and gay-lesbian-bisexual-transgendered politics.

18. James Baldwin, *Tell Me How Long the Train's Been Gone* (New York: Dell Publishing, 1968) and *Just above My Head* (New York: Dell Publishing, 1979). The language of erotic attraction is, of course, pathetically insufficient. Like desire itself, it is impossible to track or describe adequately the simultaneous fixity and fluidity of individuals' tendencies toward (un)predictable sexual objects.

19. Chester Himes, *Cast the First Stone* (1952; reprint, Chatham, N.J.: Chatham Bookseller, 1973).

20. The original version of *Cast the First Stone*, titled *Yesterday Will Make You Cry*, has been published for the first time this year by W. W. Norton & Co. See H. Bruce Franklin's insightful review "Self-Mutilations," *The Nation*, 16 February 1998, 28–31.

21. H. Bruce Franklin, *Prison Literature in America: The Victim as Criminal and Artist* (New York: Oxford University Press, 1978; expanded ed., 1989), 207–10.

22. See, for instance, the very interesting treatment of black and interracial homosexuality in Chester Himes, *Blind Man with a Pistol* (1969; reprint, New York: Vintage Books, 1989). In integrating "deviant" sexuality into his

Harlem novel in this manner, Himes is working in a rich tradition in African American men's writing that goes back to James Weldon Johnson's *Autobiography of an Ex-Coloured Man* (1912; reprint, New York: Vintage Books, 1989) and includes novels by Rudolph Fisher, Claude McKay, Langston Hughes, George Wylie Henderson, Charles Wright, Charles Perry, John Edgar Wideman—as well as Baldwin himself.

23. Edelman's theory of "homographesis," for instance, tackles this question, and his essay "Redeeming the Phallus" is a model of how to move beyond "the heterosexual logic of identity" (*Homographesis*, 23).

24. Prison same-sexuality is often taken as an abnormal form of homosexuality, as well as going against the dominant heterosexual norm, because of the way in which desire seems so circumstantially constructed. It raises impossible questions concerning the extent to which gay desire itself—and in fact, all desire—may be a "choice" paradoxically overdetermined by circumstance. This is crucial because prison same-sexuality, in some ways, may actually be closer culturally to the understanding of same-sexuality evident in many African American communities—especially in the urban North, and especially before Stonewall and the rise of openly gay culture. Difficulties in how to deal with such cultural deviances surrounding same-sexual practices can be glimpsed in the attempt of John L. Peterson to determine statistically the prevalence of same-sexuality among African American men, given that virtually all social scientific research has been conducted on middle-class European American homosexual men ("Black Men and Their Same-Sex Desires and Behaviors," in *Gay Culture in America: Essays from the Field*, ed. Gilbert Herdt [Boston: Beacon, 1992], 147–64). Peterson ends up going to studies on prison homosexuality, in which "81 percent of black heterosexual males reported that they had engaged in sexual activity with another male while in prison. In this random sample . . . of the prison population, black males were more likely than white males to engage in the insertor role during anal intercourse with other men" (148). Peterson goes on to point out that, like the prison inmates, "black males may have extensive homosexual experience, but it may not affect their heterosexual identity. These heterosexual men may not label themselves homosexual because of the reasons they engage in homosexual behavior" (149). What Peterson's essay fails to grasp is that "heterosexuality" itself may be defined differently in certain sectors of African American culture as a result of such differences in behavior and identification. Instead, Peterson attributes "heterosexual" black men's seeming high incidence of same-sexual contact wholly to coercive "economic" factors, for instance, black men becoming male prostitutes as a result of underemployment or "the casual exchange of sex for drugs or money" (149). Based on such broad logic, the high incidence of homosexuality among middle-class, urban, white men after World II could easily be attributed to the coercive economic

factors of postwar affluence, urbanization, and the ability to maintain respectable work alongside gay identity in the anonymous environment of the city. White male homosexuality, however, is no longer dealt with in such uncomplicated terms.

25. Stephen F. Milliken, *Chester Himes: A Critical Appraisal* (Columbia: University of Missouri Press, 1976), 160.

26. *Cast the First Stone* may have also fallen between the cracks of race and queer studies because Himes himself was uncertain about how to view the novel, in the context of both his career and his life. James Lundquist suggests that Himes changed the protagonist from black to white in order to get the novel published, which might indicate that Himes confronted the same kind of bias that Baldwin experienced when he was told that writing about homosexuality would cause him to lose his African American base (*Chester Himes* [New York: Ungar, 1976], 74, 211). As H. Bruce Franklin points out, between the first (1972) and second (1976) volumes of his autobiography, Himes seems to contradict himself, at first saying about the fictional story of the "Mississippi white boy" that "obviously it was the story of my own prison experience" but then stating that "it had nothing to do with me." Franklin hits the mark when he suggests that "Himes's motives are certainly not so clear to Himes." See Franklin, *Prison Literature in America,* 211; Chester Himes, *The Quality of Hurt: The Autobiography of Chester Himes* (1972; reprint, New York: Paragon House, 1990), 117, and *My Life of Absurdity—The Later Years: The Autobiography of Chester Himes* (1976; reprint, New York: Paragon House, 1990), 125.

27. Some recent scholars have begun to challenge this identity dualism in Baldwin criticism. See Cora Kaplan's "'A Cavern Opened in My Mind': The Poetics of Homosexuality and the Politics of Masculinity in James Baldwin" and especially Kendall Thomas's "'Ain't Nothin' like the Real Thing': Black Masculinity, Gay Sexuality, and the Jargon of Authenticity," in *Representing Black Men,* ed. Marcellus Blount and George P. Cunningham (New York: Routledge, 1996), 27–54 and 55–69, respectively. Also see Lee Edelman, "The Part for the (W)hole: Baldwin, Homophobia, and the Fantasmatics of Race," in *Homographesis,* 42–75, an essay that unfortunately uses a Eurogay-centric lens in trying to understand the relation between homophobia and racism but that still offers insights into Baldwin's *Just above My Head.* The theorists who have articulated the pitfalls of identity categorization are too numerous to list here, but for good instances, see Deborah McDowell, *"The Changing Same": Black Women's Literature, Criticism, and Theory* (Bloomington: Indiana University Press, 1995), 156–75; Judith Butler, *Gender Trouble: Feminism and the Subversion of Identity* (New York: Routledge, 1990), especially 1–34; and Diana Fuss, *Essentially Speaking: Feminism, Nature and Difference* (New York: Routledge, 1989), especially 73–112.

28. W. E. B. Du Bois, *The Souls of Black Folk* (1903; reprint, New York: Penguin Books, 1989), 1.

29. Fortunately, there is a growing scholarship on the cultural construction of whiteness across a number of disciplines. See especially the influential monograph by Toni Morrison, *Playing in the Dark: Whiteness and the Literary Imagination* (1992; reprint, New York: Vintage Books, 1993); Theodore W. Allen, *The Invention of the White Race* (London: Verso, 1994); David Roediger, *The Wages of Whiteness: Race and the Making of the American Working Class* (London: Verso, 1991) and *Towards the Abolition of Whiteness* (London: Verso, 1994).

30. Several critics have noted that race is important to *Giovanni's Room* without following up on the insight. In *Stealing the Fire: The Art and Protest of James Baldwin* (Middletown, Conn.: Wesleyan University Press, 1989), Horace A. Porter suggests that Baldwin "subliminally conflates race and homosexuality" (153). Weatherby, in *Squaring Off,* sees Baldwin's first two novels as "two sides of a coin"—"the one telling of the black condition, the other explaining how this had come about by the self-deception of the privileged"—and *Notes of a Native Son* as putting "them together, underlining this meaning" (9). In a very important early essay, George Kent stresses the importance of David's racial background for understanding Baldwin's critique of "naive rationalism" as the cause of racism and the fear of same-sex desire (*Blackness and the Adventure of Western Civilization* [Chicago: Third World Press, 1972], 140–46). Claude Summers has provided an astute and elegant analysis of the novel that demonstrates how Baldwin's "artistic vision . . . necessitated a white American as protagonist" (*Gay Fictions Wilde to Stonewall: Studies in a Male Homosexual Literary Tradition* [New York: Continuum, 1990], 173).

31. James Baldwin, quoted in Eckman, *Furious Passage,* 32.

32. James Baldwin, in Richard Goldstein, "Go the Way Your Heart Beats: An Interview with James Baldwin," in *James Baldwin: The Legacy,* ed. Troupe, 178.

33. See Porter on the distinction between inheritance and birthright (*Stealing the Fire,* 36–37). Porter writes, "Baldwin dramatizes in 'Notes of a Native Son' how inheritance can cripple and eventually destroy, particularly if that inheritance is defined by bitterness and rage. Such was the nature of his father's legacy" (37).

34. Norman Podhoretz, "In Defense of James Baldwin," in *Five Black Writers,* ed. Donald B. Gibson (New York: New York University Press, 1970), 145.

35. See, for instance, Amiri Baraka's essay "Brief Reflections on Two Hot Shots," in *Home: Social Essays,* ed. LeRoi Jones (New York: William Morrow & Co., 1966), 116–20.

36. Interestingly, when Richard Wright chooses Europe over Africa, he settles on a similar idea. In *Black Power: A Record of Reactions in a Land of Pathos* (1954; reprint, New York: Harper Perennial, 1995), a travelogue describing his

journey to Ghana during that country's bid for independence, Wright makes it clear that he is much more an alien in Ghana than in his adopted country, France. The titular phrase "black power," which coincidentally became the rallying cry for militant black nationalism in the United States and then across the globe in the later 1960s, suggests in Wright's book not the viability of nationalism but its impossibility as a saving ideology for the emergent African nation-states. Baldwin's "humanism" is very much hedged in and self-consciously undermined by his constant questioning of the fundamental assumptions of the Western heritage; Wright is much more confident that progressive Western ideology can help save people of the African Diaspora from the ideological quagmire manufactured by Western ideology (rampant capitalism versus totalitarian communism) itself.

37. My conception of desire as desiring whatever it is that desire wants is influenced by the theories of Gilles Deleuze and Félix Guattari in *Anti-Oedipus: Capitalism and Schizophrenia* (1972; reprint, Minneapolis: University of Minnesota Press, 1983), especially chapt. 1 (1–50).

38. Arnold Rampersad, *The Life of Langston Hughes*, 2 vols. (New York: Oxford University Press, 1988), 1:335.

39. Of course, the interpretation of what this "best light" was could vary greatly among those who held closely to the principles of uplift. We shouldn't overlook Du Bois's attack on the young "New Negro" writers of the 1920s, including Hughes, whom Du Bois saw as prostituting their talent and sullying the potential respect they could win for the race by cleaning up their act. On Du Bois's sometimes conflicting views and his attack on the Harlem Renaissance writers, see Arnold Rampersad, *The Art and Imagination of W. E. B. Du Bois* (1976; reprint, New York: Schocken Books, 1990), 184–201.

40. Again, one must be careful with these claims: the "some" in this sentence is crucial. It must also be noted that the controversies over homosexuality evident in black nationalist discourse stem from a variety of historical, political, and economic phenomena—including especially the emerging importance of openly gay ghettos (largely white, male, and middle-class), frequently near impoverished African American and Latino ghettos, in many urban centers during the 1960s, together with the political rivalry that sometimes stemmed from this new power bloc of "urban pioneers," as these gay white men were being called. See my discussion of this in the essay "Some Glances at the Black Fag: Race, Same-Sex Desire, and Cultural Belonging," in the special issue "Reading the Signs/Lectures des Signes," ed. Ross Chambers and Anne Herrmann, *Canadian Review of Comparative Literature* 21, 1–2 (March–June 1994): 193–219. Homosexual panic as racial rivalry was also sparked during the period by specific incidents that accrued significance beyond their seeming innocuousness. For instance, on the publication of William Styron's fictionalization of the rebellion of Nat Turner in *The Confes-*

sions of Nat Turner: A Novel (New York: Random House, 1966), some African American men responded with outrage to how a white novelist had taken liberty with the life of an African American hero by depicting him—among other things—in a homosexual liaison with one of his co-conspirators. John Henrik Clarke edited a collection of these reactions in *William Styron's Nat Turner: Ten Black Writers Respond* (Boston: Beacon, 1968). Baldwin was implicated in this controversy because he had read the novel in manuscript and defended it after its publication. Rumors also passed around that Baldwin, who had recently published *Another Country* and whose influence on Styron's novel is apparent, was the model for Styron's homosexual Nat Turner (see W. J. Weatherby, *James Baldwin: Artist on Fire* [New York: Donald I. Fine, 1989], 173–75, 282–83).

41. The controversy over the representation of black male lovers and other deviant sexual practices in Harlem Renaissance novels by Claude McKay (*Home to Harlem* [New York: Harper & Brothers, 1928]) and Rudolph Fisher (*The Walls of Jericho* [New York: Alfred A. Knopf, 1928]) was conducted with a great deal of circumspection and circumlocution even into the 1980s, when debates were still raging about whether these novels "prostituted" black culture for individual fame and fortune.

42. *The Defiant Ones*, produced and directed by Stanley Kramer (Hollywood: Stanley Kramer/United Artists, 1958). On buddy films, see Ed Guerrero, "The Black Image in Protective Custody: Hollywood's Biracial Buddy Films of the Eighties," in *Black American Cinema*, ed. Manthia Diawara (New York: Routledge, 1993), 237–46.

43. In literature, the emergence of Wright's protest fiction tends to subordinate the kinds of fascination with male-male companionship and sexuality so important to black men's narratives from the 1920s through the 1940s. Baldwin's depiction of the erotic-companionate relationship between John and Joshua in his first novel, *Go Tell It on the Mountain*, is another way in which he resists Wright's kind of protest fiction.

44. There are many examples of this way of thinking, but Cleaver's *Soul on Ice* seems seminal. An example of this idea, revised for a post-Stonewall, post–civil rights era, can be found in Nathan Hare and Julia Hare, *The Endangered Black Family: Coping with the Unisexualization and Coming Extinction of the Black Race* (San Francisco: Black Think Tank, 1994), especially 63–68.

45. It is no coincidence that Baldwin's 1974 novel, *If Beale Street Could Talk* (New York: Dell), is the only one that focuses exclusively on heterosexual romance and the reconstitution of the patriarchal family—following, as it does, on the heels of the Styron controversy and the heightened homophobic attacks by Cleaver and some other Black Power advocates.

46. In her biography, Faith Berry comes to a very different conclusion about Hughes's sexual circumspection, demonstrating confidence in his pre-

dominant homosexual disposition and attractions (*Langston Hughes: Before and beyond Harlem* (Westport, Conn.: Lawrence Hill & Co., 1983), especially 94 and 184–87. Charles I. Nero points out the contradictions in Rampersad's two-volume biography, attacking its use of psychiatry and other devices to deny—or at least, to challenge—the evidence of Hughes's homosexuality ("Re/Membering Langston: Homophobic Textuality and Arnold Rampersad's *Life of Langston Hughes*," in *Queer Representations: Reading Lives, Reading Cultures,* ed. Martin Duberman (New York: New York University Press, 1997), 188–96.

47. Langston Hughes, "Café 3 A.M.," in *The Collected Poems of Langston Hughes,* ed. Arnold Rampersad and David Roessel (New York: Alfred A. Knopf, 1996), 406.

48. One of the reasons that both Baldwin and Himes focus on the prison house as an originating or consequent site for same-gender desire in *Giovanni's Room* and *Cast the First Stone* derives from their understanding of how criminalization of African American men's ambition operates in tandem with the criminalization of homosexual desire itself.

49. Nero continues, "The fact that Hughes did not object to the reprinting of "Café 3 A.M." in two later volumes . . . implies that Hughes did not back away from that support. Rampersad's failure to discuss this poem distorts Hughes's vision of black people, their communities, the place of gay people within them, and state-enforced oppression" (193).

Chapter 2

Now More Than Ever
James Baldwin and the Critique of White Liberalism

Rebecca Aanerud

In 1963, when speaking to a group of public school teachers in New York City, James Baldwin was asked to talk about what role he felt the white liberal plays in social change. Baldwin responded, "There is no role for the white liberal, he is our affliction."[1] This chapter explores James Baldwin's complicated relationship to and critiques of white liberalism. I begin by discussing the contradictory role of white liberalism as an "antiracist" social category and then position Baldwin's work in light of that category. Throughout, I maintain that Baldwin's critique of white liberalism and white liberals and his use of concepts such as "personal incoherence," "missionary complex," "white liberal as an affliction," and "white guilt" offer an ideal opportunity to evaluate structural and individual responses to racism in a liberal state.

By the 1960s, white liberalism had reached its pinnacle of rhetorical and political power. Both the Kennedy and Johnson administrations provided a sustained federal "home" where civil rights issues maintained a central focus. Of equal importance was the Civil Rights movement itself, which had successfully swayed a largely uninformed white American public from indifference to moral indignation. In many ways, conditions were the best they had ever been to bring about fundamental and lasting change. And while certain changes did occur, most notably the Civil Rights Act of 1964 and Voting Rights Act of 1965, other forms of racial discrimination—for example, in housing—continued unabated.[2] Given white liberalism's strong position both politically and in the public civic conscience, why and in what ways did white liberalism as an "antiracist" social formation fall short? It seems to me that this is an important question to address for anyone interested in and committed to challenging (even dismantling, if possible) racism as it operates in the United States. For this reason, white liberalism is a crucial site of investigation.

James Baldwin figured prominently in the debates and conversations about race and racism. His novels and especially his essays, most of which were originally published in white mainstream publications such as *Harper's*, *Esquire*, the *New York Times*, and the *Nation*, made his voice central among the black intellectuals of his time. He was intelligent, articulate, and he knew how to speak the language of the white intelligentsia. But given his Harlem working-poor roots, he could be looked to as a legitimate voice of the nation's black urban poor. To err on the side of cynicism, James Baldwin offered his white debaters a relatively "safe" yet "authentic" black man with whom they could engage.

Perhaps of equal importance, however, was Baldwin's willingness and commitment to engage in dialogue with white people about race. Such a commitment is seen all the more clearly in light of another powerful black voice, that of Elijah Muhammad. In his famous essay "The Fire Next Time,"[3] Baldwin contrasts himself to Muhammad:

> I felt very close to him, and really wished to be able to love and honor him as a witness, an ally, a father. I felt that I knew something of his pain and his fury, and yes, even his beauty. Yet precisely because of the reality and the nature of this street—because of what he conceived as his responsibility and what I took to be mine—we would always be strangers, and possibly, one day, enemies. (367)

Although Baldwin writes with great respect for the leader, he ultimately cannot accept his philosophy because, unlike Muhammad, Baldwin felt a deep connection to white people. He writes, "I had many white friends, I would have no choice, if it came to it, but to perish with them" (363).

Baldwin possessed that unique ability to stand in the gray area— he could unleash exacting critiques of white people, white liberals, and white America and yet maintain close and meaningful relationships with white people and his nation.[4] Likely, it was Baldwin's deep connection to white people that propelled him to criticize the paradoxical nature of white people's—especially white liberals'—racism, as in the following passage:

> White Americans find it as difficult as white people elsewhere do to divest themselves of the notion that they are in possession of some intrinsic value that black people need, or want. And this assumption—which, for example, makes the solution to the Negro problem depend on the speed with which Negroes accept and adopt white standards—is revealed in all kinds of striking ways, from Bobby Kennedy's assurance that a Negro can become President in forty years to the unfortunate tone of warm congratulation with which so many liberals address their Negro equals. It is the Negro, of course, who is presumed to have to become equal—an achievement that not only proves the comforting fact that perseverance has no color but also overwhelmingly corroborates in the white man's sense of his own value. ("Fire," 367)

It is undoubtedly Baldwin's unwillingness to simplify his own complex relationship to U.S. racism that placed him at the roundtables, debates, and lecture halls.

Aspects of White Liberalism

I begin with a brief discussion of white liberalism, which is by no means a cohesive or static term. It refers to a social and political category of wide-ranging perspectives, beliefs, and agendas. Although linked to the social welfare programs of the Democratic Party, white liberalism is more accurately understood as bi- or even nonpartisan. Adherence to principles of liberty and justice, especially as they are applied to race, serves as a more accurate common denominator of white liberalism than commitment to a specific economic or social platform. Having grown in influence and status since the 1930s, white liberalism by the 1960s had reached the pinnacle of its rhetorical and political power. During the civil rights era of the second half of the twentieth century, it represented the dominant site for white people opposed to the racial ordering of the United States, and as such, white liberalism can be read as "antiracist."

The term *white liberal* has a complicated and uneven history. In Morton Sosna's study of white liberals of the South, he uses the term interchangeably with "racial liberals," "white Southern liberals," and "Southern liberals."[5] Similarly, John B. Kirby, in his work on liberalism and race in the Roosevelt era, interchanges "white liberal" with "race liberal" and "liberal interracialists."[6] Indeed, given that whiteness has historically occupied the normative cultural space in terms of racial ordering in the United States, the word *liberal* alone, if used in a racialized context, can often carry with it the assumption of "white."

One of the first writers to use the term *white liberal* in a mainstream publication was Southern writer Lillian Smith. In many ways an atypical white liberal voice, Smith urges social change in her 1944 article "Addressed to White Liberals"[7] by calling for a quick end to segregation: "I cannot endure the idea that so many liberals hold that segregation as a way of life must change slowly . . . [we] who do not believe in segregation as a way of life, must say so." For Smith, the central project of white liberalism was desegregation. However, she was a decade or so ahead of her white sympathizers, many of whom—including influential and public figures such as Eleanor Roosevelt—felt that pushing for desegregation would be too antagonistic for the long-range goals of racial equality. In a letter to her friend Pauli Murray, Roosevelt wrote: "I do not want to make [a public statement on desegregation] until we have achieved the four basic citizenship rights because I do not think it is wise to add any antagonism that we do not have to" (Kirby, 85).

Whether they viewed desegregation as politically unwise or as undesirable on some other grounds, many of Smith's contemporaries and predecessors would leave segregation in place and work instead on other, related projects. These predecessors include abolitionists, missionary teachers of the Reconstruction era, and post-Reconstruction writers such as George Washington Cable, who coined the term *the silent South* to refer to those Southern whites who opposed ongoing systematic discrimination of African Americans. Smith's white liberal successors, however, would include those generally committed to desegregation and voter's rights and, increasingly, those whose goal envisioned, as *Commentary* editor Norman Podhoretz put it, "the gradual absorption of deserving Negroes one by one into white society" ("Liberalism and the Negro," 25).

Given the range of commitments, the varying degrees of social change sought, and the absence of a historically continuous political

name, white liberalism constitutes an unwieldy social category. In his
evaluation of the white liberal, journalist Louis E. Lomax provides a
sampling of characteristics identifying the white liberal:

> He is the white Anglo-Saxon protestant marching along the road from
> Selma while his eyes dart furtively toward the rising Negro crime rate;
> he is the clergyman torn between the new gospel he must now preach
> and the conservatism of the flock he must feed and which feeds him so
> well; he is the businessman quite willing to accept change as long as
> things remain the same; he is the parent welcoming the new Negro
> neighbor and praying God that his daughter will marry one of her own
> kind; he is the [academic] peppering his lectures with liberalism and
> mumbling over why there are not more qualified minority students in
> his class . . . he is the woman sleeping with a Negro man to prove some-
> thing about herself to herself; he is the co-ed at the University of Ore-
> gon determined to have Negro babies because she is convinced that
> miscegenation is the only solution to the race problem; he is the
> wealthy scion who dropped out of Yale to become a general in the
> Negro Revolt because he felt empty within and saw the Negro's strug-
> gle as the only spiritual movement existent in Western civilization; [he
> is] a man of conflicts, not contradictions: an advocate of change, but an
> arch foe of revolution.[8]

In short, the white liberal takes many forms—forms that are inflected
by region, historical period, religion, and gender. Yet despite the variety of ways in which one can occupy the space of white liberalism, a
common denominator to this social and political category does exist.
The underlying premise constructing white liberalism is a distinction
between "good whites" and "bad whites." Lomax's contemporary
Lerone Bennett, Jr., speaks succinctly of this premise in the 1964 essay
"Tea and Sympathy: Liberals and Other White Hopes."[9] "The fundamental trait of the white liberal," Bennett writes, "is his desire to differentiate himself psychologically from white Americans on the issue
of race" (77). White liberalism, then, can be understood as a social formation meant to designate those individual whites who want to distance themselves from racism—who want to be viewed as not racist.

It is important to consider the terms under which this distancing
occurs. First, it relies on an oversimplified and dualistic notion of
racism—either one is racist or one is not. In accordance with this binary, to be a racist is to advocate an unambiguous white supremacist
ideology. This configuration, by failing to recognize the ways in

which racism is embedded in the very structure of our society, assumes that one can position him- or herself "outside" racism. Second, the designation of "good whites," with its implied "bad whites," is articulated most readily through class affiliation. In dominant discourse, terms such as *poor whites, white trash, crackers,* and *rednecks* signal, among other things, sites of blatant racism. The association of white liberalism with the middle or upper middle class is revealed in Lomax's list, which tends toward professionals. White liberalism is born not only out of the desire to distance oneself from other white U.S. Americans on the issue of race but out of the means by which to do so.

I return now to Baldwin's assessment of the white liberal as an affliction for social change. In March 1964, the magazine *Commentary* printed a partial transcript of a roundtable discussion titled "Liberalism and the Negro." While the conversation initially focused on general questions of liberalism, it did not take long for it to shift to the more limited topic of white liberalism. James Baldwin was asked to elaborate on his by then well-known, disparaging comments about white liberalism, and specifically on his recent claim that the white liberal is "our affliction." Baldwin responded that he was talking about a "certain missionary complex on the part of white liberals." Their assumption, Baldwin reflected, "basically seems to be that I am much worse off than they are and that they must help me into the light."

Baldwin's answer, with its invocation of the "missionary complex," situates white liberalism in the disciplinary and rhetorical practices of colonialist discourses—particularly that of paternalism. By the 1960s this paternalism or "missionary complex" had a well-established history in the interactions between whites and blacks. From the abolition movement before the Civil War, to the American Mission Association's establishment of colleges and secondary schools throughout the South after the Civil War, to the Roosevelt administration of the 1930s, programs specifically designed to improve conditions and opportunities for African Americans carried with them paternalistic attitudes played out at both the individual and structural levels.

Historian James M. McPherson examines one such program in his article "White Liberals and Black Power in Negro Education, 1865–1915."[10] McPherson tells of the ongoing struggle of African

Americans to benefit from the hundreds of colleges and secondary schools established and run by Protestant churches, particularly those run by the American Mission Association. Speaking about schools run by Protestant churches, Frederick Douglass, angered by condescending statements that equated African Americans with children who needed to be taught everything, spoke out: "We have been injured more than we have been helped by men who professed to be our friends" (McPherson, 1358).[11] Other black leaders similarly frustrated by the missionary complex called for the establishment of colleges funded and run by African Americans. Some such schools were established; however, obtaining funding remained a struggle, and the majority of schools continued to be those founded by Northern missionaries.

The effort to extend the availability of education in the late nineteenth and early twentieth centuries was but one of the programs debilitated by the patronizing attitudes of whites. The election of Franklin Delano Roosevelt in 1932 brought renewed hope to those working for improved racial conditions. For white liberals, the New Deal represented a national home and federal funding for reform programs unevenly supported in the first two decades of the century. Historian John B. Kirby notes that as white liberals began to interpret the meaning of the New Deal, "they gained confidence in their—and others'—ability to alter the 'Negro problem'" (12). However, he goes on to say that "blacks were more cautious than white liberals in their initial response to Roosevelt and his reforms" (11). Their caution proved well placed when, in 1933, Clark Foreman, a white man, was appointed to the newly created position of special adviser concerned with the "economic status of the Negro." This position, according to Julius Rosenwald Fund president Edwin R. Embree, would involve overseeing the "Negro's interests in all phases of recovery" (Kirby, 16).

Frustration with the ongoing pattern of paternalism fueled African American responses to the appointment of Foreman. W. E. B. Du Bois, for example, expressed anger that "again, through the efforts of our best friends [Negroes should] be compelled to have our wants and aspirations interpreted by a person who cannot understand them" (Kirby, 19). The official position of the National Association for the Advancement of Colored People (NAACP) was voiced by Roy Wilkins, who argued that "the age of paternalism" was over. Wilkins stressed that NAACP objections to Foreman were not on a personal level but "to the idea of a white adviser for Negroes." Ironically, for those in the white liberal community who supported the Foreman appointment, white paternalism was viewed not as a liability but as a strategic political tool. Kirby suggests that "white paternalism, nourished by southern racial experience and a traditional progressive faith in 'government by experts' shaped their beliefs." In a letter to William Rosenwald, Embree states that the choice of Foreman "is an attempt to work out in the most strategic fashion a method of keeping the welfare of the whole race effectively before the persons responsible for the national recovery . . . only a white man could carry the kind of influence that is necessary for results" (Kirby, 17).

These examples of white paternalism in social reform programs provide a historical context for Baldwin's perspective. Moreover, they suggest that white liberals naturalized paternalistic attitudes and underscore that the debates and tensions about white paternalism centered on its interpretation and its effects. Viewed as condescending and inconsistent with the philosophy of solidarity, self-help, and race pride, white paternalism was, at the very least, problematic for many African Americans. For white liberals, however, the interpretations of white paternalism ranged from viewing it as an obvious benefit to considering it a necessary, albeit controversial, political choice. For James Baldwin the interpretation was clear: paternalistic attitudes defined white liberalism, thereby rendering it an unsuitable ally in the struggle for civil rights. In a similar vein, Lerone Bennett, Jr., speaks to this unsuitability. The white liberal, Bennett explains, "like practically all other white Americans, [refuses] to accept Negroes as serious social actors" (81). This refusal fits neatly within the "logic" of colonial discourses. It reaffirms the African American as a dis-abled political subject and thereby ensures the centrality of the white liberal in the struggle for racial equality.

One of Baldwin's most passionate essays about white liberalism and whiteness itself concerned the issue of white guilt. In "White Man's Guilt,"[12] originally published in *Ebony*'s 1965 special issue on whiteness, Baldwin begins by wondering what it is that white people talk about when they are together. He is quite certain that whatever it is, it differs from what they talk with him about. White people—especially the white liberals who invite him to engage on the race issue— seem, in Baldwin's estimation, conflicted and uncomfortable when talking to him. "I concluded long ago that they found the color of my skin inhibiting. This color seems to operate as a most disagreeable mirror, and a great deal of one's energy is expended in reassuring white Americans that they do not see what they see. This is utterly futile, of course," he continues, "since they do see what they see, And what they see is an appallingly oppressive and bloody history known all over the world. What they see is a disastrous, continuing, present condition which menaces them, and for which they bear an inescapable responsibility" (47).

Baldwin speaks of white guilt as a "personal incoherence" and suggests that history is the site of white U.S. Americans' psychic entrapment. He argues that white Americans "are dimly, or vividly, aware that the history they have fed themselves is mainly a lie, but they do not know how to release themselves from it, and they suffer enormously from the resulting personal incoherence" (47). In a particularly moving passage, Baldwin speaks of history and the challenge it offers:

> History, as nearly no one seems to know, is not merely something to be read. And it does not refer merely, or even principally, to the past. On the contrary, the great force of history comes from the fact that we carry it within us, and are unconsciously controlled by it in many ways, and history is literally *present* in all that we do. It could scarcely be otherwise, since it is to history that we owe our frames of reference, our identities, and our aspirations. And it is with great pain and terror that one begins to realize this. In great pain and terror one begins to assess the history which has placed one where one is and formed one's point of view. In great pain and terror, because, therefore, one enters into battle with that historical creation, Oneself, and attempts to recreate oneself according to a principle more humane and more liberating; one begins the attempt to achieve a level of personal maturity and freedom which robs history of its tyrannical power, and also changes history. (47)

Baldwin's challenge for us to face history and to be willing to examine honestly the ways in which it lives in each one of us can indeed be a painful and terrifying project. Unfortunately, the conflict between white guilt and the need to construct an innocent white self does more to efface history than it does to face it. One response to this conflict is to disavow history. The familiar rejoinder to U.S. racism— "I wasn't there; my family isn't even from the South"—depends on positioning and reducing history to a set of isolated events of the past. By regulating history as something over and done with, one can deny the ways in which white U.S. Americans continue to benefit from that history. Another response does not look at history as insignificant and dismissive but, on the contrary, constructs history as monumental and beyond redress. Daunted by the overwhelming injustices carried out in the name of the nation, the white liberal takes refuge in his or her status as a mere individual. While recognizing the personal benefits of history, the white liberal uses that same history to construct a paralyzed and impotent self. Although not actually freed from white guilt, the white subject is convinced that there is nothing to be done about the history of racial injustice. Indeed, white guilt in many ways serves the purposes of white supremacy by keeping the white subject central to the racial drama. White guilt, like guilt in general, plays a distinctly self-serving role by positioning white people as the real sufferers of racism because they feel so bad.

While it is not surprising that Baldwin's appeal to face history and work through guilt has, for most white people, gone unheeded, it remains one of his most important critiques of white liberalism. And it is directly related to ongoing debates on racial equality and social change. These debates are currently waged in a changed social context and national discourse from those of the mid-1960s. The rise of conservatism, and especially neoconservatism, has had direct bearing on the content and rhetorical strategies employed in these debates. In the next section, after offering a brief overview of the shift in the political and social climate on race and racism from the 1960s to the present, I return to Baldwin's critique of white guilt and situate it in light of Shelby Steele's article "White Guilt." Published as one of the collected essays in Steele's well-known *The Content of Our Character*, "White Guilt" stands as an apt example of the changed discourse on race, at the same time maintaining some curious parallels to Baldwin's position.

White Liberal Guilt at the Century's End

The strength of white liberalism as a political force began to lose momentum by the end of the 1960s. Faith in the programs of the Great Society waned as college and urban demonstrations against

continued racial abuses took place across the United States. As the
Black Power movement gained in influence, many white liberals
found that the very people whom they sought to help began to question their position as the "good whites." At the same time they found
themselves vulnerable to the attacks of their conservative counterparts, who were quick to highlight the shortcomings of big government and ready to capitalize on white liberals' apparent naïveté.

Through the 1970s and 1980s, a new political voice came into play
in the U.S. American political discourse: neoconservatism. As with
most political categories, neoconservatism claims no single defining
description or agenda. Mark Gerson, editor of a collection of neoconservative essays, states that "the term applies broadly to a prominent
group of intellectuals who, once *considered* to be on the left, are now
on the right."[13] In part, Gerson acknowledges, neoconservatism developed as a method to challenge the tenets of the Great Society, but
he adds:

> Neoconservatism is far more that just a method of critiquing the Great
> Society, a reaction to the counterculture, or a conservative defense of a
> limited welfare state. It is an intellectual persuasion, a comprehensive
> outlook on economics, politics, culture, and society linked by common
> principles and a distinctive vision. (xiv)

In his preface to Gerson's collection, James Q. Wilson writes that
"perhaps most important of all, neoconservatives embrace the American conviction that many of the central problems of our society arise
out of a want of good character and human virtue" (ix). James Baldwin, in his characteristically succinct way, refers to neoconservatives
simply as "yesterday's Liberals, the Negro's friend."[14] Regardless of
how one defines or characterizes the neoconservative, there can be little doubt that this political newcomer has had an impact on contemporary dialogues over a wide range of social issues; certainly this is
true of issues such as racial inequities and affirmative action.

The 1990 publication of Shelby Steele's *The Content of Our Character: A New Vision of Race in America*[15] made a substantial addition to a
neoconservative position on race issues. Although Steele does not
identify himself specifically as a neoconservative, preferring instead
the term *classical liberal*, with a focus on freedom and the power of the
individual,[16] the thesis he articulates throughout the essays of his
book fits neatly in the general philosophy of neoconservatism. Blacks,

Steele maintains, continue to be plagued by poorer life opportunities because they choose to subscribe to an antiquated identity which "presumed that black opportunity was sharply limited by racism and that blacks had to 'win' more 'victories' 'against' society before real opportunity would open up. This was an identity that still saw blacks as victims and that kept them at war with society even as new possibilities for advancement opened all around" (169). For Steele, self-doubt serves more powerfully to the detriment of African Americans than does structural or institutional racism.[17]

It is not my intent or concern to examine Steele's book in total; rather, I am interested in only his chapter titled "White Guilt." At first glance it might appear that Steele's and Baldwin's positions coincide, because both recognize the need to examine white guilt and both are critical of white liberalism and white liberals. But the two writers' critical stances do not lead them in the same direction. The anti–affirmative action arguments Steele makes are informative because in them we can see some of the consequences of Baldwin's unmet challenge to acknowledge and examine white guilt. I maintain that Steele's chapter on white guilt demonstrates and confirms Baldwin's critique of white liberalism, because the unexamined white guilt of white liberals left them vulnerable to the kinds of moves neoconservative arguments make—especially in regard to affirmative action, of which approach Steele's work is emblematic.

Steele begins his discussion by situating white guilt in terms of his own experience. He writes that prior to the mid-1960s he does not recall hearing the term *white guilt* or encountering anything he would characterize as white guilt; he surmises that it was Black Power (defined by Steele as "militant fringe groups, the civil rights establishment, or big city political campaigns," 85) that brought about this change on the part of white Americans. Black Power, Steele suggests, harnessed the vulnerability of white guilt. This move to "[up] the ante on white guilt" (86) is characteristic of Black Power, which, according to Steele, given its "profound anger at what was done to blacks and an equally profound feeling that there should be reparations," is "after more than fairness" (86). Steele's discussion of white guilt is in some ways similar to Baldwin's. Like Baldwin, Steele situates white guilt in terms of history. He writes that "white guilt, in its broad sense, springs from a *knowledge* of ill-gotten advantage" (80). "White Americans," he continues, "*know* that their historical advantage comes from the subjugation of an entire people" (81). For Steele, however, this white guilt (especially that of white liberals) is directly linked to affirmative action programs, as those associated with Black Power discovered that "white guilt was black power" (81). Steele provides an example of this equation as he recounts the story of a friend of his who made use of his "power" by subtly goading a white businessman into overtipping the black men's room attendant. With this narrative, Steele attempts to demonstrate that in their eagerness to escape white guilt, white people are willing to pay for their innocence, and in this story Steele sees the blueprint of "racial policy-making in America since the sixties" (83).

While I believe one of the primary objectives and an undeniable necessity of acknowledging and working through white guilt is the looming falsehood of reinstating a mythical white innocence, I question Steele's facile analysis. Can affirmative action programs be so easily wedded to white guilt? Steele clearly thinks this is the case, but I suggest that his position is plagued by imprecision and generalizations, making it less than fully convincing. First, Steele implies an overly simplistic affiliation between the white guilt of the Great Society liberals and affirmative action. According to political scientist Robert R. Detlefsen, whose own work suggests a political position right of center, this reliance on the presumed close association of affirmative action to the white liberal agenda of the 1960s is highly disputable. Detlefsen argues that

> although its supporters often locate the origin of affirmative action in the Executive Order No. 11246, and accordingly regard affirmative action as one of the great civil-rights victories of the Johnson administration, the Johnson order itself did nothing to alter the common understanding that affirmative action meant nothing more than that employers, in addition to hiring without regard to the race or ethnicity of job-seekers . . . should also publicize job vacancies and seek to encourage job applications from members of those groups (principally blacks) who might otherwise be discouraged from applying because of widespread discrimination against them in the past.[18]

Detlefsen adds, "Contrary to conventional wisdom, contemporary federal affirmative action policy owes far more to the likes of John Mitchell, George Schultz (Nixon's secretary of labor), and Richard Nixon than to Lyndon Johnson" (26).

Second, and perhaps more important, Steele never defines affirmative action. Rhetorically, and characteristic of the political agenda his work furthers, he speaks of it as a set of "entitlements." Yet affirmative action refers to a wide range of programs, and ones not exclusively race based. In Detlefsen's examination of civil rights under Ronald Reagan, in which he explores President Reagan's inability to eliminate affirmative action programs despite his supposed mandate to do so, Detlefsen stresses that *affirmative action* is an ambiguous term and cites President John F. Kennedy's Executive Order No. 10925 as a source of its vagueness. This order, which addressed employment discrimination among federal contractors, states that such contractors should take "affirmative steps" to avoid discrimination. In 1967 the director of the Office of Federal Contract Compliance Programs commented that "there is no fixed and firm definition of affirmative action. I would say that in a general way, affirmative action is anything that you have to do to get results" (23). Given the historical inexactness associated with the term *affirmative action,* as well as the range of programs it encompasses, it would seem especially important to provide some parameters of the term when invoked currently.

For Steele, the term applies principally to the higher education of African Americans. His primary objection to affirmative action concerns the "implied inferiority" fundamental to what he refers to as "racial preferences": "I think that one of the most troubling effects of racial preferences for blacks is a kind of demoralization, or put another way, an enlargement of self-doubt" (116). This issue of self-doubt is, as Amy Gutmann writes, "difficult to evaluate." She continues, "We should not deny people otherwise justified benefits because of the paternalistic consideration that the benefits may demoralize them or enlarge their self-doubt. (Many successful people are tormented by self-doubt partly because they are more successful than they believe they deserve to be)."[19]

One reason this claim of Steele's is difficult to evaluate stems from the absence of any actual evidence or support. His writing is anecdotal and impressionistic; yet his claims are wide in scope. Characteristic of neoconservatism, Steele's discourse reveals an underlying suspicion of statistical studies and data.[20] He speaks not as an "expert" but as a man of "common sense." Perhaps the predominant appeal of his writing is its individual voice. Arguably, Steele successfully capitalizes on the ideology of individualism. The rhetorical move to invoke this ideology is an essential part of an argument that situates racism as individual and a matter of attitude—not a structural problem. Consistent with contemporary public debates on racism, Steele characterizes racism as name-calling and "slights" (111), in effect attributing ongoing racism to individuals of poor manners and thus relinquishing the need for structural or institutional remedy.

I return now to my claim that the anti–affirmative action arguments Steele posits are fruitful to look at because in them we can see some of the consequences of Baldwin's unmet challenge to acknowledge and examine white guilt. It is Steele's contention that the Civil Rights movement, and later the Black Power movement, successfully exploited the guilt of vulnerable white Americans, paving the way for the installation of questionable public policy. Yet as I have suggested above, to designate white guilt as the sole motivating force behind the policies of the 1960s is not only overly simplistic but lacks substantiation. However, I agree that white guilt continues to play a crucial role in racial discourse. Steele's narrative itself exemplifies this role. In Steele's formulation, white liberals, eager to escape discomfort of white guilt, set up and agreed to short-sighted programs. Yet twenty-five years later, Steele, perhaps inadvertently, demonstrates the ease with which one can still exploit white guilt. This time, Steele relies on the eagerness to avoid not the discomfort of white guilt, as he claims occurred in the 1960s, but looking foolish. After all, instigating policies that, according to Steele, do not work and actually harm blacks, on the basis of an emotion such as guilt, would be a bit of an embarrassment. The remedy, of course, would be not only to distance oneself politically from the policy makers of the 1960s but to dismantle affirmative action programs currently in place. In short, I propose it is Steele who capitalizes on white guilt, far more than the "entitlement" policies he criticizes—especially as that guilt is tied to a construction of white Americanness.

The point I am making is that absent any sustained and thorough examination on the part of white people of what it means to be white, conservative agendas such as that supported by Steele carry a certain degree of influential sway. To put it differently, Shelby Steele has successfully tapped into an Achilles' heel of whiteness. Had white liberals of the civil rights era been more willing to take up the difficult challenge Baldwin set out in 1965, the very basis of Steele's argument would be undercut.

Epilogue: Racial Debate in the 1990s

I close my discussion with a brief look into the current climate of racial debate, with a focus on a recently published book by Gordon MacInnes, *Wrong for All the Right Reasons: How White Liberals Have Been Undone by Race.*[21] MacInnes, who was a staff worker for a White House task force on cities for the Johnson administration, a speech writer for Walter Mondale in 1984, and elected state senator of New Jersey in 1993, describes himself as a Democrat, "albeit a frustrated one." In his book he argues that white liberals have fallen short of enacting lasting social change because they have lost their willingness to argue about racially charged issues. This loss is primarily attributed to white guilt.

MacInnes sets up his argument with a reference to President Bill Clinton's remarks about rap artist and activist Sister Souljah at a 1992 campaign talk before the Rainbow Coalition. Then-Candidate Clinton criticized Sister Souljah, and by extension Jesse Jackson, under whose auspices she performed, for her recent comments about black-white violence. (She was quoted in the *Washington Post* as saying, "If black people kill black people every day, why not have a week and kill white people?")[22] MacInnes credits Clinton's open criticism and its fallout with a significant revitalization of his campaign—especially among white working- and middle-class voters. According to MacInnes, Clinton's campaign, by distinguishing itself from those of his liberal Democrat predecessors, demonstrated "a measure of how far liberal Democrats had fallen in their standards of intellectual integrity and common sense that a candidate's criticism of someone for advocating racial violence would seem noteworthy" (15). MacInnes goes on:

> Typically, white liberals had taken to standing in quiet acquiescence in the presence of statements by black Americans, however outrageous they might be. And when these liberals were criticized by a black American, their response was to retreat, explain, apologize, or overreact. This pattern was so well established by 1992—particularly after the presidential candidacies of Hubert Humphrey, George McGovern, Walter Mondale, and Michael Dukakis—that Clinton's criticism stunned Jackson, the Rainbow Coalition audience, and the press. (15)

In brief, MacInnes's thesis is that white liberals (and for him, these are individuals associated with the Democratic Party) were unwilling to argue with black Americans and therefore "ended up supporting, at least abetting crazy ideas" (104). However, given the changed atmosphere and public debate on racial issues in general, the white liberal retreat from debate is no longer—and no longer should be—politically viable. MacInnes advocates a renewed progressive coalition, comprised of "working- and middle-class whites, minorities, and liberals" (1) and in part characterized by a willingness to discuss and argue about race and racism in a way that "need not ignore or revise our horrific racial history or diminish the influence of our very different racial, ethnic, and religious backgrounds" (203).

If MacInnes is correct that the racial climate has so significantly changed that more open dialogue and debate are possible, it is perhaps crucial now more than ever to revisit James Baldwin's cogent critiques of white liberals of the 1960s. I am less confident than MacInnes in the transformative power of his proposed new progressive coalition. However, I do believe that because we now have in place both a body of work on critical whiteness[23] and the beginnings of a national dialogue more able, or perhaps more willing, to argue about race, some of the vulnerabilities seized by those of Steele's ilk can be avoided. Of course, none of this is easy. Baldwin's challenge is indeed a great one. But his own life and writings serve as an example of what is possible.

NOTES

1. "Liberalism and the Negro: A Round-Table Discussion" *Commentary* 37, March 1964, 37.

2. See, for example, Douglas S. Massey and Nancy A. Denton, *American Apartheid: Segregation and the Making of the Underclass* (Cambridge: Harvard University Press, 1993), especially chap. 4.

3. James Baldwin, "The Fire Next Time," in *The Price of the Ticket: Collected Nonfiction, 1948–1985* (New York: St. Martin's/Merek Press, 1985), 333–379. Hereafter cited as "Fire."

4. In many ways, Baldwin's writings and discussions on whiteness foreshadow the recent work in critical whiteness studies.

5. Morton Sosna, *In Search of the Silent South: Southern Liberals and the Race Issue* (New York: Columbia University Press, 1977).

6. John B. Kirby, *Black Americans in the Roosevelt Era: Liberalism and Race* (Knoxville: University of Tennessee Press, 1980).

7. Lillian Smith, "Addressed to White Liberals," *New Republic,* September 1944, 331–333.

8. Louis E. Lomax, "The White Liberal," *Ebony* 20, August 1965, 60.

9. Lerone Bennett, Jr., "Tea and Sympathy: Liberals and Other White Hopes," in *The Negro Mood* (Chicago: Johnson Publishing, 1964).

10. James M. McPherson, "White Liberals and Black Power in Negro Education, 1865–1915," *American Historical Review* 75, 5 (1970): 1357–1386.

11. Douglass was speaking as part of the "Seventh Annual Report of the Freedman's Aid Society of the Methodist Episcopal Church" in Cincinnati, 1874. McPherson cites both the *New York Tribune,* July 7, 1874, and the *Weekly Louisianian,* July 17, 1875.

12. James Baldwin, "The White Man's Guilt," *Ebony* 20, August 1964, 47–48.

13. Mark Gerson, ed., *The Essential Neoconservative Reader* (Reading, Mass.: Addison-Wesley, 1996), xiiii.

14. James Baldwin, *Evidence of Things Not Seen.* (New York: Holt, Rinehart & Winston, 1985), 79.

15. Shelby Steele, *The Content of Our Character: A New Vision of Race in America* (New York: St. Martin's Press, 1990).

16. "Up from Obscurity," *Time,* August 13, 1990, 45.

17. Indeed, it is doubtful that Steele even acknowledges or recognizes structural or institutional racism. Throughout his book, his examples of racism are best characterized as individual or attitudinal racism. Most scholars on racism maintain that individual racism is but one (and perhaps the most benign) form of racism operating today.

18. Robert R. Detlefsen, *Civil Rights under Reagan* (San Francisco: ICS Press, 1991), 23.

19. Anthony Appiah and Amy Gutmann, *Color Consciousness: The Political Morality of Race* (Princeton: Princeton University Press, 1996), 130. In an earlier passage Gutmann points out the perils of failing to distinguish between preferential treatment and affirmative action, as Steele fails to do. "Affirmative action," she stresses, "as originally articulated, entails taking steps that would not have to be taken for members of an advantaged group in order to ensure that members of a disadvantaged group are not discriminated against. How, if at all, can preferential treatment—as distinguished from affirmative action—be justified? Once we collapse affirmative action and preferential treatment, as our contemporary public debate has done, then we cannot pose this question or clarify the controversy that surrounds the very different practices of giving preference to members of disadvantaged groups and taking positive steps that would not be necessary absent our legacy of racial injustice to prevent discrimination against them" (130–31).

20. See Wilson's preface in Gerson, eds., *The Essential Neoconservative Reader.*

21. Gordon MacInnes, *Wrong for All the Right Reasons: How White Liberals Have Been Undone by Race* (New York: New York University Press, 1996). For a related discussion of white liberals, see Jim Sleeper, *Liberal Racism* (New York: Viking Books, 1997).

22. As quoted in MacInnes, *Wrong for All the Right Reasons,* 14.

23. Despite MacInnes's clear critique of white liberalism, he says nothing about whiteness as a racialized social category. It seems curious that, given the recent work on whiteness, MacInnes would fail to address the social category in which white liberalism's primary actors are positioned.

Chapter 3

Finding the Words
Baldwin, Race Consciousness, and Democratic Theory

Lawrie Balfour

The Words of a Native Son

James Baldwin was only twenty-four when he wrote "Everybody's Protest Novel," but the essay announced his presence as a literary figure to be reckoned with. First published in *Zero* in 1949 and later that year in *Partisan Review*, "Everybody's Protest Novel" lays out Baldwin's dispute with literature that aims for social improvement by galvanizing opposition to some moral outrage. Baldwin disparages *Uncle Tom's Cabin* and, to a lesser extent, *Native Son*[1] as examples of fiction that attempt to effect social change by representing individual women and men as symbols of a social wrong. While much of the critical attention generated by "Everybody's Protest Novel" has focused on whether or not Baldwin's own novels escape his complaints about protest fiction,[2] my purpose in revisiting the essay is to highlight and explore a different dimension of Baldwin's argument. At the same time that Baldwin demolishes the literary value of the protest novel, he also demands an alternative standard for moral and political critique. He aspires to find a language to express the wrongs of racial injustice without losing sight of the complicated workings of race consciousness in American society.[3] I argue that this aspiration, and Baldwin's appreciation of the sheer difficulty of realizing it, offers valuable guidance for American democratic theory today; for the ease with which the formal equality guaranteed by the civil rights legislation of the 1960s has been deployed against the purposes of the Civil Rights movement indicates the urgency of Baldwin's warnings about the dangers of disconnecting democratic principles from the lives of the women and men who are expected to abide by them and hold them dear.

The opening passage of "Everybody's Protest Novel" re-creates a moment in *Uncle Tom's Cabin* in which Miss Ophelia, a proper Northerner, conveys her horror at the uses to which Southerners put their black slaves.[4] Miss Ophelia's reaction, according to Baldwin, provides the novel's "moral, neatly framed and incontestable like those improving mottoes sometimes found hanging on the walls of furnished rooms."[5] What Miss Ophelia responds to is indeed horrific. But Baldwin contends that her declaration of moral outrage, insofar as it distances her personally from the cause of the outrage, is no less incongruous in a world built on racial hierarchy than the cheery order implied by the "improving mottoes" set against the anonymous setting of a furnished room. This incongruity makes a larger point about invoking moral principles without investigating the sources of the suffering experienced by those to whom counsel is offered; to them, the principles may not only appear unconnected to their experience but may even serve as an affront to it. Protest novels resemble Miss Ophelia, Baldwin contends, insofar as both rely on a "medieval morality" that understands the world to be divided cleanly into good and evil. Such a morality unfailingly provides the right answers without considering their relevance in the lives of human beings who reside in the more complicated realm that is somewhere between heaven and hell. Inadequate to the task of grappling with either slavery or racial injustices, this moral vision copes with the existence of these horrors by assigning individuals and their behavior to simple categories and mouthing moral formulas. Even as the protest novel proclaims its own good intentions, it does so by providing so flat a picture of the evil it aims to overcome that readers are not required to recognize the significance of racial injustice in their own lives.

Baldwin wages war on the literature of protest because it perpetuates what he calls the myth of innocence. The innocence Baldwin decries is a deliberate ignorance, a form of moral insulation that allows Americans not to confront the deep injustices that define their society:

The "protest" novel, so far from being disturbing, is an accepted and comforting aspect of the American scene, ramifying that framework that we believe to be so necessary. Whatever unsettling questions are raised are evanescent, titillating; remote, for this has nothing to do with us, it is safely ensconced in the social arena, where, indeed, it has nothing to do with anyone, so that finally we receive a very definite thrill of virtue from the fact that we are reading such a book at all. This report from the pit reassures us of its reality and its darkness and of our own salvation. ("Everybody," 31)

Baldwin's critique is not purely an aesthetic one. His opposition stems from his observation that protest novels, far from encouraging self-examination or critique, generate the sort of indignation that comforts the comfortable in the righteousness of their opinions and the necessity of the existing moral framework. Just as the stories stretch the bounds of credibility, Baldwin asserts, the standards that undergird them prove their unreality and lose their force as guides to ethical behavior.

Protest novels, according to Baldwin, refuse to acknowledge the fundamental difficulties of moral improvement. With regard to issues of racial injustice, they have nothing to say to about why white Americans have behaved so brutally, for so long. Instead, they offer "a mirror of our confusion, dishonesty, panic, trapped and immobilized in the sunlit prison of the American dream" ("Everybody," 31). Left unasked are hard questions concerning the possibilities for multiracial democracy: What must be given up—by black and by white Americans—in the definition of a common and equal citizenry? Is it possible that the women and men whose enslavement was justified by the claim that they were less than human could become, by fiat, full members of society, either in the eyes of their oppressors or in their own? Baldwin gives us good reason to think the answer to the first question is "More than we can now imagine" and the answer to the second question is no:

It is the peculiar triumph of society—and its loss—that it is able to convince those people to whom it has given inferior status of the reality of this decree; it has the force and the weapons to translate its dictum into fact, so that the allegedly inferior are actually made so, insofar as the societal realities are concerned. This is a more hidden phenomenon now than it was in the days of serfdom, but it is no less implacable.

Now, as then, we find ourselves bound, first without, then within, by the nature of our categorization. And escape is not effected through a bitter railing against this trap; it is as though this very striving were the only motion needed to spring the trap upon us. ("Everybody," 32)

That the decree of black inferiority is not only hidden but internalized by black and white Americans indicates the depth of the harm of racial injustice and the difficulty of extirpating such injustice. According to Baldwin, genuine opposition to entrenched racial inequalities requires no less than a transformation—of Americans' understanding of themselves and of the society in which they live.

Baldwin concludes "Everybody's Protest Novel" with a plea that establishes his own vision of the relationship between writing and social change: "Our humanity is our burden, our life; we need not battle for it; we need only do what is infinitely more difficult—that is, accept it. The failure of the protest novel lies in its rejection of life, the human being, the denial of his beauty, dread, power, in its insistence that it is his categorization alone which is real and which cannot be transcended" ("Everybody," 33).[6] The project that Baldwin sets for himself in "Everybody's Protest Novel" is daunting. Simultaneously declaring the equal humanity of black and white Americans and undermining the assumption that the meaning of his claim is self-evident, Baldwin both speaks in the name of democratic principles and unsettles received understandings of what those principles mean.[7]

The challenge "Everybody's Protest Novel" poses to democratic theory is also daunting. If the failure of protest novels resides in their preference for categories over human experiences, then one might expect democratic theories to be even more remote from those experiences. Part of the task of theory, after all, is to make general claims. And one of the most powerful tools of theoretical work, particularly when the subject is controversial, is abstract conceptual analysis. By removing to the level of principle, theorists can sort out and evaluate conflicting viewpoints and devise a rational basis for mediation.[8] Baldwin's point is that race consciousness operates on many levels, coexists with earnest expressions of antiracism, and undergirds racial hierarchy in ways that are difficult to detect. Their denial that assumptions about racial identity and racial difference are thoroughly interwoven into the fabric of Americans' experience disables theorists' capacity to address the political implications of race consciousness. Abstract conceptual theory, by supposing it is possible to make arguments at the level of principle, where race is not relevant, may thus serve to protect the sort of racial innocence Baldwin attacks. This possibility ought to be of particular concern to *democratic* theorists: it suggests that "race-blind" theorizing may exclude from consideration the experiences of men and women best acquainted with racial injustice.

Baldwin's essays enlarge the capacity of democratic theories to recognize and respond to the challenges of race consciousness, by reorienting theory from the level of principle to the murky region between principle and practice. His ability to discern and describe the resonances of political principles in everyday life illuminates the meanings of the principles and evokes what Stuart Hampshire calls "the tension of unrealised possibilities."[9] Baldwin shifts attention away from moral formulas and precepts, which too often carry the weight of the neatly framed mottoes he scorns, to the furnished rooms in which they hang. The approach he offers is hermeneutical insofar as it accentuates the impossibility of escaping the bounds of context; at the same time, it is always suspicious of the authority of the traditions and of the language within which it operates.

By examining Baldwin's effort to find the words to capture and make sense of his own experiences, I suggest how his essays assist his readers in uncovering the habits of thought and the "habits of the heart" that either stymie or nurture democratic possibilities in light of the ongoing significance of race. First, I examine Baldwin's account of the difficulty of putting into words the implications of race consciousness for the realization of democratic principles. Then, I consider the story Baldwin tells in *The Fire Next Time* about the two preeminent principles of democratic theory: equality and freedom. Toward the end of *The Fire Next Time*, Baldwin muses that "people are not . . . terribly anxious to be equal (equal, after all, to what and to whom?)" Later in the same paragraph he notes, "I have met only a very few people—and most of these were not Americans—who had any real desire to be free. Freedom is hard to bear."[10] What Baldwin means by these claims and how they bear on thinking about democratic promises in a race-conscious society illuminate the difficulty of defining equality and freedom in a way that makes space for experiences of individuals who have never taken their value for granted.

"To Shape a Silence While Breaking It"[11]

When the "Ebonics" debate erupted nearly a decade after his death, Baldwin's thoughts about the uses and limits of language made news. Commentators cited his 1979 essay "If Black English Isn't a Language, Then Tell Me, What Is?" to explain what was at stake in the controversy over the use of black English in American schools. Baldwin's point—that black English reflects the experiences of African Americans in a way that "standard" English does not, and that the uproar generated by this idea reveals white Americans' unwillingness to confront the distinctiveness of those experiences[12]—may strike a reader as somewhat dishonest. Baldwin, after all, renders his own experiences in uncommonly beautiful "standard" English. Yet the fluency of Baldwin's prose disguises a deeper distrust of the language of his inheritance. As a racial outsider to the American "mainstream," Baldwin is wary about embracing the language that has functioned as an instrument of his subjugation. As an artist, he grapples with the inadequacy of any language to convey the full force of experience. As a moralist, he wrestles with the problem of expressing his convictions without sacrificing nuance. Combined, these ambivalences suggest why, as Toni Morrison observes, "in spite of implicit and explicit acknowledgment, 'race' is still a virtually unspeakable thing."[13] And they indicate the sheer difficulty of imagining alternatives to race-blind discourse that do not, at some level, reproduce discredited assumptions about racial difference. Briefly, I consider here the interlocking dimensions of Baldwin's struggle to find his own words—as a black man in a white-dominated society, as an artist, and as a moralist—recognizing all the while that it is impossible to separate any single dimension definitively from the others.

Baldwin's dispute with his native tongue resides in the suspicion that the language has not done justice to his experiences as a marginal American. Yet because the language that he distrusts is also inescapably his, he responds by claiming it and molding it to serve a critical purpose. "If the language was not my own," he muses, "it might be the fault of the language; but it might also be my fault. Perhaps the language was not my own because I had never attempted to use it, had only learned to imitate it."[14] Given Baldwin's distrust of the English language, it is no accident that *unspeakable* and *unspeak-*

ably appear so often in his essays. Words such as these acknowledge the fundamental elusiveness of human experiences, which, as he notes in his rejection of protest novels, strain human capacity for expression in *any* language. But Baldwin's emphasis on the unspeakable also conveys his sense of the costs of putting into words the hurts of racial injustice. When he writes that "for the horrors of the American Negro's life there has been almost no language" ("Down," 362), Baldwin means that American public discourse has had no way to accommodate stories that so deeply undercut the assumption that democratic ideals have been, for the most part, realized. And he recognizes that the "privacy" of black experiences protects even as it marginalizes. To break silence, he knows, is to risk exposing the details of those experiences to public scrutiny, with no assurance that they will be understood as he intends. He knows as well that the very act of finding a receptive white audience may spell his own alienation from other black Americans. Baldwin believes that everything is at stake in choosing to write. For him, language "is the most vivid and crucial key to identity: It reveals the private identity, and connects one with, or divorces one from, the larger, public, or communal identity."[15]

An artist, in Baldwin's view, is "a witness to the truth." As a writer, he strains for the words that will move his readers without either making them conscious of his efforts or presuming to control exactly how they will respond. To that end, Baldwin writes most effectively when he focuses on the smallest details, the moments that reach beyond themselves. Referring to the powerful imagery of Baldwin's "Notes of a Native Son," Alfred Kazin remarks that "there is a certain law for art: not to know as you're writing what everything means. It's being impressed with the fact, not with the significance of the fact."[16] Baldwin uses his gifts as a reporter of overlooked detail to craft his narratives in a way that allows his readers to discern and absorb their significance. Although Baldwin described himself as a novelist—and he dreamed of becoming a great playwright—his development in the essays of the persona of James Baldwin may stand as his greatest literary accomplishment. By creating and re-creating from his own life a figure whose loneliness nearly grabs the reader from the page, and whose struggles with despair express a universally human struggle, Baldwin demonstrates the force of the personal essay. He makes good on the aim to "render the transient eternal."[17]

Baldwin the moralist has a point to make. And he wrestles with the temptation to simplify for the sake of making his point compelling. While he probably does not accord *Uncle Tom's Cabin* adequate respect for its part in precipitating the Civil War, his critique of the protest novel nevertheless expresses a valid anxiety about the costs of moral or political persuasion. Causes, he notes, "are notoriously bloodthirsty" ("Everybody," 29). And crucial to their bloodthirstiness is the reduction of human complexity. Commenting on Cassius's glorification of the killing of Caesar in Shakespeare's *Julius Caesar*, Baldwin writes, "This single-mindedness, which we think of (why?) as ennobling, also operates, and much more surely, to distort and diminish a man—to distort and diminish us all, and, or perhaps especially, those whose needs and whose energy made the overthrow of the State inevitable, necessary and just."[18]

Related to this dilemma of the costs of persuasion and political action is the writer's awareness of the malleability of words that persuade. Even the most admirable ideals can be perverted without losing their formal meaning. Listen, for example, to Václav Havel, himself a fighter for the values of the French Revolution, as he describes the multiple meanings possible through the "mysterious, ambiguous, ambivalent, and perfidious phenomenon" of words: *"Liberté, Egalité, Fraternité*—what superb words! And how terrifying their meaning can be. Freedom: the shirt unbuttoned before execution. Equality: the constant speed of the guillotine's fall on different necks. Fraternity: some dubious paradise ruled by a Supreme Being."[19] Havel's point is not to discount the value or the possibility of liberty, equality, fraternity. Rather, his emphasis on the multivalence of the words is an appeal to vigilance. It provides a reminder that the proclamation of principle is no guarantee of its meaning. If the perversion Havel describes is extreme, it cannot be explained away as simply an example of the costs of revolutionary zeal. Rather, it speaks to one of Baldwin's great worries—the ease with which moral and political ideals become twisted in the course of everyday life.

In his essay about a meeting with Ingmar Bergman, Baldwin captures his own sense of the dilemmas that arise from the inseparable and yet frequently contradictory forces that shape his efforts to break silence. Baldwin notes in "The Northern Protestant," almost as an aside, that he envies the Swede's unqualified love for his home and his ability to live and work there. As soon as Baldwin makes the admission, however, he allows that maybe he does not really envy Bergman after all. There is no point in wishing for a different home, Baldwin realizes; "everything in a life depends on how that life accepts its limits: it would have been like envying his [Bergman's] language."[20]

This line from "The Northern Protestant," while it touches directly on neither political life nor race, goes to the heart of Baldwin's convictions about the possibility of fulfilling the promise of democracy. Further, it points to what he would see as the greatest obstacle to transcending race consciousness: it is "virtually impossible, if not completely impossible, to envision the future, except in the terms which we think we already know."[21] When the inherited terms are political or moral and the setting in which they are elaborated is a racially hierarchical one, he argues, the project of articulating their meanings must balance an interest in their achievement with a distrust of the ways in "which we think we already know" them. Baldwin's job as a critic is to show how the meanings of those inherited terms are deliberately unknown and to call attention to the experiences that are excluded from consideration when the content of the terms is taken for granted.

For a measure of his achievement and an exploration of its implications for the practice of political theory, I turn now to *The Fire Next Time*. Although this piece has been unfavorably compared to the earlier essays,[22] I contend that *The Fire Next Time* succeeds as an extended example of how Baldwin makes the English language his own, and how at the same time he invests it with new critical power.

Equality and Freedom, Down at the Cross

To claim for Baldwin the title "political theorist" would be to misrepresent his aims and his achievement. Not long after the publication of "Everybody's Protest Novel," Baldwin offered an assessment of theory that is compatible with his rejection of protest novels: "I think all theories are suspect, that the finest principles may have to be modified or may even be pulverized by the demands of life."[23] In addition to this antitheoretical attitude, Baldwin's unwillingness to disentangle political matters from discussions of spiritual or cultural or personal subjects makes him an unorthodox guide for political theorists.

Nonetheless, I read *The Fire Next Time* as a meditation on equality and freedom from which democratic theorists have much to learn. *The Fire Next Time*, I argue, makes a twofold contribution to the task of understanding the meaning of democratic principles: (1) through its precision of language, it evokes the lived meanings of equality and freedom for readers who are not themselves touched by the every-dayness of racial injustice and gives shape to the experiences of those who are; (2) at the same time, it calls attention to the limits of expression, insisting that change can and must be conceived within those limits.

The Fire Next Time is actually two essays—"My Dungeon Shook: Letter to My Nephew on the One-Hundredth Anniversary of the Emancipation" and "Down at the Cross: Letter from a Region in My Mind." The latter essay first appeared in the 17 November 1962 issue of the *New Yorker*, its twenty thousand words consuming nearly the entire issue and boosting sales of the magazine dramatically; the former, a much shorter piece, was published in *The Progressive* in December 1962.[24] Most of my comments focus on "Down on the Cross," but I read the essays together as parts of a whole. In "My Dungeon Shook" Baldwin explains to his nephew, who is also named James, why it is that he is growing up in poverty and why his prospects appear so limited. The essay then counsels the nephew not to accept the white world's definition of him and urges him to make the notion of freedom real. In "Down at the Cross," Baldwin interweaves a narrative about his early encounters with Christianity with a discussion of the Nation of Islam and an exposure of the emptiness of white liberal commitments. The points of connection between the two essays are many. Both are written as open letters, although one is addressed to his nephew and the other to no one in particular, coming as the letter does from an unspecified "region" in Baldwin's mind. The nephew to whom Baldwin addresses his thoughts in "My Dungeon Shook" is about fourteen years old, the age Baldwin recalls in the opening section of "Down at the Cross." And as the ensuing discussion aims to demonstrate, the notes Baldwin strikes in the shorter essay are elements of more elaborated themes in "Down at the Cross."

Equality, as it is represented from the opening paragraph of the "Down at the Cross," is terrifying. According to Baldwin, the summer he turned fourteen was one of crisis. It was the summer in which he "discovered God" and the onset of puberty convinced him of his damnation. Intertwined with these developments was another: during the summer of 1938, Baldwin recognized in the men and women in his neighborhood the future toward which he seemed inevitably to be hurtling. "What I saw around me that summer in Harlem was what I had always seen; nothing had changed. But now, without any warning, the whores and the pimps and racketeers on the Avenue had become a personal menace. It had not before occurred to me that I could become one of them, but now I realized that we had been produced by the same circumstances" ("Down," 337). The essay continues, drawing out what it was in Baldwin's surroundings that suddenly seemed to pose such great danger to him. Clearly, the dread Baldwin describes is religious. But it is not only the fear of an otherworldly hell that emerges in the opening paragraph of the essay. The observation that "in the same way that the girls were destined to gain as much weight as their mothers, the boys, it was clear, would rise no higher than their fathers" ("Down," 338) indicates how the kind of equality evident in the streets of Harlem in 1938 might feel like a trap to an ambitious fourteen-year-old boy. If the men and women who struggled not to be eaten away by "the incessant and gratuitous humiliation that one encountered every working day" ("Down," 339) and those who had long since given up the struggle and succumbed to the lure of "the Avenue" were the people against whom Baldwin measured his own prospects, and if he could see nothing standing between their present and his future, equality could only look frightening.[25]

Against this backdrop, the notion of individual agency and the significance accorded to choice seem irrelevant. According to Baldwin, the only imaginable escape from the ghetto and the certainty of sharing the fate of those around him was to find a "gimmick." Among the gimmicks he reports having considered that summer were prizefighting, singing, dancing, and preaching ("Down," 341). Baldwin does not represent his election of the pulpit over the other options as a righteous one; becoming one of the men and women "on the Avenue" was, morally, no worse than any other fate. As he tells the story, he was essentially seduced into his preaching career when a woman pastor greeted him with precisely the same question used by the street hustlers asking him to join them: "Whose little boy are you?" ("Down," 343). Furthermore, Baldwin's calling to the pulpit was contrived, a flight from the alternatives: "Out of a deep, adolescent cunning I do not pretend to understand, I realized immediately that I could not remain in the church merely as another worshipper. I would have to give myself something to do, in order not to be too bored and find myself among all the wretched unsaved of the Avenue" ("Down," 345). Baldwin's irreverence toward his own success as a preacher undercuts the moral authority of the role. His self-mocking description of "what we might call my heyday" relates how he used that authority to win an adolescent battle for power over an overbearing father ("Down," 345). In contrast to the wisdom of the improving mottoes he rejects in "Everybody's Protest Novel," Baldwin's retelling of his embrace of and by the church proffers no "neatly framed and incontestable moral." The fact that the arms into which he fell were those of the church was sheer luck; his evasion of the trap of a criminal career was narrow and arbitrary.

Although the ideal of equal opportunity, of careers open to talent and hard work, provides the basis for a critique of precisely the sort of restricted future Baldwin describes, his retelling of his fourteenth summer casts even this ideal in a sinister light. His story evokes the power of boundaries more impermeable than the physical barriers dividing uptown Fifth Avenue from the shops and museums downtown. Baldwin conveys his early premonition of the unimaginably awful implications of presuming that he could realize the same dreams as any other child:

> The fear that I heard in my father's voice . . . when he realized that I really *believed* I could do anything a white boy could do, and had every intention of proving it, was not at all like the fear I heard when one of us was ill or had fallen down the stairs or strayed too far from the house. It was another fear, a fear that the child, in challenging the white world's assumptions, was putting himself in the path of destruction. ("Down," 341)

By capturing the dread consequences of believing in equal opportunity in a society not ready for the full inclusion of African Americans, Baldwin makes it plain how, for some citizens, the most cherished democratic ideals can be experienced as ambiguous, dangerous, and real.

Does Baldwin's unsettling narrative recommend the abandonment of equality as a political principle? Not at all. In fact, Baldwin's critique is made in the name of the equal humanity of all, regardless

of race, and of the equal entitlement of all Americans to the basic
rights of citizenship. Still, what Baldwin calls for is equality radically reconceived. His use of the term is radical insofar as it demands
an examination of the question "Equal . . . to what and to whom?"
Baldwin's response to this question is to show that the full inclusion of all Americans as equal citizens means reexamining the status of those already recognized as "equals." Taking the notion seriously, he avers, requires that privileged Americans recognize their
equals in the men and women "on the Avenue." At the same time,
it demands the same from the excluded, who have good reason not
to view the men and women who have excluded them as *their*
equals. Simply to declare or assume the equality of all citizens is to
fail to grapple with the difficulty of these demands. "It is easy to
proclaim all souls equal in the sight of God," he notes in a critique
of Harriet Beecher Stowe. But, he adds, "it is hard to make men
equal on earth, in the sight of men."[26]

Baldwin's radicalism consists, moreover, in his capacity to cast
taken-for-granted concepts in new light. He does so by taking seriously questions whose answers are presumed to be uncontroversial.
For example, he repeats with approval a question raised by the
Tunisians in 1956: "Are the *French* ready for self- government?"
("Down," 354). The Tunisians' query could be extended to the American case: Are white Americans ready for equality? Alternatively, "Do
I really *want* to be integrated into a burning house?"[27] Baldwin asserts
that the fundamental difficulty, for white Americans, of seeing blacks
as their equals resides in an unwillingness to think through how that
equality requires a revaluation of white identities and whites' stake in
persistent racial inequalities. He reveals how the idea that moral
progress involves the inclusion of black Americans in an ever-ex-
panding circle of people deserving of respect or recognition leaves
the center of the circle unexamined and preserves the assumption
that that center contains some value worth having or emulating. This
idea, Baldwin declares, "is revealed in all kinds of striking ways, from
Bobby Kennedy's assurance that a Negro can become President in
forty years to the unfortunate tone of warm congratulation with
which so many liberals address their Negro equals." For black Americans, who are hardly newcomers to the United States, Kennedy's assurance insults. "It is the Negro, of course, who is presumed to have
become equal—an achievement that not only proves the comforting

fact that perseverance has no color but also overwhelmingly corrobo-rates the white man's sense of his own value" ("Down," 374). Equal-ity thus extended to the formerly unequal is robbed of its critical po-tential, for its extension leaves unaddressed the question of what al-lowed white Americans to see black Americans as their inferiors in the first place.

Corresponding to an unwillingness among white Americans to see in black Americans human beings like themselves, Baldwin identifies an unwillingness among black Americans to see whites as fully human. Indeed, he notes that many African Americans view their white neighbors as "slightly mad victims of their own brainwashing" ("Down," 378). The source of the resistance to equality, however, is not the same. Baldwin explains that the everydayness of race-based humiliation and the possibility of brutality means that "it begins to be almost impossible to distinguish a real from a fancied injury." Fur-thermore, protecting oneself against such injuries can, without one's realizing it, engender a hostile outlook toward white Americans. "Ne-groes cannot risk assuming that the humanity of white people is more real than their color," Baldwin explains. "And this leads, impercepti-bly but inevitably, to a state of mind in which, having long ago learned to expect the worst, one finds it very easy to believe the worst" ("Down," 362). Baldwin's recollection of dinner at Nation of Islam headquarters indicates just how entrenched such a state of mind can be. He recounts how he groped, unsuccessfully, for a way to counter the Black Muslims' rejection of any kind of interracial future. "In the eeriest way possible," he remembers, "I suddenly had a glimpse what white people must go through at a dinner table when they are trying to prove that Negroes are not subhuman. I had almost said, after all, 'Well, take my friend Mary,' and very nearly descended to a catalogue of those virtues that gave Mary the right to be alive" ("Down," 364).

Furthermore, Baldwin's conviction that racial hierarchies dehu-manize the privileged as much as the oppressed reveals how the premise that blacks aim to be whites' equals demeans African Ameri-cans. He captures this sentiment by using a device that he deploys in several essays. Compressing a history into a few moments that ex-pose the connections between past and present, he undermines the attempt to locate racial subjugation in the past or to deny that its legacy exists at the heart of American democratic possibilities:

The Negro came to the white man for a roof or for five dollars or for a letter to the judge; the white man came to the Negro for love. But he was not often able to give what he came seeking. The price was too high; he had too much to lose. And the Negro knew this, too. When one knows this about a man, it is impossible for one to hate him, but unless he becomes a man—becomes equal—it is also impossible for one to love him. ("Down," 378)

This reflection, which appears just before the conclusion of "Down at the Cross," casts equality in an even more unattractive light than do Baldwin's comments at the essay's opening. If the idea that the same conditions had created both him and the men and women "in those wine- and urine-stained hallways" was frightening to the fourteen-year-old Baldwin, the possibility of sharing an inheritance with creatures capable of the kind of baseness described above was nearly inconceivable. Despite the gloominess of this conclusion, however, Baldwin advances an alternative to despair: acceptance.

Acceptance, for Baldwin, does not connote passivity or fatalism. Instead, Baldwin's notion of acceptance entails an active opposition to innocence, a confrontation with life's harshest truths. Acceptance is thus the key not only to equality but also to freedom as Baldwin conceives it. It is the link between equality and freedom. In advancing his own notion of acceptance, Baldwin casts doubt on other interpretations of *what* needs to be accepted and *by whom*. Unlike the standard tale of equal citizenship, in which outsiders become members by accepting the standards of the inside and the insiders, in turn, accept the formerly excluded as their fellow citizens, Baldwin offers narratives that explore the difficulties of expanding the company of equals. When the experiences of African Americans are taken into consideration, he shows, the standards for inclusion appear at best incompletely realized and at worst fundamentally compromised. By casting his account in the light of those experiences, Baldwin provides an explanation of why black and white Americans are largely ill prepared to achieve, in fact, the ideal of race-blind equality guaranteed by law. While his discussion of equality disarms the standard usage of acceptance, his account of the meaning of freedom reloads acceptance with a new meaning.

What is freedom for Baldwin? His report of the visit to Elijah Muhammad suggests just how difficult it is to formulate a precise answer. As he relates his conversation at the Nation of Islam headquarters, Baldwin maintains a tenuous line, repeating the Muslim leader's diagnosis of American racial ills, with which he agrees, and challenging Muhammad's prescribed course of treatment, with which he cannot agree. Baldwin understands the conviction that without land, without sovereign power, black Americans have no reason to expect recognition as human beings or inclusion in American prosperity. Yet he cannot endorse the Black Muslims' call for a separate, black nation. No matter how unlikely the possibility that African Americans will be able to move or speak or reside or get an education as freely as white Americans, Baldwin objects to an ideal of freedom based on the illusion that blackness and whiteness are internally unified and externally divisible properties ("Down," 364–65). According to Baldwin, this sort of freedom merely displaces the white world's constraints through an illusion. And like the gimmick that kept Baldwin off the streets as a teenager, it is ultimately as binding as the constraints it succeeds in breaking.

Baldwin's exchange with a young Black Muslim who escorts him from Nation of Islam headquarters to his next appointment ("I was . . . going to have a drink with several white devils on the other side of town" ["Down," 367]), suggests what the writer means by freedom and why he maintains that it is "hard to bear." During the ride, he engages his driver in a discussion of the prospects for black nationhood. Afterward, Baldwin writes that

> the boy could see that freedom depended on the possession of land; he was persuaded that, in one way or another, Negroes must achieve this possession. In the meantime, he could walk the streets and fear nothing, because there were millions like him, coming soon, now, to power. He was held together, in short, by a dream—though it is just as well to remember that some dreams come true—and was united with his "brothers" on the basis of their color. Perhaps one cannot ask for more. People always seem to band together in accordance to a principle . . . that releases them from personal responsibility. ("Down," 368)

By framing the discussion in personal terms, Baldwin does not underestimate the significance of the political freedom demanded by his driver or by Elijah Muhammad. What he sees instead is that this dream of self-determination is a fantasy. It is a fantasy, moreover, that relies on the same racial logic that makes escape from the United States seem imperative. Given the fundamental interrelation of black and white Americans, neither the dream of separation (which Baldwin likens to "amputation") nor the liberal notion of integration ("gangrene," in Baldwin's parlance) grasps reality.[28] He notes, furthermore, how the appeal to the principle of freedom can actually perpetuate the evasion of difficult truths. Hence Baldwin's appeal to "personal responsibility." This phrase, whose usage in the context of contemporary debates about welfare reform is largely cynical, is, as Baldwin uses it, a radical idea.

The idea of freedom as the acceptance of responsibility appears at the conclusion of "My Dungeon Shook," preparing the way for the longer treatment in "Down at the Cross." In "My Dungeon Shook," Baldwin proceeds from a piece of advice to his nephew about how to cope with a white world that mistakenly believes its acceptance of blacks into the fold is a prize—"The really terrible thing, old buddy, is that *you* must accept *them*"—to the claim that "we cannot be free until they are free."[29] In "Down at the Cross," Baldwin inverts this statement when he asserts that "the price of the liberation of the white people is the liberation of the blacks—the total liberation, in the cities, in the towns, before the law, and in the mind" ("Down," 375). This inversion indicates the elusiveness of "freedom." Baldwin's writing takes aim simultaneously at an unjust social structure ("the price of the liberation of the white people is the liberation of the blacks") and at the assumptions and fears that undergird it ("we cannot be free until they are free" and "the total liberation . . . in the mind"). The confusion here is not causal, although his language implies that it is. Rather, it indicates that Baldwin is demanding everything—the freedom of blacks and the freedom of whites—and all at once.

Much of Baldwin's treatment of freedom is negative.[30] He spends a great deal more energy identifying what freedom is not than he does elaborating on what it is. For instance, freedom is not given but must be fought for or taken.[31] Indeed, most of Baldwin's essays emphasize the rarity of freedom. This rarity is evident not only in his descriptions of the lives of women and men trapped in the ghetto but also in the arbitrariness of his own escape. The rarity or even the absence of freedom is illustrated, moreover, in the racial innocence of so many white Americans. By contrast, Baldwin contends that freedom requires the exercise of moral agency. Hence, when he does define freedom positively, he calls it "maturity" or "flexibility" or the state of being "present" or "the fire which burns away illusion."

Underlying all these meanings is an acknowledgment of the bounds of human achievement. Baldwin's conception of freedom, finally, involves facing the terrifying fact that "the earth turns and the sun inexorably rises and sets, and one day, for each of us, the sun will go down for the last, last time"—and salvaging the will to act in spite of it.

> It is the responsibility of free men to trust and to celebrate what is constant—birth, struggle, and death are constant, and so is love, though we may not always think so—and to apprehend the nature of change, to be able and willing to change. I speak of change not on the surface but in the depths—change in the sense of renewal. But renewal becomes impossible if one supposes things to be constant that are not—safety, for example, or money, or power. One clings then to chimeras, by which one can only be betrayed, and the entire hope—the entire possibility—of freedom disappears. ("Down," 373)

Among the chimeras to which Americans cling, Baldwin avers, is the idea that the "race problem" is anything other than a way of avoiding confrontation with the tragic dimension of human life. From this willful existential innocence grows another: the evasion of responsibility for participation in an avowedly democratic society in which democratic principles bear little connection to the lives of many of its citizens. In spite of legal and social prohibitions against overt racial discrimination, the tacit acceptance of racial division props up American confidence that democratic principles have largely been realized. Consciously or not, race serves as a crutch. Baldwin's job as an essayist is to convince his readers that they are not walking until they try to walk without it but at the same time to warn them that no American can imagine what that kind of walking would feel like without interrogating his or her reliance on the crutch in the first place. If "everything in a life depends on how that life accepts its limits," then the realization of freedom at any level involves accepting the radical unfreedom of human life without being defeated by it.

By locating African American experiences at the center of an account of equality and freedom, *The Fire Next Time* delivers the message that Americans have never attempted the realization of either principle. By focusing on those experiences, "My Dungeon Shook" and "Down at the Cross" insist on the intimate relationship between equality and freedom. To more elaborate arguments about the meaning of the principles or their relative priority Baldwin offers a simple rejoinder: a democratic society is one in which no one is free until everyone is.

Finding the Words

> Color is not a human or a personal reality; it is a political reality. But this is a distinction so extremely hard to make that the West has not been able to make it yet. And at the center of this dreadful storm, this vast confusion, stand the black people of this nation, who must now share the fate of a nation that has never accepted them, to which they were brought in chains. Well, if this is so, one has no choice but to do all in one's power to change that fate, and at no matter what risk—eviction, imprisonment, torture, death. For the sake of one's children, in order to minimize the bill that *they* must pay, one must be careful not to take refuge in any delusion—and the value placed on the color of the skin is always and everywhere and forever a delusion. I know that what I am asking is impossible. But in our time, as in every time, the impossible is the least that one can demand. ("Down," 378–79)

The first sentence of this passage from the penultimate paragraph of *The Fire Next Time* is surprising. What is Baldwin's message, if not that color is a human or a personal reality and that human and personal realities and political realities are thoroughly entangled with each other? But the statement "Color is not a human or a personal reality; it is a political reality" does not indicate a lapse in Baldwin's struggle against the illusion of race blindness. It captures the tension that Baldwin strives to maintain. "The value placed on the color of the skin," while a delusion, has real effects on individual experiences; or, although whiteness and blackness have no meaning outside a context of racial domination, they are significant within such a context. Because that significance cannot be wished away, to demand the impossible is to aspire to change society fundamentally without either valorizing race or denying that a value is attached to it.[32]

Baldwin insists that racial assumptions, which serve to perpetuate racial hierarchy, pervade American society to a degree that defies simple abolition, and he urges that Americans acknowledge the ways in which those assumptions shape their experience, their identities, their language. Race-blind thinking is, by this account, an attempt at escaping the terrifying implications of American history in the name of the ideals that history is supposed to represent. It is an innocence Americans cannot afford. Race-conscious thinking, in contrast, requires that one "strive to become tough and philosophical concerning destruction and death" ("Down," 334).

Of course, becoming "tough and philosophical" is not a specific plan of action. And Baldwin offers little concrete guidance about the mechanics of social change. He has virtually nothing to say about how to construct more just political institutions and policies. Moreover, his essays challenge most solutions by revealing levels of complexity unnoticed by would-be solvers. Yet by inhabiting and describing the space between democratic principles and American practices, he lays critical groundwork for the development of political theories that do tackle the substantive moral challenges of race consciousness. He develops a vivid moral psychology that suggests why racial injustices have survived the public rejection of white supremacy. By conveying how those injustices are felt or not felt, by the subordinated and by the privileged, he provides a crucial reminder of the peculiar vulnerability of democratic societies to the assumptions, beliefs, and prejudices of their members.

"How stunning is the achievement of those who have searched for and mined a shareable language for the words to say it."[33] Toni Morrison's tribute, while not directed specifically at Baldwin, captures his gift to the society he criticized throughout his life as a writer.[34] Despite the uneven quality of his later essays, which sacrificed some of their early control as he became more vulnerable to despair, Baldwin's prolific career remained, and still remains, a strike against doom. Despite his awareness of the entrenchment of American racial innocence, his writing constitutes an expression of faith in the possibility of change. By trying to find the words, both to make his own experiences real for those to whom the message of those experiences was inaudible and to re-form the language in order to accommodate the stories that have been denied expression, Baldwin puts flesh on those democratic values he criticizes so relentlessly. The words— *equality, freedom, democracy*—are part of Baldwin's inheritance. His achievement consists in the evidence that he seized that inheritance and bequeathed it, changed, to subsequent generations.

NOTES

1. Baldwin maintained that he referred to *Native Son* as a sign of respect for the importance of Richard Wright's novel (although the timing could not have been worse, because his former mentor had agreed to publish a story in the same issue of *Zero* in which, unbeknownst to him, "Everybody's Protest Novel" would appear). In an essay written after Wright's death, however, Baldwin acknowledges that Wright had served as an idol he needed to smash, and Baldwin allows that he is not sure how he will respond when the next generation deems it necessary to destroy him. See James Baldwin, "Alas, Poor Richard," in *The Price of the Ticket: Collected Nonfiction, 1948–1985* (New York: St. Martin's/Marek, 1985), 277.

2. See Albert Murray, "James Baldwin, Protest Fiction, and the Blues Tradition," in *The Omni-Americans: Black Experience and American Culture* (New York: Da Capo, 1970), 142–68.

3. I use the term *race consciousness* to capture the myriad ways in which racial identity in general and the distinction between "black" and "white" Americans in particular get noticed. Insofar as such noticing perpetuates assumptions about racial difference, race consciousness sustains racial inequalities.

4. This discussion will not evaluate the accuracy of Baldwin's reading of Stowe.

5. For a fuller account of the sinister effect of such moralizing mottoes, see Baldwin's description of the Grimes family's living-room mantel in *Go Tell It on the Mountain*. There, the narrator reports, hang two examples of such mottoes—a hackneyed poem written in pink and blue and an excerpt from the Gospel of John "in letters of fire against a background of gold." For the novel's primary character, John Grimes, the juxtaposition of the mottoes with a green metal serpent, and more important, with an environment in which neither the saccharine poem of welcome nor the claim "God so loved the world . . . " bears any relation to the alienation of the family living there, produces a profound feeling of isolation and fear. See James Baldwin, "Everybody's Protest Novel," in *Price of the Ticket*, 27 (this essay noted hereafter in the text as "Everybody," followed by the page number); and James Baldwin, *Go Tell It on the Mountain* (New York: Signet Books, 1952), 25–26.

6. Although Baldwin's language suggests a disavowal of political struggle, Irving Howe's conclusion that the substitution of *acceptance* for *battle* aligns Baldwin with "a post-war liberalism not very different from conservatism" strikes me as unfair. Defending Richard Wright against challenges by Baldwin and Ralph Ellison, Howe, paraphrases Wright to say that "only through struggle could men with black skins, and, for that matter, all the oppressed of the world, achieve their humanity." This formulation reduces

"men with black skins" to their oppression by failing to see that the significance of their lives exceeds the terms set for them. (It may also help to account for Howe's evaluation of *Giovanni's Room*, the only Baldwin novel with no black characters, as "a flat failure.") Rather than counseling quietism, as Howe suggests, Baldwin's attack on the protest novel reminds his readers that even successful political struggle is not the full measure of a person's humanity. Furthermore, Howe's emphasis on the responsibility of the oppressed misses Baldwin's insistence that oppressed and oppressor, while living under considerably different conditions, are both implicated in the condition of their society; to endorse one-sided struggle, whether by the oppressed or on their behalf, is to miss this interrelation. See Irving Howe, "Black Boys and Native Sons," *Dissent* (Autumn 1963): 353–68.

7. Perhaps one of the best examples of this metamorphosis in contemporary discourse is the ease with which the term *discrimination* has been folded into the term *reverse discrimination* and thereby stripped of its historical association with systematic oppression. When disconnected from claims about the persistence of racial injustice in American society, the call to fight discrimination can be as easily deployed to bolster as to counter the status quo.

8. See John Rawls, *Political Liberalism* (New York: Columbia University Press, 1993), 43–46.

9. It is the drama of the ancients and the modern novel, however, not the personal essay, that Hampshire calls "the necessary arts of the moralist." See Stuart Hampshire, *Innocence and Experience* (Cambridge, Mass.: Harvard University Press, 1989), 105.

10. James Baldwin, "Down at the Cross: Letter from a Region in My Mind," in *The Fire Next Time*, reprinted in *Price of the Ticket*, 371. Subsequent references to this essay are noted in the text as "Down," followed by the page number.

11. Toni Morrison, "Unspeakable Things Unspoken: The Afro-American Presence in American Literature," *Michigan Quarterly Review* 28 (Winter 1989): 23.

12. James Baldwin, "If Black English Isn't a Language, Then Tell Me, What Is?" in *Price of the Ticket*, 649–52.

13. Morrison, "Unspeakable Things Unspoken," 3.

14. James Baldwin, "Why I Stopped Hating Shakespeare," *The Observer* (19 April 1964): 21.

15. Baldwin, "If Black English Isn't a Language," 650.

16. Alfred Kazin, quoted in "The Negro in American Culture," *Cross Currents* 11 (Summer 1961): 213. Other participants in the discussion, which was broadcast on public radio in New York City, were Baldwin, Lorraine Hansberry, Emile Capouya, and Langston Hughes. Nat Hentoff moderated the event.

17. Theodor W. Adorno, "The Essay as Form," in *Notes to Literature,* vol. 1, trans. Shierry Weber Nicholsen, ed. Rolf Tiedemann (New York: Columbia University Press, 1991), 11.

18. Baldwin, "Why I Stopped Hating Shakespeare," 21.

19. Václav Havel, "Words on Words," *New York Review of Books* 36 (18 January 1990): 6.

20. James Baldwin, "The Northern Protestant," in *Price of the Ticket,* 202.

21. This impossibility applies not only to the blindnesses of the privileged members of society. Hence Baldwin's dismissal of the Marxian dream that an entirely new and entirely egalitarian society will emerge from the triumph of the oppressed ("Everybody," 32). See James Baldwin, "Every Good-Bye Ain't Gone," in *Price of the Ticket,* 643.

22. For example, in a review originally published as the cover article of the inaugural issue of the *New York Review of Books,* F. W. Dupee criticizes Baldwin for replacing the acute analysis and critique of his earlier essays with more grandiose prophetic claims. See F. W. Dupee, "James Baldwin and 'the Man,'" in *James Baldwin,* ed. Harold Bloom (New York: Chelsea House Publishers, 1986), 11–16.

23. James Baldwin, "Autobiographical Notes," in *Notes of a Native Son* (Boston: Beacon Press, 1984), 9.

24. "Down at the Cross" first appeared in the *New Yorker* with the title "Letter from a Region in My Mind." "My Dungeon Shook" was originally titled "A Letter to My Nephew" in *The Progressive.* According to one Baldwin biographer, an editor at Dial Press understood the link between the two and recommended publishing them together, with the shorter essay serving as an introduction for the longer one. See David Leeming, *James Baldwin: A Biography* (New York: Alfred A. Knopf, 1994), 212.

25. Another story about equality, related to the first, lurks in *The Fire Next Time.* Equality not only contains dreadful possibilities but, as a comparative value, can be deployed as a critical device. By comparing institutions and principles not generally thought to be alike and declaring them moral equals, Baldwin demonstrates the appeal, and the shortcomings, that they share. Baldwin uses this sort of critical equation to great effect by showing the inhumanity of all "totems, taboos, crosses, blood sacrifices, steeples, mosques, races, armies, flags, nations" through a depiction of the similarities between Christianity, American nationalism, and the Black Muslim movement ("Down," 373).

26. Just how difficult it is to "make men equal on earth, in the sight of men" is suggested by the kinds of denigration or exclusion that affect even the most prosperous African Americans. Evidence of the barriers to the social equality of white and black Americans is so abundant that I cite only two examples here. First, Baldwin, in describing his efforts to devise a trick that

would effect his escape from the ghetto, observes that "one would never defeat one's circumstances by working and saving one's pennies; one would never, by working, acquire that many pennies, and, besides, the social treatment accorded even the most successful Negroes proved that one needed, in order to be free, something more than a bank account" ("Down," 339–40). Lucius Barker, former president of the American Political Science Association, offers a similar reflection: "That [glass] ceiling might have been broken a second time by my presidency of this association, for example, but neither that nor anything else had relevance for those who, in the past year or so, referred to me as a 'bus driver' or those who asked my wife and me upon answering our doorbell whether we were 'caretakers' of our own home." For quotations in text, see James Baldwin, "The Crusade of Indignation," in *Price of the Ticket*, 158. For the quotation above, Lucius J. Barker, "Limits of Political Strategy: A Systemic View of the African American Experience," *American Political Science Review* 88 (March 1994): 11.

27. Baldwin does not identify the source of this question, although it may be Lorraine Hansberry, according to whom it was on the minds of "all Negro intellectuals, . . . all politically-conscious Negroes" in the early 1960s ("Down," 374). See also Lorraine Hansberry, quoted in "The Negro in American Culture," 222.

28. James Baldwin, "Notes of a Native Son," in *Price of the Ticket*, 144.

29. Baldwin, "My Dungeon Shook," in *Price of the Ticket*, 335–36.

30. I do not use the word *negative* here to mean "freedom from," as it is most famously articulated by Isaiah Berlin. Rather, I distinguish between negative and positive definitions to suggest how difficult it is to pin down freedom's precise meaning. That having been said, however, Baldwin does provide a powerful definition of negative freedom, as "freedom from . . . ," in the American context: "They, the blacks, simply don't wish to be beaten over the head by the whites every instant of our brief passage on this planet" ("Down," 340). Cf. Isaiah Berlin, "Two Concepts of Liberty," in *Four Essays on Liberty* (London: Oxford University Press, 1969), 118–72.

31. James Baldwin, "Notes for a Hypothetical Novel," in *Price of the Ticket*, 243.

32. Stephen Spender's complaint that *The Fire Next Time* counsels despair by "postulating a quite impossible demand as the only way of dealing with a problem that has to be solved" misses the point in two respects. First, by saying Baldwin offers his "impossible demand" as the *only* way to deal with racial inequality, Spender mistakes Baldwin's criticism of incremental change for the assertion that such change is not an improvement. Second, and more important, the assertion that the "problem has to be solved" does not mean it is as susceptible to solution as Spender intimates. See Stephen Spender,

"James Baldwin: Voice of a Revolution," *Partisan Review* 30 (Summer 1963): 257–58.

33. Toni Morrison, *Playing in the Dark: Whiteness and the Literary Imagination* (Cambridge, Mass.: Harvard University Press, 1992), xiii.

34. Morrison does offer such a tribute elsewhere. See Toni Morrison, "Life in His Language," in *James Baldwin: The Legacy*, ed. Quincy Troupe (New York: Simon & Schuster, 1989), 75–78.

Part II

Baldwin and Sexuality

Chapter 4

Culture, Rhetoric, and Queer Identity
James Baldwin and the Identity Politics of Race and Sexuality

William J. Spurlin

While academic queer studies has played a pivotal role in shifting the politics of sexuality to the forefront of literary and cultural inquiry, it has still not sufficiently theorized queer subjectivity in relation to other axes of social positioning. Queer studies has yet to examine its own hegemonic impulses. Teresa de Lauretis points to one problem, for instance, in noting that gay male critics seldom make more than a perfunctory gesture toward feminist or lesbian studies.[1] This is especially true to the extent that many gay men assume that their own authority as gay is sufficient to articulate queer identity. Another, related problem is the uncritical lumping of lesbians and gay men together under the umbrella term *queer* along with other sexual minorities or simply referring to lesbians and gay men as a distinct group, assuming a kind of symmetry between them, as if they occupy the same political, social, and economic ground as a result of sexual identity alone. More broadly, queer studies needs to analyze seriously the political implications of the problem Eve Sedgwick identified in *Epistemology of the Closet* regarding "how a variety of forms of oppression intertwine systemically with each other; and especially how the person who is disabled through one set of oppressions may *by the same positioning* be enabled through others".[2] In addition to a masculinist bias in queer studies, white gay men in particular have focused on the ways in which they are oppressed through homophobia without sufficiently interrogating their proximity and access to white

male privilege and analyzing the specific contexts in which their oppression may or may not operate. A more thorough analysis remains
to be done on the more or less slippery relation between privilege and
struggle among white gay men.

Studying Baldwin's reception in the 1960s helps critique the notion that sexual identity is experienced in isolation from other axes of
social positioning and provides a salient site of investigation into the
politics of identity, especially the ways in which patriarchal power is
interarticulated, through more than one vector of domination. Not
only are the axes of race and sexuality important areas of investigation in a study of Baldwin's reception, but gender is included as an
intersecting axis in that nexus as well, insofar as homophobia assigns
failed or abject gender to homosexuals, and since sexuality, as Judith
Butler reminds us, "is regulated through *the policing and the shaming
of gender.*"[3] Operating on a premise of social-epistemic rhetoric,
which James Berlin has referred to as the study and critique of signifying practices in their relation to subject formation within specific
social, political, and economic conditions,[4] I (re)examine Baldwin's
literary and cultural reception in the early 1960s in the dominant culture and his reception later in the decade in the U.S. Black Power
movement, marking both receptions as themselves interpretive acts.
This chapter analyzes some of the cultural tropes and rhetorical
strategies used to read and interpret gay male identity and the relation of these tropes to early 1960s cultural conversations and institutional discourses on homosexuality prior to Stonewall, especially
pre–*DSM III* medical and psychoanalytic discourses operative at the
time.[5] The tropes used to read African American identity as they informed American civil rights discourses and the concomitant discourses of black struggle and resistance are also analyzed. The chapter refers to such texts by Baldwin as *Giovanni's Room* (1956), *Another
Country* (1962), and *The Fire Next Time* (1963); but in an effort to resist
an impulse in queer studies merely to reread canonical authors
queerly and stabilize the queer referent, my primary focus is not on
Baldwin's homosexuality per se, nor on sexual or racial themes in his
texts. Rather, I focus on a specific historicized representation of homosexuality by reading the *cultural lenses* and *rhetorical practices* that
informed interpretations of queer and African American identity in
Baldwin and in his work in the 1960s, setting these strategies and
lenses in broader social and cultural discourses on homosexuality

and race at the time and exploring their contemporary social and political implications.[6]

One interpretive act to which I refer occurred on May 17, 1963,
when *Time* magazine ran a cover story on Baldwin as part of an article
"Races: Freedom—Now." The article begins by exploring the violent
abuses of African Americans in Birmingham, Alabama, especially
those involved in freedom marches, by the police and the public
safety commissioner, Theophilus Eugene "Bull" Connor, as a means
to maintain racial segregation and to squelch black resistance. Baldwin's photograph, with the caption "Author James Baldwin," appears on the cover of *Time* under a banner across the upper left corner
that reads "Birmingham and Beyond: The Negro's Push for Equality."
The pages given to Baldwin at first appear to address his views on
race relations in light of the publication of his essay "The Fire Next
Time" as a book earlier that year and of the media's attempt to pay serious attention to civil rights struggles among African Americans.
Near the end of the story on Birmingham, the article mentions the
great chasm between "the Negro who looks with eagerness toward a
militant solution, and the unyielding Southerner who hopes not to be
further disturbed. . . . Negro Author [*sic*] James Baldwin has illuminated this grey gulf with bolts of intellectual lightning."[7]

While Baldwin's most recent biography remarks on how the *Time*
article on Baldwin, which follows the lead article on Birmingham,
casts him as a spokesman and prophet,[8] it fails to mention the rhetoric
of homophobia with which *Time* represents him, which certainly
should have been obvious by the 1990s, when the biography was
published. In less-than-subtle contrast to Dr. Martin Luther King, Jr.,
whom the entire article masculinizes as a black leader, *Time* immediately proceeds to claim that Baldwin "is not, by any stretch of the
imagination, a Negro leader. He tries no civil rights cases in the
courts, preaches from no pulpit, devises no stratagems for sit-ins,
Freedom Riders or street marchers" (26). The story goes on to speculate on Baldwin's sexuality, marking his homosexuality, as if it threatens to "pass" un(re)marked, not only through its comparison of Baldwin to King and Malcolm X but through its obviously coded description of Baldwin as "a nervous, slight, almost fragile figure, filled with
frets and fears. He is effeminate in manner, drinks considerably,
smokes cigarettes in chains, and he often loses his audience with
overblown arguments" (26). It is important to bear in mind that this

article was written a year after the publication of Baldwin's novel *Another Country*, which candidly depicts queer desire—particularly the relationship between Eric and Yves in Paris and the homoerotic relationship between Rufus Scott and Vivaldo—at the same time as it calls into question the social conflation of gender and sexuality. *Giovanni's Room*, published in 1956, would have also been part of Baldwin's critical reception in the early 1960s. While several early reviews of *Giovanni's Room* glossed over its homosexual content, by the time *Another Country* appeared in 1962, it had become increasingly difficult not to read both works from a queer perspective. The important issue at stake here, I reiterate, is not so much Baldwin's own (homo)sexuality per se but that he was read and interpreted as queer by critics and by the media, and how readings of queer desire and queer identity in his work and in him made use of and extended dominant social practices, cultural conversations, and institutional discourses on homosexuality in the early 1960s.[9]

This was all that was said—or more accurately, implied—about Baldwin's homosexuality in *Time*. To broaden the scope of the cultural conversations and institutionalized discourses on homosexuality that were put to rhetorical use to defend interpretations about Baldwin and his work in particular and about queer identity in general, I turn to an important issue of *Life* magazine, that other mass-circulated periodical that entered middle-class American homes in the 1960s. *Life* did a double feature story titled "Homosexuality in America" one year later, on June 26, 1964. Unlike the *Time* article of 1963, which reads queer identity in the context of a prominent cultural figure, the *Life* articles are an early attempt to read queer identity as a public position. Once again, as was the case with Baldwin, gay men are stereotypically represented as effeminate. One reason they are attracted to large urban areas, argues Paul Welch in the first article, "The 'Gay' World Takes to the City Streets," is that the professions most favored by homosexuals are interior decorating, hairstyling, and fashion design, the best job opportunities for which are in the cities. The article also contends that most gay men in 1964 are easily identified by their "fluffy" sweaters, tight khaki pants, and tennis shoes.[10] Though the article acknowledges that not all gay men are effeminate, it maintains the discourse of deviance in its descriptions of the leather bars in San Francisco, commenting on the "obsessive" effort of gay leathermen to appear masculine and tough "in the rakish angle of the caps, in the thumbs *boldly* hooked in belts" (70; emphasis added).

Acknowledging that effeminate gay men and gay leathermen are not representative of the majority of gay men, and that 85 percent of gay men look and act like other men and cannot be spotted for certain even by "experts," Ernest Havemann, author of the second article in *Life,* on etiology, still makes use of the rhetoric of deviance in telling readers that "often the only signs are a very subtle tendency to over-meticulous grooming, plus the failure to cast the *ordinary man's* customary admiring glance at *every* pretty *girl* who walks by."[11] The juxtaposition of *man* and *girl,* as well as the agency of the male gaze, not only attempts to produce a marker or sign with which to identify gay men and make them culturally legible but also points to gender politics in that *man* and *girl,* used simultaneously to describe and condone heterosexuality, are not invested with equal power. More important, the use of these terms reveals how homophobia and misogyny intertwine in culture, though one is not reducible to the other. But it is also important to note that the anxiety over the undetectability of homosexuality incited discursive strategies to expose it and mark its difference. In the 1950s and early 1960s, these discursive and rhetorical strategies were closely linked to the cold war political imaginary. As Robert J. Corber has noted, the possibility that gay men could escape detection by passing, whether consciously or not, as straight linked them to subversive groups who were allegedly conspiring to infiltrate the nation's cultural and political institutions and were national security risks[12] largely because they looked like "everyone else" and could easily evade social apparatuses of surveillance.

Closely related to cold war discourses on homosexuality, and largely influenced by dominant social and cultural assumptions of gender and sexuality in its representations of homosexuality as pathological, psychoanalysis, the most rigorous and elaborate institutionalized discourse on sexuality in the West, also played an influential role in the cultural management and reading of queer identity. This influence became even more decisive in 1962, a year before the *Time* article on Baldwin appeared, when Dr. Irving Bieber and his colleagues published a monograph titled *Homosexuality,* a ten-year investigation of the etiology of male homosexuality.[13] The study contested Kinsey's 1948 findings on the scope of homosexual experiences among American males and responded to growing concerns about

Kinsey's statistical evidence that men with homosexual histories could be found across social classes, occupations, and geographic locations. Bieber's study became the leading authority and standard pronouncement on male homosexuality until, after widespread criticism from within and outside the psychiatric, psychoanalytic, and medical professions against heterosexual intercourse as the standard for sexual health, the American Psychiatric Association (APA) decided in 1973 to delete homosexuality as a category of psychopathology from the *DSM III*.

Bieber and his colleagues studied the family constellations of 106 gay male patients, as reported in therapy, in an effort to shift psychoanalytic attention to early childhood experiences, particularly the relationship between the growing child and his parents, rather than studying the role of constitutional factors in the development of homosexuality, which Sigmund Freud had clearly indicated was also important to consider.[14] It was Bieber's study that promulgated the by now all-too-familiar view that a high proportion of gay men had "close-binding mothers," who demasculinized their sons and thwarted the development of their heterosexual drives, and detached, hostile fathers.[15] Bieber is quoted as an "expert" in the etiological portion of the *Life* double feature, offering what appears to be a profound medical opinion when he suggests that the use of the word *gay* by homosexuals "is only a flippant and rather pathetic attempt to cover up deep and chronic feelings of pathological depression" (Havemann, 78).

Though later in the decade, when the status of homosexuality became a subject of serious debate within the APA, strong objections would be raised for the study's sample of gay male patients with other psychological disturbances, and for its application of findings to the general population of gay men not in treatment, it is nonetheless possible to observe Bieber's clinical and analytic arguments, centered on gay men as effeminate and as pathological figures, rhetorically underlying the media's representation of gay men in general (in *Life* in 1964) and of Baldwin in particular (in *Time* in 1963). One must also speculate whether the *Time* article implies a direct correlation between its descriptions of Baldwin's smoking and drinking and of his "nervous, slight, almost fragile figure" and "effeminate" manner. Indeed, Bieber's 1962 study found "effeminacy" to be a distinguishing trait of the 106 gay male patients, compared to the one hundred heterosexual men in the control group. Examples of effeminate behavior in men were identified as exaggerated shrugging, "wrist-breaking," lisping, hand-to-hip posturing, and, interestingly, effusiveness (188–89), the last being a trope of which the *Time* article made explicit use in mentioning how Baldwin often loses his audience with overblown arguments.

Psychoanalysis, especially in the context of the Bieber study, operated in the 1960s as more than just a clinical practice, as its discourse on homosexuality was tied to political and social practices and beliefs.[16] The homophobic manner in which Baldwin and his work were read and received in the early 1960s is not simply a reflection of psychoanalytic thinking on homosexuality; psychoanalytic thinking on homosexuality ratified and largely reflected American homophobia, while its tropes of psychological and moral pathology, used to interpret the sign of homosexuality culturally and socially through the clinical literature and the media (which popularized clinical "findings"), further intensified the deployment of homophobic ideologies and concomitant discriminatory practices.

At the same time, it is important to note, as Corber does, that the stereotype of the feminine gay man was not simply externally imposed by a hostile society but that gay men strategically (re)appropriated the stereotype to make themselves visible to one another and to the dominant culture (Corber, 65). So while it may be true that gender inversion operated as a dominant cultural trope with which to mark gay men, it is not reducible to its homophobic usage by the dominant culture. But the representation of gay men as effeminate by mass media organs such as *Time* and *Life* and by psychoanalysis in the early 1960s nevertheless reproduced the homophobia of cold war political discourse and effectively reinforced Butler's point on how sexuality "is regulated through the policing and the shaming of gender."[17]

Despite *Time's* sympathetic treatment of African Americans engaged in civil rights struggle in Birmingham under King, Baldwin was nonetheless feminized—indeed, often referred to as "Martin Luther Queen" among some black nationalists—even though the book that won him acclaim and visibility in the media as a writer and lecturer in the spring of 1963 was on race relations. The *Time* feature on Baldwin occurred against the backdrop of black struggle in the spring of 1963, as he made the lecture circuit in California after the publication of his provocative *The Fire Next Time*, wherein he expresses the myths and costs of assimilation by candidly asking if white people should be taken as the model by which to live:

> White Americans find it as difficult as white people elsewhere do to divest themselves of the notion that they are in possession of some intrinsic value that black people need, or want. . . . There is certainly little enough in the white man's public or private life that one should desire to imitate. White men, at the bottom of their hearts, know this. Therefore, a vast amount of the energy that goes into what we call the Negro problem is produced by the white man's profound desire not to be judged by those who are not white, not to be seen as he is, and at the same time a vast amount of the white anguish is rooted in the white man's equally profound need to be seen as he is, to be released from the tyranny of his mirror.[18]

What is particularly worth noting in this quotation is that it can serve as a kind of master trope, as a synecdoche, for the ways in which patriarchal domination operates. Indeed, on one level, when Baldwin speaks of the self-serving fantasies of whites that they are in possession of some self-evident, intrinsic value that blacks desire, the same could be said of heterosexual fantasies with regard to lesbians and gay men, of men's fantasies with regard to women, of the fantasies of the middle class with regard to the working class, and of the fantasies of developed Western nations with regard to postcolonial nations and nations of the Third World.

Moreover, this passage from *The Fire Next Time* works to open up oppressive structures of patriarchal power across several matrices and demonstrates that power does not operate only through a single vector of domination (racism, sexism, homophobia, etc). Like bell hooks, who reminds us that feminism "must exist apart from *and as a part of* the larger struggle to eradicate domination in *all* of its forms"—particularly noting that racism cannot be eradicated while other forms of domination remain intact[19]—Baldwin questioned models of political solidarity and resistance based on one's membership in a particular community (thought of as homogeneous) and looked at the ways in which a variety of oppressions intersected with one another. Corber's analysis of *Another Country* shows how the frequent shifts in the novel's point of view encourage identifications on the part of the reader across lines of race, gender, sexuality, and class and help dismantle the split between self and Other, though these identifications are seldom realized by the five principal characters in the novel. Baldwin's use of multiple centers of intelligence, according to Corber, enabled him to stage the construction of subjectivity across several axes of difference and to critique the patterning of identity according to a single axis of difference that prevented African Americans, women, gay men and lesbians, and other disenfranchised groups from overcoming the racist, sexist, and homophobic structures of postwar American society (Corber, 178). Because the characters in *Another Country* are so deeply divided along lines of race, gender, sexuality, and social class, which are reinforced by many of the liberationist struggles of the 1960s (particularly the Civil Rights and feminist movements) and perhaps by liberal humanist views that considered subjectivity as transcending politics, they are unable, according to Corber, to form broad-based coalitions and to engage in the collective action necessary to overcome postwar structures of oppression (187).

This seems particularly significant in the context of the identity politics of race and sexuality, as both Rufus and Vivaldo are affected by racial stereotypes and therefore remain divided along racial lines. After Rufus's suicide, Vivaldo reflects on his relationship with him:

> They had slept together, got drunk together, balled chicks together, cursed each other out. . . . And yet how much, as it turned out, had each kept hidden in his heart from the other! . . . Well, perhaps they had been afraid that if they looked too closely into one another each would have found . . . the abyss. Somewhere in his heart the black boy hated the white boy because he was white. Somewhere in his heart Vivaldo had feared and hated Rufus because he was black.[20]

These racial tropes, in addition to Rufus and Vivaldo's sexual competitiveness with women and Vivaldo's later confession to Eric that his reluctance to hold Rufus in his arms shortly before the suicide was out of fear that Rufus might think him "queer" (i.e., not a "real" man), reveal, Corber argues, Vivaldo's insecurities about his own masculinity and prevent him not only from expressing love to Rufus but also from expressing solidarity with him (Corber, 187). Yet the potential for coalition, especially across boundaries of race and sexuality, is still there, and the attempts of the characters to fix identity are part of the problem Baldwin critiques.

Baldwin's poignant treatment of gay relationships and his construction of subjectivity and identity politics along intersecting and
mutually inflecting axes of difference led to intense criticism and
censure later in the decade from African American critic Eldridge
Cleaver, in his collection of essays *Soul on Ice* (1968). Speaking specifically of the Black Power and Black Aesthetic movements, Henry
Louis Gates, Jr., remarks that black national identity became sexualized in the 1960s in such a way as to engender a curious connection between homophobia and black nationalism.[21] Interestingly,
Cleaver, in spite of his embrace of the politics of black struggle,
makes rhetorical use of the dominant cultural tropes of conventional
masculinity and its causal link to heterosexual desire when he describes Baldwin's critique of these in *Another Country* and of the
stereotype of the threatening black male phallus in Richard Wright's
Native Son and in Norman Mailer's 1957 essay "The White Negro."
Cleaver saw Baldwin's critiques as attacks on a "natural" black masculinity, as a rejection of Africa, and as an *assertion* of gay superiority,[22] all of which further contributed to the emasculation of straight
black men.

In the beginning of his essay "Notes on a Native Son," Cleaver
briefly praising Baldwin's work, but then, in carefully coded terms
not unlike those used in the *Time* article, describes how he gradually
began "to feel *uncomfortable* about something in Baldwin," and how
he was personally insulted by Baldwin's "*schoolmarmish* dismissal of
[Mailer's] *The White Negro*" (Cleaver, 98; emphasis added). Cleaver
also criticizes Baldwin for making retreats to the security and "camouflage of the *perfumed* smoke screen of his prose" (100; emphasis
added). This feminization of Baldwin reaches an outrageous climax
when Cleaver declares that in their sickness, gay black men are in the
position of "bending over and touching their toes for the white
man"—a sickness Cleaver says causes them uncontrollably to "re-
double their efforts and intake of the white man's sperm" (102).
Cleaver blatantly ignores the wide range of possible roles gay men
and women play sexually, not all of which, obviously, are reducible to
the "bottom" role and which may vary between and within specific
erotic acts, and he continues to speak of Baldwin's character Rufus
Scott in *Another Country* as a "pathetic wretch . . . who let a white bisexual homosexual fuck him in his ass" (107). Yet regardless of the
race of the penetrator in gay male sexual relations, the point is that

Cleaver and others in the U.S. Black Power movement in the 1960s saw homosexuality among blacks as a form of *ideological* penetration by whites, that is, as introduced into black culture from without and inherently foreign to it. Looked at in this light, homosexuality, a white man's decadence and disease, has "deprived [the black homosexual man] of his masculinity, castrated him in the center of his burning skull" (103).

Equally important, Cleaver's homophobic reading of Baldwin as emasculated because he is gay is linked to gender oppression and misogyny, insofar as it reduces black power to the phallus and leaves one asking about the role of black women in the politics of liberationist struggle. Indeed, African American feminist thinkers such as Deborah E. McDowell, bell hooks, and Joyce Hope Scott have written on the almost exclusive focus on race in African American literary and critical discourses, often tantamount to a focus on maleness, and on the concomitant subordination or complete erasure of black women.[23] Specifically speaking about the black activist writers of the Civil Rights and Black Power movements, Joyce Hope Scott writes that black male novelists tended to portray black women "with ambivalence at best and at worst, within the Euro-American, male-dominated, exploitative framework where the male is superior, owner, controller, and defender of the female who is owned, inferior." In the latter category, she continues, black women appear as the bitch or as the "terrible mother" who "emasculates and tyrannizes the black male, depriving him of his opportunity to flourish and grow into a *healthy* American man."[24] While Scott mentions and discusses the misogynistic implications of the shift to black male virility and power in the later phase of the black nationalist movement, as opposed to an earlier preoccupation with liberty and redressing past wrongs, she nevertheless fails to connect the ways in which its masculinist and misogynistic impulses can, in some cases, be informed by homophobia. This is obviously the case in her example of the "terrible [black] mother" who threatens the healthy development of black male gender identity—a trope taken directly from the dominant culture, particularly Bieber's 1962 study, where affectionate and loving mothers supposedly demasculinize their sons and prevent them from becoming "healthy" (i.e., heterosexual) men. This myth still haunts mothers of sons today, across racial lines, despite the removal of homosexuality as a diagnostic category from the *DSM*.

Through his arguments about Baldwin's masculinity and therefore questionable status as a representative African American writer, Cleaver makes rhetorical use of cultural conversations and institutionalized discourses, including psychoanalysis, imported from the dominant Euroamerican culture (which he supposedly rejects). These tropes appear in his homophobic readings of queer identity and, as Kathleen Rout points out, in his reading of "proper" masculine gender identity, where he equates respectable masculinity with social violence.[25] Specifically, Cleaver appeals to what Judith Butler and others have referred to as the "heterosexual matrix," which legislates that a stable sex be expressed through a stable gender that is oppositionally and hierarchically defined through the compulsory practice of heterosexuality.[26] Cleaver's feminization of Baldwin and his "attribution of a damaged, failed, or otherwise abject gender" (Butler, *Bodies*, 238) to black gay men raise for speculation whether it was he or Baldwin who was the more eager for the "fanatical, fawning, sycophantic love [and acceptance] of whites" (Cleaver, 99).

One is also inclined to wonder what is really at stake in arguments that take critiques of the logic of phallic masculinity under a regime of compulsory heterosexuality as an assertion of the superiority of gay sexuality—especially where the critique (and assertion) is being launched by one who is black and perceived to be queer. Baldwin dared to speak out against racism and to write poignantly of homosexuality while not conforming to black or white social expectations about masculinity. Cleaver's attack on Baldwin's work, as well as his attack on Baldwin for being queer—which Cleaver felt alienated Baldwin from his African heritage and from his connections to black resistance—did have an effect on Baldwin's literary reputation as a black writer and as a potential black leader. While Baldwin continued to speak out militantly and passionately against racism, he never achieved the stature of other black leaders, such as Martin Luther King and Malcolm X, because he did not fit the image of (straight) black male virility that many black leaders wished to project publicly, themselves and through their spokesmen, as a way of resisting racism. Baldwin's cultural resistance (and therefore site of potential power, given the attention he received as a writer at the time and the rising momentum of the Civil Rights movement) was regarded, in the dominant cultural context of the early 1960s and in the rhetorical strategies used to represent him as homosexual, as an assault not only on "mainstream" cultural practices but on his own African heritage. This aggression of "flagrancy" simultaneously incites discursive and institutional strategies to "expose" homosexuality, to mark its difference—but always through the gaze and specification of patriarchal (and therefore homophobic) appropriation. Speaking to this point, Lee Edelman has noted that gay resistance in a homophobic regime, through assertive and unapologetic representation of gay male sexuality (i.e., "flaunting it"), signifies in the view of the dominant order "an act of aggression, an assault that sodomitically unmans the very body through which that dominant order represents itself."[27]

That sense of a loss of power through homosexual penetration resonates not only in Cleaver in the 1960s but in contemporary Afrocentric/nationalistic discourses as well, inasmuch as they embrace the idea that being queer is a way of being "un-African." Molefi Kete Asante, for instance, in his book *Afrocentricity*, writes that "homosexuality is a deviation from Afrocentric thought because it makes the person evaluate his own physical needs above the teachings of national consciousness," and he argues that homosexuality cannot be condoned for the national development of a strong people.[28] Such a perspective, however, once again makes rhetorical use of outdated (though still widely used) studies of the etiology of homosexuality, in that Asante insists that raising children Afrocentrically will give them "*healthy* self concepts" and teach the *male* child "that his manhood is attached to a mind working on important questions" (65). His position not only relegates black gays to the margins but similarly shows little concern for black womanhood and unrealistically assumes that black heterosexuals engage in sexual practices solely for the purposes of reproduction and the perpetuation of the race, at the complete expense of physical needs for pleasure (for which he criticizes homosexuals) and psychological needs for intimacy with another person. Additionally, Asante's position on homosexuality forecloses discussion on how a variety of oppressions may productively intertwine and is detrimental to the building of broader coalitions through which further to disrupt patriarchal power from a variety of locations.

Study of the critical reception of Baldwin in the 1960s through the rhetorical strategies and cultural tropes used to represent him, as queer and as African American, and through the ways in which these strategies extended social, political, and economic practices is not limited to the historical period in question but, like Baldwin's roles as writer, thinker, and activist, has wider cultural and political implications for reading emerging queer identities and cultures. This is especially the case in postcolonial contexts outside the Euroamerican axes of contemporary queer power, where the queer subject is often constructed through similar, though not reducible, signifying practices. I agree with Corber's point that Baldwin believed African American culture was the product of peculiar circumstances, but I cannot agree that African American culture can be only tenuously connected to the cultures of postcolonial Africa (Corber, 177); such a claim forecloses the possibilities of comparative analysis across cultures and across national boundaries. It is unfortunate that Baldwin did not live to see the dramatic changes that have occurred in postapartheid South Africa, where, in the context of current debates on difference and democratic community and of African National Congress (ANC) attempts at national reconciliation, previously marginalized voices, including those of lesbians and gay men, are now claiming subjectivity, cultural legitimacy, and political viability. Queer identities and cultural practices in contemporary South Africa are important in relation to the kind of identity politics Baldwin professed, because they are being shaped by resistance to fixed identities and fixed notions of culture previously imposed by the system of apartheid, and because new spaces of queer visibility and identity politics among Africans (as opposed to their confinement largely to white middle-class urban areas) have helped form broad-based coalitions to move toward ANC-initiated democratic imperatives. Though it may be difficult to connect Baldwin and African American culture to the cultures of Africa using race alone as a point of comparison, it may be possible to begin to think about comparative inquiry when we look at race through cultural constructions of sexuality and gender and focus on specific historical events—in this case, on issues pertaining to the homophobia surrounding Baldwin's reception in the 1960s and similar issues pertaining to the contemporary reception of queer struggles in South Africa since the elections of 1994—without making foundationalist claims.

The locus of comparison in this case, I believe, rests particularly in the acknowledgment or disclaimer that must be made with regard to South Africa, which is that material conditions still mitigate against the fullest realization of democratic community. As Anne McClintock,

Chris Dunton, Simon Nkoli, and others have pointed out, queer activists in South Africa have often been condemned as supporting lifestyles that are imports of empire.[29] The same appeals to loss of power through homosexual penetration of which Cleaver spoke in the 1960s are found in nationalistic discourses in the southern African region, especially those articulated by President Robert Mugabe of Zimbabwe, and are often based on the assumptions that white colonial power was emasculating for African men and that black gay men are further victims of white decadence and corruption carried over from colonialist rule. Not only do nationalistic appeals to "authentic" African beliefs and ways of being positioned in the world once again link black power to the phallus and reinvent the medicalized tropes of pathology and gender abjection, in a manner remarkably similar to Baldwin's literary and cultural reception in the 1960s (especially in the Black Power movement), but they also rearticulate a homophobic apparatus with which to read homosexuality that is not altogether different from the colonial legacy that these nationalistic discourses purport to resist. Moreover, as Kwame Anthony Appiah notes, nationalist ideologies, fueled by sentimental rhetorical appeals to a precolonial authenticity, see Africa as culturally homogeneous and fail to account for the diversity of its people and its cultures.[30] Nationalist discourses that demonize queers as enemies of the nation-state further normalize domination; fail to acknowledge the multiplicity and fluidity of African identities and cultures shaped by historical, economic, and political influences; and maintain a problematic split between Africa and the West, all of which, in addition to the censure of homosexuality, are highly characteristic of the imperialist gesture.

Black queer writers in South Africa have written on the personal limitations and psychic violence inflicted on queers of African descent, who, in a regime of compulsory heterosexuality—the material remnants of which still exist in South Africa, despite juridical changes—often assume their only choices are to take their African heritage as primary, suppressing their queer sexuality as frivolous, or to openly identify as queer while suffering a sense of wounded African identity.[31] Hein Kleinbooi, for example, writes of the intense alienation he experienced as a black gay student activist: his gay white colleagues equated the heterosexist and homophobic oppression they experienced as homosexuals with the racism he experienced growing up on the Cape Flats, thereby trivializing the violence and poverty resulting from racial oppression, and his black liberationist comrades told him he was "hijacking the struggle" for racial equality when he spoke to them of gay rights.[32] As Baldwin and others have reminded us, one cannot define one's identity only in relation to the oppressor and only from a single axis of difference. bell hooks, speaking to and for African Americans, argues in her book *Art on My Mind* that this oppositional logic prevents one from moving toward the practice of freedom and the decolonization of the mind. Like Baldwin, she asserts that "we can liberate ourselves and others only by forging in resistance identities that transcend narrowly defined limits."[33]

Finally, in ironic contrast to his reception in the early 1960s and his own preference to take a public stand more on racial than on sexual issues, Baldwin's contemporary literary stature and critical reception have had a strong and viable presence in the growing field of queer studies. It is difficult to find a syllabus for a queer studies course in lesbian and gay literature today that does not include *Giovanni's Room* or *Another Country*; an anthology of gay literature that does not contain excerpts from these and other novels, such as *Just Above My Head*; or critical work in academic queer theory that does not analyze Baldwin's work. Most important, though the U.S. Black Power movement received Baldwin as already alienated from his African heritage because he was queer, and though contemporary identity politics in the United States often articulate differences according to race, gender, class, and sexuality (as if these are in parallel relation to one another, without accounting for their differential structures and their intersecting and converging formations in the social field), Baldwin's advocacy of coalitions across multiple axes of difference seems to be taking shape in the "new" South Africa, where black lesbians and gay men are working to resist new hegemonic reifications of race and nation and are taking a visible role in helping rearticulate and redefine African identity. Baldwin's work, and especially the cultural tropes and rhetorical strategies used to represent him as queer and as black in the 1960s, become important areas of inquiry in queer studies because they enable more compelling analyses of the ways in which racism, gender oppression, and homophobia intertwine, in addition to providing culturally broadened and historicized understandings of the politics of identity.

NOTES

1. Teresa de Lauretis, "Queer Theory: Lesbian and Gay Sexualities," *Differences: A Journal of Feminist Cultural Studies* 3, 2 (1991): viii.

2. Eve Kosofsky Sedgwick, *Epistemology of the Closet* (Berkeley: University of California Press, 1990), 32.

3. Judith Butler, *Bodies That Matter: On the Discursive Limits of "Sex"* (New York: Routledge, 1993), 238; emphasis added. For a more detailed argument on the enmeshing of gender and sexuality and coalitionist alliances between queer studies and feminism, see my forthcoming essay "Sissies and Sisters: Gender, Sexuality, and the Possibilities of Coalition," in *Lesbian and Gay Studies: Coming Out of Feminism?* ed. Elizabeth Wright, Naomi Segal, and Mandy Merck (Oxford: Blackwell, 1998).

4. James A. Berlin, *Rhetorics, Poetics, and Cultures: Refiguring College English Studies* (Urbana: National Council of Teachers of English, 1996), 77.

5. *DSM* refers to the *Diagnostic and Statistical Manual*, published by the American Psychiatric Association (APA) and used to diagnose psychiatric disorders. The third edition (*DSM III*), published in 1980, removed homosexuality as a category of psychopathology as a result of the APA's historic 1973 decision.

6. With this in mind, while I am trying to understand a particular historical reception of Baldwin, I must acknowledge that contemporary work in American lesbian and gay studies, academic queer theory, and post-Stonewall activism has provided a space for me to (re)read the cultural lenses that helped interpret Baldwin and his work and constitute his reception in the 1960s, and that my readings and critique of the claims made about homosexuality in the period under discussion make rhetorical use of queercentric interpretations of gay identity by these disciplines and social practices in the present.

7. "Races: Freedom—Now," *Time*, 17 May 1963, 25.

8. David Leeming, *James Baldwin: A Biography* (New York: Knopf, 1994), 221.

9. Even though many of Baldwin's characters are bisexual, and though Baldwin often chose to represent himself as bisexual rather than as a gay man, it is my contention that interpretations of Baldwin and his work nonetheless made use of dominant cultural conversations on homosexuality that were largely homophobic.

10. Paul Welch, "The 'Gay' World Takes to the City Streets," *Life*, 26 June 1964, 68.

11. Ernest Havemann, "Why?" *Life*, 26 June 1964, 77; emphasis added.

12. Robert J. Corber, *Homosexuality in Cold War America: Resistance and the Crisis of Masculinity* (Durham: Duke University Press, 1997), 11.

13. Irving Bieber's study, originally published in 1962 under the title *Homosexuality: A Psychoanalytic Study of Male Homosexuals*, was republished in its entirety in 1988 under the revised title *Homosexuality: A Psychoanalytic Study*, under the names of the same team of coauthors, who were also the researchers in the 1962 study. All references herein are to the 1988 edition of the 1962 study. The 1988 edition contains only a new foreword by Irving Bieber and Toby Bieber and aims to familiarize the reader with the ideas and observations of the 1962 study since the time it was originally published. Even though the new foreword acknowledges some of the debates and changed thinking about homosexuality, it is still largely a defense of the original findings.

14. Sigmund Freud, *Three Essays on the Theory of Sexuality*, trans. James Strachey (New York: Basic Books, 1962), 6–7, 12n.

15. Irving Bieber, et al., *Homosexuality: A Psychoanalytic Study* (New York: Basic Books, 1962; reprint, Northvale, N.J.: Jason Aronson, 1988), 79–80, 310.

16. The same is true today, as psychiatry, psychoanalysis, and other therapeutic practices continue to conflate mental health with social conformity. This is especially evident in recent post–*DSM III* clinical work on "Gender Identity Disorder (GID) in Children." While the *DSM* has depathologized atypical sexual object choice, it has (re)pathologized atypical gender identification. The fairly new addition of GID in children as a diagnostic category, which first appeared in the *DSM III* in 1980 and remains in the current *DSM IV* (1994), is targeted at those least capable of resisting it and is often cloaked in "concern" for the "best interest" of the gender-atypical child (usually the feminine boy). What really drives this so-called concern, however, is not helping the child adapt to a world hostile to gender-atypical behavior in boys but the fear of possible queer outcome.

17. The relative exclusion of lesbians in *Life's* exposé on homosexuality enables further readings of social practices and assumptions about gender that helped constitute readings of queer identity in the early 1960s. Lesbians are mentioned only tangentially in the *Life* feature; Havemann, for instance, claims that clinical studies of homosexuality have ignored lesbians because they are not as numerous, promiscuous, or conspicuous as their male counterparts (79). As in the earlier example of gender bias, where gay men were marked by a failure to cast an admiring glance to women ("pretty girls"), the reasoning employed in this line of argument is an extension of social practices prominent in the early 1960s, prior to the sexual revolution and the oppositional impact of second-wave feminism later in the decade. Also, assumptions about a lower social profile of American lesbians in the 1950s and early 1960s are misleading. Lillian Faderman's historical work *Odd Girls and Twilight Lovers* (New York: Penguin, 1992) has shown that lesbian enclaves and subcultures proliferated through the postwar years in the United States,

and that social invisibility was not a reflection of the existence of a comparatively small population of lesbians but the "discreet" style of many middle- and professional class lesbians who escaped notice by the heterosexual world (185–86).

18. James Baldwin, *The Fire Next Time* (New York: Vintage, 1963), 94–95.

19. bell hooks, *Talking Back* (Boston: South End Press, 1989), 22; emphasis added.

20. James Baldwin, *Another Country* (New York: Vintage, 1962), 133–34.

21. Henry Louis Gates, Jr., "The Black Man's Burden," in *Fear of a Queer Planet: Queer Politics and Social Theory*, ed. Michael Warner (Minneapolis: University of Minnesota Press, 1993), 234.

22. Eldridge Cleaver, *Soul on Ice* (New York: McGraw-Hill, 1968), 109–10.

23. Deborah E. McDowell, "Boundaries: Or Distant Relations and Close Kin," in *Afro-American Literary Study in the 1990s*, ed. Houston A. Baker, Jr., and Patricia Redmond (Chicago: University of Chicago Press, 1989), 59.

24. Joyce Hope Scott, "From Foreground to Margin: Female Configurations and Masculine Self-Representation in Black Nationalist Fiction," in *Nationalism and Sexualities*, ed. Andrew Parker, Mary Russo, Doris Summer, and Patrick Yeager (New York: Routledge, 1992), 303–4; emphasis added.

25. Kathleen Rout, *Eldridge Cleaver* (Boston: Twayne, 1991), 31.

26. Judith Butler, *Gender Trouble: Feminism and the Subversion of Identity* (New York: Routledge, 1990), 151n.

27. Lee Edelman, *Homographesis: Essays in Gay Literary and Cultural Theory* (New York: Routledge, 1994), 65.

28. Molefi Kete Asante, *Afrocentricity: The Theory of Social Change* (Buffalo: Amulefi Publishing, 1980), 64–65.

29. See Anne McClintock, *Imperial Leather: Race, Gender and Sexuality in the Colonial Contest* (New York: Routledge, 1995), 384.

30. Kwame Anthony Appiah, *In My Father's House: Africa in the Philosophy of Culture* (New York: Oxford University Press, 1992), 24.

31. Addressing this point in an African American context, Max C. Smith refers to these two positions as "Black gays" and "gay Blacks," respectively. See Max C. Smith, "By the Year 2000," in *In the Life: A Black Gay Anthology*, ed. Joseph Beam, (Boston: Alyson, 1986), 226.

32. Hein Kleinbooi, "Identity Crossfire: On Being a Black Gay Student Activist," in *Defiant Desire: Gay and Lesbian Lives in South Africa*, ed. Mark Gevisser and Edwin Cameron (New York: Routledge, 1995), 264.

33. bell hooks, *Art on My Mind: Visual Politics* (New York: New Press, 1995), 8.

Chapter 5

Of Mimicry and *(Little Man Little)* Man
Toward a Queersighted Theory of Black Childhood

Nicholas Boggs

*Introduction: "Looking for Jimmy" and
Finding the "Little Man"*

Ralph Ellison's trope of the "little man at Cheshaw Station" acquires a certain vexed currency when considering the relationships between childhood, sexuality, and race in African American literature. Henry Louis Gates, Jr., has used Ellison's figure of the little man situated at the cultural crossroads of American sensibility as an allegory for the critic of African American literature reading through the historically white optic of contemporary critical theory. Such an explicitly gendered metaphor, as productive as it has been for thinking about the place of male African Americanist criticism in the academy, requires interrogation and elaboration when exploring the specificities of gender and sexuality as mapped through representations of childhood in African American literature.[1]

To utilize critical theory to engage in a queer, African Americanist exploration of childhood subjectivity risks the added marginalization of working through and against critical methodologies that not only have had little interest in children's literature but also have been marked as historically racist and heterosexist. As black feminist theory has pointed out, psychoanalytic criticism, whose Lacanian specificity of sexual difference has been so efficacious for white feminist theory, has yet to contend successfully with the complexities of racialized identity. Such a critical pitfall is compounded by the heterosex-ism of Freudian psychoanalysis and its institutional adherents, who, firmly entrenched in the Oedipal drama of adult subjectivity, disre-gard childhood identities comprised of nonconforming or nonrepro-ductive sexualities.

To further complicate such an exploration, recent black feminist theory has noted the tendency of African Americanist criticism to elide questions of gender, as Valerie Smith writes when critiquing the history of the critical discourse: "Afro-Americanists, mostly male, have assumed that one may theorize about the experience of blacks in a racist culture on the basis of the lives of black men alone."[2] In this context, if Ellison's trope of the little man at Cheshaw Station is to be extended into readings of childhood identity, then where in this mas-culinist model is the little *woman*, and where is the little *queer* subject of color? And if this trope, as Gates describes it, represents a "trickster figure surfacing when we least expect him" (64), then what unex-pected cultural site will allow us to interrogate and perhaps even eradicate the acute embarrassment generated by its universalizing pronoun?

In this context, it is only fitting that a reconstituted little visitor at Cheshaw Station should emerge, coming not from behind the little stove, as presented in Ellison's classic account, but out of the repre-sentational closet in a seldom-read children's book by James Baldwin, aptly titled *Little Man Little Man: A Story of Childhood* (1976). That this little trickster is at once a ubiquitous and invisible American fixture in Ellison's paradigm is also appropriate—the surreptitious yet om-nipresent codings of homosexuality in the narrative of *Little Man Lit-tle Man* suggest that queerness is an open secret (to borrow D. A. Miller's lovely logic) of African American childhood and, concomi-tantly, of the history of African American literature and criticism.[3]

The queer trajectory of Baldwin's text, which is accompanied by the illustrations of his close friend Yoran Cazac, can be located in its veiled attention to the lives of black children whose identifications and desires fall outside the heavily policed boundaries of white het-erosexual normativity. While a limited canon of black children's liter-ature exists, from Du Bois's short-lived children's magazine *The Brownie's Book* (1919) and the children's books of Langston Hughes, such as *The Pasteboard Bandit* (1935), to Virginia Hamilton's novel *The Planet of Junior Brown* (1971), the space for literature dealing explicitly, or even implicitly, with queer, black, juvenile characters is marked, not surprisingly, by silence and invisibility. Yet throughout the text of *Little Man Little Man*, Baldwin and Cazac complicate Du Bois's seminal formulation of double consciousness by queering the "twoness" of the black American experience into the triple consciousness of being black, American, and queer.

Apart from Du Bois, Baldwin signifies on the works of Ellison and, perhaps most aggressively, Richard Wright; *Little Man Little Man: A Story of Childhood* reproduces the subtitled structure of Wright's novel *Black Boy: A Record of Childhood and Youth*. Wright's autobiographical narrative of a young black man coming of age in the United States commences when the protagonist is four years old, an age matched by TJ, a central character in Baldwin's text. But if *Black Boy* is the canonical and paradigmatic narrative of the formation of black heterosexual masculinity, then Baldwin, experiencing something akin to Harold Bloom's anxiety of influence, revises the discursive framework of the black masculinist canon with the critical signifying difference of queerness.[4]

As the book's jacket describes the narrative, Baldwin, along with Cazac, constructs a "microcosm of his concern for our children and our future" by "making an unforgettable picture of New York as it looks to those who are black, poor, and less than four feet high."[5] The text mobilizes tropes of queer identity, including homoerotic touch, ambivalent parodies of blackface minstrelsy, and cross-racial and cross-gender identifications, as it narrates a day in the Harlem life of two black boys, WT and TJ, aged seven and four respectively, and an eight-year-old black girl named Blinky.

Such an intervention is enabled through what Kobena Mercer describes as "the artistic commitment to archaeological inquiry,"[6] the process of recuperating and constructing a counterhistory. Baldwin produces such a narrative in *Little Man Little Man* when he engages in a dialogue with his own queer black childhood.[7] Instead of producing an autobiographical representation of this childhood, however, Baldwin interfuses his lifelong interests in childhood and sexuality to construct a narrative that speaks to the unrepresented lives of those queer children in Harlem who have been silenced and marginalized by historical and institutional forces because of their "deviant" sexualities. By "looking for Jimmy" in the text of *Little Man Little Man*, instead of uncovering a replication of Baldwin's own queer youth we find the production of a queer black subjectivity; that is, Baldwin draws on fragments of his own experience to dramatize the way in which queer identity is a formation that is never complete, rather than an essential self.

Baldwin's act of personal and historical reclamation engages in the familiar queer strategy of drag, often used to rewrite mainstream representations. Baldwin reverses the terms of dominant cultural production when he writes a book that transgresses the usual demarcations separating adult literature from children's literature. Presented as a "children's book for adults and an adults' book for children,"[8] Baldwin's adults' book, in the subversive drag of children's literature (complete with a children's book type size, text design, and illustrations), outstrips and disrupts normative expectations of a children's book as it reveals that which the juvenile genre typically represses—a queer childhood sexuality.

The confounding queerness of *Little Man Little Man* has resulted in its neglected status in the canons of both black literature and children's literature. The text thus stands as one of the greatest anomalies of Baldwin's career, among his many classics and best-sellers. Hardly noticed when it was printed in London and then New York in 1976, it went quickly and quietly out of print, even though it held great significance for Baldwin, who, according to one of his biographers, considered the work a "celebration" of the self-esteem of black children.[9]

Despite the importance of the book to the author, no scholarly work has been done on the text, and only one review of it in a major national periodical exists. In the *New York Times Book Review* the black literary critic and children's book author Julius Lester dismissed it as "not especially exciting or disappointing," advising Baldwin that "those who wish to write a 'story of childhood for adults' should do that, but in the form of an adult novel."[10] Such a criticism reacts, perhaps unwittingly, to the queerness of the text, as it is the subversive drag and narrative inscriptions of queer identity and desire that cause it to appear odd, or "queer," and thus unreadable to the heteronormative reader and critic.

The genre-bending book requires that we adopt a queer lens of reading to decode its textual meanings. One of the characters, an eight-year-old black girl named Blinky, provides a model for such a practice of reading. The queer little girl reacts to the world around her by performing her female masculinity throughout the narrative and thus, I argue, functions paradoxically as the "little man" in this text. She also gazes through the racializing lenses of a pair of eyeglasses that are given to her by teachers at her school, exemplifying a model of criticism that I refer to as "queersighted," a practice that reads for the narrative formation and figuration of the social and psychic child in relation to the intersections of race, gender, and sexuality.[11]

Utilizing such a lens allows us to decode this neglected text for the obscured, queer meanings that have resulted in its apparent unreadability for other readers and critics. It allows us to take seriously the advice given to another character in the text, the four-year-old black boy, TJ, by his mother:

> "Don't believe everything you read. You got to think about what you read." His Mama say, "But read everything son, everything you can get your hands on. It all come in handy one day." TJ don't really understand none of this yet, but she say, "Don't worry. You going to understand it." (70–71)

Following the imperative to read skeptically and closely everything "you can get your hands on," this critical intervention attempts to read the text of *Little Man Little Man* queersightedly, so that, eventually, the reader "going to understand it."[12]

(Little) Man to (Little) Man: Queerness and Textual (Re)production

Collaboration and birth are major tropes both in Baldwin's career and in his literary productions. He often spoke about writing his books in terms of pregnancy and birth, describing his final novel, *Just Above My Head*, as a baby he "carried" for an unusually long time. It was so difficult to write that he even exclaimed, "Talk about shitting bricks!" Such an expletive seems to answer Leo Bersani's provocative question "Is the rectum a grave?" suggesting that Baldwin's rectum was not such at all—it was a metaphorical birth canal.[13]

Baldwin's gestation metaphors, combined with his penchant for male interracial collaboration, provide a framework for the textual production of *Little Man Little Man*. The dialogic relationship of text and image fascinated Baldwin, as reflected in his work with the white photographers Richard Avedon and Teddy Pelatowski, who was also

Baldwin's first love, with whom he collaborated on an unpublished literary-photographic exploration of Harlem churches. As a labor of unrequited love, the project with Pelatowski prefigured the collaborative effort that produced *Little Man Little Man*, since Baldwin also had unreturned romantic feelings for Cazac, who provided the colorful illustrations alongside the text.[14]

The tropes of children and childbearing are especially significant around the time of the book's production and publication. The later stages of the writing coincided with the birth of two children in Baldwin's family by his sisters, Paula and Gloria. Additionally, Baldwin eventually flew to Italy to become godfather to Cazac's third child, and he dedicated *If Beale Street Could Talk* to Cazac, just as he had dedicated *Giovanni's Room* to his lover Lucien Happersberger and served as the godfather to Happersberger's son. By dedicating the novel to the illustrator, Baldwin hoped Cazac would be the man who would not only allow him to "give birth" to *Little Man Little Man* but also provide him with a stable, loving, romantic relationship.

Though Cazac was unable to provide Baldwin with such a partnership, the double signature still assumes special significance when placed in the framework of Wayne Koestenbaum's theory of "double talk."[15] Men who write together engage in double talk, according to Koestenbaum, in that their collaboration is the metaphorical sexual intercourse that produces the text as their "child." Reimagining *Little Man Little Man* as an interracial labor of love between two men allows the children's book, with its anonymous third-person child's voice, to function as a metaphoric child, produced by their dialogic relationship. Indeed, the interplay between the title and subtitle reproduces and supports Koestenbaum's paradigm of the erotics of male literary collaboration:

$$1\ 2\ 3$$
Little Man + Little Man = a story of childhood

In this equation, the doubling of Baldwin and Cazac, as the first two terms, produces a third term, a child, whose voice relates the story of three black children exploring Harlem. The text is thus an overfathered, interracial child produced by the erotic interchange between two men.[16]

Another crucial doubling that occurs in the text's production is an autoerotic dance between the adult Baldwin and the child Baldwin.

As Stuart Hall has remarked, an identity founded through a reclaiming of the past is always an "imaginary reunification" that involves a "partnership of past and present."[17] In *Little Man Little Man*, the adult Baldwin speaks to the child Baldwin who forms an integral part of the former's sense of self. Indeed, Baldwin once remarked that "one's relationship to the past changes. Yet that boy, the boy I was, still controls the man I am. If I didn't know as much as I think I do know about that boy, I would still be his prisoner."[18] The intimacy and interplay between Baldwin's child and adult selves allow for the production of a queer childhood narrative.

The text, then, is also a work of metaphoric masturbation, the erotic, even pederastic dance of Baldwin to Baldwin, which works to uncover a missing childhood in Harlem. This is fitting since, in Freudian terms, masturbation is the "dirty" hallmark of the secrecy of repressed childhood sexuality. Further, in the heterosexist imagination, masturbation, like homosexuality, is often figured as horrific because it is allegedly nonreproductive.[19] The text of *Little Man Little Man* repudiates this homophobic stance and transforms autoeroticism into a generative act that (re)produces and tells the story of an erased queer childhood. The title itself reproduces this paradigm, as the homo/autoerotic repetition of the phallic signifier "little man" produces the third term of "a story of childhood."

Baldwin's metaphoric masturbation is manifested through the way in which he talks back to and signifies on his earlier literary works, most prominently *Another Country* and his roughly autobiographical first novel, *Go Tell It on the Mountain*. In fact, it can be argued that the transgressive desire of Baldwin and Cazac facilitates the masturbatory doubling of Baldwin himself. That is, as Baldwin is unable to engage in physical sex with Cazac, the text becomes a masturbatory substitute, excited by the unrequited homoeroticism of its production. This formulation is supported by the text of *Go Tell It on the Mountain* in the following scene involving John Grimes, the protagonist who is based, at least in part, on Baldwin himself:

> He had sinned. In spite of the saints, his mother and his father, the warnings he had heard from his earliest beginnings, he had sinned with his hands a sin that was hard to forgive. In the school lavatory, alone, thinking of the boys, older, bigger, braver, who made bets with each other as to whose urine could arch higher, he had watched in himself a transformation of which he would never dare to speak.[20]

Here, John's masturbation represents a Wildean love—or perhaps more accurately in this context, an insurgent desire that "he would never dare to speak." The passage also points to how the parental and religious repression of childhood sexuality and the designation of masturbation as a sin do not forestall and perhaps even eroticize and proliferate the boy's "transformation" from compulsory heterosexuality into his sexual desire for "older, bigger" boys. The explicitly phallic homoeroticism of the bathroom scene allows John to masturbate, a paradigm that is reproduced in the textual production of *Little Man Little Man*—the unrequited homoerotic engagement of Baldwin and Cazac facilitates the metaphoric masturbation of Baldwin that produces the "story of childhood."

Policing Queer Little Bodies

Baldwin's story of childhood is, in many ways, a story of normalization and the ambivalence of resistance, of the ways in which language is used to police bodies and subjectivities. It is no revelation that the importation of normative justice has long been a force in the constitution of both gay and black male subjectivities, as both are systematically positioned by dominant culture, in distinct but related ways, as always already criminal.[21] The thematics of Baldwin's narrative, including recurrent tropes of police surveillance, are concerned with the ways in which the children imitate, incorporate, and resist stereotyped models of black male identity as produced by regulatory regimes of race, gender, and sexuality. In the process, Baldwin prefigures the postmodern attention to the discourses of the media and film when he interrogates the ways in which the mass media act as a racial industry that manufactures stereotyped brands of black identity, which are then naturalized through filmic and televisual representations of criminality.

Of course, children do not function merely as blank slates upon which stereotyped identities are inscribed and then materialized. Rather, as Judith Butler has argued, performance can be a way of talking back[22]—and the children in *Little Man Little Man* indeed respond performatively to the way in which black subjectivity, like all subjectivity, is constituted discursively, through a multiplicity of discourses. While the children utilize bodily mimicry as both accommodational and oppositional strategies against imposed and racialized notions of black identity, the black vernacular of the narrative voice engages in an analogous strategy of resignification in the linguistic domain. The children talk b (l)ack to the hegemonic discourse of standard English through the violation of standard rules of grammar, syntax, and vocabulary, in such sentences as "Blinky and WT done stopped skipping rope, and watching him" (8). This mimicry of the master discourse is supplied by a child's third-person black vernacular voice as the narrator, in order to create the linguistic effect of a speaking child. By assuming the consciousness of various characters within the structure of free, indirect discourse, the "speakerly" narrative documents and expresses an elastic representation of a black childhood in Harlem that cannot be pinned down to any one, essentializing gender or experience.[23]

Such a process of mimicry has been described by postcolonial theorist Homi Bhabha as "a discourse uttered between the lines and as such both against the rules and within them."[24] Bhabha argues that the inappropriate and parodic imitations involved in mimicry have the effect of menacing colonial authority, and that opposition is the inevitable effect of a system of power based on cultural difference. In this sense, the vernacular voice in *Little Man Little Man* engages in a strategic resistance that establishes an enabling self through a narrative that both is implicated in and resists the surrounding culture.

In *Little Man Little Man*, this vernacular language must convey a resistance to both standard English and the racist stereotypes that are produced discursively through this hegemonic language system, since, as Baldwin writes in an essay on "black English," "language is . . . a political instrument, means, and proof of power . . . the most vivid and crucial key to identity."[25] If racialized identity is constructed through language, then the text of *Little Man Little Man* suggests it can also be resisted through the manipulation and subversion of this language system and of the mass media representations that are its effects.

Baldwin's narrative is concerned with the formation of the children's identities within the parameters of notions of black identity, as constructed by the linguistic and ideological machinery of the white racist imagination and imposed by the discourses of the mass media. The impossibility of living up to these notions of racialized masculinity is brought into an unexpected yet critical symbolic representation midway through the narrative. In this scene, TJ witnesses Miss Lee, the alcoholic wife of the building superintendent, Mr. Man, as she discards some empty liquor bottles in a trash can in front of the building. Behind the trash can, etched ever so lightly on the wall, is a piece of graffiti that consists of a peace sign above the name Rufus. Nothing in the text suggests that this graffiti is significant; indeed, it is almost invisible. Yet, as a written word placed in the visual space of Cazac's illustrations, it represents the very intersection of the textual and the visual that characterizes the dialogic (pro)creation of the book itself. Far from insignificant, this narrative inscription is Baldwin's signification on *Another Country* and the central character of that novel, Rufus Scott. Rufus represents the stereotype of the black homosexual, menaced by rigid definitions of masculinity and race. Repeating and revising the figure of Wright's Bigger Thomas in *Native Son*, Rufus acts out and perpetuates the stereotypes imposed on him.

The graffiti in *Little Man Little Man* represents a textual and visual memorial to not only Rufus, who is driven to jump off a bridge to his death by the pressures of dealing with his black, queer identity, but the very idea of the anxiety of such an abject identity.[26] In this sense, the image is something of a "Rest in Peace" sign for Rufus and, more generally, for a black masculinity that is always stereotyped and specularized in the white imagination to the point of literal collapse.

Lurking in the background of *Little Man Little Man*, the image also stands as a warning to the children as they make the difficult navigation toward black manhood. The process of mimicry is an important part of this navigation, since "blackness," as a social construct, is learned through imitation. Or as Baldwin writes in "Nobody Knows My Name" "Children have never been very good at listening to their elders, but they have never failed to imitate them" (in *Price of the Ticket*, 183). Throughout the text TJ, WT, and, significantly, the female Blinky imitate and perform numerous versions of black manhood and masculinity, with mixed results.

Many of these performative options involve "jumping the roof," an act that recalls the suicide jump of Rufus. Early in the text TJ fetches his ball from the street and dodges a speeding car. The narrator's voice then informs the reader, in its characteristic vernacular voice, that "that ain't nothing. He going to be a bigger star than Hank Aaron one of these days. Soon as he get a bit older, he going to jump the roofs" (5). The roof is cited as a location where an explicitly athletic manhood is practiced and performed, and "jumping the roof" becomes a physical act and symbol of adult masculinity.

WT also mimics male sports figures as a model of manhood: "WT going to be a boxer. Somebody told him that Sonny Liston used to skip rope while he had Night Train on his record player. So now, WT take the rope from Blinky and he start to skipping rope in time to the music" (38). WT imitates Liston, the tough and uncompromising black boxer of the 1960s, joining TJ in his imitation of a manhood explicitly linked to athletic performance. Imitation allows the boys to learn their prescribed and stereotyped social role of black athletic masculinity.

As Bhabha has argued, the stereotype is a "major discursive strategy . . . a form of knowledge and identification that vacillates between what is always 'in place,' and already known, and something that must be anxiously repeated" (66). While Liston and Aaron represent normative public, televised models of black manhood, TJ's desire to jump the roof when he gets "a bit older" points to other, darker performative paradigms that are repeated anxiously in the text. The trope of jumping the roof reappears early in the narrative, in a string of images, as a public model of black criminality. The free, indirect discourse of the narrative assumes the consciousness of TJ as he "look up and down the street . . . where he was born" (*Little Man Little Man*, 14). TJ likens the street to "the street in the movies or the TV when the cop cars come from the other end of the street" (14) and proceeds to narrate a stereotypical televisual escape scene that eventually slips into a filmic representation. The passages involving the televised escape narrative point to how the discursive strategy of the stereotype subjects the children to damaging and repeated models of black identity.

The scene involves a black man as he is chased up and down the Harlem street by the police: "The man they come to get he in one of the houses or he on the fire-escape or he on the roof and he see they come for him" (15). TJ's narrative positions black manhood as a site of criminality, although the crime is unnamed; the unarmed man is marked as criminal all the same.[27] The anonymous black man "don't know what to do. He can't go nowhere. And he sweating" (15). The black subject is under police surveillance, while TJ discusses all the places where he might be hiding as the "cops keep coming real slow and careful down this long street with their guns out" (15).

The trope of jumping the roof reappears in this narrative sequence, as TJ explains that "if he on one of them roofs don't care which side of the street he on, he going to have to run like a mother a jump a roof to get him to another block" (16). The act of jumping, which encompasses both the suicide jump of Rufus and the jumping-the-roof imitation of Hank Aaron, is reinscribed here as a model of escape and criminalized black masculinity.

The remainder of the escape scene is accompanied by illustrations that are framed explicitly in TV screens and reels of film, dramatizing the filmic and televisual qualities of the narrative. By framing the illustrations in TV screens and reels of film, the narrative shows how black male subjects become publicly visible and fixed as criminals through repetitive representations of criminality. Although this scene is a product of TJ's imagination and experience, he inevitably gains access to his athletic heroes and images of criminality through a televisual medium that is structured by the scopic drive of the white imagination—a drive that derives pleasure in the look from the place of the "other" in order to fix the black man from without by the fantasmic binary of absolute difference.[28]

TJ's narrative conflates the filmic and the real by placing the escape narrative on his actual street in Harlem. Discussing the various locations where the man hides, TJ notes that "if he ain't there, then he in TJ's house," or "he might be in Blinky's house" or "the house across from WT" (18). The televisual representation reflects the "watching" that informs TJ's notions of black subjectivity. Media-produced images and lived experience are not mutually exclusive; rather, they constitute one another through the interplay of reality and available visual representations. TJ's sense of self, and black subjectivity more generally, is formed partially through the discursive practices of filmic and televisual representations.

As the escape narrative progresses, the illustrations are framed exclusively in film reels that underscore the surveillance of the police as they "watch out for their man" (18). The possessive tone of this statement points out how the filmic and televisual mediums actually "watch" those who think they are watching them. As Ishmael Reed has claimed, "On television, black men are typically shown naked from the waist up, handcuffed and leaning over a police car."[29] The escape narrative partakes in a similar stereotyping strategy, whereby the unarmed black man embodies and enacts the expected stereotype of the criminalized black body. The film screens become a site of surveillance so that, paradoxically, black subjects who view the films are actually themselves being watched, within the bounds of a prescripted, racist narrative. Indeed, toward the end of the escape narrative, TJ informs the reader that "one thing for sure, by the time the cops get this far they know they got their man" (*Little Man Little Man,* 19). Watched by the police, the Harlem residents, and, by extension, the imaginary filmgoers, the man is "sweating and ducking but he done for" (19). His fate is inevitable in the predetermined narrative— "he not going to make it off this street alive" (19).

As the escape narrative comes to a deadly close, TJ offers several dramatic and distinctly filmic endings that inevitably result in the death of the man:

> Sometime he running down the middle of the street and the guns go *pow!* and *blam!* he fall and maybe he turn over twice before he hiccup and don't move no more. Sometime he come somersaulting down from the fire-escape. Sometime it from the roof, and then he scream. (19)

The text is accompanied by frames of film that illustrate the possible endings—hiccuping death in the street, somersaulting down the fire escape, falling from the roof. The repetition of *sometime* before each example shows how these images are repeated, both in TJ's lived experience and in the films, thereby fixing the black subject in the criminal stereotype.

The final filmic example equates jumping or falling from the roof with death, when the black man "jump from the roof and then he scream." "Jumping the roof" is part of the vocabulary of childhood that articulates a deadly scene in a childlike, almost playful manner. The chase is presented as a child's cops-and-robbers game, typified by onomatopoeia (*pow! blam!*), conflated with the serious reality of the chases the children witness in the media and on their own street. Habituated to violence and stereotypes through his everyday life and through media and film representations, TJ cannot help but represent death and black criminality as normalized to the point of a childish game.

The juvenile representation, however, should not obscure the ways in which the visual field through which the children consume the criminalized performances of black manhood is not neutral to the question of race. Rather, as Judith Butler has argued, the visual field "is itself a racial formation, hegemonic and forceful" ("Endangered/Endangering," 17). Baldwin was very much aware of how black subjects have access only to images that the racist episteme produces as the visible. In *The Devil Finds Work*, his meditations on blacks and film (published in the same year as *Little Man Little Man*), he writes that "a black man had certainly best not believe anything he sees in the movies," since the white-controlled camera "sees what you point at it, the camera sees what you want it to see."[30] Indeed, for Baldwin, the language of the camera is "the language of dreams," and in the case of television and film, the dreams of the racist white imagination.

In this sense, as TJ and WT gaze at the televisual and filmic images, they are subjected to the imagination of a racist episteme that works aggressively to suppress, stigmatize, indeed "police" the sexuality and identity of the black male body. A scene of police brutality, then, can be reified as a scene of stereotype-affirming criminality. As bell hooks has argued, discourses have the power "to do violence" to people, "a violence which is material and physical, although produced by the discourses . . . of the mass media."[31] The children's mass media models of manhood are overdetermined by a racist organization and disposition of the visible that does psychic and bodily "violence" to them, as viewers and as subjects.

Queersighted Resistance

The two boys in *Little Man Little Man*, WT and TJ, are not the only consumers of the damaging discursive regimes of race, gender, and sexuality. In many ways it is the character of Blinky who interrogates masculine subjectivity in more provocative ways and provides a compelling model for a practice of queer reading. The eldest of the children at eight years old, Blinky figures as a preadolescent butch type who cross-identifies with boys:

> One thing TJ understand about Blinky. She don't like nothing that wears dresses. She don't hardly never wear a dress herself. She always in blue jeans. But she ain't no boy. Blinky is a girl. But she don't like girls. (33)

Blinky's body, clothed in blue jeans, is a site of performed female masculinity in that she subscribes to an early form of butch identity, which Gayle Rubin describes as "women who are more comfortable with masculine gender codes, styles, or identities than with feminine ones."[32] Blinky's performance as a butch is the type of sex/gender mismatch that, according to Judith Halberstam, "is not only a repetition but one which is necessarily imperfect, flawed and rough," thereby revealing that "gender is always a rough match between bodies and subjectivities."[33] Blinky's gender performance allows her to appropriate dominant codes of masculinity with the critical signifying difference of black, cross-gender queerness.

The subjectivity of Blinky complicates a reading of the text that focuses on masculinity as necessarily and exclusively linked to men. Instead, her mimicry challenges the stability of binary sex/gender systems, especially considering that WT "do everything Blinky do" (*Little Man Little Man*, 29), often following and imitating the actions of Blinky: "WT is seven and ain't no excuse for him at all, skipping rope and following behind Blinky" (12). Skipping rope represents a performative act that is ambiguous in relation to gender. Often associated with girls jumping rope in the street, in this text it is also associated with the black masculinity of Sonny Liston, when WT jumps rope in order to imitate the boxer. WT's rope-jumping imitation of Blinky suggests a complex system of identifications occurring between the children—TJ often imitates WT, and WT often imitates Blinky, who, in turn, imitates dominant codes of masculine behavior. Hence their performances reveal how masculinity is constituted discursively and does not naturally belong to any one gender.

The queer performance of Blinky contributes to what I call her "queersightedness" that is, her position of seeing, which is privileged increasingly as the text progresses into more complicated and often darker meditations on black subjectivity. Her nickname derives from the eyeglasses she wears, which seem to racialize her field of vision:

> Them eye-glasses blinking just like the sun was hitting you in the eye. TJ don't know why she all the time got them glasses on. She say she can't see without them. Maybe that true, if she say so. But TJ put them on one time and he couldn't see nothing with them on. . . . Everything looked like it was rained on. So TJ ain't too sure about Blinky. (10)

TJ's skepticism is rooted in the fact that "some white folks at school bought her them glasses" (10), and he cannot see anything out of them. Blinky's queersightedness is a combination of her gender-bending subjectivity—her butchness—and her racialized gaze, which allows her to see things in a different way from anyone else in the text. She thus provides a suitable model for reading the text itself, a queersighted practice that pays special attention to the unstable boundaries of racial and gender distinction. Such a queer lens of reading allows for a consideration of the formation of homosexual identities in the text across various racial and gender boundaries.

The butch, bespectacled Blinky represents a paradoxical body upon which "manhood" is realized, or more precisely, upon which the contradiction of masculinity as solely male identified is revealed. As a seeming gender counterfeit, her masquerade reveals the mere "seemingness" of gender in the first place. Blinky accomplishes this feat by appropriating and subverting the stereotypes discursively produced through the mass media. The notion of a queer third term is thus realized in the "third sex" of Blinky—it is her subject position as a queer "dark body" that combines with her eyeglasses to allow for her critical queersightedness. Her ownership of the glasses, given to her by white people at her school, seems to embody Du Bois's notion of "looking at oneself through the eyes of others,"[34] yet Blinky uses the glasses to create a counterreading of the visible, just as she disrupts discursive chains of gender formation by signifying on the normative ways in which gender is coded and articulated. Blinky realizes the ways in which queer black children must be constantly "blinking" in resistance when consuming representations of their identity, such as the discourses of the television and film.

In this sense, Blinky is a paradigmatically *queer reader.* Gazing through her eyeglasses, her deadlocked double consciousness is actually tripled—she is black, American, and emphatically queer, a hybridization of man and woman through her gender performance and, through her glasses, an interfusion of black and white subjectivity. Blinky is the subversive reappearance of Ellison's "little man" at Cheshaw Station—a liminal trickster at the crossroads of gender, sexuality, and race who manipulates hegemonic, white systems of domination.

While Blinky utilizes her body to talk back to heteronormative discourse, the queer resistance of WT and TJ is not enacted principally through bodily performance and resignification; rather, they create crucial moments of rupture in the text through physical, homoerotic touch, thereby resisting the dialectic of spectatorship and identification that imprisons them in a racist, prescribed notion of black masculinity. The boys attempt to break out of the deadlock of the double consciousness that W. E. B. Du Bois describes as "this sense of looking at oneself through the eyes of others, of measuring one's soul by the tape of a world that looks on in amused contempt and pity" (*Souls of Black Folk*, 5). Following Du Bois, the boys must always feel their "twoness—an American, a negro, two souls, two thoughts, two unreconciled strivings; two warring ideals in one dark body, whose dogged strength alone keep it from being torn asunder" (5). Indeed, as the text progresses, WT and TJ attempt to attain manhood, what Du Bois describes as the "history of the American Negro"—the "longing to achieve a self-conscious manhood, to merge his double self into a better and truer self" (5). The boys' attempts to achieve this "self-conscious" manhood are acts of queer spectatorial resistance in that their response to the dominant logic, as articulated in the filmic and televisual narratives, is to perform, with hesitation, a mutual if confusing desire for each other.

After fighting with his drug-addicted older brother, who serves as yet another stereotype of pathologized black masculinity, "WT start to crying" (*Little Man Little Man,* 29) and flees from the scene. He escapes to the childhood space of the playground, followed by TJ, who "just sit there on a swing while WT cry and cry" (29). As WT cries, TJ is silent, since "he want to say something but he don't know what to say. To tell the truth, he scared" (29). TJ is reluctant to utter the truth, to speak the unspeakable—the love that dare not speak its name. Instead of words, human touch communicates desire when "WT stop crying after awhile and he put his hand on TJ's neck and they start to walking. But they don't say a word" (29). Silently, they walk out of the childhood space of the playground together.

In this scene Baldwin once again signifies on the homosexual underpinnings of his earlier work, *Go Tell It on the Mountain*, in which physical contact becomes a substitute for the voicing of queer adolescent desire. In this semi-autobiographical text the protagonist, John Grimes, desires the older, athletic Elisha. As in the relationship between TJ and WT, Elisha considers John his "little brother," yet John was "afraid. He wanted to stop and turn to Elisha, and tell him . . .

something for which he found no words" (219). Much like WT reaching out and touching TJ's neck, the unvoiced desires of John and Elisha are articulated when, at the close of the novel, Elisha "kissed John on the forehead, a holy kiss . . . like a seal ineffaceable forever" (221). Echoing the salvation of human contact between the two boys at the close of *Go Tell It on the Mountain*, WT and TJ locate a space of resistance to the dominant and specularizing discourse of black masculinity through the sanctifying power of homoerotic human touch.

This performance of homosexual desire embodies Baldwin's conception of intersubjective affection as a saving principle in a world ravaged by racism and homophobia; the boys' transformative moment in the playground allows for a moment when the trauma of double consciousness is soothed by the crucial third term of queerness. Homosexual touch allows for a provisional and tentative affirmation of a manhood based on the rejection of a damagingly self-conscious masculinity rooted in compulsory heterosexuality.[35] While it may be instinctive to posit that the transgressive desire of the two boys is a wholly subversive response to the discourses that collude in their damaging subjectification, the text of *Little Man Little Man* does not allow for such a celebratory, tidy sense of closure, which would be stereotypical of the children's book genre. On the contrary, as the text progresses, a series of events allude to a more troubling side of homoeroticism—events that culminate in a cataclysmic scene of symbolic castration that threatens to hurl the children into insanity rather than salvation. The homoerotic touch of WT and TJ sets in motion this chain of catastrophic events, recalling Baldwin's description of the social aftermath of the homoerotic embrace of two boys in his short story, "The Outing":

> But now where there had been peace there was only panic and where there had been safety, danger, like a flower, opened.[36]

Strutting African, Signifying Queer

As the narrative extends toward the dramatic concluding scene of symbolic castration, Baldwin introduces another mode of resistance alongside the sanctifying powers of homosexual touch. Baldwin presents laughter as a possibly subversive strategy to combat the deadlock of double consciousness. This strategy, however, eventually doubles back on itself in a complex system of allusions, suggesting that the deadlock of double consciousness cannot be broken, or if it can, one must indeed pay a heavy price for such an emancipation. In the process, Baldwin exposes the fact that two of the modes of resistance presented in the text, homosexual enactment and laughter, are not separate strategies but are intimately and frighteningly connected historical phenomena. The result is that there is no "storybook ending" for a children's book concerned with queer black subjectivity but rather a narrative that must be as bittersweet as it is precarious in order to explicate and encompass the beauty, pain, and struggle of growing up black and queer in Harlem.

In his essay "Alas, Poor Richard," Baldwin posits that the double consciousness of the "American Negro" allows for something of a reconciliation of the trauma of being racialized in American society. He suggests that the condition of being American and being black can expose the "hoax" of race in America, and that laughing at this hoax can be a unifying experience for two black subjects who come face to face:

> Alliances, in the great cocktail party of the white man's world, are formed, almost purely, on this basis [the realization of the hoax of racial identity], for if both of you can laugh, you have a lot to laugh about. On the other hand, if only one of you can laugh, one of you, inevitably, is laughing at the other. (281)

Laughing together, then, becomes a subversive act in that it seems to represent an "alliance" and an understanding of how racial identity is a performance. At the same time, if only one of the black subjects is laughing, it means that the other has not recognized the hoax and is instead tricked into believing that constructed racial categories are essential and natural.

In this essay Baldwin aligns himself with what Ralph Ellison describes as "the extravagance of laughter." This phenomenon occurs for Ellison when, as a black man, he comes into contact with an experience that exposes the hoax of racial identity and causes him to laugh and tremble simultaneously and gain "thereby a certain wisdom."[37] Indeed, this is the wisdom that Du Bois speaks of in Souls of Black Folk as the "special gift" of the American blacks' "second sight in this American world" (5). Ellison sees this double consciousness as a way of effecting an "infectious laughter" that becomes a way of subverting racist ideologies.

While Baldwin's discussion of laughter seems to align itself with Du Bois and Ellison, I suggest that the text of *Little Man Little Man* revises this formulation with the critical signifying difference of queerness. The Du Boisian "longing to achieve self-conscious manhood, to merge his double self into a better and truer self," produces a queer third term in the text that brings together the resistant strategies of homosexual touch and laughter, only to present them as bittersweet instead of emancipatory. The third term is a strange and parodic "African strut" that appears in the text immediately after the homoerotic encounter between WT and TJ and then reappears significantly to close the text after the confounding scene of symbolic castration.

The initial appearance of the African strut demonstrates a sense of unity through laughter. Blinky, deploying the familiar chain of imitation and identification, facilitates the strut after WT and TJ return from the playground site of their homoerotic encounter:

> They hear Mr. Man's record player from the basement, and Blinky start go fooling around, and dancing. WT, he do everything Blinky do, and so he start dancing too.
> "Come on, TJ!" WT say, and TJ start doing his African strut.
> WT love to see TJ strut. It crack him up every time.
> "Go on, TJ!" WT say, laughing, and just moving to the music, him and Blinky. (29–30)

Once again, it is the chain of masculine identification from Blinky to WT to TJ that results in the appearance of the African strut, when WT imitates Blinky dancing and then implores TJ to join them. When "TJ start doing his African strut," he causes WT to "crack up." Cracking up can signify both laughter and insanity, and in this sense, WT's reaction to the African strut exemplifies Ellison's notion of the "wisdom" gained through laughing and crying at the same time.

The accompanying illustrations depict Blinky, TJ, and WT dancing in the street, with musical notes floating through the air. A colorful, presumably African wilderness scene appears to be exploding out of the side of the building. Watching WT enables TJ to do his strut after repeated encouragement, and eventually "TJ move like *he in a jungle where he can't get no satisfaction*" (30). The highly overdetermined nature of the sentence fragment (boldface in the text) seems to point to

TJ's parodic performance of African identity, his "African strut," as an act that elicits laughter from the other children. The effects of the strut are highly reminiscent of Baldwin's and Ellison's discussions of laughter as a moment of bonding and healing of the trauma of double consciousness. However, I suggest that the overdetermined, boldface words offer a darker, more complex reading of this parodic practice and its relation to the supposed "twoness" of the black American experience.

Baldwin writes about the ambivalence he feels when he comes face to face with an African: "An American Negro, however deep his sympathies, or however bright his rage, ceases to be simply a black man when he faces a black man from Africa," for he is "facing the unspeakably dark, guilty, erotic past which the Protestant fathers made him bury—for their peace of mind, and for their power—but which lives in his personality and haunts the universe yet" ("Alas, Poor Richard," 287). The disjunction between being an *African* and being an African American forces Baldwin, like TJ, to "move like *he in a jungle* where *he can't get no satisfaction.*" The lack of satisfaction arises out of what Bhabha describes as the *ambivalence* of colonial discourse—as the black American looks at the African, he sees both himself and a body that must be cited as a location of irreducible difference, an otherness and a sameness that he must both claim and disavow in order to occupy his uniquely doubled American identity. The black American, by virtue of his absorption into an American identity, must both claim and disavow his African self; hence Baldwin's tension between "envy, despair, attraction, and revulsion." This ambivalence is distinctly "dark, guilty, and erotic," as Baldwin put it, suggesting that identification and desire of and for an other that is a part of the discursively stereotyped self creates this fantasmic ambivalence in the African American subject. Not at all mutually exclusive, identification and desire play off each other furiously in the doubled consciousness of the black American psyche.

The double consciousness of the black American subject produces the African strut as a tripled term, a parodic performance of racial identity and dissatisfaction with the ambivalence of binding categories of identity. But is WT "cracking up" a sign of mirth, or is it a symptom of the insanity of living behind Du Bois's "veil," of always looking at oneself through the eyes of others? This question forces us to take seriously the fact that *Little Man Little Man* is dedicated to

Beauford Delaney, whose mental deterioration and eventual death Baldwin saw as the price of the struggle of being black, American, and loving other men (Leeming, 337). In this context, the insanity of double consciousness gains a certain urgent and immediate currency in a text dedicated to a man who, like the abject Rufus, literally "cracked up" under the strain of triple consciousness.

The loaded "jungle where he can't get no satisfaction" suggests that the ambivalence of the African strut calls on a tradition of homo-eroticism and laughter that, while parodic, can hardly be described as wholly subversive. On the contrary, by alluding to the Rolling Stones' 1965 hit "Satisfaction," Baldwin also alludes to the minstrelsy tradition of the nineteenth century, of which Mick Jagger is a latter-day manifestation. This chain of allusions is substantiated by the fact that the words are written in boldface on the white page—*jungle where he can't get no satisfaction*—as if boldface equals blackface.[38] I argue that the allusion to Jagger, while brief and of seemingly marginal narrative importance, actually structures a complex system of meanings and historical significations that resonate throughout the text of *Little Man Little Man* and many of Baldwin's other works.

Jagger represents a paradigmatic manifestation of white appropriation of black musical and cultural forms.[39] Such appropriations, as Eric Lott argues in his book *Love and Theft: Blackface Minstrelsy and the American Working Class*, are modern resonances of blackface, which was an "established nineteenth century theatrical practice, principally in the urban North, in which white men caricatured blacks for sport and profit."[40] This type of cross-racial appropriation has been habitual, even career making and sustaining for Jagger, as he modeled his campiness self-consciously on another "little man," Little Richard, wearing similar makeup and incorporating many of Little Richard's signature moves in Little Richard's performances. Jagger also appropriated James Brown's patent lurches, shuffles, twists, and slides. The Rolling Stones' lead singer thus imitated and learned a certain kind of African strut, and his cultural borrowing (to put it generously) allowed him access to the virility, humility, and abandon that enabled him to write self-descriptive songs such as "Primitive Cool," thereby affirming, through appropriation, the racist white ideologies of black manhood that structured blackface minstrelsy and continue to structure much of the white imagination today.

Jagger's African strut is reappropriated by TJ in the text when he dances to the music of the "Night Train," moving like "he in a jungle where he can't get no satisfaction." What is registered through the parodic African strut, vis-à-vis the intersecting allusion to Jagger and blackface minstrelsy, is not simply a subversive, laughter-inducing result of TJ's doubled identity as black and American, in the model of Du Bois and Ellison, but a realization and expression of the explicitly *sexual* condition of being black, American, and queer. The near un-readability of the strut points to the various ways in which desire is racialized. The song "Satisfaction," after all, as Jagger puts it, is about "frustration and sex" (Sandford, 92), and fittingly enough, so is the practice of blackface minstrelsy so clearly alluded to in the boldface-as-blackface words.

As Lott argues in his book, the practice of blackface minstrelsy was very much tied up in the quest for white male sexual "satisfaction." In fact, white male investment in the black penis defined minstrelsy, as the pleasure of the show was derived from an ambivalent interest in "blackness" and the always present threat of castration—a threat brutally reversed in white lynching rituals (9). According to Lott's formulation, the minstrel show was in many ways a cover for the ex-plicitly homoerotic charge of the pleasure in the specularization of black male bodies. The "fixing" of the black subject had everything to do with the white racist mythology of the huge black penis and white male desire for and disavowal of the stereotyped phallicism of black masculinity. The anxiety of this colonial fantasy precipitated the lynchings and literal castrations of the Other's "strange fruit," and the minstrel show served as a way of appropriating and thus taming the raging phallicism of the black male subject. This containment of the threat of black masculinity allowed the minstrel show to trans-form fear into libidinal gratification—a reading supported by much of Baldwin's writing on race and sexuality.

A striking example of Baldwin's concordance with Lott's formula-tions is his short story "Going to Meet the Man," in which Baldwin interrogates the historical and psychological dimensions of castration through a lynching scene, as told from the position of a white sheriff. It is only by recalling a lynching viewed in childhood that that narra-tor can "perform" with his white wife: "Come on, sugar, I'm going to do you like a nigger, come on, sugar, and love me just like you'd love a nigger" (*Going to Meet the Man*, 249). The sheriff can engage in sexual intercourse—or in Jagger's words from "Satisfaction," he can "make some girl"—only through the recollection of a black man hanging from a tree. The black victim is deprived of his masculinity by virtue of a castration that is enacted through the white man's myth of black sexuality; by castrating the black man, the white sheriff gains access to the sexual power he otherwise lacks (Leeming, 249). For Lott and Baldwin, then, black masculinity in the white imagination represents, paradoxically, both emasculation and a rampant, phallic masculinity. Indeed, it is the perception of having the phallus or losing it through castration that animates the sexual nature of blackface minstrelsy.

The overdetermination of the African strut, and its accompanying boldface/blackface text thus calls on a historical tradition from the nineteenth century that lives on in white rock and pop stars, even producing parodic songs such as Lou Reed's 1979 hit "I Wanna Be Black." In doing so, the parodic strut dramatizes the interdependency of whiteness on otherness and the way in which whiteness is a specific, culturally constituted racial identity. Kobena Mercer, in *Welcome to the Jungle*, points out how this notion was articulated by Jean Genet when Genet said that "in white America, the blacks are the characters in which history is written . . . they are the ink that gives the white page its meaning" (218). Genet's sentiments are literalized in the text of *Little Man Little Man* through the *jungle where he can't get no satisfaction,* where the boldface words function as an inscription of blackness on whiteness, in order to convey the historical allusions to minstrelsy and its modern manifestation in Jagger.

These allusions suggest that the complicated African strut resists the categorical designation of a subversive performative and is instead a decidedly bittersweet and ambivalent practice of queer resignification. The strut's implicit queerness, which can be located in the almost unreadable homoerotic allusion to Jagger and blackface, is a product of the condition of double consciousness tripled into a parodic third term. The "thirdness" of this queer, black, American identity creates a queersighted lens for looking at the instability of a white heterosexual subjectivity that must tame the threat of blackness through ridicule and castration. As the complex workings of blackface minstrelsy demonstrate, white subjectivity depends on the constant and repetitive production of an otherness that must be alienated precisely because it implicates itself, through the interplay of identification and desire, as a part of the white self. As Lott points out, this is the color line Du Bois discusses as the decisive factor in double consciousness, a line both transgressed and reified through Jagger and blackface minstrelsy.

Might the African strut allow for a specifically queersighted lens to expose the interlocking systems of race and sexuality in the constitution of white and black subjectivity, the equation that entraps both races in a fearful, interdependent bind? The strut signifies on Jagger's appropriations, singing the queer childhood blues and asking, Why is it that *we* can't get any satisfaction? Overdetermined almost to the point of saturation, the strut requires aggressive decoding to get to its textual meanings, work that can be completed only by examining its final manifestation in the text after WT's symbolic castration, a scene that is haunted by the spectacle of blackface minstrelsy.

Castration, Closure, and Little "Bodies That Matter"

The scene of castration, as a paradigmatic, historical manifestation of racist violence and a major preoccupation of the defensive tactics of blackface minstrelsy, is reinscribed in the text of *Little Man Little Man* through the metonymic relation of feet to genitalia. While WT is not literally castrated in the text, he suffers a horrifying wound that tropes on the Freudian fetishistic displacement of phallus to foot, an oscillation between the literal and the figurative that is distinctive of fetishism as a mode of defense against castration. Such a narrative structure is utilized in the closing pages of the text, which involve the reappearance of the African strut as a defensive and ambiguous performative reaction to this symbolic castration, culminating in a distinctly ambivalent and queer sense of narrative closure.

After TJ throws WT's ball up in the air, all three children are shocked when the ball does not come back down but rather there is a "big explosion, like a bomb falling" (78). TJ is knocked, crying, to the ground, and WT is standing in a pool of blood. Not only has he "done lost his ball"—arguably a tropological allusion to castration—but, more convincingly, "WT got that hole in his sneaker and he done stepped on the glass and his foot be bleeding something awful" (79). The "hole," as Lee Edelman has argued, signifies the negation of the penis, "the fetishized part in which the wholeness and coherence of the subject's identity is invested" (Edelman, 64). The impeded closure of the "hole" in the sneaker, which results in the cutting of the foot and thus the "pool of blood," represents WT's symbolic castration; it thereby signifies, in the heterosexist imaginary, the emasculation of WT and his concomitant transformation into the stereotyped "feminized fag" (*Bodies That Matter*, 96), in Judith Butler's blunt phrasing, who lacks phallic masculinity.

The explosion also has potentially devastating consequences for Blinky, who says, "WT, your foot! Look at your foot! You standing in a pool of blood!" (*Little Man Little Man*, 79). The accompanying illustration depicts TJ on the ground with Blinky, her eyeglasses enlarged and "blinking," pointing emphatically at WT's bleeding foot. Following a Freudian narrative, Blinky should respond to WT's castration by realizing her own castration, what would be a shocking contradiction of her preadolescent female masculinity—or, to borrow Butler's terminology again, her "phallicized dyke identity" (*Bodies That Matter*, 103). Yet the focus on the looking and the pointing of Blinky, which substantiates the privileging of the scopic drive in the psychic structuring of sexual difference, also demonstrates how her queer-sightedness allows for a refutation of the heterosexualizing symbolic with its taboo on homosexuality (*Bodies That Matter*, 167).

More specifically, if, as Butler has argued, the Oedipal scenario depends on the threat of castration in order to sex and heterosexualize subjects (167), then Blinky's phallic lesbianism—that is, her ownership of the phallic "little man"—enacts a subversive rearticulation of the symbolic; her abject phallic dyke identity exists in contradistinction to the normative female reaction to castration. Her critical queer-sightedness allows for a resistant, "blinking" reading of the scene of castration—by refusing to identify with the feminine position and instead claiming ownership of the "little man," Blinky shows how such normative identification (which, according to Butler, is produced and consolidated through repetition) can be resignified and subverted when, as in Blinky's case, it fails to repeat.

Blinky's ownership of the phallus, and thus of the little man as its signifier, contradicts the fact that it is WT, and not her, who is described repeatedly as the "little man" in the text. The phallus is thus actually located where it is nominally absent in the text—in Blinky as the budding phallic dyke and the subversively liminal little man. In a Lacanian sense, then, where power is wielded by the feminine position of not-having, WT, as an ostensibly masculine subject, requires the existence of the female Blinky as Other to confirm and "be" the phallus.[41] Only Blinky does not embody the lack of phallus in order to represent WT's phallic possession; instead, through her phallic lesbianism, she "owns" the phallus that WT "loses" by way of his symbolic castration. The pointing at WT's sudden phallic lack enables Blinky's queersighted recognition of her own phallic masculinity.

With TJ crying and WT "about to vomit" (79) in reaction to his violent emasculation, Blinky, as usual, assumes command by saying "Come on!" (*Little Man Little Man*, 79) and leading the others away toward refuge and the possibility of rectifying their horrific experience. Once again the chain of identification by way of Blinky is enacted, when "she take WT by one hand and TJ hold him by the other and she lead them down the steps, to the basement, to Mr. Man's house" (82). It is in the underground space of the "basement" where the children—signifying on, among others, Ellison's Invisible Man and Wright's Fred Daniels in "The Man Who Lived Underground"—make their escape from the white-controlled aboveground world. The basement becomes a space where they attempt to come to terms with the symbolic castration and construct a narrative of ascent by forging a new and authentic triple consciousness of queer, black American identity.

Mr. Man's anger, it is revealed as the narrative unfolds, is directed at his wife, Miss Lee, because she was responsible for WT's wound, and thus his symbolic castration, when, in a drunken stupor on the roof, she dropped a liquor bottle that hit the ball and shattered on the sidewalk.[42] Due to her error, "WT's foot just keep dripping and dripping blood. It a big cut" (83). Experiencing guilt over her castrating actions, Miss Lee applies peroxide to WT's foot and tells him to "take it like a man" (85), furthering the imposition of a manhood and masculinity as what Baldwin once called "an embattled, blood-stained thing."[43] Yet, even as this heterosexual imperative is launched at WT by the mother figure of Miss Lee, "he lean hard against TJ" (*Little Man Little Man*, 85) for support. Indeed, as Miss Lee bandages WT's foot, the two homoerotically bonded boys, clinging to the sanctifying intersubjective touch initiated in the playground, do not let go of each other's hands.

The compulsory heterosexuality that Miss Lee implicitly espouses as she attempts to heal and bandage the emasculating injury is enforced performatively when she takes WT's face in her hands and says to him, "Little Man, Little Man" (92). The reiteration of the phallic signifier "little man" enforces, through the regulatory power of repetition, his expected yet disrupted budding heteromasculinity—it is as if she hopes that she can fill in his supposed lack through the excess of her phallic utterances. As the maternal figure who inadvertently castrates and thus emasculates her "child," Miss Lee desperately tries to reinsert WT back into the heterosexual economy through her insistent, performative utterances of "Little Man." But her normalizing speech acts are ineffectual, as WT stares at her "and then tears start rolling out his eyes" (92)—a realization of the disjunction between the phallicized, heteronormative manhood she is imposing on him and his actual desires, signified stereotypically through his little man lack.

As Miss Lee kisses WT and holds him in her arms, "he more scared than he ever been . . . and he don't know why" (93). The maternal embrace of Miss Lee is not a safe haven but rather a location of fear. While WT cannot articulate the terms of his bondage in the "fearful mathematic" of black masculinity mandated by Miss Lee, the queersighted Blinky, with her "glasses just shining like diamonds" (93), realizes that WT must be freed from the binding logic of compulsory heterosexuality. While it may seem Blinky is more than a bit too precocious for her age (after all, how many eight-year-olds are familiar with psychoanalysis and Judith Butler, in however cloudy an extrapolation?), the text stresses how she is mature far beyond her years: "Blinky look hard at WT and finally she say, just like she older than time, 'You better start to walking, little man'" (93). A blurring of the lines between childhood and adulthood is thus a crucial component of Blinky's "older than time" queersightedness; this wisdom allows her to call on her privileged position in the children's chain of identification by telling WT to "start to walking, little man," thereby commanding him to walk away from and reject the suffocating embrace of the threatening, castrating, and then heteronormalizing (m)other, Miss Lee.

In an attempt to bring WT to an understanding of the possibility of queer masculinities in opposition to the damagingly self-conscious masculinity of heteronormativity, Blinky "start moving, dancing to the music. She putting on a show for WT, really, she want to make him smile" (93). Realizing that the desperate bandaging is a futile attempt to reinstate WT's black masculinity within the heterosexual economy of having the phallus, or having the "little man," Blinky hopes to "make him smile" through her queer bodily performance. Instead, Blinky inadvertently brings together the fractured heterosexual pairing of Mr. Man and Miss Lee: "Pretty soon, Blinky do something to the music to make Mr. Man laugh. Then, Miss Lee laugh, and Mr. Man put one arm around her shoulder" (95). Blinky's dance, a performative act that is meant to be subversive, instead goes awry and reconsolidates the heterosexual norm. Despite Blinky's realization of the ways in which her queer body matters, it is not enough to convince WT that the castration anxiety is part of a fictive, racist, and heterosexualizing logic that substitutes the little man part for the (w)hole of black male identity,[44] as "WT still just lying there, and watching" (95).

The chain of identification, still in place as WT watches Blinky and "TJ watching WT" (95), is broken as the text concludes when "TJ think *Shucks*, and he start into doing his African strut and WT just crack up" (95). The punctuating reappearance of the parodic African strut once again oscillates between the subversion of "cracking up" as laughter and the darker notion of insanity, as exemplified through Beauford Delaney and the looming graffiti image of Rufus, the black abject. What is at stake in this final manifestation of the African strut is whether this queer resignification can, in fact, parody racist, minstrelsy-like ideologies or whether, instead, it will fail to displace these conventions, thereby hurling WT into a "cracked-up" insanity instead of a subversive, Ellisonian "extravagance of laughter."

As discussed earlier, the African strut alludes to the history of blackface minstrelsy in the antebellum North. I argue that the final appearance of the strut is an aggressive "queering" of the already demonstrably homosocial practice of blackface minstrelsy.[45] Just as *queer* has been deployed to reterritorialize a term that historically has been used to isolate a group of people based on "deviant" sexual object choice, TJ's "queering" performance is a site of resistance and resignification of abjectifying racial stereotypes enacted through the practice of blackface minstrelsy. The tension lies in that this attempt to enable a social and political resignification is a parodic mimicry that makes its claim for intelligibility through and against a model and discourse of racist oppression—blackface minstrelsy. Just as the vernacular narrative seeks to rearticulate and subvert the hegemonic discourse of standard English, TJ can be read as performing what Bhabha describes as "a discourse uttered between the lines and as such both against the rules and within them" (89). My concern here is whether TJ's "queering" practice enables a subversive position, or whether he simply reifies the racist, ambivalently homophobic/homoerotic ideological "lines" of blackface minstrelsy, thereby ensuring that WT's laughter is a sign of insanity—a decidedly nonsubversive, paroxysmal reaction to a failed effort toward subversive resignification.

TJ's African strut recalls Lott's discussion of "seeming counterfeits" in *Love and Theft*. These black men, such as Juba (William Henry Lane), mocked white men through credible imitations of white men imitating blacks (13). Juba utilized stereotyped "black dances"—graceless, stammering, laughter-inducing movements that could be aptly described as African struts—in a display of black irony toward whites. When TJ "think *Shucks*, and he start into doing his African strut," I argue that he is one-upping modern "white Negroes" such as Mick Jagger by offering, much like Juba, a possibly subversive parody of white stereotyping constructions of black identity as the African "other." Indeed, TJ's "seeming counterfeit" performance finally elicits a reaction from the castrated WT, who "just crack up" in the final line of the book. Yet, as suggested earlier, I am unconvinced that this performative, or any performative for that matter, is categorically subversive; rather, I argue that it is the indeterminacy of the strut's queer resignification that characterizes the closure of the text.

While, as Lott argues, blackface images substituted in complicated ways for the castrating threat of the (b)lack (15), here TJ deploys his imitation of an imitation as a healing defense to the castration that WT has suffered metonymically in the wounded foot episode. It appears that WT can be brought out of his castration-induced despondency only through the parodic African strut. If, following Lott, the black male in blackface minstrelsy is white people's referent for Lacan's threatening (m)other, then here TJ operates within the same normative, phallocentric logic by attempting to heal WT's castration through the ridicule and specularization, and thus threatened castration, of a white masculinity that itself imitates and polices black masculinity to substantiate its own coherence. As such, TJ's performance is still very much invested in the reductive logic of castration anxiety, which figures masculinity as intrinsically connected to the ownership of the phallus and femininity—and by extension, homosexuality—as the lack of the transcendental signifier, the "little man."

bell hooks offers a succinct definition of the historical and political problematic that is deeply entrenched in TJ's strategy of resignification:

> The discourse of black resistance has almost always equated freedom with manhood, the economic and material domination of black men with castration, emasculation. Accepting these sexual metaphors forged a bond between oppressed black men and their white male oppressors. They shared the patriarchal belief that revolutionary struggle was really about the erect phallus.[46]

TJ's "seeming counterfeit" strut is deployed in an attempt to heal WT's castration by deflecting the threat of castration back at the white imagination through a parodic, ridiculing performative. As such, TJ is heavily invested in a patriarchal "discourse of black resistance" rooted in the masculinist logic that structures castration rituals and, by extension, the practice of blackface minstrelsy. Extrapolating from hooks's argument, TJ's performance is structured around the homosocial bond forged between black and white men through the struggle to own and control the erect "little man."

Arguably, such a position is subverted through Blinky's female masculinity, which contests the phallocentric notion that only men can "own" the phallus (since she is, as I have argued, the female yet phallic little man in the text). And yet the question remains as to whether WT and TJ are sufficiently queersighted at this point to comprehend the positive implications of this subversion for the formation of alternative sexual and gender identities, or whether they remain imprisoned in the phallocentric logic of castration, whose racist reduction of the black man to his genital part is reinscribed through the "seeming counterfeit" of blackface minstrelsy.

The fact that earlier in the text TJ, when looking through Blinky's glasses, was unable to "see nothing" and "everything looked like it was rained on" (*Little Man Little Man*, 10) suggests he is not yet proficiently queersighted. At the same time, early in the text his biological mother advised him to read "everything you can get your hands on" but to read it skeptically, so that "one day . . . you going to understand" (70–71). TJ, then, is learning to become a queer reader, striving toward a critical queersightedness.

For this reason, the conclusion of the text is radically indeterminate—when WT "just crack up," he could either be laughing extravagantly at the possibly deconstructive effects of the parodic strut or losing his mind due to his castrated position in the binding logic that posits masculine identification through lack of castration. Both possibilities could even be acting in furious and contradicting simultaneity. Since having or losing the phallus animates both blackface minstrelsy and its subversively intended redeployment by TJ, the parodic performance fails to recognize that, as Butler argues and Blinky exemplifies, the desire to have the phallus represents "that vain striving to approximate and possess what no one can ever have, but anyone can sometimes have in the transient domain of the imaginary" (*Bodies That Matter*, 105).

Just as Blinky's butch performance reveals the mere seemingness of gender, the African strut, in its failure to displace its conventions outside the problematics of phallocentric discourse, uncovers the mere seemingness of phallic possession—the fact that having or being the little man is a phantasmic identification, a counterfeit that is at all times a performative strut toward a phallic authenticity that can never be consolidated precisely because it is fictive. Paradoxically, then, the strut's subversive power lies in its inevitable failure.

As if to punctuate this point, after WT's ambiguous "cracking up," the text concludes with the "end of Little Man." More than a straightforward, normative sign of the text's conclusion, the "end of Little Man" is perhaps a signal of the end of "little man" as a conceptual tool. That is, the text's conclusion rejects little man as a phallic signifier that partakes in the heterosexualizing symbolic, mandates distinct genders, and demeans homosexual identities. This rejection allows for the proliferation of queer identities, such as those of the children, whose formations within and across gender and racial boundaries constitute what Butler might describe as "subversive rearticulations of the symbolic" (*Bodies That Matter*, 109). In the illustration accompanying the phrase, "the end of Little Man," the three children stand, holding hands, in the familiar ordering of identification: WT in the middle, TJ and Blinky on either side. The text thus concludes with a gesture toward a queer solidarity that is tainted, as it must be, by a laughter whose indeterminacy betrays the precarious and bittersweet nature of a queer black childhood.

Such a conclusion points to the ambivalence of queering practices in general, insofar as the parodic mimicry of systems of domination always risks the reification of those linguistic and discursive systems. And yet, what other recourse is there in a world where reductive, heterosexist imperatives structure the barometer determining that which is considered normative for both children and adults? Baldwin's adults' book in the drag of a juvenile text is itself like the African strut, an ambivalent resignifying practice, a powerfully parodic mimicry and queering of the children's book genre that is nonetheless an indeterminately subversive performative. In this context, it is relevant to question whether this book elicits laughter, tears, or both from its readers.

Such a question is difficult to answer conclusively, due to the text's marked paucity of readers. Since the book went quickly out of print, at least in part because of its only seemingly unreadable queerness, the possibilities of its resignifying effects, for the most part have been neutralized. If no one reads the text, it cannot do its subversive work. While the "unreadable" book attempts to strut as a children's book, to "dance along with a child's rhythm and resilience,"[47] as its jacket describes its narrative, the text's failure to do so allows for a queersighted—and thus, one hopes, a *clearsighted*—counterreading of the visible and the legible. What would it mean, then, to bring this neglected text back into print and thereby to bring childhood queerness into some form of visibility that allows for queersighted readings in all their subversive potentialities? What would it mean to reprint a text whose veiled "deviant" sexual content, whose very queerness, resulted in its virtual extinction?

To reprint and reread this text queersightedly would represent a gesture, albeit a small one, against the normalizing censorship, even attempted extermination, of a childhood queerness forced every day, in big and small ways, *to go out of print*, as it were. To reprint this text would mean to reproduce the queer, interracial child of two men, essentially to make more and more metaphoric queer babies, through the mechanical and (homo)sexual reproduction of a text that contests racist and heterosexist constructions of racial, sexual, and gendered subjectivity.

While this position may come across as melodramatic, I argue that, as the high suicide rate among queer youth demonstrates, such a childhood is itself more often than not an exceptionally dramatic experience. In light of the myriad ways in which mainstream cultural representations systematically obviate any significantly positive queer presence, resurrecting and rereading this emphatically queer text would represent a provisional statement that the welfare of queer children is relevant in this pressing postmodern moment. Such a rebirth just might signify an oppositional—indeed, a queersighted—recognition that queer little bodies do, in fact, matter.

NOTES

1. Both Henry Louis Gates, Jr., and Houston Baker have privileged Ellison's figure of the little man at Cheshaw Station, a whistle-stop near Tuskegee, Alabama, in their contributions to African American literary theory: the former in conjunction with his theory of African American "signifyin(g)" and the latter with his conception of the "blues matrix." Neither, however, has fully explored the gendering of this figure and its implications for a feminist and queer approach to African American literature. See Henry Louis Gates, Jr., *The Signifying Monkey: A Theory of African American Literary Criticism* (New York: Oxford University Press, 1988), 64–65; and Houston Baker, *Blues, Ideology, and Afro-American Literature: A Vernacular Theory* (Chicago: University of Chicago Press, 1984), 12–13.

2. Valerie Smith, "Gender and Afro-Americanist Literary Theory and Criticism," in *Speaking of Gender,* ed. Elaine Showalter (New York: Routledge, 1989), 57.

3. The phrase "open secret" is drawn from D. A. Miller's paradigmatic work *The Novel and the Police* (Berkeley: University of California Press, 1988), which resonates in a queer reading of the little man at Cheshaw Station, whose existence is truly a "secret that is known to be known" in Ellison's account of a teacher and her young black pupil:

"All right," she said, "you must *always* play your best, even if it's only in the waiting room at Cheshaw station, because in this country there'll always be a little man behind the stove."

"A what?"

She nodded. "That's right," she said, "there'll always be the little man whom you don't expect, and he'll know the *music,* and the *tradition,* and the standards of *musicianship* required for whatever you set out to perform." Ralph Ellison, "The Little Man at Cheshaw Station," in *Going to the Territory* [New York: Vintage Books, 1986], 4)

4. Baldwin's relationship to his African American male literary predecessors, such as Du Bois, Ellison, and especially Wright, is well documented as at once filial and antagonistic. The dialogue between Baldwin and Wright takes on a decidedly Freudian slant when Baldwin follows his scathing critique of Wright's Bigger Thomas with the admission that Wright's work was "an immense liberation and revelation for me . . . he became my ally and my witness, and alas! my father!" James Baldwin, "Alas, Poor Richard," in *The Price of the Ticket: Collected Nonfiction, 1948–85* [New York: St. Martin's/Marek, 1985], 274). What is at stake here is not merely a Freudian struggle, where the younger artist slays his metaphorical father, but also a dramatic reconfiguration of black masculinity.

5. James Baldwin and Yoran Cazac, *Little Man Little Man: A Story of Childhood* (New York: Dial Press, 1976).

6. Henry Louis Gates, Jr., quoting Kobena Mercer in "Looking for Modernism," in *Black American Cinema*, ed. Manthia Diawara (New York: Routledge, 1993), 204.

7. The term *queer* may be something of a misnomer when referencing Baldwin's sexuality; yet his attitude toward social construction of sexual subjectivity is certainly more aligned with the identity sign of "queer" than with any other system currently available. He consistently rejected the self-designation "gay." He once said in an interview that "the phenomenon we call 'gay' . . . has always rubbed me the wrong way . . . I never understood exactly what was meant by it" (Richard Goldstein, "Go the Way Your Blood Beats: An Interview with James Baldwin in *James Baldwin: The Legacy*, ed. Quincy Troupe [New York: Simon & Schuster, 1989], 182). Indeed, Baldwin's refusal to mark himself as a gay writer has vexed many—especially white gay critics. A salient recent example of this tendency can be found in the chapter "The Agony of Black Literature," in David Bergman, *Gaiety Transfigured: Gay Self-Representation in American Literature* (Madison: University of Wisconsin Press, 1991), 163–187.

8. James Baldwin and Yoran Cazac, *Little Man Little Man: A Story of Childhood* (London: Michael Joseph, 1976), jacket description.

9. David Leeming, *James Baldwin: A Biography* (New York: Henry Holt, 1994), 330.

10. Julius Lester, "Little Man Little Man," *New York Times Book Review*, September 4, 1977, 22.

11. Another example of a paradigmatically queersighted reader is Audre Lorde, whose reflections in *Zami: A New Spelling of My Name*, stress the important differences of race, class, and gender within the queer community. Fittingly enough, her severe nearsightedness forced her, like the queersighted Blinky, to wear eyeglasses at a very young age.

12. Perhaps I am being paranoid, but I am somewhat hesitant to label this reading practice "skeptical," when in fact what it aims to be is closer to what Eve Kosofsky Sedgwick, drawing on the work of Melanie Klein, calls "reparative reading." In many ways Blinky functions as a model figure for Sedgwick's notion of reparative reading, which Sedgwick suggests can be represented by the image of "the interpretative absorption of the child or adolescent who . . . if she reads at all—is reading for important news about herself, without knowing what form that news will take; with only the patchiest familiarity with its codes." I see Blinky as such a reader, and I imagine that a queersighted reading practice strives to be a manifestation of the reparative mode that Sedgwick describes as a "speculative, superstitious, and methodologically adventurous state where recognitions, pleasures, and discoveries seep in only from the most stretched and ragged edges of one's competence." See Eve Kosofsky Sedgwick's introduction, "Paranoid Reading and Reparative Reading; or, You're So Paranoid, You Probably Think This Introduction Is about You," in *Novel Gazing: Queer Readings in Fiction,* ed. Eve Kosofsky Sedgwick (Durham: Duke University Press, 1997), 2–3.

13. Leo Bersani, "Is the Rectum a Grave?" in *AIDS: Cultural Analysis, Cultural Activism,* ed. Douglas Crimp (Cambridge, Mass. and London: MIT Press, 1988).

14. Leeming writes in his biography that after returning from a vacation with Cazac, Baldwin related that he was "happier than I have ever thought I could be, happier than I have ever been in my life" (54).

15. Wayne Koestenbaum, *Double Talk: The Erotics of Male Literary Collaboration* (New York: Routledge, 1989).

16. All this queer repetition, resulting in the textual birth of a metaphoric child, draws attention to the way in which gay men have often been equated with mechanical, not sexual, reproduction. As Koestenbaum has pointed out, citing the way in which the term *clone* is used to "subtly deride gay male nonreproductive sexuality and define homosexuality as replication of the same . . . gay criticism needs to develop a theory that wipes the tarnish off of clones" (182). The text of *Little Man Little Man* (its very title a "cloning") provides a locus for such theorizing, as the homophobic analogy of gay men as clones, signifying mechanically reproduced masculinity, finds the unwelcome resistance of a text that is both mechanically and (homo)sexually reproduced. See Wayne Koestenbaum's "Wilde's Hard Labor and the Birth of Gay Reading," in *Engendering Men: The Question of Male Feminist Criticism,* ed. Joseph Boone and Michael Cadden (New York: Routledge, 1990).

17. Stuart Hall, quoted by Henry Louis Gates, Jr., in "Looking for Modernism," in *Black American Cinema,* ed. Diawara, 201.

18. In *Conversations with James Baldwin,* ed. Fred Stadley and Louis Pratt (Jackson: University Press of Mississippi, 1989), 278.

19. A good example of this phenomenon is the conception of homosexuality promoted by Anita Bryant in her 1977 anti–gay rights campaign in Dade City, Florida: "As a mother, I know that homosexuals, biologically, cannot reproduce children; therefore they must recruit our children" (cited in Richard Meyer, "Warhol's Clones," *Yale Journal of Criticism* 7, 1 [spring 1994]: 108 n. 24.

20. James Baldwin, *Go Tell It on the Mountain* (New York: Doubleday, 1953), 19.

21. See D. A. Miller's *The Novel and the Police* for an elaboration of the role of the police in the constitution of the gay subject and the modern liberal subject more generally. For an extended exploration of criminal stereotypes in relation to black and gay male identities, see Kobena Mercer's *Welcome to the Jungle: New Positions in Black Cultural Studies* (New York: Routledge, 1994). See also Maurice Wallace's *Constructing the Black Masculine: Identity and Ideality in African American Men's Literature and Culture* (forthcoming).

22. Judith Butler, *Bodies That Matter: On the Discursive Limits of "Sex"* (New York: Routledge, 1993), 225.

23. Baldwin's use of free, indirect discourse recalls a similar strategy in Zora Neale Hurston's *Their Eyes Were Watching God*. According to Gates, Hurston utilizes free indirect discourse to "evoke a 'voice' or 'presence' that supplements the narrator's." That is, the syntactic and semantic structures and the enunciative properties of her language create the linguistic effect of a speaking character. This type of orality is at work in the "speakerliness" of Baldwin's text, in which a child's ungendered vernacular voice seems to move among the consciousnesses of the three children without ever claiming its own identity. The narrative effect is that of a child who assumes various subject positions by oscillating among multiple points of view as he or she talks aloud to the reader about the events of the day. See Gates, *The Signifying Monkey*, 209.

24. Homi K. Bhabha, "Of Mimicry and Man: The Ambivalence of Colonial Discourse," in *The Location of Culture* (New York: Routledge, 1994), 89. The logic of Bhabha's essay structures much of this chapter, and my title obviously signifies on the title of Bhabha's essay.

25. Placing the speaking black child in a (post)colonial framework is consistent with James Baldwin's ruminations in his essay "If Black English Isn't a Language, Then Tell Me What Is," in which he argues that the black vernacular "comes into existence by means of brutal necessity, and the rules of the language are dictated by what the language must convey." The child's narrative voice can thus be described as what Houston Baker terms *supraliteracy*— "the vernacular invasion and transcendence of fields of colonizing discourse in order to destroy white male hegemony" (in *Price of the Ticket*, 651). Indeed, in the 1970s, Baldwin began to write many of his works in black vernacular, feeling he had "paid his dues" in the language of the oppressor and now

should write by "the beat of the language of the people who produced him," according to Leeming (343). See Houston Baker's "Caliban's Triple Play," in *"Race," Writing, and Difference,* ed. Henry Louis Gales, Jr., (Chicago: University of Chicago Press, 1985), for a discussion of supraliteracy; see also Baldwin's "If Black English Isn't a Language, Then Tell Me What Is."

26. For a discussion of Rufus as the "black abject," see Robert Reid-Pharr's "Tearing the Goat's Flesh: Crisis, Homosexuality, Abjection, and the Production of a late Twentieth Century Black Masculinity," in *Novel Gazing,* ed. Sedgwick, 353–76.

27. I cannot help but think of Rodney King in this context, especially the way in which, even as he was being beaten, he was somehow positioned as dangerous, as if the armed white police were the victims. See Judith Butler's "Endangered/Endangering: Schematic Racism and White Paranoia," in *Reading Rodney King/Reading Urban Uprising,* ed. Robert Gooding Williams (New York: Routledge, 1993).

28. For an elaboration of the role of colonial fantasy in mass-media stereotypes of black male identity, see Kobena Mercer's *Welcome to the Jungle.*

29. Ishmael Reed, quoted in Lee Edelman's *Homographesis: Essays in Gay Literary and Cultural Theory* (New York: Routledge, 1994), 53.

30. James Baldwin, *The Devil Finds Work* (New York: Dell Publishing, 1976), 41.

31. bell hooks, "The Oppositional Gaze: Black Female Spectatorship," in *Black American Cinema,* ed. Diawara, 298.

32. Gayle Rubin, "The Traffic in Women: Notes on the 'Political Economy' of Sex," in *Toward an Anthropology of Women,* ed. Rayna Reiter (New York: Monthly Review Press, 1975), 467.

33. Judith Halberstam's work on drag kings provided a model for this project, and conversations with her while I was her student enabled me to think about Blinky in relation to female masculinity. See Judith Halberstam, "Lesbian Masculinities: Even Stone Butches Get the Blues," *Women and Performance: a Journal of Feminist Theory* 8:2, 16, special issue, "Queer Acts" (1996) 66. See also her *Female Masculinity* (Durham: Duke University Press, 1998).

34. W. E. B. Du Bois, *The Souls of Black Folk* (New York: Random House, 1986), 5.

35. For a discussion of homosexual enactment as a response to double consciousness in Baldwin's fiction, see Lee Edelman's "The Part for the (W)hole: Baldwin, Homophobia, and the Fantasmics of 'Race,'" in *Homographesis.* Edelman argues that Du Bois's "self-conscious manhood" is actually an unconscious identification with the hegemonic white model of manhood, in which the acquisition of a masculine identity depends on the ability to specularize other men and render them the irreducible "other." He argues further that homosexual desire in Baldwin's fiction creates the opportunity to

affirm "the possibility of a 'manhood' predicated on . . . shedding the deforming self-consciousness of a 'masculinity' enacted through a performative display of homophobia" (69). I am arguing, essentially, that TJ and WT are engaged in an a preadolescent manifestation of such an affirmation.

36. James Baldwin, "The Outing" in *Going to Meet the Man* (New York: Dell, 1965), 47.

37. Ralph Ellison, "The Extravagance of Laughter," in *Going to the Territory*, 197.

38. The notion of "blackface as boldface" was brought to my attention in a conversation with Elizabeth Teare, a graduate student at Yale who provided helpful readings of drafts of this essay.

39. Jagger's musical development was marked by an obsession with "real music," which for him meant black music, as he once told the *Evening Standard*: "I don't really even like white music anyway—it's never been my inspiration. Not even Elvis . . . " (in Christopher Sandford, *Mick Jagger: Primitive Cool* [London: Victor Gollancz, 1993], 227).

40. Eric Lott, *Love and Theft: Blackface Minstrelsy and the American Working Class* (New York: Oxford University Press, 1993), 3.

41. Here I draw explicitly, as I do implicitly throughout this chapter, on Butler's arguments regarding Lacanian psychoanalysis in *Bodies That Matter* and in *Gender Trouble: Feminism and the Subversion of Identity* (New York: Routledge, 1990), 44.

42. The lack of a "Mrs." prefix suggests the couple may not be legally married, pointing to the mere seeming of the performative heterosexual norm in this text.

43. James Baldwin, *Just above My Head* (New York: Bantam Books, 1964), 342.

44. For an elaboration of the logic of synecdoche at play in such a racist, fetishizing conception of black male subjectivity, see Edelman's "The Part for the (W)hole," 42–75.

45. See Lott's *Love and Theft*, 136–68, as well as earlier arguments in this chapter, for a discussion of the homosocial/homoerotic underpinnings of blackface minstrelsy.

46. bell hooks, "Reflections on Race and Sex," in *Yearning: Race, Gender, and Cultural Politics* (Boston: South End Press, 1990), 58.

47. Baldwin and Cazac, *Little Man Little Man*, London ed., jacket.

Chapter 6

Sexual Exiles
James Baldwin and Another Country

James A. Dievler

> For what this really means is that all of the American
> categories of male and female, straight or not, black
> or white were shattered, thank heaven, very early in
> my life. Not without anguish, certainly; but once you
> have discerned the meaning of the label, it may seem
> to define you for others, but it does not have the
> power to define you to yourself. This prepared me for
> my life downtown, where I quickly discovered that
> my existence was the punch line of a dirty joke.
> —James Baldwin, "Here Be Dragons"

"Hear Be Dragons," written in 1985 and near the end of his life, is
James Baldwin's look back to the sexual culture he experienced in
Greenwich Village in the 1940s. He explains that an affair with a
gangster he had as a teenager in Harlem had the effect of obliterating
any sense of his own sexual identity in terms of the categories that
dominated American culture then (and today). Writing in distant retrospect, Baldwin claims in this essay that, as a result of having no desire to define himself in terms of the socially constructed identity categories that dominated not only the sexual culture but the culture of
New York City as a whole, he was "prepared" for "life downtown."
But he also remembers that, as a result of most others seeing him only
in terms of these categories—black, gay, male—his "existence was the

punch line of a dirty joke." In fact, he did not last very long in the Village, and the time he spent there he describes as his "season in hell."

In "Here Be Dragons," Baldwin describes American sexual culture as having "created cowboys and Indians, good guys and bad guys, punks and studs, tough guys and softies, butch and faggot, black and white. It is an ideal so paralytically infantile that it is virtually forbidden—as an unpatriotic act—that the American boy evolve into the complexity of manhood."[1] In addition to restating the categorical nature of American sexual culture, in this passage Baldwin characterizes that culture as immature. It may also be worth noting that he is primarily concerned with male identities.

The essay is significant because Baldwin is directly addressing the conflict he had with New York's sexual culture in the time period that directly preceded his departure for Paris in 1948. Further, Baldwin identifies the essence of that conflict: his inability to live within a sexual culture defined by rigid categories that were trouble for him, not only because he could not find his own identity within them but also because he viewed their cost as devastating—preventing Americans from ever experiencing anything approaching Baldwin's idea of mature love. He describes New York's sexual culture as a "hall of mirrors" that "threw back only brief and distorted fragments" of himself. He states that he was "miserable" and that he "moved through that world very quickly."[2] Indeed, his time in the Village was relatively brief (1944–1948), and once he left for Paris, he would never live permanently in his native city and country again. He described his state of mind before leaving to an interviewer:

> I no longer felt I knew who I really was, whether I was really black or really white, really male or really female, really talented or a fraud, really strong or merely stubborn. I had become a crazy oddball. I had to get my head together to survive and my only hope of doing that was to leave America.[3]

When Newland Archer and Ellen Olenska of Edith Wharton's *The Age of Innocence* are taking their sad carriage ride, they wonder about a "country" where "categories" that prohibit their love from living do not exist. Baldwin echoes their wistfulness in his third novel, *Another Country* (1962). Here he portrays the devastation wrought in a country dominated by a categorically limited sexual culture and offers both a view of and the means of transport to "another country," beyond the confines of the narrow identity categories that imprisoned Americans in the immediate postwar period and still do so today.[4] Further, in *Another Country*, Baldwin asserts that all these categories are intertwined and most effectively transcended through love-based sex—sex that is itself taking place beyond the socially constructed senses of sexuality that have dominated the twentieth century. He is, I believe, advocating a postcategorical, poststructural concept of sexuality that we might call "postsexuality." And he believes it is only in such a "country" that the other categories (race, gender) will cease to exist as well.[5]

Baldwin began *Another Country* in Greenwich Village in 1948. He continued working on the book throughout the 1950s and finally completed it in Istanbul in 1962. As such, the production of *Another Country* spans the primary period of Baldwin's expatriation—he moved to Paris in 1948 and remained there until returning home (but not permanently) in 1957.

For Baldwin, the need to leave was particularly acute. He told interviewers over the years that he had to go or he would have killed someone or been killed. He also expressed the fear that he would end up like a friend who had killed himself by jumping off the George Washington Bridge.[6] Baldwin wrote for *Esquire* in 1961: "I was absolutely certain, from the moment I learned of his death, that I, too, if I stayed here, would come to a similar end."[7] In *Another Country* such a suicide is, indeed, Rufus's fate, and Rufus can be viewed as a James Baldwin who did not escape. In any event, one reason for Baldwin's expatriation was simple physical survival.

Baldwin's exile was an attempt to escape and come to terms with the socially categorical sense of identity construction that he found so limiting and destructive in New York. A Baldwin biographer, James Campbell, calls this "a remarkable moment in Baldwin's development," because not only is he "seeing himself from the outside" but "by detaching himself from his own dislocation, he has started to transcend the condition."[8] For Baldwin, then, the process of expatriation was one of transformation from "the previous condition" of captivity within America's identity constraints to a new level of freedom and self-knowledge in Paris that allowed him to create. Paris had its own identity categories, but Baldwin could live there on the periphery. He was critical of the limited way in which the French assigned identity, but less was at stake for him there than in New York.

In Baldwin's words: "From this void—ourselves—it is the function of society to protect us; but it is only this void, our unknown selves, demanding, forever, a new act of creation, which can save us."[9] Paris for Baldwin was, in a sense, this "void," from which he could contemplate the damaging way in which his native society "protected" him from himself.

The characters in *Another Country* are almost all artists, and as such their success or failure is tied to their ability to "read or write" stories—their own and those of others. A critical moment in *Another Country* is when Vivaldo, in the midst of a night of troubled drunken reverie (he does not know where Ida is and suspects she is with Ellis), apprehends the idea of a world without categories and understands the role of storytelling in achieving that world. He has been eyeing a blonde woman in the bar—seeing her as he saw most women before he met Ida—when he thinks of Rufus and changes his mind:

> And something in him was breaking: he was, briefly and horribly, in a region where there were no definitions of any kind, neither of color, nor of male and female. There was only the leap and the rending and the terror and the surrender. And the terror: which all seemed to begin and end and begin again—forever—in a cavern behind the eye. And whatever stalked there *saw*, and spread the news of what it saw throughout the entire kingdom of whomever, though the eye itself might perish. What order could prevail against so grim a privacy? And yet, without order, of what value was the mystery? Order. Order. *Set thine house in order.* He sipped his whiskey, light-years removed now from the blonde and the bar and yet, more than ever and most unpleasantly present. When people no longer knew that a mystery could only be approached through form, people became—what the people of this time and place had become, what he had become.[10]

Vivaldo enters a world without racial and gender categories, but additionally, he realizes the importance of "spreading the news" and that the "mystery" of that world can "only be approached through form." Thus, for Baldwin, it was critical for him not only to escape New York but also to write about his sense of the city as derived from his experience there.

Writing thus has two functions for Baldwin both of which are also manifest in Vivaldo. First, on the personal level, writing is attached to the individual struggle to step free of the constraints of identity categories. Second, a society can move beyond a culture dominated by such categories only if the people in it understand their own histories and the histories of those around them. (Baldwin argued that there was no difference in these histories.) The second point is further understood in light of the Henry James epigraph that Baldwin chose for his novel:

> They strike one, above all, as giving no account of themselves in any terms already consecrated by human use; to this inarticulate state they probably form, collectively, the most unprecedented of monuments; abysmal the mystery of what they think, what they feel, what they want, what they suppose themselves to be saying.

In Paris, then, Baldwin through his own writing is facing his conflict with New York's sexual culture, and in doing so, he points out the importance of "terms already consecrated by human use"—not just his story but everyone's—in changing the deeply problematic nature of that culture. And the act of writing is also, in a sense, a productive recognition of one's state of exile. In other words, only by actually emigrating was Baldwin able to come to terms with the fact that he was disconnected from his native culture—actual exile and its attending creative productivity enabled Baldwin to understand where he came from. For his characters—Peter, Rufus, and Vivaldo in particular—the struggle lies in their ability or inability to articulate their feeling of being exiled. For other characters, such as Eric, the actual exile experience (that of living abroad, like Baldwin) mitigates this articulation problem.

The immediate postwar period in New York, and particularly in the Village, saw a heightened fixing of identity categories, sexual and otherwise, for a variety of reasons.[11] Throughout American history, "European migrants to America had merged racial and sexual ideology in order to differentiate themselves from Indians and blacks."[12] The Village emerged from the war still largely an enclave for immigrant Italians, although by 1945 many of the Italians in the Village were several generations removed from the immediate immigration experience. As such, the assimilation process had already taken its toll in terms of the immigrant's need to identify and disparage another ethnic or racial group so as not to be the lowest. The Village also remained the locus for artists and bohemians, and after the war, gay Americans flocked there as well. There were, however, very few African Americans living downtown at this time. (Baldwin tells the story of being the first black man served in the San Remo in "Here Be Dragons.") In *Another Country*, this Village mix is observed by Vivaldo along McDougal Street:

> He walked along McDougal Street. Here were the black and white couples, defiantly white, flamboyantly black; and the Italians watched them, hating them, hating, in fact, all the Villagers, who gave their streets a bad name. The Italians, after all merely wished to be accepted as decent Americans and probably could not be blamed for feeling that they might have had an easier time of it if they had not been afflicted with so many Jews and junkies and drunkards and queers and spades. (297)

Baldwin's postwar Village Italians lived in a time when African Americans were beginning to assert their civil rights and gay Americans were forming their own subculture. Women were experiencing new economic and educational opportunities, which would blossom into the feminist movements of the 1960s and 1970s.[13] These developments were largely tied to the war itself. Black Americans returned from the war with the knowledge of having helped defeat fascism, only to be reminded of their second-class status at home. Still, Truman's move to integrate the army just after the war and the vast migration of blacks to Northern cities in search of war-related manufacturing jobs resulted in not only the initial stirrings of the Civil Rights movement but also large numbers of blacks living in close proximity to whites. Northern, urban whites were increasingly exposed to black culture, and in a more intimate way than had occurred in the late-night forays to Harlem that whites had undertaken during Prohibition. But as in the 1920s, in the postwar period whites were particularly drawn to black sexual culture (a fact embodied in Vivaldo in *Another Country*), and once again, this culture was used by whites—despite their attraction to it—as a definition of sexual immorality: "Blacks found themselves again labeled as promiscuous and dangerous, their sexual mores categorized as symbols of immorality."[14]

World War II also directly effected "the articulation of a gay identity and the rapid growth of a gay subculture." The armed services, in which millions of men lived closely together, allowed gay men to find and associate with other gay men in a way that previously had not been available to them in their small towns and cities. The increased urbanization of the mid twentieth century created the same proximity factor. As a result, and particularly in the Village, the gay lifestyle became more openly apparent to mainstream culture. As happened with greater exposure to blacks, a backlash resulted. Homosexuality was linked to the threat of communism—people were simultaneously accused of both—and the gay subculture was viewed as a threat to traditional morality and the stability of the family.[15]

Though more and more gay people settled in the Village after the war because of the community there, they were still stigmatized and threatened. Additionally, because the presence of the community in the Village was widely known, gay men from other parts of the city and the suburbs flocked there for sex that was often anonymous and degrading, as Baldwin describes in "Here Be Dragons":

> At bottom, what I had learned was that the male desire for a male roams everywhere, avid, desperate, unimaginably lonely, culminating often in drugs, piety, madness or death. It was also dreadfully like watching myself at the end of a long, slow-moving line: Soon I would be next. All of this was very frightening. It was lonely and impersonal and demeaning. I could not believe—after all, I was only nineteen— that I could have been driven to the lonesome place where these men and I met each other so soon, to stay.[16]

In Baldwin's time, then, homosexuality as an identity was a negative one from the standpoint of mainstream culture. And further, it was viewed as negative perhaps because it suggested possibilities that those otherwise considered—and who considered themselves— heterosexual were drawn to, and therefore it became a marker for immorality in much the same way that black sexuality did for whites.

While these changes and their corresponding backlashes were taking place for blacks and gays, the primary engine of influence on American culture remained capitalism, and the consumer-based economy that emerged in the first part of the twentieth century hit full throttle during the postwar boom. The consumption-fed boom had a significant effect on the sexual culture. The economy was heavily reliant on the stable, heterosexual family for purchasing the torrent of consumer goods that the retooled war machine was turning out. Therefore, business advertising intensely defined and reenforced a domestic role for women, and individuals and groups who did not fit the consumer norm were further marginalized. Advertising became the primary way through which Americans gained a sense of identity, and it was a source that offered only the most rigid, categorical definitions. New York, as the center of commerce, was for Baldwin the dwelling place of people lost to identities that were at once narrow and vacuous:

> It was a city without oases, run entirely, insofar, at least, as human perception could tell, for money; and its citizens seemed to have lost entirely any sense of their right to renew themselves. Whoever, in New York, attempted to cling to this right, lived in New York in exile—in exile from the life around him; and this, paradoxically, had the effect of placing him in perpetual danger of being forever banished from any real sense of himself. (316)

Beyond establishing Baldwin's perspective on the connection between capitalism and identity, this passage reveals Baldwin's sense of exile: it is both a state of mind and a physical experience. The reality of not "fitting in" at home allows for a certain naturalness about living in a different country. And further, the psychological sense of exile, the disconnectedness from one's home, loses its crisis nature when one is truly disconnected. Baldwin was able to contemplate and write about what it means to be an exile when he actually was one in Paris and was distanced from the cultural forces that created the "condition" in the first place. In his writing, Baldwin prescribes a visit to "another country"—the experience of exile—as an almost necessary way of coming to terms with an exclusive culture.

The postwar period also saw the ascendancy of popular culture and the advent of sexual liberalism. Movies and music, for example, became eroticized in new and blatant ways; but this phenomenon was closely linked to the consumer culture (sexy products bought by sexy people) and was held in check by the new sexual liberalism that "celebrated the erotic, but tried to keep it within a heterosexual framework of long-term, monogamous relationships." Again, both blacks and gays were marginalized:

> As sexual liberalism took hold among the white middle class, it raised new issues for the maintenance of sexual order. . . . But as black urban communities grew, the black family and black sexual mores appeared as a convenient counterpoint, identifying the line between what was permissible and what was not.[17]

Gays, meanwhile, because of their marginalization, "were freed from the social controls placed on heterosexuals,"[18] but as Baldwin points out, their sex, despite its apparently greater freedom, was not without its stigmatization. And most important to Baldwin, for both the mainstream and the marginalized, the very existence of identity categories in the culture ruins the prospect of mature, healthy sexual relationships. As someone who might be described as "categorically enhanced," Baldwin, the black, gay man, had a particularly vivid awareness of this cultural problem, which led to his expatriation and which is both the inspiration for and subject of his writing.

Two other components of postwar culture fed the development of rigid identity categories in the postwar period: existentialism and psychoanalysis. Questions about "the self," "identity," and "alienation," as raised by philosophical existentialism, were pervasive throughout intellectual and popular discourse in the 1940s and 1950s.[19] Also, psychoanalysis became part of middle-class, mainstream experience.[20] Baldwin's own writing throughout this period employs the language of these schools of thought. Twentieth-century culture—consumerism, war, genocide, technology, nationalism, colonialism, postcolonialism, nuclear weapons—created a profound disjunction between consciousness and meaning. It is not surprising, then, that existentialism and psychoanalysis flourished in the postwar period, and that intellectuals and artists became highly interested in "questions of identity."[21] But the same culture that gave birth to these questions also offered ready answers: rigid identity categories. While these categories served (and still serve) an important political function—the attainment of social and economic equality for those from whom it has been withheld—they are also, for Baldwin, fatally limited and lead only to a more permanent disjunction between individual fulfillment and cultural experience.

Another Country contains three characters who are, to varying degrees, manifestations of Baldwin himself. Rufus represents Baldwin before his departure for Paris. He feels as though he is in exile from the world around him, but he never actually leaves. He simply wanders around in it, a lost soul perpetually being punished by the cultural forces that precipitated his "homelessness." After his death, he remains in the novel suggesting to the other characters how they, too, are disconnected from their worlds and what they might do to overcome this condition. Eric is the Baldwin who went to live in France.

He is disconnected too, but it is a distance from his "previous condi-tion" of exile at home, fostered by his sexual orientation. His actual exile experience allows him, even after he physically returns to New York, to function as a symbolic interloper, alerting the other charac-ters—as the memory of Rufus does—to the devastating hazards of their rigid, identity-based culture. Vivaldo is Baldwin the writer. His exile experience (in the state-of-mind sense) is attached to his ability or inability to write—to "approach the mystery through forms." His struggles with writing are equated with his struggle to connect with his world—a connection painted by Baldwin mostly in terms of Vi-valdo's sex life. In the end, it is not so much a connection he achieves as an understanding.

When he lived in the Village, Baldwin spent a great deal of time both working and socializing in bars. It is not surprising, then, that a great deal of *Another Country* takes place in bars, and that Baldwin portrays them as galleries displaying the "lamentable" sexual culture he bemoaned. The characters' favorite hangout is Benno's:

> The bar was terribly crowded. Advertising men were there, drinking double shots of bourbon or vodka, on the rocks; college boys were there, their wet fingers slippery on the beer bottles; lone men stood near the doors or in corners, watching the drifting women. The college boys, gleaming with ignorance and mad with chastity, made terrified efforts to attract the feminine attention, but succeeded only in attract-ing each other. Some of the men were buying drinks for some of the women—who wandered incessantly from the juke box to the bar—and they faced each other over smiles which were pitched, with an eerie precision, between longing and contempt. Black-and-white couples were together here—closer together now than they would be later, when they got home. These several histories were camouflaged in the jargon which, wave upon wave, rolled through the bar; were locked in a silence like the silence of glaciers. Only the juke box spoke, grinding out each evening, all evening long, syncopated, synthetic laments for love. (73)

In this passage, Baldwin virtually lists the components of his con-flict with New York's sexual culture—all the categories of gender, race, and sexual orientation and the resulting disconnectedness among the people there. The patrons at Benno's want love, but they can't find it because their "histories" are "camouflaged in jargon," and they are separated by the categories that did not include Baldwin when he was in New York. The jukebox, which suggests the possibility of love through its music, is like the sex the New Yorkers are used to—"grinding," "syncopated," and "synthetic," and ultimately noncommunicative. This scene in Benno's is a culturally specific articulation of the "exiled" nature of Baldwin's New York social scene. The characters are distanced from one another and are oblivious to their condition.

During his last night, Rufus goes into the bathroom at Benno's and witnesses the nature and extent of the communication that Baldwin sees in his New York:

> It smelled of thousands of travelers, oceans of piss, tons of bile and vomit and shit. He added his stream to the ocean, holding that most despised part of himself loosely between two fingers of one hand. *But I've got to stay there so long.* . . . He looked at the horrible history splashed furiously on the walls—telephone numbers, cocks, breasts, balls, cunts, etched into these walls with hatred. *Suck my cock. I like to get whipped. I want a hot stiff prick up my ass. Down with Jews. Kill the niggers. I suck cocks.* (83)

This violent, despairing scene is, for Baldwin, the direct result of New Yorkers' inability to apprehend the humanity of others. Rufus is the most victimized by this short-sightedness—he dies early in the novel. But his presence remains throughout the novel, reminding and offering hints to the other characters about the cost of socially constructed identity categories. The others struggle, with varying degrees of success, to overcome this destructive cultural milieu. Further, their efforts in this regard are closely tied by Baldwin to their creative, expressive efforts, just as the two were linked for him in his life. In other words, the challenge for them of relating and loving on a human level is directly tied to their ability to get passed the "jargon" and fully express their own "secrets" and apprehend those of another. "Another country" is both the other person, who is distant and hidden by a sexual culture falsely defined by rigid categories, and a place where those categories no longer exist. The scribblers on the bathroom wall at Benno's are trapped in the noncommunicative language of their sexual culture.

As stated above, Rufus Scott is the character most damaged by his city and its sexual culture. He is also the incarnation of a James Baldwin who never left New York. This time he is a jazz musician, but he is still trapped in the racial void between uptown and downtown New York, perilously negotiating the gap on the "A" train. At one point Rufus is at a loss as to how to "move beyond the emptiness and horror," and Vivaldo suggests, "Maybe it would be a good idea for you to make a change of scene, Rufus" (49)—in other words, transcend the feeling of being an exile in your own country by actually going into exile. But Rufus never does because "he ain't got no place to go," and eventually he kills himself.

Before he does, though, he apprehends the "imprisoned" masses of New Yorkers trapped in the "A" train void. He fantasizes that the tunnel fills with water, but a "motorman gone mad" (God?) drives the train blindly forward anyway. The crazed passengers turn on one another,

> everything gone out of them but murder, breaking limb from limb and splashing in blood, with joy—for the first time, joy, joy, after such a long sentence in chains, leaping out to astound the world, to astound the world again. (85)

The passengers are freed by their violent outburst, and they leap "out to astound the world." These lines echo Baldwin's assertion that if he had remained in America, he would have killed someone or been killed. But this is just a fantasy that Rufus has while waiting for the train. Eventually, the real train arrives:

> They all got on, sitting in the lighted car which was far from empty, which would be choked with people before they got very far uptown, and stood or sat in the isolation cell into which they transformed every inch of space they held. (85)

The train is moving from downtown (white) to uptown (black), but the passengers are not able to bridge this division because they exist in "isolation cells." Rufus stays on the train, past Thirty-fourth Street, which is described as "his stop." At the beginning of the novel—which is also the beginning of Rufus's last night—Rufus is in midtown, allowing a white man who wants to have sex with him to buy him a meal. The linking of Rufus with midtown is meant to position him in a void space, not only physically between Harlem and the Village but between the race, gender, and sexuality categories. The subway train takes him under and past this place and is the conveyance taking Rufus to his death. The figurative expression of racial division and its attending interpersonal alienation, the train, is also the literal means by which Rufus travels to the George Washington Bridge so that he can jump off. Baldwin escaped this fate by going to Paris—where he came to understand why this might be someone's fate—and thereby was able to express it in this novel.

The subway ride is also used to symbolize the relationship between New York's racial divide and its sexual culture:

> Many white people and many black people, chained together in time and in space, and by history, and all of them in a hurry. In a hurry to get away from each other, he thought, but we ain't never going to make it. We been fucked for fair. . . . The train, as though protesting its heavier burden, as though protesting the proximity of white buttock to black knee, groaned, lurched, the wheels seemed to scrape the track, making a tearing sound. . . . The train rushed into the blackness with a phallic abandon, into the blackness which opened to receive it, opened, opened, the world shook with their coupling. . . . The train gasped and moaned to a halt. (86)

Rufus, as the manifestation of Baldwin's view of the most extreme result of New York's troubled culture, views that culture in sexual terms. He also experiences New York that way. The specific narrative events that lead Rufus to his state of utter despair are his sexual relationships, primarily the one with Leona. The difficult terms of their sexual relationship are racial, and therefore, for Baldwin, the relationship is doomed. Rufus expresses his anger toward whites through his maltreatment of Leona; she embodies the stereotypical white liberal sentiment of "being nice" to the black person. In their relationship, Rufus and Leona perceive only their racial selves—they are imprisoned in them. They cannot overcome the wall of racial discourse of which they are products, and therefore they end up as they do—Rufus dead and Leona committed.

When Rufus and Leona first have sex, Rufus is violently reacting to racist history and not exactly "making love": "And, shortly, nothing could have stopped him, not the white God himself nor a lynch mob arriving on wings. Under his breath he cursed the milk-white bitch and groaned and rode his weapon between her thighs." He "felt the venom shoot out of him, enough for a hundred black-white babies" (22). Leona, in contrast, once their relationship is underway, treats Rufus with the surface pity and charity that is akin to the stereotypical way in which white liberals are viewed as treating blacks. In any event, neither character is able to get past the most superficial sense of the other's identity, and the situation is compounded by the fact that the people in Baldwin's Village see them that way too. Baldwin ironically describes the Village as "the place of liberation" in a scene where Rufus and Leona are passed by a white couple. The man gives them a "nearly sheepish glance" as they pass; "the face of his wife, however, simply closed tight like a gate" (28). Later they are passed by an Italian boy, who looks at Rufus with hatred because he is with Leona (31). Rufus and Leona are doomed because they see each other as the world sees them. They are the starkest example of how New York's sexual culture was problematic for Baldwin because of its categorical nature.

Rufus's now-finished affair with Eric further adds to his reactive stance toward sexual orientation as a category of identity. Unlike the other characters—Vivaldo and Cass—who manage to involve themselves with Eric in an almost symbolic way, Rufus views that experience as a threat to his self-definition, which is not a self-definition at all because of its cultural source. His view is further compounded by his having had to prostitute himself with men in order to survive, and because white men desire him more because he is black. At one point Rufus is talking with Vivaldo:

> "Have you ever wished you were queer?" Rufus asked, suddenly.
> Vivaldo smiled, looking into his glass. "I used to think maybe I was. Hell, I think I even *wished* I was." He laughed. "But I'm not. So I'm stuck."
> Rufus walked to Vivaldo's window. "So you been all up and down that street, too," he said.
> "We've all been up the same streets. There aren't a hell of a lot of streets. Only we've been taught to lie so much, about so many things, that we hardly ever know *where* we are." (52)

Rufus is looking to Vivaldo for a compatriot in sexual confusion. Though Vivaldo seems secure in his "heterosexuality" (he later transcends that category), they are both stuck in confusion. It is a world without "a hell of a lot of streets"—with only a few, fixed identity categories—and they don't know where they are. Vivaldo spends the rest of the novel trying to find out, and Rufus kills himself, although he remains with Vivaldo and the others throughout the rest of the novel as they grapple with the sexual culture that destroyed him.

As a struggling writer, Vivaldo is also an incarnation of Baldwin, particularly since his writing difficulties are linked to his relationship to New York's sexual culture. At one point Vivaldo is talking to Rufus and his typewriter at the same time: "'A lot of things hurt you that I can't really understand.' He played with the keys of his typewriter. 'A lot of things hurt me that I can't really understand'" (50). It is only through writing that Vivaldo is able to mitigate the sense of exile that kills Rufus.

The story of Vivaldo's writer's block parallels his relationship with Ida. When Vivaldo can't write, he raves that he just doesn't "know" his characters. After making love with Ida for the first time, he studies her face in bed:

> Her face would now be, forever, more mysterious and impenetrable than the face of any stranger. Strangers' faces hold no secrets because the imagination does not invest them with any. But the face of a lover is an unknown precisely because it is invested with so much of oneself. It is a mystery, containing, like all mysteries, the possibility of torment. (172)

Baldwin links self-knowledge with knowledge of another by way of the experience of love. The inability to understand oneself becomes an inability to love, and for Vivaldo (and a pre-Paris Baldwin), an inability to create.

Toward the end of the novel, after Vivaldo and Ida's climactic, revelatory exchange, Ida strokes his back and Vivaldo cries because "she was stroking his innocence out of him." Then, "by and by, he was still. He rose, and went to the bathroom and washed his face, and then sat down at his work table" (431). Vivaldo and Ida, through the infliction of great pain and suffering on each other, achieve a degree of knowledge of themselves and each other (they overcome the culture's categories), and their love survives. But further, Vivaldo is able to write. Baldwin overcame the same culture by leaving it and then by writing about it in *Another Country*.

Like Baldwin, Vivaldo feels "homeless" in New York until he experiences mature love and is able to write:

> He felt totally estranged from the city in which he had been born; this city for which he sometimes felt a kind of stony affection because it was all he knew of home. Yet he had no home here—the hovel on Bank Street was not a home. He had always supposed that he would, one

day, make a home here for himself. Now he began to wonder if anyone could ever put down roots in this rock; or, rather, he began to be aware of the shapes acquired by those who had. He began to wonder about his own shape. (60)

Vivaldo's condition of not fitting in is established clearly in the novel as the direct result of his sexuality. His failure to overcome identity categories in his love life leaves him lonely and unable to write. Apart from an affair with a burned-out, drunken artist, Jane, Vivaldo's sexual experiences are limited to black prostitutes in Harlem. Rufus tells Vivaldo that "everybody's on the A train," and for Vivaldo this refers to his taking the subway to Harlem for sexual adventure and, symbolically, to his resulting "isolation cell" abode. Cass also assesses Vivaldo's pre-Ida sex life: "Only, I've told you, you always seem to get involved with impossible women—whores, nymphomaniacs, drunks—and I think you do it in order to protect yourself—from anything serious. Permanent" (96). Additionally, as a young man Vivaldo, with his friends, picked up a gay man in the Village, forced him to perform oral sex, and then beat him (112).

Before his relationship with Ida women are merely sex objects for Vivaldo (except Cass, who Vivaldo does not realize is a "woman" until later in the novel), black women are "inexpensive sex objects," and gay men are objects of mockery and disdain as well as sex. As the novel progresses and Vivaldo becomes more aware, he ponders his sexual past:

> Yes, he had been there: chafing and pushing and pounding, trying to awaken a frozen girl. The battle was awful because the girl wished to be awakened but was terrified of the unknown. Every moment that seemed to bring her closer to him, to bring them closer together, had its violent recoil, driving them farther apart. Both clung to a fantasy rather than to each other, tried to suck pleasure from the crannies of the mind, rather than surrender the secrets of the body. The tendrils of shame clutched at them, however they turned, all the dirty words they knew commented on all they did. These words sometimes brought on the climax—joylessly, with loathing, and too soon. The best that he had ever managed in bed, so far, had been the maximum of relief with the minimum of hostility. (132)

Vivaldo and his lovers are in a state of exile from each other. There is a distance between them because of their failure to see each other as human, and Baldwin describes their communication as limited to "dirty words" (like Rufus in the bathroom), which only serve to achieve physical relief and "loathing." Again, sexuality and language are linked, in the sense of language's role in enabling people to truly know each other and in the sense of creative writing—Vivaldo and Baldwin's craft. Writing is also the vehicle, then, for overcoming the state of exile that can manifest itself between two people in the same bed.

In the end, Ida confesses her affair to Vivaldo and also realizes how society's racial and sexual configurations have damaged her and prevented her from loving:

> There was only one thing for me to do, as Rufus used to say, and that was to hit the A train. So I hit it. Nothing was clear in my mind at first. I used to see the way white men watched me, like dogs. And I thought about what I could do to them. How I hated them, the way they looked, and the things they'd say, all dressed up in their damn white skin, and their clothes just so, and their little weak, white pricks jumping in their drawers. You could do any damn thing with them if you just led them along, because they wanted to do something dirty and they knew that you knew how. All black people knew that. Only, the polite ones didn't say dirty. They said real. I used to wonder what in the world they did in bed, white people I mean, between themselves, to get them so sick. Because they *are* sick, and I'm telling something that I know. (419)

While Ida is perhaps insightful in understanding this incarnation of the white male, as she admits in the end, that was *all* she could see in them at one point. Her "hitting of the A train" is, as it was for Rufus and Vivaldo, just another attempt to negotiate the distance between black and white through sex. She is unable to love Vivaldo freely because she is still trapped in the above-expressed way of "seeing" (or not seeing), as evidenced by her relationship with Ellis.

It is only after she rejects the role she is playing with Ellis, by expressing it to Vivaldo, that Ida comes to understand herself and is able truly to love Vivaldo. Her confession also raises Vivaldo to a new level of understanding:

> He stared into his cup, noting that black coffee was not black, but deep brown. Not many things in the world were really black, not even the night, not even the mines. And the light was not white, either, even the palest light held within itself some hint of its origins, in fire. He

thought to himself that he had at last got what he wanted, the truth out of Ida, or the true Ida; and he did not know how he was going to live with it. (431)

Baldwin describes them as "two weary children" and writes that Ida had "stroked the innocence" out of Vivaldo. Their relationship achieves a new level of maturity and reality—expressed figuratively by Baldwin through the reality of coffee cups, cigarettes, sugar, and milk—and Vivaldo is finally able to write: "Smoke poured from his nostrils and a detail that he needed for his novel, which he had been searching for for months, fell, neatly and vividly, like the tumblers of a lock, into place in his mind" (427). An important component of Baldwin's experience in Paris, as well as of the narrator's of Baldwin's short story "This Morning, This Evening, So Soon," in *Going to Meet the Man*, was the experience of love. This aspect of Baldwin's expatriation is connected to his writing through Vivaldo's character. He finally becomes a writer when he is able to participate in a mature relationship.

In the simple sense that he sleeps with almost all the other characters in the novel, Eric is a significant character. But beyond giving him a special narrative place, Eric's ranging sexual role operates in *Another Country* in a way that defines him differently from the other characters. He is an *actor*, and as such, his behavior in the novel is symbolic, interpretive, and cathartic. His defining moment occurs when the others accompany him to a screening of a film he appeared in while in France:

> Yet, the director had so placed him that his drunken somnolence held the scene together, and emphasized the futility of the passionate talkers. . . . He seemed to be made of rubber, and seemed, indeed, to be fleeing from the controversy which raged around him—in which, nevertheless, he was fatally involved. . . . It was very strange—to see more of Eric when he was acting than when he was being, as the saying goes, himself. . . . And the director had surely placed Eric where he had because this face operated, in effect, as a footnote to the twentieth century torment. . . . It was the face of a man, of a tormented man. Yet, in precisely the way that great music depends, ultimately, on great silence, this masculinity was defined, and made powerful, by something which was not masculine. But it was not feminine, either, and something in Vivaldo resisted the word *androgynous*. It was a quality to which great numbers of people would respond without knowing to what it was

they were responding. There was great force in the face, and great gentleness. But, as most women are not gentle, nor most men strong, it was a face which suggested, resonantly, in the depths, the truth about our natures. (330)

Eric's filmic representation is an explanation of his role in the novel. The "director" is also the writer—Baldwin. The scene describes Eric's strategic role, his position with regard to the other characters— he "holds the scene together" and thereby "emphasizes the futility of the passionate talkers"—and also offers an explanation of the meaning of Eric's character in the novel. Eric's face defies categorical placement. He is not even "androgynous"; that would only be another limited identity. Further, this description of Eric is termed, by Baldwin, as a "footnote to the twentieth century torment." In other words, Baldwin is stating that the nature of his conflict with New York's sexual culture is not widely or commonly thought of as the primary problem with the twentieth century. (Why would it be, given this century's overt cataclysms?) Still, Baldwin believes it is paramount—his humanism locates the source of societal ills within individual hearts, and Eric, as the "unidentified," noncategorical character, offers the other characters a suggestion of a different way to live and love, in much the same way as a film or a play or, indeed, a book might.

Eric is not a victim of a culture based on identity categories as the other characters are, at least not in the novel's present tense. (He was while a boy in the South and while in New York, before he left for France.) He has lived in another country, both literally and symbolically, and he offers that experience to the other characters. Eric has, in a sense, gone through Baldwin's exile cycle: a sense of homelessness at home; actual physical exile and a corresponding love experience; and a return to home with a detached awareness and maturity about the culture that caused the trouble in the first place. Eric tells Ida that he "grew up" in Paris (266). His relationship with Yves is idyllic and free of the lack-of-understanding problems that plague the other relationships. Eric equates Yves with home. And just as Baldwin did, Eric has found love in exile and understands America better as a result (184). Eric's relationship with Yves is cast in symbolic and religious terms: "This sex [Yves's penis] dominated the long landscape of his [Eric's] life as the cathedral towers dominated the plains" (223). The nature of the love that Eric has with Yves is redemptive. Baldwin is not suggesting that love between two men is the highest form (cf. Plato) but rather that because Eric and Yves are free of race, gender, and sexual orientation constraints (there is no point of conflict between them—they are the same in each category), they are able to transcend these culturally based categories.

Eric's role in the novel and his relationship to Baldwin are revealed in the books on his coffee table in his home in the south of France: *An Actor Prepares, The Wings of the Dove,* and *Native Son.* Eric is preparing for his role "as an actor" when he returns to New York. Baldwin was a devoted Jamesian and considered himself the successor to Richard Wright.[22] Back in New York, Eric's most significant actions are having sex with Cass and Vivaldo. The consequences of these affairs vary. As stated earlier, the affair with Cass has the effect, on the practical level, of ending her marriage with Richard, and psychologically, it liberates Cass from the identity constraints of her marriage. Cass tells Richard that the reason she went to Eric is that he has a "sense of himself" (374).

Interestingly, Eric's affair with Vivaldo seems to operate on an exclusively symbolic level. It is foreshadowed (badly, I believe) when Vivaldo recalls a blues song, on the night Ida is out with Ellis, that ends with the lines "'Cause the sun's going to shine / In my back door someday," and he wonders, "Why *back* door?" (313). Later that night, when Vivaldo rejects Harold's advances on a rooftop, he is still symbolically defining himself categorically and denying that part of him which could find sexual pleasure with a man. In other words, he is not there yet (fully human), and it will take the affair with Eric to achieve that. Vivaldo's lovemaking with Eric begins in a dream state, suggesting the affair's symbolic status. But much more significant, Eric and Vivaldo's affair can *only* be read as a symbolic event. Otherwise the novel does not cohere. Why, for example, is it incumbent on Ida to confess her affair with Ellis, while Vivaldo does not have to come clean about what he was doing the night before? Baldwin asserts throughout the novel that people have to reveal their secrets, share their stories with others, to overcome stereotypes and have mature relationships. Should not Vivaldo then have to confess to Ida? *Another Country's* realism does not seem able to accommodate that degree of honesty. (One can imagine Ida's response after Vivaldo tells her he had sex with Eric: "Excuse me? You did what with whom?") In the end, then, the affair can only be seen as a metaphorical rendering of Vivaldo's transcendence beyond a categorical approach to identity. Ida has helped him past the race hurdle, and knowing Eric (literally or not) helps him past gender and sexual orientation. He is then "positioned" for a fully human relationship with Ida.

Still, there is another interpretation for Vivaldo's lack of complete honesty in the end. He is *the writer* and, as such, must sustain a degree of exiled status, of distance from those around him. It makes sense that he should know the truth about Ida. She is one of his characters, in the sense that they are all Baldwin's characters. But Vivaldo is allowed the secret dalliance with Eric, the character who has completed the "exile cycle," because keeping that secret positions him in the same place as a Baldwin who was able to understand just what his conflict was with New York's sexual culture by moving abroad. While, according to Baldwin, the separation—the state of exile—that exists between New Yorkers and ruins their capacity for loving sex must be overcome, for the writer this state of exile, which has the same ruinous effect on him, leads perhaps to actual physical exile but, more significantly, to the kind of exile that is the artist's detached stance.

Baldwin urges his New Yorkers forward to "another country" where they have relationships free of the identity categories that created the sexual culture he lamented. And further, by going to Paris, Baldwin reached that "other country," and "another" one, too—the position from which he was able to write as he did about his New York.

NOTES

1. James Baldwin, "Here Be Dragons," in *The Price of the Ticket: Collected Nonfiction, 1948–1985* (New York: St. Martin's/Marek, 1985), 678.

2. Ibid., 685.

3. Cited in W. J. Weatherby, *James Baldwin: Artist on Fire* (New York: Donald I. Fine, 1989), 62.

4. This is not to discount the necessity of group formation along identity lines for political and economic purposes and the important gains such groups have made. Baldwin recognized that need (e.g., the Civil Rights movement) but regretted that his culture required that kind of alignment, because of its cost in human terms. His literary agenda throughout his work, and its political orientation, is humanism. He seeks to illuminate the

universal by showing how historical, social, and cultural formations have muted and distorted the commonality of human experience.

5. I do not believe, as some writers have suggested, that Baldwin's views are so historically rooted as to be anachronistic. While there is no question that Baldwin was very much a part of postwar liberal ideology, as is evidenced by his place in the integrationist-nationalist debate within the African American community, his ideas resonate strongly today, when one considers that politics have grown more divided along lines of identity and that maybe his ideas were too early. In other words, given his own blind spots (women, women's sexuality), a rereading of Baldwin that includes the effect of *all* identity categories and a historical awareness that positions him near the end of this type of approach to sexuality may help us understand what postsexuality might be like.

6. James Baldwin, "The Art of Fiction LXXVIII," *Paris Review* (Spring 1984): 51.

7. James Baldwin, "The New Lost Generation," *Esquire*, July 1961, 113.

8. James Campbell, *Talking at the Gates: A Life of James Baldwin* (New York: Penguin, 1991), 49.

9. James Baldwin, "Everybody's Protest Novel," in *Price*, 32.

10. James Baldwin, *Another Country* (New York: Dial, 1962), 302. Subsequent citations from this work will be in text.

11. See Robert J. Corber, *Homosexuality in Cold War America: Resistance and the Crisis of Masculinity (New Americanists)* (Durham: Duke University Press, 1997), for a discussion of gay culture in the postwar era and its effect on Baldwin.

12. John D'Emilio and Estelle B. Freedman, *Intimate Matters: A History of Sexuality in America* (New York: Harper & Row, 1988), 86.

13. Baldwin, particularly in *Another Country*, does not address gender in the same way as he does race and sexual orientation. He seems less concerned with the strictures of gender categories than he does with others. While he is interested in both the social and the symbolic implications of men having sex with each other, he does not include lesbian sex, and the problems his female characters face seem mostly due to their race, rather than to the culture's categorization of women. (Though Cass is affected by Richard's chauvinism, Baldwin allows her only a very limited understanding of this through her apprehension of an African American couple in a club in Harlem and her affair with a gay man, Eric.)

14. D'Emilio and Freedman, *Intimate Matters*, 295.

15. Ibid., 289, 292, 294.

16. Baldwin, "Dragons," 683.

17. D'Emilio and Freeman, *Intimate Matters*, 300, 298.

18. Steven Seidman, *Romantic Longings: Love in America, 1830–1980* (New York: Routledge, 1991), 158.

19. See Anatole Broyard's *Kafka Was the Rage: A Greenwich Village Memoir* (New York: Vintage, 1993) for an interesting personal account of Village life in the immediate postwar era, which includes discussions of popular existentialism, psychoanalysis, and abstract art.

20. The film *Rebel without a Cause* (1955) is an example, among many others, of the role of psychological discourse in middle-class life and popular culture.

21. Among the many discussions of this, and one that relates particularly well to this discussion of Baldwin because of its confluence of race and sex, is Frantz Fanon's *Black Skin, White Masks* (London: Pluto, 1986).

22. Indeed, Baldwin's writing in *Another Country* and in other works is something of a blend of James's humanism and psychological realism with Wright's social realism and naturalism—Bigger Thomas in the drawing room.

Part III

Baldwin and the Transatlantic

Chapter 7

Baldwin's Cosmopolitan Loneliness

James Darsey

The spiritual haughtiness and nausea of every man
who has suffered profoundly—it almost determines
the order of rank *how* profoundly human beings can
suffer—his shuddering certainty, which permeates
and colors him through and through, that by virtue
of his suffering he *knows more* than the cleverest and
wisest could possibly know, and that he knows his
way and has once been "at home" in many distant,
terrifying worlds of which "*you* know nothing"—this
spiritual and silent haughtiness of the sufferer, this
pride of the elect of knowledge, of the "initiated," of
the almost sacrificed, finds all kinds of disguises necessary to protect itself against contact with obtrusive
and pitying hands and altogether against everything
that is not equal in suffering. Profound suffering
makes noble; it separates.
                —Friedrich Nietzsche, *Beyond Good and Evil*

The term *cosmopolitanism* intimates knowledge of Paris in the spring-
time, facility with chopsticks, appreciation of Ashanti rituals and
Mahler's Fourth Symphony, confidence when ordering shrimp with
achiote, and skill at ballroom dancing; grace in every situation. But as
Nietzsche—self-described free spirit, having been "at home, or at
least having been guests, in many countries of the spirit"[1]—understood, cosmopolitanism is also a kind of exile. To be everywhere is to
be nowhere; to be above it all is to be groundless, recognizing the

fragility and relativity of all laws and mores. As Pico Iyer, member of "a transcontinental tribe of wanderers," "transit lounger"[2] par excellence, describes it:

> For us in the transit lounge, disorientation is as alien as affiliation. We become professional observers, able to see the merits and deficiencies of anywhere, to balance our parents' viewpoints with their enemies' position. Yes, we say, of course it's terrible, but look at the situation from Saddam's point of view. I understand how you feel, but the Chinese had their own cultural reasons for Tiananmen Square. Fervor comes to seem to us the most foreign place of all.[3]

The loneliness entailed in cosmopolitanism has kinship with the loneliness of oppression. In Iyer's description of the emotional numbness and alienation of the contemporary citizen of the world, I hear the voice of the slave:

> But there are some of us, perhaps, sitting at the departure gate, boarding passes in hand, who feel neither the pain of separation nor the exultation of wonder; who alight with the same emotions with which we embarked; who go down to the baggage carousel and watch our lives circling, circling, circling, waiting to be claimed.[4]

Indeed, the cycle is such that cause and consequence become the same: escape from provincial oppression compounding the difference that originally encouraged the exile.

If cosmopolitanism can be oppressive, oppression can be perversely liberating. Oppression makes of certain conditions—gender, race, sexual orientation—incorrigible outlaws, who may as well do as they please (and who are expected to) since their fate is sealed; they will be oppressed for what they are, regardless of what they do. In other cases, oppression provides the oppressed the motive for transcendence, what Nietzsche calls ennoblement, the seeking an alternative standard—black pride and gay pride, for example—but this liberation is not without costs, and as long as the dominant culture has the power of legitimate definition, it is never complete.

James Baldwin lived his life in this borderland—this not-quite-anyplace, this on-the-way-to-somewhere, this geopsychical warp where oppression and liberation overlap—the figmental world of "escape," with its dual freight of necessity and opportunity. If Iyer is a transit lounger, Baldwin was a "transatlantic commuter."[5] It only seems that Baldwin, in emigrating to Paris, escaped to freedom, the life of the international literary figure and bon vivant. "What's most difficult is that you are penalized for trying to remain in touch with yourself," he warns against the seductive illusion.[6] Though Baldwin emphatically declared in "Everybody's Protest Novel," an essay most famous for marking Baldwin's break with Richard Wright, that "literature and sociology are not one and the same,"[7] he went on to provide, in that same essay, one of the most incisive analyses of the nature of oppression on record, an analysis so nuanced and sensitive that the reader is led to believe that the failed identity of literature and sociology is rooted in the poverty of the latter:

> It must be remembered that the oppressed and the oppressor are bound together within the same society; they accept the same criteria, they share the same beliefs, they both alike depend on the same reality. Within this cage it is romantic, more, meaningless, to speak of a "new" society as the desire of the oppressed, for that shivering dependence on the props of reality which he shares with the *Herrenvolk* makes a truly "new" society impossible to conceive.[8]

Baldwin recognizes the falseness in the promise of Nietzschean freedom. Perhaps he is, from Nietzsche's perspective, simply not strong enough to disregard society entirely. In "this impossibility," this shared "cage," Baldwin recognizes Kenneth Burke's grand dialectic, whereby the moment that God fashions order out of chaos, a relationship is established that contains not just the possibility of the negative but its necessity; the fall from grace is contained "in the beginning. . . . " So it is that the cycle is established from order to disobedience to guilt to victimage to redemption in a new order. Logically, thesis and antithesis, Christ and Antichrist, are coeval and symbiotic.[9] In the dominate white American version of this dialectic lie the roots of self-oppression, including "the heritage of the Negro in America":

> *Wash me*, cried the slave to his Maker, *and I shall be whiter, whiter than snow!* For black is the color of evil; only the robes of the saved are white. It is this cry, implacable on the air and in the skull, that he must live with. Beneath the widely published catalogue of brutality—bringing to mind, somehow, an image, a memory of church-bells burdening the air—is this reality which, in the same nightmare notion, he both flees and rushes to embrace.[10]

The simultaneous urge to flee and to embrace captures Baldwin's psychotic equilibrium, always tensed, unable to find places of rest, ever indecisive. There is no quiet refuge, even in the self; for as Baldwin recognizes, even the self has been invaded, sabotaged, by the prevailing ideology. The measure of true oppression lies in this estrangement: "And the extraordinary complex of tensions thus set up in the breast, between hatred of whites and contempt for blacks, is very hard to describe," Baldwin writes. "Some of the most energetic people of my generation were destroyed by this interior warfare."[11]

As a black man in a white culture, Baldwin was estranged: "You can only be destroyed by believing that you really are what the white world calls a *nigger*," he notes.[12] As a black man and a homosexual, Baldwin was doubly burdened, doubly estranged; as a poor black homosexual, triply estranged; and as a poor black homosexual who never knew his biological father or, until well into his adulthood, his broader paternity in the American South, estranged once again.[13] To this list Kenneth Kinnamon adds Baldwin's vocation and suggests that the combination provided a volatile mix:

> As a black man, he could not identify with a white racist society. As an artist-intellectual, he thought that he could not identify with black people. This double estrangement, together with the hectic pace of working by day and writing by night and his troubling questions of sexuality, intensified his nervous condition to an intolerable degree.[14]

And estrangement has the remarkable capacity to reproduce and compound itself through withdrawal, as Baldwin was to demonstrate in a life punctuated by emigrations. In the first of these, Baldwin symbolically quit the ghetto by refusing the fate inscribed for him there and giving himself over to God:

> What I saw around me that summer in Harlem was what I had always seen; nothing had changed. But now, without any warning, the whores and pimps and racketeers on the Avenue had become a personal menace. It had not before occurred to me that I could become one of them, but now I realized that we had been produced by the same circumstances. Many of my comrades were clearly headed for the Avenue, and my father said that I was headed that way too.[15]

The sense of determinism adumbrated in the phrases "nothing had changed" and "we had been produced by the same circumstances" is corroborated and amplified elsewhere in this letter: "One did not have to be very bright to realize how little one could do to change one's situation";[16] "One would never defeat one's circumstances by working and saving one's pennies."[17]

Baldwin's response to this "religious crisis" is generally consistent with his analysis of the conditions in which he finds himself; it is, significantly, a strategy not of outward resistance but of passivity, though the question of underlying deliberation is left unresolved. About a conversion that sounds strikingly like a nervous breakdown Baldwin first confesses that, in retrospect, "everything I did seems curiously deliberate, though it certainly did not seem deliberate then."[18] He notes that "every Negro boy—in my situation during those years, at least"—needed "a gimmick to lift him out, to start him on his way."[19] He later refers to his short career as boy evangelist as part of "the church racket."[20] But about the moment of conversion itself Baldwin maintains complete innocence:

> I fell to the ground before the altar. It was the strangest sensation I have ever had in my life—up to that time, or since. I had not known that it was going to happen, or that it could happen. One moment I was on my feet, singing and clapping and, at the same time, working out in my head the plot of a play I was working on then; the next moment, with no transition, no sensation of falling, I was on my back, with the lights beating down into my face and all the vertical saints above me. I did not know what I was doing down so low, or how I had got there. And the anguish that filled me cannot be described. It moved in me like one of those floods that devastate counties, tearing everything down, tearing children from their parents and lovers from each other, and making everything an unrecognizable waste.[21]

The metaphor of the flood tearing child from parent is revealing. The event described here laid the foundation for Baldwin to leave his father, paradoxically by usurping the father's place,[22] and then, having vanquished the father, to leave the father's house. The pattern is repeated throughout Baldwin's life: in his periodic departures from the United States; in his break with Richard Wright, his artistic father (again, a competition); in the nervous breakdown for which he removed himself to Switzerland to recuperate; and in the scores of romantic relationships about which so little is known except that they were not lasting.

Baldwin's problem is fundamentally one of place, *topos*, and it manifests itself in his writing as a problem of *topoi* and as a problem of *ethos*. On the one hand, Baldwin is irremediably American. "The Negro," he writes "has been formed by this nation, for better or for worse, and does not belong to any other—not to Africa, and certainly not to Islam."[23] America is always "my country," the common legacy of black and white. "For this is your home, my friend," Baldwin writes to his nephew James, "do not be driven from it; great men have done great things here, and will again, and we can make America what America must become."[24] On the other hand, Baldwin cannot allow himself to be restricted to the stunted place that America has allowed him; he cannot "go back to my people where I belong and find me a nice, black nigger wench and raise me a flock of babies";[25] in the story "Sonny's Blues," he feels the inarticulate rage of the high school boys who "were growing up with a rush and their heads bumped abruptly against the low ceiling of their actual possibilities."[26] Much as Baldwin cannot forsake America, neither can he "go on uptown" as if he belongs:[27]

> I was icily determined—more determined, really, than I then knew—never to make my peace with the ghetto but to die and go to Hell before I would let any white man spit on me, before I would accept my "place" in this republic. I did not intend to allow the white people of this country to tell me who I was, and limit me that way, and polish me off that way.[28]

J. Gerald Kennedy expresses optimism that criticism and theory, having long neglected questions of place, are at last ready to confront such questions as central. "This process of orientation," he writes, "of situating ourselves in space and coming to know the surrounding environment, seems indispensable to the recognition of the self as a self. The elements of place to which we are most responsive (consciously or unconsciously) comprise the physical signs of our deepest intentions and desires."[29] If ever a writer required, perhaps demanded, such attention to place, it is Baldwin. Throughout Baldwin's writing is an awareness of the relationship between place and self. In one interview, in response to the question "How would you define identity?" Baldwin responds:

> I don't know. It's some respect for the self, which has something to do—as my good friend Sidney Poitier says—with knowing whence you came. And really knowing that. And in some way, if you know that, you know something else, too. I can't tell precisely what it is you know then, but if you know where you were, you have some sense of where you are.[30]

There is vacillation here between the temporal—"came," the movement from "were" to "are"—and the geographical—"whence," "where"—but there is no mistaking the urge to locate the self. Yet Baldwin cannot accept the location provided by white America: "Any effort, from here on out, to keep the Negro in his 'place' can only have the most extreme and unlucky repercussions," Baldwin avers.[31] The rejection of place as given requires the creation of an alternative, an emigration. To where? And the alternative place Baldwin must create must deal with problems more complex than race, as though that, in itself, were not complex enough. It seems an unlikely project that no one, existing in no place, can create someone with a home in the world.

Following in the great tradition of American artists of all sorts, Baldwin went to Paris, where he did not so much find an alternative place as realize the profundity of his displacement. Though his surrogate in "This Morning, This Evening, So Soon," the black American expatriate artist living in Paris, can rhapsodize about his love for Paris—"And I love Paris, I will always love it, it is the city which saved my life. It saved my life by allowing me to find out who I am"[32]—Baldwin himself, in a more sober mood, confesses that the French personality "which had seemed from a distance to be so large and free had to be dealt with before one could see that, if it was large, it was also inflexible and, for the foreigner, full of strange, high, dusty rooms which could not be inhabited."[33] His thoughts during his incarceration for the alleged theft of a bedsheet "flew back to that home from which I had fled,"[34] and he is confronted with the awful realization that "the laughter of those who consider themselves to be at a safe remove from all the wretched"[35] is a universal laughter, not the peculiar sufferance of blacks in America. Paris may have exhibited a certain largeness on the issue of race that allowed Baldwin more room than he would have had in the United States, but that extra space was purchased at the expense of the security offered by a permanent address; Baldwin could never be more than a squatter on the Left Bank. The actor Eric in *Another Country*, wandering the Rue des St. Pères, understands that "whoever prolongs his sojourn in that city—who tries, that is, to make a home there—is doomed to discover that there is no one to be blamed for whatever happens to him":

Contrary to its legend, Paris does not offer many distractions; or, those distractions that it offers are like French pastry, vivid and insubstantial, sweet on the tongue and sour in the belly. The discontented wanderer is thrown back on himself—if his life is to become bearable, only he can make it so.[36]

"It turned out that the question of who I was was not solved because I had removed myself from the social forces which had menaced me," Baldwin affirms; "anyway, these forces had become interior, and I had dragged them across the ocean with me."[37]

Michel Fabre writes of Baldwin's Parisian exile: "He had been liberated in Paris from becoming merely a Negro writer, but he realized that he was inescapably American. Even though his fellow Americans were no more at home in Europe than he, Europe was to a greater degree part of their inheritance."[38] And David Leeming notes that "Baldwin spoke of the importance of being forced early in his life to recognize that he was a kind of bastard of the West."[39] In his "Autobiographical Notes," Baldwin elaborates:

> In some subtle way, in a really profound way, I brought to Shakespeare, Bach, Rembrandt, to the stones of Paris, to the cathedral at Chartres, and to the Empire State Building, a special attitude. These were not really my creations, they did not contain my history; I might search in them in vain forever for any reflection of myself. I was an interloper; this was not my heritage. At the same time I had no other heritage which I could possibly hope to use.[40]

A writer who does not know where he or she is, who does not know who he or she is, cannot hold a position and has nothing to say.

The problem is not new to Baldwin. W. E. B. Du Bois, a man who might be seen as Baldwin's logical predecessor but about whom Baldwin has little to say,[41] gives eloquent voice to the agony of "double-consciousness":

> It is a peculiar sensation, this double-consciousness, this sense of always looking at one's self through the eyes of others, of measuring one's soul by the tape of a world that looks on in amused contempt and pity. One ever feels his twoness,—an American, a Negro; two souls, two thoughts, two unreconciled strivings; two warring ideals in one dark body, whose dogged strength alone keeps it from being torn asunder.[42]

Du Bois's resolution is transcendence, to live "above the veil," "in a region of blue sky and great wandering shadows."[43]

Du Bois's abstract idealization, however, is too easy for Baldwin, perhaps a product of their very different beginnings. Baldwin grew up in Harlem amid hardship and the caste of color. Du Bois only gradually awakened to the onus of being black in America. Baldwin read as a child but never retreated to the campus and its Platonic world of ideas, as Du Bois did. Du Bois, looking down upon his mandala, sees the grand design; Baldwin, looking up from the gritty details of life on the street, walking beneath "the great buildings, unlit, blunt like the phallus or sharp like the spear," down among the fallen,[44] struggles to make meaning out of the myriad details of life, of living, breathing, earthy biological organisms, whose very bodies are controlled by laws they do not understand.[45] "This is the only real concern of the artist," Baldwin writes, "to recreate out of the disorder of life that order which is art."[46]

The differences reflect themselves even in titles of works. Du Bois's titles promise authoritative pronouncements: "The Negro and Communism," *The Souls of Black Folk*, "Negro Education," "The Present Leadership of American Negroes," *Darkwater: Voices from within the Veil*. Baldwin promises only his own unsparing self-examination: *Nobody Knows My Name*, "A Question of Identity," *One Day When I Was Lost*, *No Name in the Street*, *If Beale Street Could Talk*, *Tell Me How Long the Train's Been Gone*. It is more than difficult to imagine Du Bois confessing to one of his biographers, as Baldwin did, "I no longer felt I knew who I really was, whether I was really black or white, really male or female, really talented or a fraud, really strong or merely stubborn."[47]

The theme of escape or flight in Baldwin's life and work represents a refusal of constraints, an urge to freedom. Escape derives from the garment in which those fleeing persecution or prosecution would cloak themselves—denial of the self as a condition of freedom. And flight, too, is a form of release—from pedestrian limitations, from the law of gravity, from the boundaries imposed by the weight of color or sexual orientation or homeliness or physical frailty. Pico Iyer knows this; this is why the airport becomes his metonym for postmodern cosmopolitan life. Baldwin, too, knows this. In *Another Country*, the passengers on the flight that brings Yves to New York are transformed as the plane touches down; they revert to their earthbound selves:

> The housewife, traveling alone, who had been, during their passage, a
> rather flirtatious girl, became a housewife once again: her face re-
> sponded to her proddings as abjectly as her hat. The businessman who
> had spoken to Yves about the waters of Lake Michigan, and the days
> when he had hiked and fished there, relentlessly put all of this behind
> him, and solemnly and cruelly tightened the knot in his tie.[48]

Similarly, Baldwin's flight from the United States releases him from
the weight of racial oppression. As C. W. E. Bigsby writes:

> Europe's function was precisely to release him from an identity which
> was no more than a projection of his racial inheritance. It was not . . .
> that he wished to deny his colour but rather that he recognized the dan-
> ger implicit in allowing public symbols of oppression or resistance to
> stand as adequate expressions of the self.[49]

But there is no identity in absolute freedom. Charles Newman provides the solemn reminder: "To say that the self is not what we commonly thought, even to say it again and again, is not to say what the
self is."[50] There is, in *Another Country*, a moment in which Vivaldo
finds himself "equal" to Cass and Richard, in which he finds "something in him was breaking" (the destruction of the self? the loss of vir-
ginity, of innocence?). Vivaldo describes that moment as one in which
he was "briefly and horribly, in a region where there were no definitions of any kind, neither of color, nor of male and female. There was
only the leap and rending and the terror and the surrender. And the
terror: which all seemed to begin and end and begin again—forever—
in a cavern behind the eye."[51] It is the very essence of definition that it
sets limits, boundaries, and at some level we need and want the sense
of placement and differentiation that those boundaries provide.

The effect of Baldwin's European exile is to allow him to replace
himself in America: "I proved, to my astonishment, to be as American
as any Texas G.I."[52] "Once I was able to accept my role—as distinguished, I must say, from my 'place'—in the extraordinary drama
which is America, I was released from the illusion that I hated America."[53] How cruel, then, that at the moment Baldwin is reconciled to
America, the moment that he can finally go home, America dissolves
from under him. American society, Baldwin comes to understand, is
"perpetually shifting," home to a "bewildered populace";[54] "the very
word 'America' remains a new, almost completely undefined and extremely controversial proper noun. No one in the world seems to

know exactly what it describes, not even we motley millions who call ourselves Americans."[55] America presents the writer who would capture it in words the challenge of a moving target. "American writers do not have a fixed society to describe," Baldwin proclaims. "The only society they know is one in which nothing is fixed and in which the individual must fight for his identity."[56] Baldwin chooses to see this failure of place to provide a foundation for identity as an opportunity, as unmolded chaos waiting to be shaped into meaningful form.

In the absence of firm *geographical* boundaries, Baldwin's response to oppression and its way of grinding him into pieces, its repeated fracturing of him, is profoundly *rhetorical*. The two domains come together under the term *describe*. The single part of Baldwin's identity that remains intact against the assaults, the one irrefragable fact of his being, is his identity as a writer.[57] "I do not think," he writes, "if one is a writer, that one escapes it by trying to become something else. One does *not* become something else; one becomes nothing. And what is crucial here is that the writer, however unwillingly, always, somewhere, knows this."[58] If one *is* a writer—the statement is ontological, genetic, basal; it is more certain in Baldwin's case than race, sexuality, patrimony, or national identity. If one is a writer, there is, Baldwin maintains, "no structure he can build strong enough to keep out this self-knowledge."[59] And Baldwin is not just a writer but one with an evangelical Christian past and a correspondingly infinite and mystical faith in the power of the word, the *logos*, the truth: "In the beginning was the Word. . . . " (John 1:1). Note the concatenation of elements in his credo: "I want to be an honest man and a good writer."[60]

Words, for Baldwin, are the raw material out of which his creation will be built. It is the privilege and the burden of great writers, he believes, to "help to excavate the buried consciousness of this country."[61] His conception of his task as a writer is directly proportional to his conception of the power of his art: to construct a narrative in which the hard truths of American society are revealed in such a way as to inspire their amelioration, and in which he can find the coherence of his character. Baldwin must write himself into an order, a plot, that seems to have no place for him, and he must reorganize the world around that beginning, around the ineffable material of his own experience. "I had tried, in the States," Baldwin notes with the weariness of compulsion, the dead weariness of the cross, "to convey something of what it felt like to be a Negro and no one had been able to listen: they wanted their romance."[62] His clearest statement of his vocation occurs not in a discussion of writing but in a moment where he imagines himself to be manipulating symbols through the medium of film. His film "would begin with slaves, boarding the good ship *Jesus*: a white ship, on a dark sea, with masters as white as the sails of their ships and slaves as black as the ocean," and it would follow the fate of succeeding generations to the present day. The story would be made whole by Baldwin's daring to envision "the tragic hero for whom I was searching—as myself."[63] If Baldwin could not find a home and a self, then he would write one; he would re-create himself through words.[64] "To become a Negro man, let alone a Negro artist, one had to make oneself up as one went along," Baldwin alleges. "This had to be done in the not-at-all-metaphorical teeth of the world's determination to destroy you. The world had prepared no place for you, and if the world had its way, no place would ever exist."[65]

It is Baldwin's first task as a writer to find himself, to find his place within himself. "Don't many of us know what's going on in our own hearts for the matter of that," intones the Reverend Foster at the funeral after Rufus's suicide.[66] But this process has its own limits and can survive interrogation only up to a point. I am reminded of the famous Escher drawing of two hands drawing themselves into existence. Escher intends the drawing to be maddening in its ultimate finessing of the question of origins. Similarly, the world Baldwin sets out to unveil in *Another Country* is a terrifying world of inherited rage and profoundest alienation, always verging on madness.[67] "Something's got all twisted up in his mind and he can't help it," Leona protests to Vivaldo of Rufus,[68] and the weight of Rufus's insanity drives Leona to her own breakdown. Vivaldo's father pretends that everything is well "while his wife was going crazy in the hardware store we've got."[69] Ida declares Vivaldo to be "crazy."[70] Cass begins to think "that growing just means learning more and more about anguish. That poison becomes our diet—you drink a little of it every day. Once you've seen it, you can't stop seeing it—that's the trouble. And it can, it can . . . drive you mad."[71] and with Eric's inexorable confrontation of his love for Vivaldo comes a larger, more terrifying understanding: "He had not known because he had not dared to know. There were so many things one did not dare to know. And were they all patiently waiting, like demons in the dark, to spring from hiding, to reveal themselves, on some rainy Sunday morning?"[72]

Driven to confront those demons in himself, Baldwin faces his own inherited rage, the now-overripe fruit of his oppression, and he partakes fully of its bitterness preparatory to employing the power of revelation, however unwelcome, to liberate others; for as he notes with apparent resignation, "One can only face in others what one can face in oneself."[73] So it is, as Randall Kenan observes, that however wide the superficial range of Baldwin's subject matter—movie reviews, William Faulkner, Baldwin's life in Paris, his stepfather's death, Ingmar Bergman, Richard Wright—"the primary recurring theme" that preoccupied Baldwin throughout much of his written work, particularly his essays, is "his struggle to form and maintain an individual artistic identity in a society that puts very little value on the life and contributions of its black citizens."[74]

Virtually every essay, regardless of its ostensible subject matter, becomes an occasion for considering Baldwin's own condition and thereby the condition of all who are like him—despised, alone, afraid, devalued.[75] Consider this rumination from Baldwin's essay on Ingmar Bergman. Baldwin, black beyond any doubt, sits in a very white country, interviewing a very white filmmaker; yet what he finds in his subject is largely his own reflection: "I felt identified, in some way, with what I felt he was trying to do," Baldwin writes. "What he saw when he looked at the world did not seem very different from what *I* saw."[76] Though he confesses his envy of Bergman's sense of place—"I am at home here," Bergman tells him—Baldwin consoles himself with the thought that "everything in a life depends on how that life accepts its limits."[77] What is left is a common "landscape": "I thought how there was something in the weird, mad, Northern Protestantism which reminded me of the visions of the black preachers of my childhood."[78] Similarly, when the slight, somewhat fey Baldwin writes of the would-be heir to Ernest Hemingway's mantle of machismo in American letters, Norman Mailer, he ventures that he knows something of Mailer's "journey" "from my black boy's point of view because my own journey is not really so very different."[79] "I wanted to find out in what way the *specialness* of my experience could be made to connect me with other people instead of dividing me from them," Baldwin writes.[80]

The tension in Baldwin's enterprise between solipsism and mythology, his insistence that his own story is somehow everyone's story, is mirrored in jazz and blues—the tension between the soloist and the group, between the composition and improvisation, between the individual and the community, between the precise placement of the notes and soaring freedom. In "Sonny's Blues," Baldwin's portrait of Sonny playing at the club while his brother watches and listens is a beautiful statement of the power of the artist as poet, the power of *poietes*—the ability to create out of the self, to take the chaos of the world into the self and represent it as universal narrative:

> And Sonny went all the way back, he really began with the spare, flat statement of the opening phrase of the song. Then he began to make it his. It was very beautiful because it wasn't hurried and it was no longer a lament. I seemed to hear with what burning he had made it his, with what burning we had yet to make it ours, how we could cease lamenting. Freedom lurked around us and I understood, at last, that he could help us to be free if we would listen, that he would never be free until we did. Yet, there was no battle in his face now. I heard what he had gone through and would continue to go through until he came to rest in earth. He had made it his: that long line, of which we knew only Mama and Daddy. And he was giving it back, as everything must be given back, so that, passing through death, it can live forever.[81]

Baldwin survives; he thwarts madness; he is reincarnated. His literary legacy, so personal, so painfully intimate, escapes irrelevancy, self-indulgence, and "the prison of my egocentricity"[82] to the degree that it is unsparing and truthful. Baldwin's angst is the angst of all of us. The problem of oppression, the problem of alienation, the problem of self-hate—all this, he reminds us, "is not special to the Negro. This horror is also the past, and the everlasting potential, or temptation, of the human race."[83]

But it is not enough, in the end, to find in Baldwin's work a chronicle of our shared destruction and despair. If this is all there is, then we are indeed merely victims of great forces beyond our control, and the shattering of the individual player says nothing about the human condition except to testify to our helplessness and our lack of responsibility, obviating any motive toward moral change, even its possibility. And "a moral change is the only real one."[84] "There's nothing here to decide," Eric concedes to Vivaldo in *Another Country*. "There's everything to accept."[85] Often, Baldwin sees place only as the cage, a locus of activity in which the individual player, especially if he or she is black, is merely a prop. "What happens up here," Cass reflects "happens *because* they are colored."[86]

Baldwin's characters are, more often than anything else, afraid. They are afraid because they are helpless, their humanity diminished by their lack of efficacy in the world. They are overwhelmed by place. The incorrigible nature of the ghetto is a major theme in Baldwin's work. In "Sonny's Blues" the narrator repeatedly observes that nothing has changed across generations, not the buildings or the lives of those who grow up in them: "But houses exactly like the house of our past yet dominated the landscape, boys exactly like the boys we once had been found themselves smothering in these houses, came down into the streets for light and air and found themselves encircled by disaster. Some escaped the trap, most didn't."[87] It is, in Burkean terms, a scenic "way of placement," and it entails "the reduction of action to motion"[88]—thus, exemption from moral evaluation and responsibility.[89] Human beings, in such a view, a merely products of material conditions. Ida in *Another Country* is not responsible for her hatred of white people; it is an inevitable reflex:

> Wouldn't you hate all white people if they kept you in prison here? . . . Kept you here and stunted you and starved you, and made you watch your mother and father and sister and lover and brother and son and daughter die or go mad or go under before your very eyes? And not in a hurry, like from one day to the next, but every day, every day for years, for generations.[90]

It is even worse, in a peculiarly but unmistakably misogynistic way, for black men, whose identity as men depends on their ability to exercise power in the world, to alter conditions and to protect their women and families, and who are denied that power in white society[91]—denied, sometimes quite literally in Baldwin's grisly representative anecdote, their manhood.[92]

But Baldwin cannot accept. He simultaneously desires and resists placement. We are all products of the past and its matrix of torment, Baldwin argues, we are "what time, circumstance, history have made of [us]," but we are also much more than that.[93] "If we do not know this," Baldwin continues the argument elsewhere, "it seems to me, we know nothing about each other; to have accepted this is also to have found a source of strength—source of all our power. But one must first accept this paradox, with joy."[94] The paradox, the apparent contradiction between living in a place that determines our destiny and living in that alternative, more truthful "vast reality"[95] that we create for ourselves, is the site of Baldwin's struggle. The title *Notes of a Native Son*, emphasizing as it does the relationship between one's nation of birth and one's identity, is posed against the subtitle of the essay "Down at the Cross: Notes from a Region of My Mind." Baldwin wants to insist on the value of the ideal, of the possible; on the reality of the interior life, and on the power of "intangible dreams . . . [to] have a tangible effect on the world."[96] And all that he has to put between himself and "the fact that life is tragic . . . the fact of death, which is the only fact we have"[97]—all that anyone has—is his own moral center.[98]

Nietzsche reminds us of the great burden of such independence; it is "for the very few; it is a privilege of the strong," he repeatedly pronounces.[99] It is far too fragile a place for most of us to feel at home. It is, Nietzsche assures us, an extremely lonely place.[100] Baldwin's artist, "the lonely . . . singular intelligence on which the cultural life—the moral life—of the West depends,"[101] has much in common with Nietzsche's exceptional man, though Baldwin's moral purpose represents, from a Nietzschean perspective, a stubborn tether to the community, to the desire to reform place rather than overthrow it. The fragility of Baldwin's own identity as an artist is captured in an incident related by Michel Fabre:

> One evening when the French police were checking papers as usual, Baldwin found he had forgotten his *carte de séjour*. But he had a copy of his book [carrying "a big photograph of the author on the dust jacket"] and he hesitantly showed it to the *agent*; it was accepted as proof of his identity.[102]

It is a more assertive moment than the one in which Kafka's Joseph K., called on by the authorities to provide evidence of his identity, finds he can produce nothing better than his bicycle license; but it is still very tenuous indeed.

Perhaps if Baldwin had been able to do as he repeatedly called on himself and all of us to do—"follow the line of my past,"[103] back to the genetic code, back to the source—perhaps if he had been able to make a full confession, "to tell the whole story, to vomit the anguish up,"[104] including the truth of his homosexuality,[105] he would have found solid ground on which to stand; he would not have, as he accuses Harriet Beecher Stowe and the long line of protest novelists that followed of doing, retreated into a simplistic analysis wherein race seemed to become the paramount reality, the ultimate mode of placement.[106] But to say Baldwin never fully surmounted the paradox he knew so deeply is not a fair evaluation of his achievement. He articulated that paradox, the tensions among place, freedom, and identity, more fully than any contemporary American writer, and he struggled to resolve them. In that lonely struggle is something admirable. "Ain't many trying and all that tries must suffer," intones Reverend Foster.[107] Amen, amen.

NOTES

1. Frederich Nietzche, *Beyond Good and Evil: Prelude to a Philosophy of the Future,* trans. Walter Kaufmann (New York: Vintage, 1989), 55.

2. Pico Iyer, "Nowhere Man: Confessions of a Perpetual Foreigner," *Utne Reader* (May–June 1997): 78.

3. Ibid., 79.

4. Ibid.

5. Eve Auchincloss and Nancy Lynch, "Disturber of the Peace: James Baldwin—An Interview" (1969), reprinted in Fred L. Standley and Louis H. Pratt, eds., *Conversations with James Baldwin* (Jackson: University of Mississippi Press, 1989), 80. Baldwin uses the same description in a 1961 interview with Studs Terkel ("An Interview with James Baldwin," reprinted in Standley and Pratt, eds., *Conversations,* 15).

6. Auchincloss and Lynch, "Disturber of the Peace," 80.

7. James Baldwin, "Everybody's Protest Novel," in *Notes of a Native Son* (1955; reprint, Boston: Beacon Press, 1984), 19.

8. Ibid., 21.

9. Kenneth Burke, *The Rhetoric of Religion: Studies in Logology* (Berkeley and Los Angeles: University of California Press, 1970), passim.

10. Baldwin, "Everybody's Protest Novel," 21.

11. James Baldwin, *Nobody Knows My Name* (1961; reprint, New York: Vintage Books, 1993), 81.

12. James Baldwin, *The Fire Next Time* (1963; reprint, New York: Vintage Books, 1993), 4. In an interview with Studs Terkel, Baldwin elaborates: "Every Negro in America is in one way or another menaced by it. One is born in a white country, a white Protestant Puritan country, where one was once a slave, where all the standards and all the images when you open your eyes

on the world, everything you see; none of it applies to you" ("Interview with James Baldwin," 5). See also his account of black shame of blackness in *Nobody Knows My Name*, 80.

13.

I am, in all but in technical legal fact, a Southerner. My father was born in the South—my mother was born in the South, and if they had waited two more seconds I might have been born in the South. But that means I was raised by families whose roots were essentially southern rural and whose relationship to the church was very direct because it was the only means they had of expressing their pain and their despair. (Kenneth B. Clark, "A Conversation with James Baldwin" (1963), reprinted in Standley and Pratt, *Conversations,* 39; see also *Nobody Knows My Name*, 98–99).

14. Kenneth Kinnamon, "Introduction," in *James Baldwin: A Collection of Critical Essays,* ed. Kenneth Kinnamon (Englewood Cliffs, N.J.: Prentice-Hall, 1974), 4; see also Irving Howe, "James Baldwin: At Ease in the Apocalypse," 99 in the same volume.

15. Baldwin, *Fire Next Time,* 16.

16. Ibid., 19.

17. Ibid., 21.

18. Ibid., 27.

19. Ibid., 24.

20. Ibid., 29.

21. Ibid., 29–30.

22. Ibid., 32.

23. Ibid., 81.

24. Ibid., 10.

25. James Baldwin, "Previous Condition," in *Going to Meet the Man* (1965; reprint, New York: Vintage Books, 1995), 97.

26. James Baldwin, "Sonny's Blues," in *Going to Meet the Man,* 104.

27. Baldwin "Previous Condition," 91.

28. Baldwin, *Fire Next Time.*

29. J. Gerald Kennedy, *Imagining Paris: Exile, Writing, and American Identity* (New Haven, Conn.: Yale University Press, 1993), 8.

30. In Auchincloss and Lynch, "Disturber of the Peace," 74.

31. Baldwin, *Nobody Knows My Name,* 81.

32. James Baldwin, "This Morning, This Evening, So Soon," in *Going to Meet the Man,* 157.

33. Baldwin, *Notes of a Native Son,* 141.

34. Ibid., 150.

35. Ibid., 158.

36. James Baldwin, *Another Country* (1962; reprint, New York: Vintage Books, 1933), 215.

37. Baldwin, *Nobody Knows My Name*, xii.

38. Michael Fabre, *From Harlem to Paris: Black American Writers in France, 1840–1980* (Urbana: University of Illinois Press, 1991), 200.

39. David Leeming, *James Baldwin: A Biography* (New York: Henry Holt, 1994), 4.

40. James Baldwin, "Autobiographical Notes," in *Notes of a Native Son*, 7.

41. In "Down at the Cross: Letter from a Region in My Mind," Baldwin does quote Du Bois's famous proclamation "The problem of the twentieth century is the problem of the color line" (in *Fire Next Time*, 107). And in "Princes and Powers," Baldwin describes the reception of a letter Du Bois sent to be read at the 1956 Conference of African-Negro Writers and Artists. Du Bois was prohibited from attending the conference by the U.S. State Department (see *Nobody Knows My Name*, 17–18).

42. W. E. B. DuBois *The Souls of Black Folk* (New York: Bantam, 1989), 3.

43. Ibid., 2. See also James Darsey, "'The Voice of Exile': W. E. B. Du Bois and the Quest for Culture," in J. Michael Hogan, ed., *Rhetoric and Community: Case Studies in Unity and Fragmentation* (Columbia: University of South Carolina Press, 1998).

44. Baldwin, *Another Country*, 4.

45. Ibid., 54.

46. Baldwin, "Autobiographical Notes," 7.

47. Quoted in Randall Kenan, *James Baldwin* (New York: Chelsea House, 1994), 56.

48. Baldwin, *Another Country*, 433–34.

49. C. W. E. Bigsby, "The Divided Mind of James Baldwin," in Harold Bloom, ed., *James Baldwin: Modern Critical Views* (New York: Chelsea House, 1986), 122.

50. Charles Newman, "The Lesson of the Master: Henry James and James Baldwin," in Kinnamon, ed., *James Baldwin*, 61.

51. Baldwin, *Another Country*, 301–2.

52. Baldwin, *Nobody Knows My Name*, 4.

53. Ibid., 5.

54. Ibid., 20.

55. Ibid., 3.

56. Ibid., 11.

57. See, for example, Baldwin, *Fire Next Time*, 61, 70.

58. Baldwin, *Nobody Knows My Name*, 239.

59. Ibid.

60. Baldwin, "Autobiographical Notes," 9.

61. Baldwin, *Nobody Knows My Name*, 238.

62. Ibid., 221.

63. Ibid., 179.

64. I am indebted to Richard Hall's short story inspired by Baldwin, "The Language Animal" (in *Fidelities* [New York: Penguin, 1992], 163–87), for this insight, and to Valdan Pennington for pointing this story out to me.

65. Baldwin, *Nobody Knows My Name*, 232.

66. Baldwin, *Another Country*, 121.

67. Ibid., passim.

68. Ibid., 59.

69. Ibid., 111.

70. Ibid., 146.

71. Ibid., 405.

72. Ibid., 393.

73. Baldwin, *Nobody Knows My Name*, xiv.

74. Kenan, *James Baldwin*, 77, see also 94, 101.

75. Ibid., 77.

76. Baldwin, *Nobody Knows My Name*, 168.

77. Ibid., 175, 176.

78. Ibid., 177.

79. Ibid., 217.

80. Ibid., 3–4.

81. Baldwin, "Sonny's Blues," 140.

82. Baldwin, *Nobody Knows My Name*, 223.

83. Ibid., 213.

84. Baldwin, *Notes of a Native Son*, xiii.

85. Baldwin, *Another Country*, 339.

86. Ibid., 113.

87. Baldwin, "Sonny's Blues," 113.

88. Kenneth Burke, *A Grammar of Motives,* campus ed. (Berkeley and Los Angeles: University of California Press, 1969), 131.

89. Ibid., 136.

90. Baldwin, *Another Country*, 350–51.

91. Baldwin, *Fire Next Time*, 98–99; see also the incident related in "This Morning, This Evening, So Soon," 174–75; and in *Nobody Knows My Name*, 110, 115.

92. Baldwin, *Nobody Knows My Name*, 100, 109, 213.

93. Baldwin, *Notes of a Native Son*, xii.

94. Baldwin, *Nobody Knows My Name*, 213.

95. Baldwin, "Everybody's Protest Novel, in *Notes of a Native Son*, 15.

96. Baldwin, *Nobody Knows My Name*, 12.

97. Baldwin, *Fire Next Time*, 91.

98. Baldwin, "Autobiographical Notes," 9; see also *Nobody Knows My Name*, 88, 116.

99. Nietzsche, *Beyond Good and Evil*, 41, 72.

100. Ibid., 139.

101. Baldwin, *Nobody Knows My Name*, 26.

102. Fabre, *From Harlem to Paris*, 206.

103. Baldwin, "Autobiographical Notes," 6.

104. Baldwin, *Nobody Knows My Name*, 179.

105. See, for example, Baldwin's discomfort with André Gide's homosexuality in *Nobody Knows My Name*, 155–56.

106. I heard Baldwin in person on only one occasion, near the end of his life in the spring of 1986 at DePaul University in Chicago. Asked by a white woman to extend his analysis of racial oppression to women in the United States, Baldwin flatly responded that white women were not oppressed; they were white. And black women, to the degree that they were oppressed, suffered the oppression of race. Questions were closed before I had the opportunity to ask if he would say the same about gay white men.

107. Baldwin, *Another Country*, 122.

Chapter 8

"Alas, Poor Richard!"
Transatlantic Baldwin, the Politics of Forgetting, and the Project of Modernity

Michelle M. Wright

Introduction

On November 11, 1948, James Baldwin took a significant step toward becoming one of our most important writers on African American identity: he moved to Paris. Alternatively, as Baldwin put it several years later, "I didn't go to Paris, I left New York." As James Campbell writes in *Exiled in Paris: Richard Wright, James Baldwin, Samuel Beckett, and Others on the Left Bank,* this statement calls attention to the life he left, one in arrears, where an overbearing climate of racism only heightened family and personal crises.[1] It also highlights Baldwin's representation of himself in two important ways: first, how his status as an African American and an openly gay man—in short, his multiple identity—was far from welcome in the United States, even in a metropolis as large, impersonal, and diverse as New York City;[2] and second, on a more abstract, theoretical level, how his arrival in Paris is framed by a life left in New York. In other words, to understand Baldwin in Paris, one must simultaneously reference the Baldwin who had lived in and fled from New York: the transatlantic James Baldwin.

All the same, it is difficult to understand the why and how of Baldwin in Paris, especially if one considers the thought-provoking situation of Baldwin's public split from Richard Wright upon the publication of Baldwin's essay "Everybody's Protest Novel." Given the very different ideologies of these two men (which I elaborate on shortly), this rift is logical. Yet, if one considers that Baldwin arrived in Paris with no useful contacts apart from Wright, and even further, that Wright had been so convinced of Baldwin's prosaic talents that he had recommended him for an award back in New York, many questions arise. On the basest level: Why bite the hand that feeds you, especially in such an undiplomatic manner? And if Baldwin disagreed with Wright so strongly, why voice that disagreement in so public a forum as a journal?

It is clear Baldwin wished to make a clean, irrevocable break from Richard Wright, in a gesture, it should be noted, significantly disproportionate to his actual tie. It is also clear that the nature of the disagreement was important to Baldwin; indeed, it is important to any scholar in African American and postcolonial studies. In "Everybody's Protest Novel," Baldwin attacked Wright for perpetuating a tradition of African American representation in which the humanity and diversity of the "Negro" is sacrificed to antislavery or antiracist discourse. Although extremely young at the time, Baldwin's critique intelligently outlines the irony of protesting the inhumane treatment of the African American by structuring him as Other. By "Other," I mean the representation of the black as wholly the result of white racism. Theoretically speaking, the black as Other is structured as the antithesis of the white Self, as all that the white Self rejects, hates, fears, and secretly (and consciously) desires.

According to Baldwin, Wright's protagonist in the novel *Native Son*, Bigger Thomas, is victim to a far more pertinent tragedy than the one Wright has so narrowly portrayed:

> Bigger's tragedy is not that he is cold or black or hungry, not even that he is American, black; but that he has accepted a theology that denies him life, that he admits the possibility of his being sub-human and feels constrained, therefore, to battle for his humanity according to those brutal criteria bequeathed him at his birth. But our humanity is our burden, our life; we need not battle for it; we need only to do what is infinitely more difficult—that is, accept it. The failure of the protest novel lies in its rejection of life, the human being, the denial of his beauty, dread, power, in its insistence that it is his categorization alone which is real and which cannot be transcended.[3]

This passage is striking not only for the eloquence of its idea but for its careful rhetoric. Part of what is significant here is the absence of the term *Negro,* which was beginning to acquire poignant political significations informed by (to name just a few) Richard Wright, Ralph Ellison, and the *négritude* writers. By 1948 the term *Negro* conjured up not only centuries of violent oppression and white hatred but active political, cultural, and social resistance to continued racial repression. In both popular and intellectual circles, *Negro* was a term that reclaimed "blackness" from the wholly derogatory attitudes with which it had been infused—quite consciously—by white segregationists and—we will assume, unconsciously—by those who championed integration, both white and black. Discursively speaking, *Negro* was being deployed by writers such as Wright, Ellison, Frantz Fanon, Aimé Césaire, and Léopold Sédar Senghor to move beyond the simplistic meaning of an inferior, exotic people marked by color and into a shorthand for the complex, sometimes celebratory, sometimes agonizing identity informed by history, geography, language, culture, and nationality. But in 1948, in one of his first essays about the black in America, James Baldwin does not use this term in the grand finale of his scathing critique on *Native Son,* the protest novel to end protest novels.

What is the alternative? Baldwin refers to the trope of Bigger, the archetypal Negro, as "black" and as "American" before moving into many variations on the term *human* to close his argument. Throughout the rest of the essay, *Negro* is used liberally to discuss the tradition of the protest novel, from *Uncle Tom's Cabin* to *Native Son. Negro* becomes tied to Baldwin's critique, to signify this Other that Harriet Beecher Stowe—and now, Richard Wright—deployed in the American literary genre of protest fiction. In his conclusion, Baldwin pulls Bigger away from Wright and Stowe—Bigger's literary parents, the essay seems to suggest, who created him in the midst of a gruesome copulation that conjures up a twentieth-century version of Dr. Frankenstein, the monster, and his bride, described in a distinctly American vernacular:

> Bigger is Uncle Tom's descendant, flesh of his flesh, so exactly opposite a portrait that, when the books are placed together, it seems that the contemporary Negro novelist and the dead New England woman are locked together in a deadly, timeless battle; the one uttering merciless exhortations, the other shouting curses. And, indeed, within this web of lust and fury, black and white can only thrust and counter-thrust, the longing making the heavier that cloud which blinds and suffocates them both, so that they go down into the pit together.[4]

What this rhetoric immediately calls to mind, with its references to white and black, lust and fury, exhortations and curses, and an unhappy, doomed lust, is an inversion of the rape of black bondwomen by their white American "masters."[5] Baldwin's scenario clearly entails a black man and a white woman fornicating, but it is unclear who is raping whom or if, indeed, a rape is taking place at all. In fact, the deliberate ambiguity of the scene suggests this copulation is based on mutual consent, although "mutual consent" is misleading, given that these two figures—specifically, Wright and Stowe—are engaged not in making love but in a destructive struggle fueled by hatred. The nature of this sexual act as compulsory is suggested in that although the man and woman to whom Baldwin refers are clearly Wright and Stowe, and therefore specific individuals with individual wills, rather than just raced and gendered tropes, both the fame of their novels and the nature of those novels as protest fiction return them to a narrative that they themselves have framed—one where there are no individuals, just Uncle Toms and Bigger Thomases, whose race and gender status overshadow any individuality or (as Baldwin would put it) any humanity they might possess. This is an ironic and enormously clever rhetoric, because the authors of the novels are forced to share the same punishment they have meted out to their characters, namely, being reduced to subhuman status.

By depicting Wright and Stowe as engaged in a strangely compulsive sexual act infused with both sadistic and masochistic tendencies, and also as framed by the rape narrative that left crucial marks on both American literature and American history, Baldwin also suggests that any encounter between two people that is primarily understood by race and gender (and, most likely, any other socially determined identity) is a "rape" of some sort. Race and gender, deprived of a humanizing context, are removed to their most basic function: that of articulating power and powerlessness. The effect of this is to transform the sexual act to one of mutual rape. It is a dehumanizing (and it should be noted, farcical) scene between two monsters, recalling the hideous violence that marks both *Uncle Tom's Cabin* and *Native Son*. Baldwin's description deliberately recalls the unforgettably base and perversely detailed violence that played no small part in catapulting both novels into the American literary canon, where, in disturbing ways, those scenes of violence became synonymous with the "Negro problem."

We come full circle: the manner in which these two novels became metaphors for the "Negro problem"—specifically, the sadistic care with which their narratives offer up the abused black body to the hungry imagination of the reader—only perpetuates the dehumanizing cycle of lust and violence that the protest genre supposedly condemns. By ending the last few lines of his essay with *American, black,* and *human* while omitting the term *Negro,* Baldwin seems to be offering alternatives to what he perceives to be the destructive and vicious cycle of protest fiction. The alternatives are not just the business of writers who concern themselves with the "Negro," nor even just the business of writers; as the essay's title states, we are all complicit with and victimized by this literal and figurative tradition of thinking about and acting on the "Negro problem." After all, it is a problem that concerns the author of this essay—and he is in Paris.

Why was "Everybody's Protest Novel" the first essay that Baldwin finished and published while in Paris? At this point we understand that Baldwin is bridging two continents, obviously preoccupied with the problems from which he was also escaping. We also understand that it was important for him to renounce publicly an ideology and a literary tradition that discussed racism in terms that focused on socially constructed identities at the expense of the Subject's "humanity." So how does one discuss the African American Subject in a way that does not render that Subject as "Other," especially when one is so far removed from America and has severed ties with the leading (and practically the only recognized) figure in African American fiction? If Baldwin will not speak *as* subaltern, one many ask, can he speak *to* the subaltern?

The Politics of Forgetting

"Everybody's Protest Novel" argues for a discourse that reaches beyond the confines of race as determined and framed by racism. It is difficult to speculate what Baldwin means by "accepting our humanity"; it is safe to assume he does not mean anything specific, given the rhetorical flourishes of his essays, which are aimed at causing the reader to think rather than at espousing a new theory of the African American Subject. But by leaving New York, Baldwin is already expanding the definition of the African American Subject, moving be-

yond the geographical confines of the "Negro question." By emphasizing his move to Paris as a move *from* New York, and by splitting
with Wright publicly, Baldwin suggests that his own understanding
of the African American Subject moves beyond national borders. This
is not to say his understanding of this Subject transcends geographical boundaries but rather that it is at least partially located in the link
between transit; that in one sense at least, the African American Subject is a transatlantic Subject.

I want to make a chronological leap forward to a text where Baldwin explicitly identifies himself and his understanding of the African
American Subject as transatlantic, moving beyond mere conjecture
and into a concrete position. In understanding the African American
Subject as transatlantic, Baldwin was in a small but August company,
one that includes Chester Himes and, interestingly enough, Margaret
Mead.

In *A Rap on Race,* James Baldwin and the anthropologist Margaret
Mead discuss the "Negro problem" from a vantage point both had
helped shape: that is, one that is cross-cultural. Unfortunately, as the
reviews at the beginning of the 1971 book indicate, only Mead was
understood in this respect; Baldwin is noted for his intellect and,
ironically, for the emotional force that is so often linked to the American stereotype of the Negro as Other. If nothing else, this reminds us
of the controlling discourse, (represented here by critics from America's most prominent journals and newspapers who can understand
Baldwin in only one trope, albeit in two modes: he is either a Negro
or a Negro in Paris. Only whites, it seems, can be transnational. Yet,
as the six hours of transcribed dialogue indicate, both Baldwin and
Mead frame their discussion of America's racial climate in a cross-
cultural, transnational context. It would be impossible to summarize
the range of topics and arguments that this transcription entails; it is
easier to focus instead on a provocative and complex trope that the
two return to again and again in their discussion: forgetting.

In the first hour of their conversation, Baldwin and Mead situate
the African American in a transatlantic context. The African American
possesses a white ancestry, figuratively or literally, which ultimately
can be traced back to Europe. Both Baldwin and Mead agree it is important that black and white Americans claim this shared ancestry for
both its interracial and international ramifications, so that we may
begin to defuse the racial antagonisms enshrouded in a mythological

narrative of segregated blood and histories. As the conversation proceeds, *interracial* and *international* become almost synonymous, linked to an epiphanic moment they have both shared.

> *Baldwin:* . . . It took me a long time to [ignore race], and perhaps I would never have been able to do it if I hadn't left America. I *know* I wouldn't have been able to do it if I hadn't left America. It was a great revelation for me when I found myself finally in France among all different kinds of people—I mean, at least different from anybody I had met in America. And I realized one day that somebody has asked me about a friend of mine who, in fact, when I thought about it, is probably North African, but I really did not remember whether he was white or black. It simply had never occurred to me. The question had never been in my mind. Never in my mind.
>
> I really had a terrible time. I suddenly felt as though I were lost. My whole frame of reference all the years I was growing up had been black and white. You know, you always knew who was white and who was black. But suddenly I didn't have it; suddenly that frame of reference had gone. And in a funny way—and I don't know how to make sense of this—as far as I could tell, as far as I can tell this hour, once that happened to you, it never comes back.
>
> *Mead:* I had to make it come back.
>
> *Baldwin:* Well, I came home.
>
> *Mead:* Well, I had to move from advocating integration only to the meaning of black power.
>
> *Baldwin:* I've had to do that, too.[6]

When analyzed in conjunction with "Everybody's Protest Novel," this moment of conversation may appear puzzling, possibly problematic. Is Baldwin advocating that we ignore or forget race, that any and all differences between black and white, French and North African, are superficial at best, deserving of obliteration so as to erase those troubling structural positions of Self and Other? Baldwin seems to suggest that in the United States, this racially determined frame of reference is unsalvageable, and that we should attempt to replicate the freeing space of forgetting that France seems to have created and sustained. There is the suggestion that racial identities are at best useless, at worst wholly derogatory; that the African American Subject, paradoxically, is fully achieved upon forgetting s/he is black; that transit or travel can (or perhaps, *will*) erase racial borders. How can we read beyond this move?

In this exchange Baldwin links his move from New York to his "ignoring" or "forgetting" of racial designations—specifically, the racial designation of a North African friend. Of course, "ignoring" and "forgetting" are very different things, and it is difficult to tell whether this slippage is simply due to the immediacy of a spoken conversation, where one does not have the luxury of time to mull over and select the perfect word but must communicate with the first word that comes to mind, or whether this difference is significant. When Baldwin first uses the term *ignore*, it suggests he was aware of his friend's race on some level but chose to disregard it when asked about him. The rest of the anecdote, however, points to having *forgotten* that friend's racial designation, an obviously freeing moment that Baldwin locates as specific to being in Paris—or, given the final exchange in this excerpt, *not* being in the United States.

Although Baldwin is discussing "forgetting race" in this exchange, he uses not racial but geographical references to frame his story. Consequently, the exchange remains race-less: we do not know the race of the inquirer who unwittingly prompted this epiphany, nor do we know the race of Baldwin's friend. We do know the friend is North African, but given the complex history of that region (which, no doubt, Baldwin is aware of and assumes Mead is aware of)—involving invasions by ancient Romans (themselves racially mixed and indeterminate), then Arabs, and finally the Portuguese, Dutch, French, and Germans—it is not safe to assume this friend was "black." This is significant because it directly relates to the nature of Baldwin's forgetting and his construction of the transatlantic Subject.

For Baldwin, the Subject's frames of reference are determined geographically; that is, he positions the binary construction of "black and white" as his frame of reference both before and after his moment of "forgetting" in Paris. Furthermore, these geographic frames of reference do not simply transfer values (i.e., move from "black and white" in America to "no race whatsoever" in Paris); they transform their structure when "accessed" in a different locale. Finally, this change in structure appears to be scenario specific; that is, Baldwin's epiphanic moment achieves significance in its shift from a racial to geographical frame of reference not only because he is in Paris but because he is an African American in Paris being queried about a friend from North Africa.

For the moment we will relinquish the third term, or geographical reference (North Africa), in this triangulation of forgetting, because

this term did not occur to Baldwin until he returned to that moment
and thought about it. Instead, we will concentrate on the immediate
dynamic in place at that moment, namely, Baldwin as an African
American in Paris. Paris is filled with "different people" Baldwin relates, he but goes on to qualify this statement with "different from
anybody I had met in America," thereby rendering difference a two-
sided term that comes into play in a transatlantic context. By qualify-
ing what he means by different, Baldwin is indicating two separate
moments of reference for his transatlantic Subject. As an African
American newly arrived in Paris, he found the people different; as an
African American who eventually acclimated himself to Paris, he
finds that the people are no longer different—although at the risk of
becoming too complicated, it must be pointed out that this second
understanding of difference is always already contingent upon the
first. Similarly, Baldwin's moment of forgetting achieves meaning
only retroactively, for the simple reason that the moment in which
one forgets is, by definition, unmemorable. It lacks significance; it remains empty of meaning until one remembers. In Baldwin's anecdote, one remembers as a transatlantic Subject simultaneously within
two frames of reference: as the African American who understood
only black and white and as the African American who now recalls a
moment of forgetting coupled with that previous moment in which
black and white constituted the sole frame of reference.

Now that we have established that the significance of forgetting
can be achieved only retroactively, we can bring back our third term
in the triangulation of forgetting, the North African. In the moment
that Baldwin forgets, he is forgetting his past frame of reference and
his future recollection that his friend is North African.[7] Forgetting,
then, moves through and achieves significance not only in a locational sense but also in a temporal one. The transatlantic Subject's
moment of forgetting is one that points not to the wholesale removal
or erasure (however one might imagine it) of race but instead to a different frame of reference within which we can come to understand
race. Harriet Beecher Stowe and Richard Wright use the racial frame
of reference to double back on itself (it is Bigger Thomas's blackness,
as it has been framed by racism, that makes him the "nigger" that
racist whites already presuppose him to be) and thus erase the temporal and locational considerations that inform the racial identity of
the African American Subject, distinguishing him or her from that

black Other projected by the white Self. This adds yet another meaning to the scandalous depiction of Wright and Stowe lustily writhing around in "Everybody's Protest Novel," in that the anachronistic presence of Stowe copulating with Wright reflects both parties' failure to consider, let alone respect, how time and history inform the black Subject. Baldwin and Mead, by contrast, although eerily paralleling the construct posited in "Everybody's Protest Novel" (a black man and a white woman sharing a connected view on the "Negro problem"), make clear that this moment of forgetting is meaningful for what one then goes on to remember. Even further, both agree that it is important to continue to remember how time and location inform the Subject, rather than to try to forget. This is the most striking difference between Stowe's Uncle Tom and Wright's Bigger Thomas, on the one hand and Baldwin's transatlantic African American, on the other; this is, quite possibly, the "humanity" to which the young James Baldwin referred.

Let us return to Baldwin's anecdote about his epiphany and the triangulation of forgetting to focus on time and place, or more specifically, on the historical and geographical significance of the African American Subject in the middle of the twentieth century forgetting at the nexus of the United States, France, and North Africa. The combination of these factors inevitably recalls the Middle Passage, American slavery, French colonization, and the African American in exile, all of which inform the transatlantic Subject and comprise this moment of forgetting. In other words, this moment of forgetting encapsulates the three major factors that inform the transatlantic African American Subject: race, nationality, and culture. As is the way with any normal conversation, Baldwin and Mead do not launch into a structured analysis of these terms in descending order; they move on to another subject. And we must look elsewhere in Baldwin to understand how these three factors inform his transatlantic Subject.

"A Question of Identity" and the Question of Nationality

Just as Baldwin does not use the term *Negro* at the end of "Everybody's Protest Novel," the most striking aspect of his essay "A Question of Identity" is also an absence. One would expect, on reading the title, having at least a vague familiarity with James Baldwin, and glancing at the first few sentences, that this essay would focus on the complexity of identity formation for the African American intellectual in Paris. In other words, given that we now understand what distinguishes Baldwin's structure of the Subject from Wright's formation is an awareness of time and place—and their entire retinue of race, nationality, and culture—it stands to reason this essay would address these factors.

Not so. The question of identity Baldwin is addressing in this text is the American identity, or more specifically, the American nationality as it plays out in Paris. By "omitting" color from consideration here, Baldwin already is making a conspicuous statement. He is writing about the American, but not just, as our familiarity with American discourse would imply, the white American. Baldwin is writing about both the black and the white American GIs who have chosen to remain in Paris on the GI Bill and attend university, rather than return stateside. He has not changed the structure of his transatlantic Subject; he is looking at it from another vantage point, from the point of view of the French—or more exactly, from the point of view of the American who comes to understand what it means to be an American by what is refracted back through his structures of meaning from the French point of view.

This makes perfect sense. How can one understand what it means to be an American until one is outside America, until one is given or has experienced a contradistinction? This dynamic falls into line with the politics of forgetting, in that significance is achieved once one is removed from a solipsistic frame of reference—à la Wright, one may note, when one considers that the novels Wright penned abroad do not appear to be affected by the change in scenery. Even Wright's travelogues, such as *Black Power* and *Pagan Spain*, are entirely self-referential: in the effort to come to understand what Ghana and Spain, respectively, mean to the African American, the reader first fails to learn *what makes the African American*, so as to understand the viewpoint Wright is supposedly affording us. I do not argue that this therefore renders Wright's texts useless, only that the definition of the African American is never fully realized, and we are, at the very least, handed a narrative created under false pretenses.

Where Wright fails to expand, Baldwin expands to the point of frustrating ambiguity. His opening paragraph in "A Question of Identity" warns us that this topic is not so clearly demarcated, remarked, and therefore remarkable as we might expect:

> The American student colony in Paris is a social phenomenon so amorphous as to at once demand and defy the generality. One is far from being in the position of finding not enough to say—one finds far too much, and everything one finds is contradictory. What one wants to know at bottom, is what *they* came to find: to which question there are—at least—as many answers as there are faces at the café tables.[8]

Whereas the figures of Uncle Tom and Bigger Thomas suffer from an underdetermined identity, Baldwin's understanding of the American GI, within the framework of the transatlantic Subject, suffers from being so diverse and diffuse as to defy categorization. There is so much to relate, Baldwin seems to be hinting, that he cannot relate it all. Yet we know he will seek a controlling structure—otherwise this project, the essay, would have been abandoned. As I have indicated, the common denominator he finds to round up the maddening diversity of GIs is those for whom there is no diversity: the French men and women among whom the GIs and the narrator now live.

Yet there is one more theoretical move to make before the essay launches into a discussion of the American GI experience in Paris. At first the move strikes us as counterintuitive, in that the first step is to deconstruct "experience" by raising the possibility that experience is meaningless. Baldwin moves on to narrate what becomes of the American in Paris—having shed the two most helpful terms one could deploy, namely, *experience* and *commonality*. So how is one to speak of nationality without the assumption of a common experience? The answer, it seems, is to *invert* the idea of the shared experience:

> The best that one can do by way of uniting these so disparate identities is simply to accept, without comment, the fact of their military experience, without questioning its extent; and, further, to suggest that they form, by virtue of their presence here, a somewhat unexpected *minority*. *Unlike the majority* of their fellows, who were simply glad to get back home, these have elected to tarry in the Old World, among scenes and people *unimaginably removed from anything they have known.*[9]

What Baldwin is doing is not new, but it is significant for how he underscores the theoretical ramifications. The maneuver is not new

simply because we are all familiar with categorization or group formation through negativity: those who were not selected; those who
stand outside the margins. The rhetoric in this passage is especially
important in that it forsakes the passive dynamic underlying commonality for the more active concept of "uniting." At the same time,
this unity is achieved not through positivism (those that do stay) but
through negativism (those that do not go). Although this may strike
the reader as a difference without distinction, Baldwin uses it to posit
these American GIs as a minority, deliberately linking negativity to
the concept of experience in order to distinguish minority and majority experience from each other. This dynamic immediately calls to
mind the African American identity, especially in the 1990s, when
many black intellectuals have deconstructed the idea of the "black experience" by arguing that the only common bond most African Americans share is rejection by mainstream society. We have spun out from
the center into the margins, where we have discovered "Others" like
us.[10] It also recalls Baldwin the individual, the one who described his
move to Paris in negative terms (he didn't *go to* Paris, rather he *did not
stay* in New York).

Another important concept distinguishes minority experience
from majority experience: the concept of individual experience. Just
before the passage quoted above, Baldwin argues that experience "is
a private, and a very largely speechless affair," further underscoring
that we are looking at a group that did not come together but rather
fell off from the majority by not going home. Returning home, then, is
the default action, and the minority experience is achieved by failing
to actively engage in that action; falling off, as it were, onto the tiny,
winding cobblestone streets of Paris "to pursue," Baldwin wryly
adds, "some end, mysterious and largely inarticulate, arbitrarily
summed up in the verb *to study*."[11]

This distinction between minority and majority experience (and it
should be noted that Baldwin leaves the concept of majority experience *sous rature* (under erasure), in that he has not definitively determined its existence) is further underscored by what becomes of this
small band united through negativity. Some discover Paris is not for
them and return home, indicating that the minority experience is defined by a dynamic (uniting through negativity) and not by the ho-
mogeneity of its members. Others, Baldwin writes, stay on and become so thoroughly ensconced in what they perceive to be "French"

that they, too, fail to achieve the as-yet-unspoken promise the narration quietly structures, mimicking the "ten little bunnies, a-layin' in the bed."[12] They, too, "fall off the bed" (or fall into the bed, if we stick closely to the structure of the minority experience), because their Francophilic tendencies become, Baldwin charges, "nothing more or less than a means of safeguarding [their] American simplicity."[13]

Although the minority experience is grounded in negativity, this does not mean its dynamic is passive. It is clear one must actively pursue this experience to achieve whatever it is Baldwin wishes to discuss as soon as he gets all the other "bunnies" out of the way. What "it" is, is an understanding of what it means to be an American—but "American" as it is understood by the transatlantic Subject:

> Hidden . . . in the heart of the confusion he encounters [in Paris] is that which he came so blindly seeking: the terms on which he is related to his country, and to the world. This, which has so grandiose and general a ring, is, in fact, most personal—the American confusion seeming to be based on the very nearly unconscious assumption that it is possible to consider the person apart from all the forces which have produced him. This assumption, however, is itself based on nothing less than our history of the total, and willing, alienation of entire peoples from their forebears. What is overwhelmingly clear, it seems, to everyone but ourselves is that this history had created an entirely unprecedented people, with a unique and individual past. It is, indeed, this past which had thrust upon us our present, so troubling role. It is the past lived on the American continent, as against that other past, irrecoverable now on the shores of Europe, which must sustain us in the present. The truth about the past is not that it is too brief, or too superficial, but only that we, having turned our faces so resolutely away from it, have never demanded from it what it has to give. It is this demand which the American student in Paris is forced, at length, to make, for he has otherwise no identity, no reason for being here, nothing to sustain him here. From the vantage point of Europe he discovers his own country. And this is a discovery which not only brings to an end the alienation of the American from himself, but which also makes clear to him, for the first time, the extent of his involvement in the life of Europe.[14]

Here, Baldwin reveals the importance of the minority experience and what it reveals about nationality. Above all else the minority experience imparts a sense of responsibility; and this is key, the essay argues, given the enormous military and economic forces America has and continues to unleash upon a war-torn, exhausted, starving, and above all else vulnerable Europe. Just as the moment of forgetting entails a sense of loss and confusion, so this prolonged minority experience hinges on a moment of confusion—a confusion that is largely informed by the experience of being a minority, inverting, as it were, the gigantic, impersonal power attached to an American passport. To understand where s/he comes from, the transatlantic Subject must first return, figuratively speaking, from where s/he arose: the Old World. Once there, s/he must look back to American shores from the vantage point of an individual. This is an experience littered with traps along the way, a rare and valuable moment that is easy to miss. One could return home and, ironically, remain ignorant about what it is—what nation, what nationality—one is returning to. One also could stay and reject the Old World, then return home with a bad taste in one's mouth, appreciating neither what it is to be an American nor the value and importance of the Old World.

One also could stay and ensconce oneself so utterly in this apparition of "being French" that one remains, at the most simplistic level, an American. This moment needs to be unpacked, for at this moment Baldwin is stating there are two ways to be an American: complex and simple. The simple American is the one produced through a binary: in rejecting all that is "not French," the transatlantic Subject is never fully achieved, in that s/he becomes utterly self-referential, determining what is and is not French and American through a meaningless "either-or" process. It is a process based on rejection rather than on exploration and discovery. It bears resemblance to the Negro of Richard Wright and Harriet Beecher Stowe in that both nationalities, French and American, are underdetermined, empty of a sense of time or place. The "simple American" is undetermined by time because s/he fails to understand the Old World, the war, what is past, and what lies ahead. S/he fails to understand that as an American, one is necessarily transatlantic and bound to two continents; it is nonsensical to submit oneself to a self-referential either-or process when, in both time and place, America and Paris overlap many times over.

For Baldwin the complex American identity is a series of negotiations, both loving and painful, whose greatest telos is understanding at the price of comfort. In a nation built upon slave labor and the genocide of its indigenous population, the complex citizen cannot, as we have often been exhorted, leave these crimes behind—dismiss them, ironically, as "history" and as therefore forfeiting any claim to relevance. As the following pages will show in detail, the complex American identity is not a static quantity, but an ever changing process that asks us continually to reclaim ugly and brutal actions, to consider their place and future cost, and to reevaluate both the meaningful and meaningless aspects of an identity we must hold dear even as we dread the consequences of such an action. The complex identity is a restless one, wounded, confused, and determined.

The dynamics indicated in the above passage from "A Question of Identity" are complicated, taking their energy from what appear to be contradictions or impossibilities. For example, the past "lived on the American continent" is also somehow "irrecoverable now on the shores of Europe," and yet that "which must sustain is in the present." Baldwin suggests that the looming presence and absence of the past, its grotesque distortions through time and location, squeezed at the margins (shores of Europe) and laid flat in awesome immensity across margin and center (the American continent), are the result of our refusal to acknowledge the past's eternal presence. The past is repressed, and just as in Freud's theory of repression, it is simultaneously pushed down into murky depths and overflowing on the surface, like water pushed down by an enormous rock that splashes upward even as it is displaced. This repression of time leads to gruesome results, whether the progeny of Richard Wright and Harriet Beecher Stowe engaged in violent, clawing sex or a past removed from its stately tomes and edifices, now rendered a distorted substance in order to achieve its many mutations. To remember the past, Baldwin writes, is to "demand from it what it has to give." This is what the transatlantic Subject must and will do, for s/he needs to remember the past as desperately as the past needs to be remembered. As the next section reveals, however, this does not mean all that is remembered is either pleasant or positive.

Given all these caveats, we now come to understand that Baldwin's transatlantic Subject is an ideal Subject formation, one that entails procedures and the apprehension of knowledge. One can seek it and fail. One must know when to deploy the moment of forgetting and when to deploy the moment of recovery. It is also a Subject whose aspects are not restricted to race; as "A Question of Identity" has revealed, some transatlantic Subjects are white. This causes us to ask if Baldwin's deployment of "minority experience" can speak to anyone willing to submit to a dynamic and place him- or herself in a situation in which that person is a minority—which, in turn, allows for enormous conflation between minorities and majorities. "A Question of Identity" conflates white and black Americans, implicitly stating that their experience is common, irrespective of race. We must now ask, with regard to the African American Subject as s/he is structured through Baldwin's transatlantic structure: Is the transatlantic Subject subaltern?

Race and Baldwin's "Encounter on the Seine: Black Meets Brown"

Race, of course, does play a role for the American in Paris, or rather, it plays a wide variety of roles. The complexity of the discourse on the transatlantic Subject status of the African American is belied by the introduction to Baldwin's "Encounter on the Seine: Black Meets Brown." It opens on a chord that is both melancholy and wry, noting the decline of what was once (and given the hyperbole of nostalgia, what was never) a unique cultural center in Paris: namely, "le Jazz hot" arts scene and its key players, the African American musicians, painters, and dancers who came to Paris at the turn of the century and well into the 1930s in search of a supportive environment relatively free from the debilitating racial prejudice that plagued the United States. After briefly noting what is left of the scene, Baldwin focuses on what is left for African Americans in Paris, both entertainers and GIs.

It is a minority experience, although it lacks the romance and touching insight narrated in "A Question of Identity." Small in number and bereft of the black communities they had been raised in back home, the African Americans in Paris whom Baldwin depicts are lonely, roaming individuals who are careful rather than welcoming of the black American expatriate they meet, as these encounters conjure up the dramas and tragedies of the American racist state with which they are only too familiar. "The American Negro in Paris," Baldwin notes, "is very nearly the invisible man."[15]

Yet invisible from whose vantage point? In only five pages, Baldwin has packed into this piece on the African American in Paris a se-

ries of contrasts that invoke race, culture, and nationality in a dizzying array of combinations. The structure Baldwin puts into place is
telling, in that he begins by isolating the African American Subject,
framing him as a lone wanderer who encounters, one by one, various
combinations of race, culture, and nationality that (to paraphrase W.
E. B. Du Bois in *The Souls of Black Folk*) cause him ever to feel his
twoness."

The central trope around which these encounters are narrated is
the Eiffel Tower, a symbol that does not function as simplistically as
one might hope. We must first consider how this tower functions in
a transatlantic context, framed as it is by peoples from a different
cultures, races, and nations. First, the tower is symbolic of Paris,
specifically, of a Paris that confidently had entered the modern age,
capable of dizzying architectural feats built on an equally impressive iron output. The erection of the tower signaled France's entry
into modernity, thus linking her with "the West."[16] Here the transatlantic functions as the means by which we have moved into a progressive era, one in which nations are no longer isolated—nor are
peoples, for better or worse, given that "Encounters of the Seine"
considers how this expanding, confident West came to envelop those
beyond her borders and forced them to work toward building her
greatness.

It is the white and the black American who first reference this
tower—a stunning comment on the transatlantic process and modernity, when one considers how each of the players finally arrived at
this scene. The white and black Americans evoke the Middle Passage,
webbed together by this impressive tower that stands for the goal of
modernity. Quite significantly, however, lacking something to say
that would not be "dangerous," as Baldwin puts it, they turn lamely
to the Eiffel Tower as a conversation piece, agreeing that it is not as
impressive as they had imagined it. Not impressive! This is an ironic
move; for if this tower represents modernity and thus stands as the
ultimate (and quite frankly, the only) symbolic justification, however
lame, for the viciously determined and brutal harnessing of black
bodies to Western delusions of grandeur, as the *raison d'être* for the
uncomfortable and loaded silence—and all it represents—between
the white and black Americans, and it has been pronounced unim-
pressive, then this whole project of modernity, roughly three hundred

years in the making, has been for naught. This scene, so loaded with meaning, also discusses meaninglessness.

The Eiffel Tower, possessed of such symbolic importance that it has achieved fame worldwide, also comes to resemble the African American experience that is so troubling to our African American in Paris. That experience has followed him here; it has isolated him from both fellow black Americans and white Americans; and though ever present, it remains intangible, difficult to define.

> His past, he now realizes, has not simply been a series of ropes and bonfires and humiliations, but something vastly more complex, which, as he thinks painfully, "It was much worse than that," was also, he irrationally feels, something much better. As it is useless to excoriate his countrymen, it is galling now to be pitied as a victim, to accept this ready sympathy which is limited only by its failure to accept him as an American. He finds himself involved in another language, in the same old battle: the battle for his own identity.[17]

The black American experience is like the Eiffel Tower in that both possess overwhelming symbolic importance and yet, when approached directly and literally, escape meaningful definition and even seem to avoid any particular importance whatsoever. Nevertheless, once one concedes defeat and withdraws from the attempt to make a large and concrete claim as to the significance of either, both loom up again, as imposing and domineering in their overdetermined symbolic frames as they ever were.

This is not coincidental, for both the African American experience and the Eiffel Tower are built on lies and mythologies, impacted on and shaped by small, deceived minds and larger, utterly corrupt ones. Baldwin seems to suggest that the fanfare has been so large, appropriated immediately and eternally by those who have decided to accept its enormous importance at face value, that this importance will continue to overshadow its much smaller and depressing realities. At this point Baldwin is not writing this about the African American but, specifically, his "experience," as it, like the Eiffel Tower, has been recorded, interpolated, analyzed, and determined by those both involved with and utterly removed from its construction.

The introduction to this essay suddenly makes much more sense. The rhetoric of the first paragraph and its choice of topic, the Paris

Jazz Age, is stunningly deliberate. Like the Eiffel Tower and its symbolic importance, the jazz era, even in its own time, came to represent the dizzying genius of Negro artistry now unleashed from the land of Puritanism and revealed in its full, frenzied fury in a city renowned for excess. The corresponding freedom these jazz musicians supposedly found in Paris simultaneously highlighted the gruesome systems of repression they had suffered beneath the vile thumb of evil white Americans who lacked the sophisticated understanding of race so native to the French. Crowds flocked to the razzing music filling Montparnasse and its environs to celebrate a musical people once enslaved but now free in their new Canaan—or at least, some of them now free. As Baldwin notes at the beginning of this essay, the fame of that era still draws visitors and young hopefuls, albeit ones who are disappointed by a relatively empty and bleak neighborhood that has since passed the age that, the sarcastic hyperbole makes clear, never existed in the first place. "In Paris nowadays it is rather more difficult for an American Negro to become a really successful entertainer than it is rumored to have been some thirty years ago. For one thing, champagne has ceased to be drunk out of slippers, and the frivolously colored thousand-franc note is neither as elastic nor as freely spent as it was in the 1920's."[18]

The transition from this mythic age of vibrant musicians lighting up the Paris evenings to the lonely, isolated stragglers who are now, as far as Baldwin is concerned, "nearly invisible" is constructed by the enveloping specter of the African American experience. The contrast between the single black American and the burgeoning symbolism of his experience is all the more striking as the essay reveals how it determines his encounters—on both sides. It renders him and the white American nearly mute, their shared nationality even more of a dividing line as the latter greets him and tries very hard, with some relief, to interact outside the prescribed, racist boundaries of which both are so painfully aware. Significantly, it causes the white Frenchman, long since bored by the Eiffel Tower, to turn from it toward the African American with a bevy of goodwill, concern, and sympathy, dying to be released and heaped on this black American. In each scenario, Baldwin makes clear that the black American experience, now realized in its full, looming entirety across the Atlantic, is uniform only in that it is ever present. Its importance, its scope, its nature, and even its meaning continually escape the painfully transatlantic African American Subject.

The essay looks at one more encounter: that between the African American and the French African colonial. The former functions as a means for the French to display their humanity and goodwill and simultaneously to condemn the effects of racism, with which, it seems, the French are even more familiar than the African American. Perhaps so; but not from the vantage point of the colonized, this essay argues, noting the racist treatment the French African colonial receives in the country that is supposedly his or her "home country"—although that home is the colonial's only as long as he or she fills the role of subaltern. In the encounter between these two in Paris, experiences pass between these men; but though they attempt, in stutters, to bond through "the black experience," this common ground is undercut by nationality and culture. Where they have come from and its immediate relation to where they are—in short, their *transatlantic* differences—prevent an easy familiarity, an instinctive bonding. After all, Baldwin notes, the African American, in facing the African colonial, feels the divisive nature of his nation status, contrasted to what the essay argues is the African's enviable one-to-one correspondence with his African homeland. The African American is a cousin "once removed" and, as a result, experiences his blackness in that scenario-specific Du Boisian double consciousness, which the African has not experienced.[19]

"Encounter on the Seine" underscores the transatlantic structure of the African American Subject, pointing to the ways in which geographic displacement brings to the fore the meanings and meaninglessness of modernity and its civilizing project. Through these encounters Baldwin posits the importance of transatlantic discourse in cutting through the simplistic mythologies of oppressed and oppressor pinned to the linear chronology of progress. Instead, through the eyes of the transatlantic African American Subject, we can see how the short-sightedness and even farcical idiocy of certain facets of modernity have bequeathed us a complicated series of relationships whose humanity and seriousness are often directly disproportionate to that which brought them into being. In contrast to the impulsive understanding of the white Frenchman and the embarrassed white American, the transatlantic African American Subject embodies and reflects the complicated ties between the Old World, the New World, and the African Diaspora.

"Stranger in the Village" and the Concluding Future

The transatlantic African American Subject also ushers in the future. Although here I do not delve too deeply into the essay "Stranger in the Village," so as to avoid repeating the many important analyses that have already been performed, I cannot avoid its importance to my analysis of the "transatlantic Baldwin."

It is the final paragraph of this essay that speaks the loudest and the longest. After narrating his experience as Other in a Swiss village that reveals many parts of the West have not yet been touched by the project of modernity, Baldwin argues that this experience is a significant moment for the West. First, the connection between the isolation of this village, its laughable and disturbing ignorance about blacks, and its atavistic, premodern civilization quietly indicates the degree to which Africans and peoples of African descent are, contrary to the perception of the villagers and (by obvious extension) the narrow-minded West, primary contributors to modernity. Second, Baldwin indicates that his arrival in this village presages the advent of rest of the project of modernity—something the villagers, and most certainly the racist West, deliberately ignorant of the inextricable tie that binds blacks to modernity, wish to avoid.

> The time has come to realize that the interracial drama acted out on the American continent has not only created a new black man, it has created a new white man, too. No road whatever will lead Americans back to the simplicity of this European village where white men still have the luxury of looking on me as a stranger. I am not, really, a stranger any longer for any American alive. One of the things that distinguishes Americans from other people is that no other people has ever been so deeply involved in the lives of black men, and vice versa. This fact faced, with all its implications, it can be seen that the history of the American Negro problem is not merely shameful, it is also something of an achievement. For even when the worst has been said, it must also be added that the perpetual challenge posed by this problem was always, somehow, perpetually met. It is precisely this black-white

experience which may prove of indispensable value to us in the world we face today. The world is white no longer, and it will never be white again.[20]

There is little to add to this eloquent and far-seeing quote, one that serves as a useful ancestor to Paul Gilroy's work and, by extension, to the postcolonial project of the "Black Atlantic." This quote answers the rather narrow-minded question I posed at the beginning of this piece, when I asked if the transatlantic Subject speaks as subaltern. According to the essays from Baldwin cited in this chapter, this speech *is* subaltern but our understanding of the subaltern as one who stands at the nexus of modernity, the future of the West and, by extension, the world, renders this question moot. The transatlantic Subject is black because the West, unwittingly, made him black. By "making" him black, categorizing race, and inventing the slew of stereotypes and mythologies the black Subject must bear, they attempted to contain that Subject as Other. As Baldwin has shown us, the ironic effect of this attempted containment was to make the Subject a significant and visible force in the transatlantic. This is why, Baldwin argues, it is important that the African American come to acknowledge his or her transatlantic status:[21] not only because it is preexistent, a primary and central aspect of the black Subject, but also because an exploration of the nature of this transatlantic status allows us to understand that which we have previously misunderstood as specific only to our particular nations, cultures, and races.

NOTES

1. James Campbell, *Exiled in Paris: Richard Wright, James Baldwin, Samuel Beckett, and Others on the Left Bank* (New York: Scribner's, 1995).

2. I insert Baldwin's status as a gay writer and thinker into my framing of this chapter, although I also fail to move beyond the significance of this fact with regard to transatlantic Subject status—unless one is so kind as to assume, by extension of the theory I propound, the inference.

3. James Baldwin, "Everybody's Protest Novel," in *Notes of a Native Son* (1955; reprint, Boston: Beacon Press, 1984), 23.

4. Ibid., 22.

5. I put this in quotes so as not to infer that blacks were actually some sort of subhuman property, owned and mastered—as whites so desperately claimed and often wished.

6. Margaret Mead and James Baldwin, *A Rap on Race* (New York: Dell Publishing, 1971), 7–8.

7. It could be argued that the term *North African* is not a future but a past frame, because Baldwin already knew that his friend was from North Africa; he has simply forgotten it in that moment. But there is a distinction between the past in which Baldwin knew only black and white and the past in which Baldwin knew his friend to be North African. In the case of the former, Baldwin has signified that this is, explicitly, a frame of reference. Baldwin most certainly knew his friend was from North Africa, but not as a frame of reference—simply as a geographical fact.

8. James Baldwin, "A Question of Identity," in *Notes of a Native Son*, 124.

9. Ibid., 125; emphasis added.

10. This is one of the most interesting dynamics that constructs the experience of "passing," in that those who pass are not, literally, part of the "black experience." Fear of discovery, the knowledge that one is participating in a sham that is not a sham (pretending to be white while knowing, by virtue of passing successfully, that there is no such thing as "white"), bars them from claiming the white experience—or does it? Baldwin's dynamic might prove useful to a study on passing that contrasts those who pass not against those who cannot but against those whites the Subject lives among.

11. Baldwin, "Question of Identity," 125.

12. I suspect most people are more familiar with this narrative in the "ten little Indians" or "ten little niggers" version. For reasons that are now obvious, I prefer to stick to the innocuous little bunnies.

13. Baldwin, "Question of Identity," 133.

14. Ibid., 136–37

15. James Baldwin, "Encounter of the Seine: Black Meets Brown," in *Notes of a Native Son*, 118.

16. I am aware of the psychoanalytic ramifications of my rhetoric here. At the risk of being thought perverse, I would like the luxury of using this suggestive sentence to invoke the very masculinist discourse that accompanied modernity and nation building—especially with regard to the gendered discourse of race and colonization, which plays no small role in the discourses that are the focus of this project.

17. Baldwin, "Encounter on the Seine," 121.

18. Ibid., 117.

19. This is not to say Africans have not experienced a complex psychological "splitting" through the experience of colonization; only that the experience of the African American, as it has been outlined by Du Bois, is, according to Baldwin, specifically American.

20. James Baldwin, "Stranger in the Village," in *Notes of a Native Son*, 175.

21. Throughout these essays Baldwin has a tendency to use the masculine

pronoun to the point of absurdity, at one juncture even writing on the moment when "the black man bears his child," which suggests it is not just the rhetorical style of the time with which we are dealing. At the same time, the prominence of women of color writing on and about black identity in the African Diaspora demonstrates that even if Baldwin could think only of men as Subjects, his essays become useless unless we frame them within an understanding of the roles both sexes have played in the development of the postcolonial Subject.

Chapter 9

The Parvenu Baldwin and the Other Side of Redemption
Modernity, Race, Sexuality, and the Cold War

Roderick A. Ferguson

He walked the streets of New York, tired of what he would later call New York's "ceaseless racial pressures," tired of being barred from this theater and that restaurant. Friends of his had gotten tired. One friend—Eugene—flung himself off the George Washington Bridge. Continuing to meander through the city's streets, he thought also of his father's recent death and the burden that fell on him to care for his mother and his eight younger siblings. "Looking for a place to live. Looking for a job. You begin to doubt your judgment, you begin to doubt everything," he said years later. "You become imprecise. And that's when you're beginning to go under. You've been beaten, and it's been deliberate. The whole society has sought to make you *nothing*. And they don't even know they're doing it."[1] New York—America—had destroyed Eugene, and it was beginning to destroy him. So on November 11, 1948, he, James Arthur Baldwin—black, gay, and male—left New York for Paris and became a writer.

In 1949, just a year after his arrival, Baldwin published two essays, "Everybody's Protest Novel" and "Preservation of Innocence," as companion pieces in the spring and summer issues of a little magazine called *Zero*. In "Everybody's Protest Novel," Baldwin discusses the image of the African American in American literature, particularly in the protest novel. In "Preservation of Innocence," Baldwin analyzes representations of the homosexual in American literature. That Baldwin originally wrote these two articles as companion pieces is interesting in and of itself—interesting sociologically because he did so at the very moment in which the United States was rife with "anxieties" about race and sexuality.[2]

In this chapter I historicize Baldwin's dual interest in race and sexuality within the context of the racial and sexual anxieties of post–World War II America. In *Talking at the Gates: A Life of James Baldwin*, James Campbell writes that, if read together, "'Everybody's Protest Novel' and 'Preservation of Innocence' make some crucial assertions: that colour and sex are the defining preoccupations of the American mind and . . . of American history."[3] This chapter attempts to address Baldwin's interest in the United States' preoccupation with color and sex and situates that preoccupation in the cold war—that is, in the rise of the United States as a world power and the emergence of the Soviet state as a threat to that power. More specifically, I argue that Baldwin's companion pieces symbolized the social contradictions operating in and reconstituted by the post–World War II era.[4] These contradictions included the constitution of an American gay subculture during World War II and the denial/negation of that subculture by the American state immediately after the war. This negation was part of the state's efforts to universalize heterosexual culture and thereby to construct the liberal citizen-subject of the United States as implicitly masculine and heterosexual. Universalizing heterosexual culture was a means of challenging the emergence of the Soviet state and of fostering capitalist relations of production worldwide.

Another contradiction was the American state's promotion of itself as the embodiment of democratic ideals at the same time that the United States promoted *de jure* racial segregation—a contradiction sustained by state interests that equated communism with antisegregationist movements and by a legal-political discourse that defined the liberal citizen-subject against the image of the black male rapist. The ideological confrontation between a capitalist United States and a communist Russia relied on sexual and racial discourses about gays and African Americans. Out of the anxieties caused by these discourses, Baldwin signifies on the aesthetic principles of an emerging American avant-garde and simultaneously challenges essentialist constructions of the gay and the African American, as well as the liberal citizen-subject, implied within the American avant-garde movement. While insisting on a representational complexity that demands narrative strategies that challenge essentialist constructions of race and sexuality, Baldwin revises the aesthetics of the avant-garde to challenge the modernist conception of race and sexuality as stable and objective. Baldwin's symbolic moves in "Preservation of Innocence" and "Everybody's Protest Novel" point to the ideological and material confrontations between the United States and the Soviet Union during the years after World War II. Baldwin's personal and professional life allows us to examine one of the constituent elements of modernity—the interaction between "globalising influences and personal dispositions."[5]

"Preservation of Innocence" and Cold War Heterosexism

World War II opened the period in which James Baldwin began to write in earnest and to explore his sexual identity. Understanding Baldwin's intellectual preoccupations necessitates exploring the relationship between World War II and gay sexuality. According to John D'Emilio, World War II was a "nationwide coming out experience." The war took place after the Great Depression, which had seen a drop in marriage and birth rates. Moreover, the war uprooted millions of young men and women from their families and placed them in nonfamilial and sex-segregated contexts; it encouraged civilians in rural areas to leave their communities and families and to migrate to urban areas in the North in search of jobs. Those civilians now were beyond the watchful eyes of family and neighbors. Such a migration to the often impersonal atmosphere of cities encouraged greater sexual permissiveness.[6] Hence, by fostering the expansion of free labor, capitalist growth during the war disrupted the structure of the nuclear family, providing greater mobility to family members who were interested in homosexual expression.[7]

Indeed, World War II fostered a "substantially new 'erotic situation'" that opened the doors for the constitution of homosexual identity and gay subculture (D'Emilio 1989, 233–34). By disrupting the heterosexual and nuclear family, American participation in the war effort allowed new social relations to emerge. Those social relations were due to a large extent to the rise of "homosexual" institutions, such as the gay bar. These institutions were sustained by individuals who, because of an expanding economy, now had the freedom to

frequent them. Gay bars allowed men and women to evolve and exercise a personal and collective identity as gays and lesbians (D'Emilio
1993, 470–71). It was in the gay bars of Greenwich Village that Baldwin, often the only black, became a local celebrity, an exotic figure
who enjoyed many brief sexual liaisons (Weatherby 1989, 46). Hence,
Baldwin—like many others—came of age in the wake of a capitalist
economy shaped by World War II and its promotion of homoerotic
and homosocial spaces, and in a city that attracted men and women
who were exploring and constituting a gay identity.

But after World War II, national anxiety about sexuality in general
and homosexuality in particular increased. It was in this climate that
homosexuality became of national concern. In 1948, New York gover-
nor and Republican presidential hopeful Thomas Dewey accused
President Harry Truman of "condoning the presence of sexual offenders on the federal payroll" (D'Emilio 1989, 227). The presence of these
"sexual offenders" was deemed an issue of national security, particularly since U.S. officials believed homosexuals were vulnerable to
blackmail and hence to manipulation by Soviet spies.

Shortly after the war, American attention turned away from defeating Nazi Germany and toward defeating America's former ally the
Soviet Union and its international effort to establish world communism. Of particular interest was the vulnerability of Greece to communist infiltration. As Undersecretary of State Dean Acheson argued,
"Like apples in a barrel infected by the corruption of one rotten one,
the corruption of Greece would infect Iran and all to the East, . . .
Africa . . . Italy, and France." On March 12, 1947, President Truman
addressed a joint session of Congress, stating that at "the present moment in world history nearly every nation must choose between alternative ways of life. The choice is too often not a free one."[8] According
to Truman, those choices were "between a way of life 'distinguished
by free institutions, representative government, free elections, guar-
antees of individual liberty, freedom of speech and religion, and freedom from political oppression,' and a way of life that relies upon terror and oppression, a controlled press and radio, fixed elections, and
the suppression of personal freedoms" (Dudziak 1988, 73).

Truman's speech culminated in the adoption of the Marshall Plan.
On June 5, 1947, in a speech at Harvard University, the plan's author
George C. Marshall, appealed to European nations to join the United
States in an international effort to rehabilitate nations that the war

had devastated. The plan was part of an elaborate campaign to fend off communist advances in France and Italy. Truman, like other American politicians, saw the plan as a defense and promotion of capitalism:

> If we leave these countries of western Europe to shift for themselves and say, "We are sorry, we can't help you any more," I think conditions will quickly ensue there which will, in effect, bring about a substantial blackout of that market for goods and for the goods of the rest of the world for Latin America, for example. If Latin America loses its markets in Western Europe, we lose ours in Latin America.[9]

In effect, the Marshall Plan helped formalize an anti-Soviet policy in the United States and Western Europe and ensure the economic supremacy of the United States in the postwar era.

To sell American-style capitalism, the United States had to sell American culture as well. Economic supremacy had to be assisted by an ideological offensive. Thus the political interest in capitalist expansion and the rhetoric of democratic freedoms were accompanied by the emergence of an American avant-garde around such periodicals as *Partisan Review, Harper's, New Leader*, and *Commentary*. The avant-garde movement was the aesthetic and the ideological opponent to Stalinism and the Popular Front. As Serge Guilbaut notes in *How New York Stole the Idea of Modern Art*, this movement was the product of the de-Marxianization of the American Left during the 1940s. In opposition to the obligations between the intellectual and the Communist Party laid down by the Popular Front, American avant-garde artists espoused the rights of the individual, particularly the right of individual artists "to be free of all political influence." In an effort to distance themselves from what were believed to be hackneyed representations in the literature that Popular Front writers produced, avant-garde writers insisted on a representational complexity that strained toward the unique and the unpredictable.

One need only look at the magazines in which Baldwin wrote (e.g., *Partisan Review, Commentary, New Leader*) to establish a link between him and the avant-garde. Later on in life, Baldwin would remember the editors of these publications—Randall Jarrell of *The Nation*, Sol Levitas of the *New Leader*, Elliott Cohen and Robert Warshow of *Commentary*, and Phillip Rahv of *Partisan Review*—and remark that these "men are all dead now and they were all very important to my life. It is not too much to say that they helped to save my life" (Weatherby 1989, 51). As a matter of fact, after joining the Young People's Socialist League during World War II, Baldwin had become a Trotskyite—he was an anti-Stalinist even when the United States and Russia were still allies (52).

One can also detect Baldwin's use of avant-garde principles in his critique of representations of gays in American literature. We can begin to see Baldwin's indebtedness to the literary avant-garde in "Preservation of Innocence." Baldwin challenges the idea of the naturalness of gender and sexual identities; underlying this challenge is the avant-garde demand for representational complexity.

> While at one time we speak of nature and at another of the nature of man, we speak on both occasions of something of which we know very little and we make the tacit admission they are not one and the same. Between nature and man there is a difference; there is, indeed, perpetual war. It develops when we think about it that not only is a natural state perversely indefinable outside of the womb or before the grave but that it is not on the whole a state which is altogether desirable. . . . We spend vast amounts of our time and emotional energy in learning how not to be natural and in eluding the trap of our own nature and it therefore becomes very difficult to know exactly what is meant when we speak of the unnatural.[10]

Baldwin proceeds by relating this issue of nature to the homosexual:

> We arrive at the oldest, the most insistent and the most vehement charge faced by the homosexual: he is unnatural because he has turned from his life-giving function to a union which is sterile (Baldwin 1949, 15–16)

By arguing that "nature" is a concept that is elusive and fraught with contradiction, then relating this to the idea of the unnaturalness of sexuality, Baldwin frustrates the assumption that there is some essence that defines sexuality. Such essentialism impedes the kind of representational complexity that Baldwin will later demand.

Baldwin is also interested in gender's relationship to essentialist notions of sexuality:

> Let me suggest that [the homosexual's] present debasement and our obsession with him corresponds to the debasement of the relationship between the sexes; and that his ambiguous and terrible position in our society reflects the ambiguities and terrors which time has deposited

on that relationship as the sea piles seaweed and wreckage along the shore. (16)

Rather than heterosexuality being natural and homosexuality being unnatural and thus worthy of stigma and rejection, Baldwin argues that the notion of the unnaturalness of homosexuality is the outcome of our understandings of the relationship between men and women. By suggesting that anxiety about the homosexual arises out of anxieties about the relationship between men and women, Baldwin implies that "heterosexual relations [are] 'the primary site where gender difference is reproduced.'"[11] Hence, by questioning the naturalness/unnaturalness of sexuality, Baldwin is also questioning the naturalness of gender identity and heterosexuality.

This concern about the naturalness of gender identity and sexuality emerges out of a post–World War II ideological climate that witnessed the emergence of a cold war hysteria about the homosexual. During this time, there emerged a "congruence between the stereotype of Communists and homosexuals," to use John D'Emilio's language (D'Emilio 1989, 232). According to right-wing ideologues, communists and homosexuals possessed no easily identifiable physical characteristics, which made it easy for them to move about without detection. And both leftists and homosexuals were dangers to the sanctity of hearth and home. As D'Emilio writes, "Communists taught children to betray their parents; 'mannish' women mocked the ideals of marriage and motherhood" (232). It was this threat to domesticity and to the naturalness of gender identity that made communists and homosexuals dangerous to the nation-state. As D'Emilio puts it, "Lacking toughness, the effete men of the eastern establishment lost China and Eastern Europe to the enemy, while weak-willed, pleasure-obsessed homosexuals—'half men'—feminized everything they touched and sapped the masculine vigor that had tamed a continent" (232). For Thomas Dewey and others who perceived homosexuals as threats to national security, gays and lesbians compromised the security of the United States at the very moment when that security was most essential *and* most vulnerable. The United States needed to deploy an image of itself as the virile "tough guy" that could withstand the advances of the Soviet Union. Thus the state exploited discourses of heterosexual masculinity in an effort to promote global capitalism.

Talking about the state's promotion of universalist discourses in "On the Jewish Question," Karl Marx argues that the liberal state posits the citizen as its abstract subject and guarantor of that state. The citizen, as a representation of the state, is "divested of [real,] individual life, and infused with an unreal universality,"[12] given the state's bias toward universalism. This bias toward universalism informed the American state's attitude toward gays and lesbians during the latter half of the 1940s. As a figure of upheaval—a threat to the stability of capitalist society and the campaign for global capitalism—the homosexual was constructed as the antithesis of the liberal citizen-subject. Therefore, homosexuals were excluded from the universalist properties of that subject.

Baldwin is aware of the prevalence of heterosexist discourse about the universality of gender and (hetero)sexual identity. In an attempt to challenge that universality and expose the instability and ambiguity of those identities, he writes:

> Directly we say that women have finer and more delicate sensibilities we are reminded that she is insistently, mythically, and even historically, treacherous. If we are so rash as to say that men have greater endurance, we are reminded of the procession of men who have gone to their long home while women about the streets—mourning, we are told, but no doubt gossiping and shopping at the same time. (Baldwin 1949, 17–18)[13]

To challenge the universality of gender and heterosexuality is to acknowledge the ambiguity of gender and sexual identity. Acknowledging that ambiguity promotes complex representations of gender and sexuality.

Discussing the relationship between ambiguity and American national identity, Baldwin writes:

> One may say, with an exaggeration vastly more apparent than real, that it is one of the major American ambitions to shun this metamorphosis. In the truly awesome attempt of the American to at once preserve his innocence and arrive at a man's estate, that mindless monster, the tough guy, has been created and perfected. (18)

For Baldwin, acknowledging the ambiguity that characterizes gender identity and sexuality is antithetical to American identity, which suggests that American identity, as it was framed toward the latter portion of the 1940s, was implicitly a heterosexual and masculine identity. Moreover, Baldwin suggests that the "tough guy" has been "created and perfected" in opposition to the ambiguity of gender and sexual identity. Indeed, the image of the tough guy helps foster the universality of gender and sexuality. As the function of the tough guy in the American imaginary attests, the national narrative of the United States has privileged heterosexual masculinity. Indeed, we may say that the tough guy is the metaphor for how the United States during the 1940s and throughout the cold war wanted to present itself.

Through a review of James Cain's novel *Serenade*—which, according to Baldwin, exhibits a "remarkable preoccupation with the virile male"—Baldwin discusses how American literature was also a kind of "technology of gender,"[14] one that made it difficult for non-essentialist representations of gender and sexuality to emerge:

> One may suggest that it was the dynamism of [Cain's] material which trapped him into introducing, briefly, and with the air of a man wearing antiseptic gloves, an unattractive invert, in . . . *Serenade*, who was promptly stabbed to death by the hero's mistress, a lusty and unlikely senorita. This novel contains a curious admission on the part of the hero to the effect that there is always somewhere a homosexual who can wear down the resistance of the normal man by knowing which buttons to press. This is presented as a serious and melancholy warning and it is when the invert of *Serenade* begins pressing too many buttons at once that he arrives at his sordid and bloody end. (Baldwin 1949, 20)

Cain's novel engraves a particular representation of the heterosexual male as one who is vulnerable to the sexuality and potential sexual advances of the gay man. One among many social technologies of gender operating in the 1940s and thereafter, the novel is a "representation of a relation, that of belonging to a class, a group, a category" (de Lauretis 1987, 4). More to the point, *Serenade* constructs a relation between straights and gays—that is, assigning them antagonistic positions in the social world generated within that text. Thus Cain's novel is part of the social technology that would later inspire a 1950 Senate investigative committee to advocate the exclusion of gays and lesbians from government service, arguing that gays and lesbians lacked "emotional stability" and possessed a moral fiber that had been "weakened by sexual indulgence. As the committee observed, homosexuality was a contagious disease that jeopardized the health and stability of anyone—any heterosexual—who came near it (D'Emilio 1989, 228).

Social technologies of gender can also be witnessed in the American avant-garde. Talking about visual art in a 1947 article, the American art critic Clement Greenberg contrasted the paintings of Jackson Pollock with the work of Parisian painter Jean Dubuffet. Greenberg argues that

> Pollock . . . is able to work with riskier elements. . . . Dubuffet's sophistication enables him to "package" his canvases more skillfully and pleasingly and achieve greater instantaneous unity, but Pollock, I feel, has more to say in the end and is, fundamentally, and almost because he lacks equal charm, the more original. . . . [Pollock] is American and rougher and more brutal, but he is also completer. In any case he is certainly less conservative, less of an easel painter in the traditional sense than Dubuffet. (Guilbaut 1983, 176)

Equating Americanness with brutality, roughness, and virility, Greenberg casts American artistic culture within a complex of masculine attributes. Juxtaposing the "brutality" and "roughness" of American art to the "charm" of Parisian art, the critic feminizes Parisian culture in order to construct its products as unequal to American art. As Guilbaut suggests, the American art world roundly exploited this discourse of masculinity at the very moment when the U.S. government wanted to persuade an international audience of American influence in political and cultural realms.

The avant-garde's complicity in the production of masculinity and in the U.S. government's effort to spread American economic, political, and cultural hegemony suggests that Baldwin's use of avant-garde aesthetics is a "signifyin(g)" strategy. That Baldwin would use an aesthetic that privileged the individual as a means to promote non-essentialist representations of gays suggests he is using that aesthetic for "essentially polemic and subversive strategies,"[15] that he is "revising the received sign"[16] of the American avant-garde to critique the heterosexist nature of the American national narrative. Instead of using the category of the individual implied in the liberal citizen-subject, Baldwin—under the guise of liberal political rhetoric—suggests a notion of the individual that preserves homosexual identity. Informed by this notion of the individual as irreducibly complex, Baldwin argues that

> James M. Cain tells us nothing of men and women, so one may read any current novel concerned with homosexual love and encounter merely a procession of platitudes. . . . It is quite impossible to write a worthwhile novel about a Jew or a Gentile or a Homosexual, for people refuse, unhappily, to function in so neat and one-dimensional a fashion. . . . A novel insistently demands the presence and passion of human beings who cannot ever be labeled. (Baldwin 1949, 22)[17]

Segregation and "Everybody's Protest Novel"

American avant-garde artists of the 1940s distinguished themselves from the Popular Front of the 1930s, in part, by focusing primarily on the individual and the freedoms of the individual. Such a focus was believed to be an effective counter to the authoritarianism of the Popular Front. As an anti-Stalinist, Baldwin was opposed to the Popular Front in general and to the cultural forms of the Popular Front in particular. For literary artists the principal cultural form of that movement was the naturalist fiction of the protest novel. In the minds of avant-garde artists, naturalist fiction could not evolve the representational complexity that the literary avant-garde favored.

Baldwin uses the essay "Everybody's Protest Novel" to critique protest fiction's inattention to the freedoms of individual artists. In "Everybody's Protest Novel," he begins his critique of protest fiction by looking at Harriet Beecher Stowe's *Uncle Tom's Cabin* and Richard Wright's *Native Son*. Referring to the former he writes:

> [Stowe] was not so much a novelist as an impassioned pamphleteer; her book was not intended to do anything more than prove that slavery was wrong; was, in fact, perfectly horrible. This makes material for a pamphlet but it is hardly enough for a novel. . . . [*Truth*], as used here, is meant to imply a devotion to the human being, his freedom and fulfillment; freedom which cannot be legislated, fulfillment which cannot be charted. This is the prime concern, the frame of reference; it is not to be confused with devotion to Humanity which is too easily equated with a devotion to a Cause; and Causes, as we know, are notoriously blood-thirsty.[18]

Baldwin's use of "truth" is instructive in that it implies that the truth of the individual is in the individual's freedom. This freedom transcends legislation and representation and is instead an ontological, universal quality of all human beings.

Baldwin's understanding of truth as the truth of individual freedom is derived from the American avant-garde and evokes the liberal ideology of the cold war. That ideology is probably best summed up by Arthur Schlesinger's *The Vital Center*, published in 1962. This book charted and advanced the new liberalism of the post–World War II period. Schlesinger argued that a new intellectual formation was taking place in the states, enabled by the defeat of Henry Wallace's Progressive Party and the communists in the 1948 presidential elections and by the destruction of the Popular Front. A new vital center, situated between fascism and communism, was emerging in the states. Liberals who made up that center saw themselves as opposed to both fascism and communism and believed that freedom was inextricably bound to individualism. As Schlesinger put it, "The essential strength of democracy as against totalitarianism lies in its startling insight into the value of the individual" (Guilbaut 1983, 189–92). It is this understanding of the individual as the standard-bearer of freedom that motivates Baldwin's critique of protest fiction, which he regards as insufficiently attentive to the freedoms and agency of the individual.

Discussing the irreducible complexity of the human being and the requirement of literature to represent that complexity, Baldwin says:

> We have, as it seems to me, in this most mechanical and interlocking of civilizations, attempted to lop this creature down to the status of a time-saving invention. He is not, after all, merely a member of a Society or a Group or a deplorable conundrum to be explained by Science. He is—and how old-fashioned the words sound!—something more than that, something resolutely *indefinable, unpredictable*. In overlooking, denying, evading his complexity—which is nothing more than the disquieting complexity of ourselves—we are diminished and we perish; only within this web of ambiguity, paradox, this hunger, danger, darkness, can we find at once ourselves and the power that will free us from ourselves. (Baldwin 1983, 15; emphasis added)

Behind Baldwin's insistence on the complexity of the individual, the indefinable and unpredictable quality, is a critique of the academicism of the protest novel—a particular critique of the sociological contours of proletarian literature.

In 1935, when the Communist International launched the Popular Front to encourage liberal intellectuals to join the Communist Party, the party also announced its intentions about how the art of these intellectuals was to be used. The artist was no longer aiming for the creation of "revolutionary literature" but for the revolutionizing of society. Literature was only a means to this end. Hence literature was a tool for propaganda, a means of revolutionizing the masses.[19] To revolutionize society, and to evolve fiction that could meet this demand, writers had to avail themselves of the cutting-edge academic writings of the times. Such a use allowed Marxist literary writers and critics to articulate the social roots of the artistic process and to "puncture the myth of individualism" (Glicksberg 1941, 453). The cutting-edge theories about urban society, poverty, and race relations that allowed such artistic innovations were being developed within the discipline of sociology at the University of Chicago, by that group of intellectuals now referred to as the Chicago School.

Hence in 1945 the former communist writer Richard Wright observed that "it was from the scientific findings of men like the late Robert Park, Robert Redfield, and Louis Wirth that I drew the meanings for my documentary book *Twelve Million Black Voices*; for my novel *Native Son*." Wright and other black writers of the 1930s, influenced by the writings of the Chicago School, were convinced that the Depression foreshadowed the economic collapse of American capitalism.[20]

It is this legacy of the protest novel that Baldwin attacks. The sociological contours of the novel rendered literary representation of human beings "mechanical," "[lopping] the human down to the status of a time-saving invention" (Baldwin 1983, 15). The current of sociological discourse running throughout protest fiction prevented readers from witnessing the "indefinable" and "unpredictable" quality that was the sine qua non of what makes a human being human. For Baldwin, the sociological contours of the protest novel can be witnessed in its adoption of sociology's "passion for categorization":

> Literature and sociology are not one and the same; it is impossible to discuss them as if they were. Our passion for categorization, life neatly fitted into pegs, has led to an unforeseen, paradoxical distress;

confusion, a breakdown of meaning. Those categories which were meant to define and control the world for us have boomeranged us into chaos; in which limbo we whirl, clutching the straws of our definition. (Baldwin 1983, 19)

According to Baldwin, sociology's passion for categorization threatens any project aimed toward representational complexity. By referring to the outcome of sociological theorizing as "a breakdown of meaning," "chaos," and "confusion," Baldwin revises the understanding of sociology as a science that arches toward truth and suggests instead that sociology was the horizon of error.

But Baldwin's antipathy to the "passion for categorization" that sociological discourse generated was not simply due to his bias toward the avant-garde. It was also the outcome of his anxieties about the protest novel's investment in essentialist discourses about the African American male. Discussing *Uncle Tom's Cabin*'s use of racial discourses, Baldwin writes:

> The figure from whom the novel takes its name, Uncle Tom, who is a figure of controversy yet, is jet-black, wooly-haired, illiterate; and he is phenomenally forbearing. He has to be; he is black; only through his forbearance can he survive or triumph. . . . His triumph is metaphysical, unearthly; since he is black, born without the light, it is only through humility, the incessant mortification of the flesh, that he can enter into communion with God or man. . . . Here black equates with evil and white with grace; if, being mindful of the necessity of good works, [Stowe] could not cast out the blacks—a wretched, huddled mass, apparently, claiming, like an obsession, her inner eye—she could not embrace them either without purifying them of sin. She must cover their intimidating nakedness, robe them in white, the garments of salvation. . . . Tom, therefore, her only black man, has been robbed of his humanity and divested of his sex. It is the price for that darkness with which he has been branded. (Baldwin 1983, 17–18)

By inscribing blackness as the sign of evil and regarding the black male body as the physical embodiment of that sign, Stowe's representation of Uncle Tom operates within a racial discourse that "represents the [black male] as a sexual instinct in its raw state" and as the "incarnation of a genital potency beyond all moralities and prohibitions."[21] For Baldwin, *Uncle Tom's Cabin* invests in and reinscribes the "racist mythology of the black male rapist."[22]

Uncle Tom's Cabin was not the only target of Baldwin's criticism. Baldwin also attacked the most celebrated African American novel of the mid- to late 1940s—Richard Wright's *Native Son*—for its use of that same racist mythology:

> In *Native Son*, Bigger Thomas stands on a Chicago street corner watching airplanes flown by white men racing against the sun and "Goddamn" he says, the bitterness bubbling up like blood, remembering a million indignities, the terrible, rat-infested house, the humiliation of home-relief, the intense, aimless, ugly bickering, hating it; hatred smolders through these pages like sulphur fire. All of Bigger's life is controlled, defined by his hatred and his fear. And later, his fear drives him to murder and his hatred to rape; he dies, having come, through this violence, we are told, for the first time, to a kind of life, having for the first time redeemed his manhood. Below the surface of this novel there lies, as it seems to me, a continuation, a complement of that monstrous legend it was written to destroy. . . . Bigger is Uncle Tom's descendant, flesh of his flesh. (Baldwin 1983, 22)

As flesh of Uncle Tom's flesh, Bigger, too, is enslaved to the dictates of his sex. Bigger—a murderer, a rapist—is also the "incarnation of a genital potency beyond all moralities and prohibitions."

Native Son emerges out of the economic and social upheavals of the Depression era. Moreover, the basis for Wright's construction of Bigger is, in part, Robert Park's theory of "social disorganization." Park argued that the impersonal and industrial quality of urban life breaks down the traditional mores of migrants and ethnic minorities. City life also causes a breakdown in the family, leading to antisocial behavior in the individual (Bell 1987, 363). Here, Park suggests that the behavior of ethnic minorities and migrants is determined by an oppressive and depressed environment. Likewise, Bigger is determined by such an environment. In reducing Bigger to the dangers of his environment, Wright essentializes Bigger—constructing him as someone who embodies the pathologies of that material environment. In the mythology of race, the pathology of African American males is most often inscribed as sexual pathology.

The coupling of sociology and the novel presents an interesting moment in the history of the novel. As a representation of the "fictive," or that "ensemble of cultural imaginings, affective experiences, animated objects, marginal voices, narrative densities, and eccentric traces of power's presence," the novel has historically symbolized that from which sociology must constantly distance itself in order to claim access to objective knowledge.[23] But the 1930s novelist's interest in sociology and other related social science disciplines represents an attempt to abridge the distance between the novel and the scientific. Such an abridgment elides the boundaries between science and fiction, rendering the naturalistic fiction of the protest novel into textual evidence of a reality that exists outside the text. Rather than fiction being the proper and presumed obligation of the novel, the novel now strains toward a truth established in the academy. Hence the novel ceases to be a "novel" and becomes, in the words of Baldwin, a "pamphlet," a "catologue of violence and brutalities."

This veneer of truth allowed the protest novel to impart legitimacy and authority to the racial discourses operating within the text. Discussing protest fiction's ability to grant authority and legitimacy to these discourses, Baldwin writes:

> It is the peculiar triumph of society—and its loss—that it is able to convince those people to whom it has given inferior status of the reality of this decree; it has the force and the weapons to translate its dictum into fact, so that the allegedly inferior are actually *made* so, insofar as the societal realities are concerned (Baldwin 1983, 20; emphasis added)

Continuing to read sociology as the horizon of error, Baldwin, in apocalyptic tones, argues:

> Now, as then, we find ourselves bound, first without, then within, by the nature of our categorization. And escape is not effected through a bitter railing against the trap; it is as though the very striving were the only motion needed to spring the trap upon us. We take our shape, it is true, within and against that cage of reality bequeathed us at our birth; and yet it is precisely through our dependence on this reality that we are most endlessly betrayed (20).

Baldwin implies here that sociological discourse becomes a kind of technology of race.[24] This technology of race draws on other sets of power relations—class, sexuality, and gender—to produce racial knowledge. Hence, Baldwin suggests that the racial knowledge of protest fiction manipulates racial, sexual, gender, and class discourses in the framing of the black male rapist. Inasmuch as protest fiction invested in and deployed essentialist representations of African Americans, it could not illustrate the complexity of African American subjectivity.

With its concerns about lynching and American national identity and its position within the specific anxieties about capitalist property relations during the 1940s, "Everybody's Protest Novel" affords us the opportunity to think about the intersections of racial categories, racial violence, and property. Historically, liberal political theory has denied any bias toward the particularities of race, class, gender, and sexuality and has alternatively postulated the abstract and universal citizen-subject as the basis of democratic and economic rights. Indeed, the U.S. Constitution states that the "right of property is that which belongs to every citizen of enjoying and disposing as he will of his goods and revenues, of the fruits of his work and industry." Marx argued that the imaginary universalization or "political emancipation" of the citizen-subject permits the reproduction of capitalist property relations, thus making the state the guarantor and author of rights such as the right to property. But inasmuch as they rely on abstract and universal propositions, neither the Constitution nor Marx can articulate the means by which racialized property interests have provided the foundation for most of U.S. history.[25] While Marx does allow us the means by which we can critique the liberal political theory on which the U.S. was founded, he does not provide access to a critique of the racialization of property relations during the post–World War II era.

Legal scholar Cheryl Harris's essay "Whiteness as Property" provides such access. She argues that "though the law is neither uniform nor explicit in all instances, in protecting settled expectations based on white privilege, American law has recognized a property interest in whiteness."[26] As Harris suggests, the consolidation of property in the United States has always been assisted by racial discourses. Indeed, "the interaction between conceptions of race and property played a critical role in establishing and maintaining racial and economic subordination" (Harris 1993, 1717).

The postwar period of the 1940s was one of increased anxiety about the status of capitalist property relations. It was also a period of de facto racial segregation, legalized in 1896 by the Supreme Court of the United States in *Plessy v. Ferguson.* By ruling that racial segregation did not suggest blacks were inferior or promote feelings of inferiority among blacks, and by denying that Homer A. Plessy, a phenotipically white man, was white, the Supreme Court protected "whiteness from intrusion and maintained the appropriate boundaries around property"

(Harris 1993, 1750). If Harris's claim about the interaction between conceptions of race and property is correct, then we may presume that that interaction was at work during the post–World War II period—that is, at a moment in which the status of property was of national concern because of legalized segregation and of international import because of the struggle between capitalist and communist interests during the latter part of the 1940s.

Harris argues that whiteness and property emerge out the same "conceptual nucleus"—the right to exclude (1714). I presume that this nucleus of exclusion also includes certain representations of the African American, one of which is a representation of the African American male. I also presume that this image, like the image of the white, helped rationalize and foster the exclusions that produced segregation. We must situate Baldwin's critique of the image of the Negro that emanated from protest fiction within this period of anxiety about property interests and of legalized exclusions based on race. Indeed, "Everybody's Protest Novel" is a symbolic move that emerges out of the social contradiction of a state that boasted of freedom and equality for all its citizens while many of those citizens endured actual economic inequalities.

Indeed, the danger of the racial discourses that defined the African American as a sexual threat lies in how those discourses assisted racial violence and the exclusions of segregation. To understand this dynamic of exclusion, one must turn to the racial violence that held it in place. As Baldwin observes:

> Uncle Tom's Cabin, then, is activated by what might be called a theological terror, the terror of domination; and the spirit that breathes in this book, hot, self-righteous, fearful, is not different from that spirit of medieval times which sought to exorcize evil by burning witches; and is not different from that terror which activates a lynch mob. (Baldwin 1983, 18)

Baldwin's passage points to the fact that the mythology of the black male rapist motivated actual violence against African American men—in Baldwin's words, it "activate[d] lynch mobs." If lynching is "the historical background against which the brutalization of black men has taken place,"[27] and if the mythology of the black male rapist helped shape that history, then representational complexity was, for Baldwin, literally a matter of life and death.

Baldwin's concern about the racial discourses surrounding the figure of the black male and the ability of those discourses to aid in
racial violence coincides with actual lynchings that took place in the
mid- to late 1940s. A tide of beatings and lynchings washed over the
South as African-American GIs returned home from the war. In the
summer of 1946, Sergeant Isaac Woodward returned home to Aiken,
South Carolina, after three years of military service and was beaten
shortly afterward by the chief of police. That same summer Macio
Snipes was killed in his home in Georgia by four whites. On July 25,
1946, in Monroe, Georgia, Roger Malcolm, his wife, and two friends
(all of whom were African American) were driven down a back road
by Malcolm's employer, to be killed by a waiting mob. Malcolm's
crime was that he had been fighting with a white man (Dudziak 1988,
77–78).

These acts of violence ignited protests throughout the country. Letters were sent to President Truman's office. The National Association
of Colored Women marched on the White House and picketed for
over a week. In addition, civil rights groups, religious organizations,
and labor unions formed the National Emergency Committee Against
Mob Violence in response to the lynchings. This committee met with
President Truman on September 19, 1946, to call for federal intervention. Because of mounting pressure, Truman decided to assume a posture in favor of civil rights (Dudziak 1988, 77–78).

Lynching has historically been justified by evoking the image of
the black male rapist. As Robyn Wiegman has argued, lynching operates within "the logic of borders" and "figures its victims as the culturally abject."[28] We may say that the figure of the culturally abject
black male rapist was the symbolic expression of an anxiety among
whites about the possibility of African Americans, particularly
African American men, transgressing privilege and property boundaries. And if lynchings operated within the logic of borders, then segregation was the material expression of that logic.

Segregation guaranteed a system of white privilege. Hence there is
little wonder that protests over the lynchings of 1946 were met with
anxieties about the status of white property and about some possible
change in "the borders" of a segregated society. In retaliation to Truman's decision, Southern politicians threatened to break away from
the Democratic Party if its convention adopted a pro–civil rights
stance and named Truman as its presidential hopeful. When the party

did nominate Truman as its candidate and did adopt a pro–civil rights platform, Southerners formed the States' Rights Party and nominated South Carolina segregationist Strom Thurmond as their presidential candidate. As the name of the party attests, the right to property—as it was distributed under segregation—was the right of whites (Dudziak 1988, 79).

The platform for the States' Rights Party denounced "totalitarian government" and racial integration. Indeed, often in the political discourse of segregationists, efforts to end racial segregation were communist inspired. According to segregationists (many of whom were educated), only those forces intent on social upheaval would advocate the end to racial segregation (79). The discourses about black male sexuality fueled the threat of social upheaval. *Native Son*, as a naturalistic form that rendered racial knowledge an objective fact, legitimated the discourse of the black male rapist—a discourse that activated the racial violence and materialist practices of segregation. The image of the black male rapist helped constitute the "racist fantasy" that names the racial other as part of the "they" that, "by means of their excessive enjoyment, pose a threat to 'our way of life.'"[29]

For the white murderers of those African Americans who died in the summer of 1946, white privilege—the white "way of life"—was at stake. We may understand those murders not as violations of the explicit rules of American law but as supports and accompaniments to that law. In *The Metastases of Enjoyment*, Slavoj Žižek argues:

> Superego emerges where the Law—the public Law, the Law articulated in the public discourse—fails; at this point of failure, the public Law is compelled to search for support in an *illegal* enjoyment.
>
> Superego is the obscene "nightly" law that necessarily redoubles and accompanies, as its shadow, the "public" Law. . . . Superego represents the "spirit of community" at its purest, exerting the strongest pressure on the individual to comply with its mandate of group identification. (Žižek 1994, 54)

Žižek's understanding of "nightly law" and "public Law" affords us the opportunity of analyzing the relationship between the obscene events of the summer of 1946 and legal segregation during the 1940s. To begin with, the murders and the subsequent protests to end segregation suggest that in the eyes of their murderers, the victims had transgressed those borders held sacred by popular opinion and by

American law. The transgression of the borders between blacks and whites was thus interpreted as a failure of American law and required the "nightly," unwritten, and illegal law of racist murderers. The fact that the chief of police who beat Isaac Woodward was acquitted to the loud cheers of a packed courtroom illustrates how "illegal enjoyment" often became the basis of white communal solidarity. That solidarity could not have emerged without this split within American law. Such a split was sustained by the racial underpinnings of American law during the 1940s. Therefore, the discourse of the black male rapist helped foster the racial violence that was the shadow support of the American legal system. As Baldwin says, "This panic motivates our cruelty, this fear of the dark makes it impossible that our lives shall be other than superficial" (Baldwin 1983, 18).

Just as the image of the black male rapist helped foster racial violence that was the underside of official American law, the racial other operating in *Native Son*—like its gay counterpart—serves as the antithesis of the modern citizen-subject of liberal democratic theory. Whereas the black male rapist is constructed as a being enslaved to the logic of his phallic member, and therefore bound to unlawfulness, the citizen-subject is possessed by reason and the rationality of democratic law. Hence, when Baldwin argues that the protest novel buys into a "medieval morality" that frames whiteness as good and blackness as evil, he is suggesting how the protest novel employs and deploys the racial binaries arising out of modernity.[30] Bigger, as the figure of irrationality, represents the belief in the other's incapacity to found and sustain a rational democratic and capitalist culture. This exclusion of the racial other from the bounds of rationality coincides with the actual exclusion of African Americans from property rights. Expressing an awareness of the dialectic between the liberal citizen-subject and the racial other, Baldwin's states, "The 'protest' novel, so far from being disturbing, is an accepted and comforting aspect of the American scene, ramifying that framework we believe to be so necessary" (Baldwin 1983, 19).

Such a belief about the other's irrational and chaotic nature is suggested in white responses to efforts to end segregation. For instance, the NAACP was constantly attacked by segregationists for being subversive; and Southerners were not the only ones to conflate antisegregation efforts with communist subversion. In May 1948 the Shanghai newspaper *Ta Kung Pao* covered the arrest of U.S. Senator Glen Taylor for using a bathroom designated for blacks and thereby violating Alabama segregation laws. Criticizing U.S. segregation, the paper argued, "If the United States wants to 'lead' the world, it must have a kind of moral superiority in addition to military superiority." In response to the *Ta Kung Pao*'s criticism, the American consul general in Shanghai stated that the *Ta King Pao* editorial "discusses the Negro Problem in the U.S. in a manner quite close to the Communist Party Line" (Dudziak 1988, 83–84).

This national anxiety about communist infiltration and the abolition of segregation created an ideological environment in which the stereotype of the Negro was symbolically congruent with the stereotypes of the communist and the homosexual. The Negro, like the homosexual, was the figure of social upheaval and irrationality. Indeed, the image of the Negro inspired national anxieties among whites, now that the United States was concerned about any potential domestic disturbance as it tried to bolster its position on the international scene and compete with communist Russia. The cold war can be read as a moment in which the racial and sexual other was symbolically congruent with the stereotype of the communist.

Mimicking cold war ideology, the American avant-garde believed true liberation could come about only through aesthetic individualism. Hence the principles of the American avant-garde coincided closely with the ideology of the American state during the cold war (Guilbaut 1983). Inasmuch as the aesthetic agenda of the American avant-garde suggested the liberal citizen-subject, it was the ideological complement of cold war politics. In liberal democracies, the liberal citizen-subject is *the* symbol of human complexity. There is little wonder, then, that the avant-garde privileged this liberal citizen-subject. In its demand for a representational complexity that conformed to liberal ideology, the avant-garde provided an opening through which that subject could enter. The citizen-subject camouflages particularities of race, class, gender, and sexuality while boasting of universal status. But the universal status of that citizen-subject is held in place by the racial and sexual other, who contradicts universality and human complexity. We may say that Baldwin signifies on the aesthetic of the American avant-garde, because he calls for complex representations of African Americans and gays while assailing the liberal citizen-subject and the national narrative that has sustained it.

Recognizing how the image of the Negro and the homosexual functioned in the American imaginary, Baldwin called for representations of African Americans and gays that resisted essentialism. In "Preservation of Innocence" he wrote:

> Once the novelist has created a human being he has shattered the label and, in transcending the subject matter, is able, for the first time, to tell us something about it and to reveal how profoundly all things involving human beings interlock. Without this passion we may all smother to death, locked in those airless, labeled cells, which isolate us from each other and separate us from ourselves; and without this passion when we have discovered the connection between that Boy-Scout who smiles from the subway poster and that underworld to be found all over America, vengeful time will be upon us. (Baldwin 1949, 22)

And in "Everybody's Protest Novel" he says:

> Our humanity is our burden, our life; we need not battle for it; we need only to do what is infinitely more difficult—that is, accept it. The failure of the protest novel lies in its rejection of life, the human being, the denial of his beauty, dread, power, in its insistence that it is his categorization alone which is real and which cannot be transcended. (Baldwin 1983, 23)

But if these two essays are shaped by a desire for modes of representation that resist essentialism, they are also troubled by their own essentialist failures. Baldwin deploys the categories of "the homosexual" and "the Negro" as if they represent the experiences of all persons who fall into these designations, but in fact, his essays betray a masculinist interest. "Preservation of Innocence" and "Everybody's Protest Novel" are really concerned about the racial and sexual discourses having to do with gay and African American men. This masculinist inscription of "the homosexual" and "the Negro" does not permit Baldwin to ask how lesbians and black women have historically been framed as the antitheses of American domesticity. Moreover, it does not allow him to ask how such representations shaped the contours of American literature written by women who were black and/or gay.

Such a failure should not be an occasion for the abandonment of anti-essentialist political and cultural practice. Indeed, we may read the possibility for such a practice as always connected to the historical failures of modernity's reflexive project.[31] One of the constituent features of modernity has been the impulse to narrate, but the narrative contours of modernity's reflexive project have never been complete. Something—someone—has always been excluded in that project. Approaching our own cultural and political practice as always connected to historical failures means that every "destination . . . becomes inadequate with our arrival, just as the historic shape of our arrival transforms the destination into an emblem of our own contingent historicity" (Wiegman 1995, 202). Contemporary anti-essentialist cultural and political practice must locate itself within the historic essentialist dilemmas that make up our reflexive enterprise. Such a gesture requires a "radical acceptance of our vulnerability,"[32] instructing us to negotiate with and strive against those restless historical failures that constitute, haunt, and compel our practice.

That Baldwin leaves the segregated United States to become a writer at the end of the 1940s, after the United States has fought to end fascism in Europe and during a period operating under the legal conventions established by *Plessy v. Ferguson*, is of the utmost significance. Indeed, Baldwin's decision illustrates Lisa Lowe's argument about culture's relationship to social contradictions. In *Immigrant Acts: On Asian American Cultural Politics*, Lowe argues that the "state governs through the political terrain, dictating in that process the forms and sites of contestation. Where the political terrain can neither resolve nor suppress inequality, it erupts in culture" (Lowe 1996, 22). Hence, Baldwin's decision to leave the United States because of segregation and to become a writer suggests that the literary text becomes, for Baldwin, an oppositional practice, whose oppositionality is measured by the text's distance from the dominant national narrative. "Preservation of Innocence" and "Everybody's Protest Novel" become means of exposing the contradiction between the United States' liberal-democratic claims and its practices. Even though Baldwin invests in an avant-garde aesthetic that was the ideological complement of cold war liberalism, he deploys that aesthetic as a means to illustrate the contradictions within liberal-democratic rhetoric, contradictions generated by discourses of race and sexuality.

In "Parvenu and Pariah: The Heroes and Victims of Modernity," Zygmunt Bauman places this relationship between mobility and cultural production within modernity. He writes that "modernity is the impossibility of staying put. To be modern means to be on the move."

Relating this desire for mobility to identity and definition, the products of cultural practice, he argues:

> Definitions are *born with*; identities are *made*. Definitions tell you who you are, identities allure you by what you are not yet but may yet become. Parvenus were people in frantic search of identities. They chased identities because, from the start, they *had been denied* definitions. . . . For parvenus . . . the desire of belonging could only point towards the future, beyond the suffocating crampedness of here and now. There [is] . . . no belonging in sight except on the other side of redemption . . . or . . . [that] authority to enforce new canons and new norms.[33]

Marx addresses this issue of the dialectical relationship between definition and identity in *The Eighteenth Brumaire:*

> What makes [petty-bourgeois intellectuals] the representatives of the petty bourgeoisie is the fact that *in their minds* they do not get beyond the limits which the latter do not get beyond in life, that they are consequently driven, theoretically, to the same problems and solutions to which material interest and social position drive the latter politically. This is, in general, the relationship between the political and literary representatives of a class and the class they represent. (In Jameson 1981, 52; emphasis added).

Marx suggests that the intellectual's affiliation with a particular social class is predicated on a *subjective* affiliation between the intellectual and that social class. Such an affiliation presumes this process of definition and identity formation. Through this process, intellectuals inherit the universe of problems of particular groups. Baldwin's subjective affiliation with African Americans and gays arises out of this dialectical process of being defined as a "Negro" and as a "homosexual" and then identifying with those groups that have been named as such. As Teresa de Lauretis notes, representations express relations between an individual and other individuals, "previously constituted as a group" (de Lauretis 1987, 4). The relations expressed in this dialectical process of definition and identity can be summed up in the word *naming*. Naming best describes the "reflexive project" that constitutes modernity and the ensuing anxieties of modernity's project (Giddens 1991, 9). Out of the anxieties caused by such naming and the universe of problems caught within names, Baldwin critiques the "Negro" and the "homosexual" as categories and demands that literary intellectuals revise them. Naming James Baldwin by means of

Zygmunt Bauman's category of the "parvenu" implies that identity is always in flux, and that naming is a contradictory process emerging out of the interaction between the definitions that are imposed on us and the identities that we make. The contradictory nature of naming provides the conditions by which Baldwin could call for a new and emerging subject, a literary intellectual whose business it is to recognize and oppose the racial and sexual discourses that define us.

Thus the parvenu Baldwin, suffering an impossibility of staying put and the crampedness of segregation, leaves New York to write—to write against the racial and sexual definitions that tried to "put him in his place," and to write of the necessity for new, more "redemptive" representations. Writing for a future on the other side of the crampedness, away from the definitions, he says that "in order to survive . . . you have to really dig down into yourself and re-create yourself, really, according to no image which yet exists in America. You have to impose, in fact—this may sound very strange—you have to *decide* who you are and force the world to deal with you, not with its *idea* of you."[34]

NOTES

I thank Steven Epstein, Jonathan S. Holloway, and Jeanne Powers for their helpful suggestions at the beginning stages of this chapter. I also thank John Berteaux for reading and commenting on a prior draft.

1. James Baldwin, cited in William J. Weatherby, *James Baldwin: Artist on Fire* (New York: D. I. Fine, 1989), 59.

2. My use of *anxieties* is derived from Anthony Giddens's *Modernity and Self-Identity: Self and Society in the Late Modern Age* (Stanford: Stanford University Press, 1991). In this text Giddens argues that modernity is a period of structural change and self-reflection, both of which lead to existential anxiety. I want to illustrate how these anxieties draw on certain racial and sexual discourses.

3. James Campbell, *Talking at the Gates: A Life of James Baldwin* (New York: Penguin Books, 1991), 72.

4. By arguing that "Preservation of Innocence" and "Everybody's Protest Novel" are symbolic moves emerging out of the contradictions of the cold war, I do not mean to suggest that the essays are mere reflections of those contradictions. As Fredric Jameson notes in *The Political Unconscious: Narrative as a Socially Symbolic Act* (Ithaca: Cornell University Press, 1981), "the

conventional sociology of literature or culture, which modestly limits itself to the identification of class motifs or values in a given text, and feels that its work is done when it shows how a given artifact 'reflects' its social background, is utterly unacceptable" (81). The type of interpretation here proposed is more satisfactorily grasped as the rewriting of the literary text in such a way that the latter may itself be seen as the rewriting or restructuration of a prior historical or ideological subtext, it being always understood that that "subtext" is not immediately present as such, not some commonsense external reality or even the conventional narratives of history manuals, but rather must itself always be (re)constructed after the fact.

5. Giddens, *Modernity and Self-Identity*, 1.

6. John D'Emilio, "The Homosexual Menace: The Politics of Sexuality in Cold War America," in *Passion and Power: Sexuality in History*, ed. Kathy Peiss, Christina Simmons, and Robert Padgug (Philadelphia: Temple University Press, 1989), 224.

7. John D'Emilio, "Capitalism and Gay Identity," in *The Lesbian and Gay Studies Reader*, ed. Henry Abelove, Michele Aina Barale, and David M. Halperin (New York: Routledge, 1993), 472.

8. Mary L. Dudziak, "Desegregation as a Cold War Imperative," *Stanford Law Review* 41, 61 (November 1988): 73.

9. Quoted in Serge Guilbaut, *How New York Stole the Idea of Modern Art: Abstract Expressionism, Freedom, and the Cold War*, trans. Arthur Goldhammer (Chicago: University of Chicago Press, 1983), 144–45.

10. James Baldwin, "Preservation of Innocence," *Zero* 1 (summer 1949): 14–15.

11. Teresa de Lauretis, *Technologies of Gender: Essays on Theory, Film, and Fiction* (Bloomington: Indiana University Press, 1987), 15.

12. Karl Marx, "On the Jewish Question," in *The Marx-Engels Reader*, 2d ed., ed. Robert C. Tucker (New York: W. W. Norton & Co., 1978), 34.

13. Though Baldwin is aware of the constructedness of gender and sexual identity, as a historical agent he is not invulnerable to the effects of sexist ideologies, as his comment about women being historically "treacherous" attests.

14. In *Technologies of Gender*, Teresa de Lauretis states:
In order to begin to specify this other kind of subject and to articulate its relations to a heterogeneous social field, we need a notion of gender that is not so bound up with sexual difference as to be virtually coterminous with it and such that, on the one hand, gender is assumed to derive unproblematically from sexual difference while, on the other, gender can be subsumed in sexual differences as an effect of language, or as pure imaginary—nothing to do with the real. This bind, this mutual containment of gender and sexual difference(s), needs to be

unraveled and deconstructed. A starting point may be to think of gender along the lines of Michel Foucault's theory of sexuality as a "technology of sex" and to propose that gender, too, both as representation and as self-representation, is the product of various social technologies, such as cinema, and of institutional discourses, epistemologies, and critical practices, as well as practices of daily life. (2)

15. Jameson, *Political Unconscious,* 81.

16. In *The Signifying Monkey: A Theory of African-American Literary Criticism* (New York: Oxford University Press, 1988), Henry Louis Gates, Jr., says this about the linguistic phenomenon known as "signifyin(g)": "[Signifying] represents the nature of the process of meaning-creation and its representation. . . . To revise the received sign (quotient) literally accounted for in the relation represented by signified/signifier at its most apparently denotative level is to critique the nature of (white) meaning itself, to challenge through a literal critique of the sign the meaning of meaning" (47).

17. Baldwin's capitalization of *Jew, Gentile,* and *Homosexual,* suggests he is referring not to actual Jews, Gentiles, and homosexuals but to their representations.

18. James Baldwin, "Everybody's Protest Novel," in *Notes of a Native Son* (1955; reprint, Boston: Beacon Press, 1983), 14–15; emphasis added.

19. Charles Glicksberg, "The Decline of Literary Marxism," *Antioch Review* 1 (winter 1941): 452–62.

20. See Bernard W. Bell, *The Afro-American Novel and Its Tradition* (Amherst: University of Massachusetts Press, 1987), 150.

21. Frantz Fanon, *Black Skin, White Masks,* trans. Charles Lamm Markmann (New York: Grove Press, 1967), 177.

22. Kobena Mercer, *Welcome to the Jungle: New Positions in Black Cultural Studies* (New York: Routledge, 1994), 147.

23. Avery Gordon, *Ghostly Matters: Haunting and the Sociological Imagination* (Minneapolis: University of Minnesota Press, 1997), 25.

24. My use of the technology of race is derived from de Lauretis's understanding of the technology of gender as "the product of various social technologies . . . and of institutionalized discourses, epistemologies, and critical practices, as well as practices of daily life," that produce gender (de Lauretis 1987, 2).

25. Lisa Lowe, *Immigrant Acts: On Asian American Cultural Politics* (Durham: Duke University Press, 1996), 25.

26. Cheryl Harris, "Whiteness as Property," *Harvard Law Review* 106 (June 1993), 1713–14.

27. Robert Staples, *Black Masculinity: The Black Man's Role in American Society* (San Francisco: Black Scholar Press, 1982), 85.

28. Robyn Wiegman, *American Anatomies: Theorizing Race and Gender* (Durham: Duke University Press, 1995), 81.

29. Slavoj Žižek, *The Metastases of Enjoyment: Six Essays on Women and Causality* (London: Verso, 1994), 71.

30. For a thorough analysis of the emergence of racial discourses in the Enlightenment, see David Theo Goldberg's *Racist Culture: Philosophy and the Politics of Meaning* (Oxford: Blackwell, 1993).

31. My use of the historical failures of the modern reflexive project as a productive site for contemporary anti-essentialist cultural and political practice is inspired by Robyn Wiegman's chapter "The Alchemy of Disloyalty" in *American Anatomies*. In that chapter Wiegman argues that contemporary antiracist feminist practice must be grounded in the historical failures of American feminism.

32. Gayatri Chakravorty Spivak, "The Post-Modern Condition: The End of Politics?" interview by Geoffrey Hawthorn, in *The Post-Colonial Critic: Interviews, Strategies, Dialogues*, ed. Sarah Harasym (New York: Routledge, 1990), 18.

33. Zygmunt Bauman, *Postmodernity and Its Discontents* (New York: New York University Press, 1997), 73.

34. James Baldwin, in *Conversations with James Baldwin*, ed. Fred L. Standley and Louis H. Pratt (Jackson: University of Mississippi Press, 1989), 5.

Part IV

Baldwin and Intertextuality

Chapter 10

(Pro)Creating Imaginative Spaces and Other Queer Acts

Randall Kenan's A Visitation of Spirits *and Its Revival of James Baldwin's Absent Black Gay Man in* Giovanni's Room

Sharon Patricia Holland

Someone once said that if man is but a figment in God's mind then the characters in men's imagination are no less real than we are. Perhaps. No one can say for certain. But we cannot deny the possibility.

Consider the demon. Regard him with awe and loathing, for he is what men despise. Or think they despise. Themselves.

—Randall Kenan, *A Visitation of Spirits*[1]

Those who saw the paucity of their own imagination in the two-way mirror you held up to them attacked the mirror, tried to reduce it to fragments which they could then rank and grade, tried to dismiss the shards where your image and theirs remained— locked but ready to soar.

—Toni Morrison, "Life in His Language"[2]

When *The Lesbian and Gay Studies Reader* was published, I followed my usual practice and searched for the articles on black women's sexuality. This reading practice has become such a commonplace in my life I have forgotten how and when I began it. I never open

> a book about lesbians or gays with the expectation
> that I will find some essay that will address the con-
> cerns of my life.
> —Evelynn Hammonds, "Black (W)holes and the
> Geometry of Black Female Sexuality"[3]

Bringing back the dead (or saving the living from the shadow of death) is the ultimate queer act. My observation of this is informed by the powerful political slogan, taken from the early days of ACT UP's fight against AIDS: "Silence = Death." Since more than a decade of political activism and academic theorizing has revealed a plethora of silences in the national discourse on sexuality, it would be prudent here to engage the conundrum "silence = death" in yet another conversation; for the "war" is not won, and AIDS most certainly is not the last frontier.[4] There are those who still remain "dead" to political and theoretical national musings about sexuality, about the removal of silence from the space of death. The disciplines of feminist, lesbian-gay, and African American studies have imagined for themselves appropriate subjects to be removed, at least theoretically, from such a contentious space into the place of recognition. These bodies/subjects are either white but not heterosexual or black but not homosexual. In the crack between discourses, the black and queer subject resides. It is the task of this chapter to devise a means by which "black" and "queer" can speak to each other.

My first reading of Randall Kenan's *A Visitation of Spirits* in the fall of 1992 illuminated the problem and provided a way to force emerging queer theory and African American discourse to converse. I knew that I wanted to write about Kenan's novel—to make the pain and experience of that novel become somehow tangible for me. I also knew that writing about this book involved an intense personal need to have the tradition—the African American literary tradition, to which I had directed my life's work for the previous ten years—acknowledge and embrace Kenan's novel as hopeful progeny in a long line of sons and daughters. But complicating this desire was a recognition that there was no precedent, almost no place, for the wounded black gay youth (Kenan's Horace) who kills himself in the bosom of the South and returns as a ghost to witness his own story, because others cannot or simply will not speak his name. The lesbian-gay canon, with its consistent emphasis on white bodies, was not an adequate resource from which to glean a possible approach to this particular story, and no appropriate precedent appeared to prepare the way for theory. I then returned to James Baldwin's *Giovanni's Room*, and the tradition unfolded itself in a queer configuration of black and white.

Before reading *Giovanni's Room*, I had a conversation with a colleague and a few students who were explicating the plot of the novel, Cliffs Notes style. I began to have a fantasy of what the characters Twuan and Reggie of Fox Television's *In Living Color* would say about Baldwin's second novel. In their parody of black gay men through a spoof, "Men On Books," Keenan Ivory Wayans's comedians performed campy reviews of American classics. In this particular parody, I imagined their conversation would be something like: "*Giovanni's Room* is a lovely book about two men who find themselves in the beautiful landscape of gay Paree, the wilderness of white folks. Their love is put to an impossible and tragic test and one of the boys is killed by the French government for indecency and the lover is cast out onto the sea of emotions that only the love of men can rescue him from. We loved it." Even the comforts of throwing shade cannot dispel the desperate and taunting reality of being black and queer that articulates itself throughout Kenan's and Baldwin's books, regardless of the masking of skin color in the latter. In evaluating the intricacies of both novels, and the critical attention paid to *Giovanni's Room* in particular, it is clear that the word *tradition*, in the Afro-American sense, encompasses all that is surely black and procreative.

Robert Bone's *The Negro Novel in America* contextualizes *Giovanni's Room* both in Baldwin's personal canon and in the "tradition" itself:

> *Giovanni's Room* is by far the weakest of Baldwin's novels. There is a tentative, unfinished quality about the book, as if in merely broaching the subject of homosexuality Baldwin had exhausted his creative energy. Viewed in retrospect, it seems less a novel in its own right than a first draft of *Another Country*. The surface of the novel is deliberately opaque, for Baldwin is struggling to articulate the most intimate, the most painful, the most elusive of emotions. The characters are vague and disembodied, the themes half-digested, the colors rather *bleached*

than vivified. We recognize in this *sterile* psychic landscape the un-
processed raw material of art.[5]

We recognize, as contemporary critics, how the tradition can police
manifestations of its own desires. Bone is in a powerful position, enabling him to define not only the tradition itself but what is useful
within the tradition. This passage is filled with sublimated sexual references, creating a belief that "the lady doth protest too much."
Bone's homophobic fears are palpable, but his lack of an appropriate
critical context is even more noticeable than his latent fear/desire.
Not only is *Giovanni's Room* not worthy in light of Baldwin's other
novels, professes Bone, but it only counts as a "first draft" of what
Bone later terms as "a failure on the grand scale," Baldwin's *Another
Country*. However, Bone constructs a contentious cast of players in
this assessment: the themes are "intimate" but "half-digested," the
characters are "vague" but "painful." What appears as his most stinging criticism of this book is its "bleached" and "sterile" (translate as
white and gay, respectively) landscape, fit only for the "raw" (as in
meat) and undigested stuff of "art." Bone defines for the tradition
what can and cannot take place within it; moreover, in a tradition rich
with signification, tropes, and simple back talk, this novel, he asserts,
is in no need of critical attention.

Bone's one noteworthy perception about *Giovanni's Room* is that it
"simply transposes the moral topography of Harlem to the streets of
Paris" (226). Basically, these are black characters in whiteface. I believe the accusation has some truth in it, but the simplicity of this
statement undermines the creative and emotional energy of Baldwin's novel. If we are to take this as fact, we will also have to digest,
however raw the knowledge, that gayness does exist under the
mask(s) of blackness.

I want first to ground this discussion as a response to the absolute,
nightmarish fear of "homosexuality" figured in the African American
imagination and mirrored in the contexts of both novels. Critic and
poet Charles I. Nero has broken ground with his essay "Toward a
Black Gay Aesthetic: Signifying in Contemporary Black Gay Literature," by presenting a chronicle of the presence/absence of black gay
men in African American literature. The purpose here is not to reproduce Nero's study but to elucidate the particular imaginative
place/space that black gay men occupy in the literary "tradition" and

specifically in Kenan's *A Visitation of Spirits*, which signifies on Baldwin's earlier text and attempts to re-create an imaginative place for black gay experience in the African American tradition.

In his examination of Kenan's novel, Robert McRuer places Horace in the space between discourses:

> Horace Cross, as a black gay teenager, always finds himself at the intersection of contradictory identities: in his own family, he is "black," but not "gay"; at the community theater where he works, he is openly "gay," while his "blackness" is rendered invisible, particularly by the production itself, which is about the history of the Cross family (the *white* Cross family) in North Carolina; with his "alternative" and white high school friends, he is neither "black" nor "gay."[6]

McRuer poses no challenge to existing African American literary studies; rather, he concerns himself with the obsessive "regionalism" found in queer studies, where "big-city" experiences are continually privileged over cultural work performed in the marginal space of rural America. However, McRuer's placement of Horace is useful in that it envisions a black gay Horace who is everywhere but nowhere. At the time of the writing of this chapter few critical essays have been written that attempt to explicate Kenan's first novel, let alone to envision a place for it in the present terrain of the African American Renaissance. Perhaps this is the result of the uneven critical response to the presence of gay men in African American literature.

For example, critics approach Baldwin's work with often ambivalent or hostile feelings toward his gay characters or endeavor to place Baldwin in a tradition of black struggle that completely decontextualizes the importance of his portrayal of sexuality. In assessing Baldwin's contribution, critic James Oliver Horton writes:

> Baldwin's message and even some of his words echoed antebellum debates among black intellectuals, writers and political leaders who, in their time, provided a voice for many of their fellow Afro-Americans during earlier stages in the struggle for racial justice and the power of self-defined identity. It also reflected many of the values of those who voiced, through their actions, clear statements of their *dreams for themselves and their children.*[7]

Horton places this movement toward self-determination in the site of a procreative dream—an imaginative project that implicitly views itself as sustained by (in this scenario) a black family, defined in the

narrowest and most heterosexist terms, and supported by a dangerous allusion to the ideology of American "values," at once both a neb-
ulous and a realistic destructive force that has been pitted against the
very black family it is invoked to rescue here. Even the noted critic
Houston A. Baker, Jr., subscribes in part to this genre of interpretation. In novels such as *Invisible Man, Native Son,* and *Go Tell It on the
Mountain,* Baker recognizes that "the arts, institutions, and leaders of
black America are normally lauded for their role in insuring the survival and growth of a culture and in providing maturation and *value*
for its artists."[8] Again, the word *value* is given mythical meaning in
the development and definition of a still-emerging literary tradition.
The meaning of a specifically "black" literary product is encased in
the relative "value" attached to both the product and its cultural fodder—signifying a masculinist discourse (in which Baldwin is certainly guilty of participating) and a heterosexual paradigm.

Tracing the intersection of the African and the pagan in gay black
literature, David Bergman offers evidence that another contemporary
critic, Henry Louis Gates, Jr., does not escape the trap of using a heterosexual paradigm to explicate black literary production. In using
the figure of Esu-Elegbara as a signifier of African American literary
expressivity, Gates "somehow [looses] the polymorphous perversity
of Esu . . . and the continuum of African thought [is] reduced to the
[male/female] binarism of western ideology."[9] It is not so much that
contemporary scholars have not politicized the gay and lesbian presence in the African American *community,* but rather that the gay, lesbian, or bisexual (sub)text of critical and literary endeavors, and
therefore the African American *canon,* is somehow treated as secondary to developing a literary project with an emphasis on its procreative aspects. The relegation of queer subjects to the unproductive
end of black literary production places them in a liminal space. Such
disinheriting from the procreative process contradicts a communal
desire to bring back (all) black subjects from the dead, from the place
of silence. The African American scholarly discussion of itself as a
canon lays bare the attempt to manifest blackness, to bring it back
from the dead, with the attending agenda of normalizing whiteness.
In Cheryl Clarke's assessment of this tradition, she observes: "I realized that the major contradictions between Blackness and lesbianism
were the sexist and heterosexist postures of the Afro-American (bour-
geois) community."[10]

But this is not to say that critics completely ignore the intersection of "tradition" and "homosexuality" found in Baldwin's works. At the outset of his discussion of *Giovanni's Room*, Horace Porter reminds his audience that the novel "is as significant among Baldwin's works as it is in Afro-American literature in general. And we can certainly argue that if *The American* reasserts itself throughout [Henry] James's career, so *Giovanni's Room* has played a similar part in the complex continuing drama of Baldwin's life and work."[11] In fact, Porter argues that the novel's focus on homosexuality is what primarily "distinguishes [Baldwin] from among his influential literary forebears" (146).

Historically, the heterosexual paradigm in African American culture was primarily nurtured by the black church, and it is impossible to launch a critique of Baldwin or Kenan without some attention to this most profound of forces. In an essay titled "Some Thoughts on the Challenges Facing Black Gay Intellectuals," Ron Simmons chronicles the extent of homophobic sentiment in African American literature and its relationship, both direct and indirect, to religious ideologies from the traditional black church and the Nation of Islam. Simmons notes that scholars and religious figures such as Louis Farrakhan, Molefi Kete Asante, Haki R. Madhubuti, Amiri Baraka, and Brent Staples often "equate homosexuality and adultery with rape and child molestation"[12] and interpret religious[13] and critical texts to fit this equation. More important, Simmons distinguishes between motive and method in his analysis of homosexuality in the black community; he writes that "'homophobia' is not so much a fear of 'homosexuals' but a fear that homosexuality will become pervasive in the community. Thus, a homophobic person can accept a homosexual as an individual friend or family member, yet not accept homosexuality" (211). This distinction has special meaning for the trajectory of this work.

People in the queer community often assert that people of color are more sensitive to lesbian-gay concerns than their white counterparts. Simmons dismantles this myth by sharpening the differentiation between accepting and tolerating. In addition, the fear of the "pervasiveness" of homosexuality is clearly equally a fear of the potential pollution of a sacred project—the construction of a black intellectual ideology steeped in a Judeo-Christian tradition—by the spread of the dis-ease of black gay subjectivity.[14] In essence, the black imaginative project can embrace difference, but only in small doses; and most striking, it appears to mirror its white counterparts in feminist and queer studies whose work also clandestinely maintains that blackness in small doses demonstrates diversity but that it ultimately impedes the critical process. As Nero so eloquently reminds us, "Many . . . [black] intellectuals would also argue that the Judeo-Christian tradition is a major tool of the Western-Eurocentric view of reality that furthers the oppression of blacks. Paradoxically, by their condemnation of homosexuality and lesbianism, these intellectuals contribute to upholding [such] an oppressive Eurocentric view of reality."[15]

There is evidence that the mantle of oppression encompasses lesbian subjectivity as well. In reading a copy of Nikki Giovanni's now out-of-print *Gemini: An Extended Autobiographical Statement on My First Twenty Years of Being a Black Poet*, I came across this incredible passage:

> I couldn't decide between school and an agency job and it must have been on my mind because I had a really terrible dream. There was a university chasing me down the street. I turned the corner to get away from it and ran right into the mouth of an agency. It gobbled me up but it couldn't digest me. When it tried to swallow me I put up such a fight that it belched me back into life. *As I hit the street there was the university again, waiting for me like a big dyke with a greasy smile on her lips who has run her prey into a corner. I woke up screaming. Both of them would destroy me!* And furthermore, what did I need with a master's degree?[16]

Due to the ambiguity of the antecedent "them," it is hard to tell whether Giovanni's worst fears are the "agency" and the "university," as is originally posited, or the "dyke" and the "university." It is as if, in the "revolutionary" mind-set of Black Power ideology, the prospect of being consumed by the sexual love of another "sister" is as dangerous as the threat of serious consumption at the hands of mainstream institutions. Most intriguing is the position the dyke serves in this "terrible dream." She becomes the metaphor for the university—the agent that makes it tick, the driving force behind one revolutionary's oppression. In this scenario, Giovanni's real fears are subverted under the code of a metaphor, and the dyke has no real, physical presence in the dreamscape, as do the university and the agency; she is literally a product of their existence. As Simmons observes, "Heterosexual brothers and sisters . . . often think of homosexuality as one more problem caused by white oppression."[17]

A contemporary complement to Giovanni's metaphorical night-mare is the "spectacle" referred to by Shahrazad Ali in the infamous *The Blackman's Guide to Understanding the Blackwoman,* where she states that the "lesbian Blackwoman [*sic*] . . . just as male homosexuals . . . overdoes it and makes herself a spectacle that is not welcome among civilized people. . . . She needs a special exorcism."[18] Both Giovanni and Ali allude to the lesbian as a manifestation of a life in direct contradistinction to the creative project. Furthermore, the "exorcism" of Ali parallels the nightmare of Giovanni, in that Giovanni's dream work is the unconscious process by which she attempts to exo(/e)rcise the specter/spectacle of the lesbian from her evolving imaginative project—a project that is, according to Ali's contemporary mapping, much in need of an old-fashioned cleansing in the tradition of the black church.[19]

This envisioning of black gay or lesbian subjectivity as a "product" of "white" institutions is a relatively old phenomenon. In terms of the African American literary imagination and its attendant aesthetic, evaluating same-sex behavior and attaching to it a negative value can be traced back to W. E. B. Du Bois's stinging reply to Claude McKay's *Home to Harlem.* While Nero has done an excellent job of explicating this reply, it is still necessary to recall that Du Bois's particular interest lay in defining what constituted a national literature, and black gay presence not only is named as outside this shaping tradition but also is painted as a "product" of whiteness. It is hard not to see the parallel between Du Bois's feverish criticism of McKay and the conservative Right's recent recruitment of the black church in the fight against the passage of lesbian-gay civil rights.[20] On both accounts, it is the need to claim ownership of a particular tradition, be it imaginative or legal, that moves us into territories where power is utilized in its most "traditional" form.

Paying tribute to James Baldwin, Nigerian playwright Wole Soyinka remarks that in Baldwin's work there is "this near-evangelical commitment to the principle that rules all being—love sought, denied, waiting in the wings or hovering on the wing, a veritable deus ex machina, lacking only a landing permit from a blinkered humanity that hesitates at the door of salvation."[21] While I do not doubt that Soyinka's insight is gleaned from Baldwin's own testimony[22] about his novels and the centrality of "love" and the human condition (especially in *Giovanni's Room*), I argue that viewing Baldwin's works filtered through this sophomoric conceptualization occludes the prominence and problematic of sexuality, and especially "homo"sexuality, in his novels. It is precisely in Kenan's imaginative revisioning of Baldwin's most maligned and forgotten novel that we can unearth a sense of the importance of *Giovanni*'s most persistent and haunting images.

Stay Down, Brown; Git Back, Black

In the opening pages of *Giovanni*, Baldwin's narrator, David, recalls his simultaneous affair with Giovanni and his fiancée, Helen. Trying to reconcile himself with past mistakes, David muses that "these nights were being acted out under a foreign sky, with no one to watch, no penalties attached";[23] however, in a few paragraphs we learn that David's flight to Paris is but a flight from himself—a self that sleeps not only with a man but with a "brown" one at that. The palpable panic after a grade school affair with a boy named Joey is with David throughout *Giovanni*, reminding him that while he assumes there is "no one to watch, no penalties attached," he has neglected to consider the powerful fear and hysteria his coupling with Joey has left on his imagination. Conjuring the memory of his first homosexual experience, David remembers that

> the desire which was rising in me seemed monstrous. . . . I saw suddenly the power in his thighs, in his arms, and in his loosely curled fists. The power and the promise and the mystery of that body made me suddenly afraid. That body suddenly seemed the black opening of a cavern in which I would be tortured till madness came, in which I would lose my manhood. (15)

Here, Baldwin constructs a dual hell for David—one in which he has the distinct pleasure of experiencing his own self mirrored in the physiological sameness of their bodies and in the difference marked by the making of a "black . . . cavern." David remembers this moment as a "sweet disorder," and it assumes almost nightmarish proportions, a steady reminder of his brush with both an identity that is queer and black.

Later this encounter becomes fodder for David's own imaginings—each homosexual act brings him closer to a recognition of his own whiteness, his own gay identity, and its conception fostered in connection with a "brown" body. David admits:

> The incident with Joey had shaken me profoundly. . . . I could not discuss what had happened to me with anyone, I could not even admit it to myself; and while I never thought about it, it remained, nevertheless, at the bottom of my mind, as still and as awful as a decomposing corpse. And it changed, it thickened, it soured the atmosphere of my mind. (24)

Like Beloved in Toni Morrison's novel of that name, the brown body in David's mind is a dead being who resides at "the bottom." In *Giovanni*, Baldwin displaces the tension of queer presence in the black community by involving a white character in a significant struggle with both his "manhood" and the "atmosphere of [his] . . . mind." I contend that this displacement does little to dispel the parallel reality of this struggle occurring in the traditional landscape of the African American novel—somewhere below the Mason-Dixon line. For David, mere contemplation, albeit forfeited by his own denial, is masked by a most horrible death. It is a parasitic death that internalizes the "black . . . cavern" alluded to earlier and prompts David to make a decision, literally in Joey's bed, that he would "allow no room in the universe for something which shamed and frightened me. I succeeded very well—by not looking at the universe, by not looking at myself, by remaining, in effect, in constant motion" (30–31). Fleeing to another country, avoiding introspection and "remaining . . . in constant motion," David's privilege of being both American and white is alluded to in the novel's first lines: "My ancestors conquered a continent." The attendant imaginative project—manifest destiny, bootstrap diplomacy—actualized through the machinations of colonial enterprise, is of little use to David outside his familiar territory. These traditional tools do not serve, to borrow a phrase from Audre Lorde, either "to dismantle the master's house"[24] or, in this case, to function as its superficial signifiers.

As the opening chapter ends, it is quite clear that Baldwin intends in part to use David's flight as a trope for a larger issue. David closes his primary flashback with the following observation:

> Perhaps, as we say in America, I wanted to find myself. This is an interesting phrase, not current as far as I know in the language of any other

people, which certainly does not mean what it says but betrays a nag-
ging suspicion that *something has been misplaced*. I think now that if I had
had any intimation that the self I was going to find would turn out to
be only the same self from which I had spent so much time in flight, *I
would have stayed at home.* (31; emphasis added)

When Baldwin writes "something has been misplaced," it is difficult
not read it as a clue to the veiled attempt in *Giovanni* to deal with both
the imaginative and the physical effects of embracing a very black
and gay identity. Moreover, the passage expresses David's desire to
escape from America as both home and institution; "America," even
though "conquered," is tainted by a queer act with a "brown" body.
This leaves the possibility of viewing David's retreat as a curative to
the "homosexual" behavior caused by or springing from the place
that is America, now soiled. Europe offers David another space of
privilege and becomes a new symbol of whiteness.

Early in *Giovanni*, it is made perfectly clear to us that escape to another country is an imaginative "out" for those who, like David, fear
their queer acts will somehow divest them of their whiteness. David's
flight is entirely possible because the world has been given to him as
a territory to be explored and conquered—a landscape upon which
he can work out his fearful imaginings, avoiding responsibility and
consequence at leisure. Because of his age, sex, and blackness,
Kenan's protagonist in *Visitation* has none of these advantages. As if
refusing to camouflage the importance of having a simultaneously
black and gay subjectivity, Kenan places Horace's struggles in a
changing South, at the table of not only a black family but one with a
churchgoing legacy to fulfill. These realities serve to shift much of
Baldwin's "misplaced" project onto the landscape that engenders it,
challenging notions of "blackness" and bringing the imaginative project back "home."

In contrast to *Giovanni*'s opening, we are not told until late in *A
Visitation of Spirits* that the cause of Horace's pain is his misgivings
about his homosexuality. We are first introduced to Horace as he
contemplates an impossible but necessary transformation. Inverting
the flight of Baldwin's protagonist, Kenan has Horace specifically
state that "he could not see transforming himself into anything that
would not fit the swampy woodlands of Southeastern North Carolina. He had to stay here" (11). Moreover, the resulting object of
Horace's transformation is a bird—an obvious allusion to the dom-

inance of birds as both grotesque and sacred figures in Baldwin's novels. As the first pages progress, it becomes clear that Horace *is* the "black . . . cavern" that David imagines in *Giovanni*. Contemplating his own sanity, Horace is haunted by a dual identity. Kenan writes:

> Had he gone mad? Somehow slipped beyond the veil of right reasoning and gone off into some deep, unsettled land of fantasy? . . . Of course, he was not crazy, he told himself; his was a very rational mind, acquainted with science and mathematics. But he was also a believer in an unseen world full of archangels and prophets and folk rising from the dead, a world preached to him from the cradle on, and a world he was powerless not to believe in as firmly as he believed in gravity and the times table. The two contradicting worlds were not contradictions in his mind. (16)

It is quite apparent that Horace has inherited this particularly black imaginative landscape, but he is denied access to it nonetheless. In Horace's cosmos, "folk rising from the dead" constitutes a normative occurrence, and he sees his own suicide as a rebirth rather than a death. Seeking salvation from his gay identity through the rough science of the occult, Horace believes he can transform his material essence into something *other*, with the aid of an imagination fostered in the understanding of the duality of existence. This duality is also present in Baldwin's universe. As critic David Bergman argues, Baldwin's relationship to a distinctly "African" past is complicated by his understanding of a black gay identity coupled with the pronouncements of a Pentecostal heritage.[25] Reevaluating the struggle of a gay Pentecostal, the Reverend James Tinney, Bergman notes that "one of the more difficult problems faced is how African a Black Christian Church can be before it descends into paganism."[26]

The irony of Kenan's novel is that it attempts to demonstrate— through Horace's use of paganism to transform his gay, African self into "another" (88)—the problematic of fostering a procreative black imaginative terrain that renders black gay subjectivity invisible. As Simmons suggests:

> While it is critically important to rebut homophobia and heterosexism, the most crucial challenge . . . is to develop an affirming and liberating philosophical understanding of homosexuality that will self-actualize black gay genius. Such a task requires a new epistemology, a new way

of "knowing," that incorporates the views our African ancestors had about the material and the metaphysical world.[27]

Simmons's claim is made manifest in Horace's failed project of "transformation"; he undertakes this experiment as an intended act of complete self-possession, as an act of self-determination.

Horace awakens at the close of the novel's first section in the company of "aberrations like himself, fierce and untamed" (28), believing himself born again and beckoned by "the voice." For the remainder of the novel a nude Horace, clutching a gun and smeared with mud and dust from his fireside ritual, performs a visitation, like some Dickensian figure, to his recent and painful past. It is significant that the opening section is titled "White Sorcery" and the next is called "Black Necromancy." While the obvious difference between sorcery and necromancy is that the former solicits the help of flagitious spirits for the purposes of divination, whereas the latter involves the conjuration of ancestors for both divination and manipulation of current events, Kenan implies that black magic is just as harmful as white incantation. By placing Horace at the mercy of white magic in the novel's opening pages and having him bear witness to the playbook of black necromancy, Kenan challenges the community-wide notion that black gay identity is a result of the horrors of slavery or evidence of pollution by white culture. The sanctity of the cultural product—essential and essentialized blackness—is interrogated in these first chapters.

Witnessing the past, Horace journeys to the First Baptist Church of Tims Creek, which is both his place of baptism and his family's inheritance. He becomes an eyewitness to a scene of his own humiliation as the Reverend Barden preaches on the sinfulness of homosexuality:

> They was talking about men and women, men and men, women and women—help me, Jesus—living together in sin. Like it wont nothing. Normal. Tolerable. Righteous. Lord, yes, it was on TV in between 'Little House on the Prairie' and 'The Waltons' so your children, my children could have been up watching this filth, as if it were as natural as a horse foaling or a chicken molting. But, dearly beloved . . . it ain't. (78)

It is not so much the indignity of the mention of homosexuality during prime time that is outrageous to Barden here as its tainting presence in the midst of *Little House* and *The Waltons*—two programs that promote the mythology of the white family as the repository of moral righteousness in America. In contradistinction to Morrison's effort to name the Beloveds, to bring them back from the place of silence, Reverend Barden's reference to the congregation as "beloved" places queer subjects in the space of the unnamed. Not only is Barden's black jeremiad undermined by his allusion to white families, but it is also shadowed by Horace's visitation. Later, Barden intones, "Satan and his demons, they come around to taint the soul, to make it unfit, O yes he does, he come, come on in and he whispers . . . in your ear, and he tells you—ha-ha—to do wrong" (80).

This fantastic scenario is actualized by Horace's ghostlike presence in the company of "his devilish crew [and] surrounded by fiends" (28); but Kenan reminds us that "demons" are conjured and not merely self-manifested. For Barden, homosexual presence, as stated in the Bible, is evidence of the "vanity" of the "imagination." Barden gives the young Horace a sermon borrowed from the same source that was used to justify slavery while naming any imaginative project with a homosexual genesis as demonic and nightmarish. Faced with Barden's empty rhetoric as fodder for his own creative genius/genesis, Horace is forced to envision an alternative creative project, a dream of transformation:

> He found himself seduced by this new world. . . . It all called to him, the numbers, the governments, the history, the religions, speaking to him of another, another, another . . . though he could never quite picture that other, the thing that called him so severely. Yet he labored and longed for it; as if his very life depended on knowing it; as if, somehow, he had to change his life. (88)

Unfortunately, Horace's creative project, his search for "another," is futile; how can he find an image of gay subjectivity, a mirror for himself, when this particular presence has been erased from the body of knowledge or given to him as a manifestation of the depraved inducements of Satan? Horace therefore attempts to become that which he knows himself to be—the grotesque companion of a multitude like himself, a figure not suggested by the dominant society but given to him in a preacherly text. The *source* of black gay identity is not white *sorcery* (and I do think Kenan intends this play on words) but the subtle manipulation and command of a "white" text in the black pulpit.

Kenan's concentration on the refiguration of a grotesque image is most likely suggested by Baldwin's usage of the grotesque as a prototype for David's self-hatred in *Giovanni's Room*. On the night of his first encounter with Giovanni, David remembers that

> someone . . . came out of the shadows toward me. It looked like . . . something walking after it had been put to death. . . . It glittered in the dim light . . . the eyelids gleamed with mascara, the mouth raged with lipstick. The face was white and thoroughly bloodless with some kind of foundation cream; it stank of powder and a gardenia-like perfume. The shirt, open coquettishly to the navel, revealed a hairless chest and a silver crucifix. (54)

Confronted with the specter of himself, David sees a nightmarish figure, a "zombie" painted white and marked with a cross of salvation, which it later uses tauntingly to signify on David's own ignorance and descent. In Kenan's *Visitation*, toward the conclusion of his personal salvation/transformation, Horace encounters an uncannily similar figure:

> He was a black man, dressed in a sun-bright costume, orange and green and blue and red, like a harlequin's. As Horace looked into the mirror, the face appeared more and more familiar, though it was becoming obscured by milky white greasepaint. He realized. Saw clearly. It was him. Horace. Sitting before the mirror, applying makeup. Of all things he had seen this night, all the memories he had confronted, all the ghouls and ghosts and specters, this shook him the most. Stunned and confused, bewildered, he could only stare at his reflection, seeing him and him and him. (219)

David's nightmarish image is reconstructed in Kenan's text. Horace recognizes himself—the white paint becomes a masking of his self, a self that becomes, because of its generational legacy through his grandfather's church, the signifier of salvation itself and the heralding of whiteness as the genesis of queer identity. The "another" that he begins his imaginative quest for is reduced here to "him and him and him." Left to himself as both source and resource, Horace decides that a movement from his human form to that of a bird will complete a creative project that he does not want to abandon. This transformation also signifies a belief that his humanity is not synonymous with his gay identity; the new "body" is better suited to both his creative expression and his self-actualization. Moreover, in a racist society, becoming a bird deracinates Horace completely from the problems associated with phenotypical arrangements. The parallel between Baldwin and Kenan here is in the ultimate erasure of black subjectivity in order to actualize a queer project.

(Im)Proper Objects and Misplaced Queers

In her introduction to the special double issue of *differences*, "More Gender Trouble: Feminism Meets Queer Theory," Judith Butler outlines the pitfalls of relegating "gender" to feminism and "sexuality" to lesbian and gay studies. Tracing a trajectory of feminist inquiries into sex/gender/sexuality from Gayle Rubin's "Thinking Sex" (1983) to the editors' introduction to the *Lesbian and Gay Studies Reader*, Butler argues that

> to restrict the proper object of feminism to gender, and to appropriate sexuality as the proper object of lesbian/gay studies, is either to deny this important feminist contribution to the very sexual discourse in which lesbian and gay studies emerged or to argue, implicitly, that the feminist contributions to thinking sexuality culminate in the supersession of feminism by lesbian and gay studies.[28]

In the impending turf war between feminism and lesbian-gay studies, Butler ultimately believes that the battlefield involves an inherent invalidation of both projects.

Butler also observes that, for the editors of *The Lesbian and Gay Studies Reader*,

> lesbian and gay studies will be derived from feminism, and yet, the editors argue, there will continue to be important communication between the two domains. . . . How is it that this framing of lesbian/gay in relation to feminism forecloses the field of social differences from which both projects emerge? In particular, terms such as "race" and "class" are ruled out from having a constitutive history in determining the parameters of either field. (6)

But in her own analysis, "race" and "class" refuse to intersect with feminism or lesbian-gay studies. Where they do overlap is in the margins of her work, where she highlights Biddy Martin's influence on her thinking in "Against Proper Objects." Butler footnotes Martin's "Sexualities without Genders and Other Queer Utopias" and surmises:

She claims as well that there are problems with theories that tend to foreground gender at the expense of sexuality and race, sexuality at the expense of gender and race, and race at the expense of sexuality and gender . . . those very theories are weakened by their failure to broach the complex interrelations of these terms." (22n. 1)

In contemporary feminist discourse, the conversation between race and feminism most often occurs in the future or in the footnotes.[29]

In my view, it is not feminism's or lesbian-gay studies' ownership of the categories of "gender" and "sexuality" that matters to the future of feminist and queer theory; it is the fact that neither field wishes to interact with its African Americanist counterparts. This lack of cross-pollination is ironic, given that the development of African American studies programs provided an institutional foundation for establishing subsequent programs with "minority" interests.

This lack of interaction, of conversation, has had devastating effects on all fields, as evidenced here in my reading of black gay presence in the midst of the African American canon. While it is true that, to some extent, African American studies has paid attention to feminism, it is abundantly clear that there is no room in the closet for discussions of sexuality that move beyond a heterosexist paradigm. With African American studies having chosen its "proper object" of inquiry, and with feminism and lesbian-gay studies debating what theirs should be, there is ample room in *all* fields for a ghosting of certain black bodies. Black queer subjectivity is the body that no one wants to be beholden to. Like Horace and his countless rituals for transmutation, in order to speak, queer black bodies have to search in outrageous places to find voice—they have to come back from the dead to get 'nuff respect due.

In all respects, feminists and their theoretical allies have ignored the first sexual revolution in this nation, which, I would argue, was more intriguing than the second. The first "outrage," to borrow from both Toni Morrison and William Faulkner, occurred during slavery, when white subjects experienced an unprecedented period of sexual revolution—a space where black bodies opened to them under the lash, in the fields and sometimes even in bedrooms.[30] Wouldn't an interplay of sexuality and gender find a remarkable stomping ground in the field of relations during slavery? Critics such as Hortense Spillers, as Butler suggests, have already broken ground with similar observations. It is not that race needs to be added to the equation; rather, it is that race cannot be excised from it. The question, as Morrison reminds us, is not why but how.[31] And why is it that the "proper object" of feminism is reduced to the terrain of gender and sexuality? What will it take for theorists to begin to move across critical boundaries? Why are certain black subjects such dead weight in feminism, in lesbian-gay studies, in African American criticism?

In Butler's piece race is, to borrow from Spillers, "vestibular" to feminism and its lesbian-gay allies. And if race is vestibular to discussions of sexuality and even gender, then we have some tacit explanation for why black gay bodies are so absent in the founding paradigm of African Americanist discourse. If lesbian-gay studies or feminism isn't having a conversation about "race," why should African Americanists reconfigure their own work to narrow the distance between points? Black (queer) bodies never get to determine the way in which discursive boundaries are organized. Like the countless understudies who know all the lines but rarely get to perform, they constantly wait in the wings for the appropriate time to be *somebody's* "proper object."

For example, in her analysis of the social and the symbolic in "Against Proper Objects," Butler notes, "The symbolic is understood as a field of normativity that exceeds and structures the domain of the socially given" (19). She later asks, "How ought the relation between the social and symbolic to be reconfigured?" (19). Perhaps the space of reconfiguration exists where whiteness and blackness intersect. Perhaps we might not only ask if the lesbian has appropriated the phallus (dildo?) but be so bold as to inquire about what that phallus (dildo?) looks like. Given that owning the phallus, or at least a replica, is as easy as a trip to your local "girl toy" shop, and given that sales of "colored" dildos outstrip those of "white" ones, the question "What does the phallus look like, what 'color' does it own?" might be outrageous but absolutely the only queer act left to those seeking a conversation at the margin—those seeking to bring back the dead from the space of silence.

My work here is proof that connections between fields are important to revitalizing a terrain seemingly evacuated of its conversational value. A conversation at the borders between African American, lesbian-gay, and feminist studies might be especially dangerous, because focus on race, sexuality, and gender threatens to catapult us into a past we prefer to remain ignorant about. If looking at black bodies (and white bodies, for that matter) through the lens of slavery dissolves gender difference, to remember Spillers's assessment, then the place of contact of the three fields of inquiry is revolutionary indeed. As Spillers maintains: "Under these conditions, we lose at least *gender* difference *in the outcome*, and the female body and the male body become a territory of cultural and political maneuver, not at all gender-related, gender specific."[32] The central query here is whether or not we are still laboring "under these conditions." We might ask if we have reclaimed the space of difference, less than 140 years after emancipation.

In the confrontation between fields, some things will most certainly be lost. The loss of "gender difference" could prove dangerous to an African Americanist position, solidly entrenched in its masculinist posturings, as well as thoroughly destabilizing to a feminism reputed to herald gender as the determining norm. But feminism ought to cease grieving over the residual effects of coalition building, and African American studies ought to challenge itself to look beyond the gender/sexuality binary it has borrowed from feminism.

In an essay on Randall Kenan's work, Robert McRuer comments on the placement of queer bodies in *Visitation*, arguing that Tims Creek, North Carolina, is

> not the most conducive atmosphere for the expression of queer desire, certainly. But as liberal gay and lesbian thought likes to remind us, "we are everywhere," and rather than conceding that "everywhere" *actually* means New York and San Francisco, I'm interested in what (perhaps more radical) cultural work can be done when that "everywhere" includes such an apparently marginal and inhospitable place.[33]

McRuer moves on to discuss the extent to which Kenan's novel is a "veritable treatise on the unstable opposition between sameness and difference" (227). Indeed, there is another place that Kenan travels to in the novel, in order to have Horace circumvent the problem of "apparently marginal" and "inhospitable" places. Kenan places Horace in the position to narrate the story of his own death—in much the same way that the Hughes brothers position the black youth Caine in their film *Menace II Society* (1993). While all black people experience the inhospitable racial climate that is America, Kenan's return of David/Horace to a black South challenges our critical placement of black (male) subjects such as Horace and Caine—one gay, one straight; one barren, one procreative—at such opposite ends of the spectrum of blackness.

Narration from the grave, or the space of death, prepares these characters to consider a conversation with one another in the context of a figurative death we all share. McRuer agrees that in all the spaces he occupies, Horace can find no peace—no space in which his many selves exist together. Horace's answer to this is to escape the harsh fact of his life for the more pleasant, agreeable realization of (him)self in death. By relocating Baldwin's tale of first encounters in the black South, Kenan allows for a twofold project to emerge: a commentary on the community that engenders Horace's macabre answer to his own life and a mechanism or back door through which black folks, hetero- or homosexual, can speak and be heard. In their deaths, we see the stories of Horace and Caine as tragically aligned—without their bodily demise, we would be unable to see any parallel in their narratives.

In a sense, Kenan's use of Horace's suicide escapes the triviality of queer theory's obsession with "sameness" and "difference." Death marks the point of absolute difference; it is a sameness we'd rather not recognize. While Horace's psyche is embattled with, as McRuer argues, competing pictures of his sense of belonging and being recognized as belonging, we find an end point to this internal and external bickering in his suicide. By crossing the line into (an)other space, Horace comes alive, in the flesh, for the first time—like Beloved before him, he appears naked and visible and haunts our imaginative attempts to erase him from a our fruitful landscapes, and our canons, if you will. Horace's suicide and his narrative journey challenge our attempts not to read him as the "proper object" of African American, feminist, and/or lesbian-gay critical endeavors.

NOTES

1. Randall Kenan, *A Visitation of Spirits* (New York: Doubleday, 1989), 252.
2. Toni Morrison, "Life in His Language," in *James Baldwin: The Legacy*, ed. Quincy Troupe (New York: Touchstone Books, 1989), 76.
3. Evelynn Hammonds, "Black (W)holes and the Geometry of Black Female Sexuality," *differences* 6, 2 and 3 (1994): 127.
4. See Michael S. Sherry, "The Language of War in AIDS Discourse," in

Writing AIDS: Gay Literature, Language and Analysis, ed. Timothy F. Murphy and Suzanne Poirier (New York: Columbia University Press, 1993), 39–53.

5. Robert Bone, *The Negro Novel in America* (New Haven: Yale University Press, 1965), 226; emphasis added. I give thanks and grateful credit to my colleague Ann duCille who brought *Giovanni's Room* to my attention and opened her classroom to me so that I could participate in a discussion about this wonderful book. Many of the ideas in this chapter have been inspired by that discussion.

6. Robert McRuer, "A Visitation of Difference: Randall Kenan and Black Queer Theory," *Journal of Homosexuality* 26, 2 and 3 (1993): 227–228.

7. James Oliver Horton, "In Search of Identity: James Baldwin and the Black American Intellectual Tradition," in *James Baldwin: His Place in American Literary History and His Reception in Europe,* ed. Jakob Köllhofer (Frankfurt am Main: Peter Lang, 1991), 98; emphasis added.

8. Houston A. Baker, Jr., *Long Black Song: Essays in Black American Literature and Culture* (Charlottesville: University of Virginia Press, 1972), 108.

9. David Bergman, "The African and the Pagan in Gay Black Literature," in *Sexual Sameness: Textual Differences in Lesbian and Gay Writing,"* ed. Joseph Bristow (New York: Routledge, 1992), 159.

10. Cheryl Clarke, "Living the Texts Out: Lesbians and the Uses of Black Women's Traditions," in *Theorizing Black Feminisms: The Visionary Pragmatism of Black Women,* ed. Stanlie M. James and Abena P. A. Busia, (New York: Routledge, 1993), 216.

11. Horace Porter, *Stealing the Fire: The Art and Protest of James Baldwin* (Middletown, Conn.: Wesleyan University Press, 1990), 133.

12. Ron Simmons, "Some Thoughts on the Challenges Facing Black Gay Intellectuals," in *Brother to Brother: New Writings by Black Gay Men,* ed. Essex Hemphill (Boston: Alyson Publications, 1991), 222.

13. For an excellent analysis of biblical references that explicitly prohibit same-sex relations, see Gary David Comstock, *Violence against Lesbians and Gay Men* (New York: Columbia University Press, 1991), 120–40.

14. Arthur Flannigan Saint-Aubin's "TESTERIA: The Dis-ease of Black Men in White Supremacist, Patriarchal Culture," *Callaloo* 17, 4 (1994): 1054–1073, gives a fascinating psychoanalytic reading of black masculinity in American culture. His work provides an interesting (heterosexual) parallel to this argument.

15. Charles I. Nero, "Toward a Black Gay Aesthetic: Signifying in Contemporary Black Gay Literature," in *Brother to Brother,* ed. Essex Hemphill, 235.

16. Nikki Giovanni, *Gemini: An Extended Autobiographical Statement on My First Twenty Years of Being a Black Poet* (Indianapolis: Bobbs-Merrill, 1971), 41.

17. Simmons, in "Some Thoughts," 211.

18. As quoted in Essex Hemphill, *Ceremonies: Prose and Poetry* (New York: Plume, 1992), 54.

19. For a discussion of "exorcism" and its relationship to the black Pentecostal church, see Nero, in "Toward a Black Gay Aesthetic," 238–43.

20. I am particularly referring to the distribution of the video *The Gay Agenda* (1992), produced by the Antelope Valley Springs of Life Ministries and distributed to black churches in an effort to spearhead an attack on gay and lesbian peoples from within the black community. For an examination of the video in the context of the military ban against gay men and lesbians, see Alycee J. Lane, "Black Bodies/Gay Bodies: The Politics of Race in the Gay/Military Battle," *Callaloo* 17, 4 (1994): 1074–1088. The group produced another video, released in 1996, entitled *The Ultimate Target of the Gay Agenda: Same Sex Marriages.*

21. Wole Soyinka, "Foreword: James Baldwin at the Welcome Table," in *James Baldwin,* ed. Troupe, 11–12.

22. In a 1984 interview with Richard Goldstein, Baldwin comments that *"Giovanni's Room* is not really about homosexuality. It's the vehicle through which the book moves. *Go Tell It on the Mountain,* for example, is not about a church and *Giovanni* is not really about homosexuality. It's about what happens to you if you're afraid to love anybody. Which is much more interesting than the question of homosexuality" ("'Go the Way Your Blood Beats': An Interview with James Baldwin," in *James Baldwin,* ed. Troupe, 176).

23. James Baldwin, *Giovanni's Room* (1956; reprint, New York: Dell Publishing Co., 1964), 9–10.

24. Audre Lorde, *Sister Outsider* (Trumansburg, N.Y.: Crossing Press, 1984), 110–113.

25. When a young man, James Baldwin became a youth minister in the local Pentecostal church.

26. Bergman, "The African and the Pagan," 158.

27. Simmons, "Some Thoughts," 224.

28. Judith Butler, "Against Proper Objects," *differences* 6, 2 (1994): 8; see also the special issue on Queer Theory in *differences* 3, 2 (1991).

29. This is not the first time Butler has sequestered her comments about the place of "race" or the work of women of color. In "Against Proper Objects," these theorists are constantly listed but never engaged; earlier, in *Bodies That Matter: On the Discurvise Limits of Sex,* (New York: Routledge, 1993) Butler's discussion of Nella Larson's *Passing* includes the work of Deborah McDowell and others as a segue into her own discussion.

30. I am thinking here about the film *Mandingo* (1975) which chronicled an aspect of slavery that all of us would rather forget. Nonetheless, the sexual life of white men and women in the film, fictional though it might be, awaits

appropriate attention from the critical community. Lodged in the psyche of all Americans is that memory of the "first" revolution. Butler's use of the tension between Foucault and psychoanalysis and the role of "kinship" and "sexuality" is ripe terrain for an examination of kinship systems under slavery—a move that Hortense Spillers makes in "Mama's Baby, Papa's Maybe: An American Grammar," *Diacritics* 17, 2 (1987). It is ironic that Butler refers to Spillers in passing, but when she interrogates systems of kinship and their relationship to sexuality, she finds no room to engage with Spillers's findings on the subject. This represents one of the most troubling missed opportunities in Butler's article.

31. In her examination of the Africanist presence in American literature, Toni Morrison writes: "Looking at the scope of American literature, I can't help thinking that the question should never have been 'Why am I, an Afro-American, absent from it?' It is not a particularly interesting query anyway. The spectacularly interesting question is 'What intellectual feats had to be performed by the author or his critic to erase me from a society seething with my presence, and what effect has that performance had on the work?'" ("Unspeakable Things Unspoken," *Michigan Quarterly Review,* 28, 1 [winter 1989]: 11–12).

32. Spillers, "Mama's Baby, Papa's Maybe," 67.

33. McRuer, "Visitation of Difference," 221–232.

Chapter 11

"I'm Not Entirely What I Look Like"

*Richard Wright, James Baldwin,
and the Hegemony of Vision;
or, Jimmy's FBEye Blues*

Maurice Wallace

> That old FB eye
> Tied a bell to my bed stall
> Said old FB eye
> Tied a bell to my bed stall
> Each time I love my baby, gover'ment know it all
> —Richard Wright, 1949

The year was 1943 when Richard Wright sketched out a plan for a monthly serial conceived, in his words, to "clarify the personality and cultural problems of minority groups" by "using the Negro question as an abstract and concrete frame of experience to reflect a constructive criticism upon the culture of the nation as a whole."[1] Schematically, "American Pages"[2] was to have offered an inexpensive, intelligent corrective to the culturally atrophying influence of popular magazines on the American reading public. For the project's prospectus, Wright compiled a list of one hundred or more possible issues. Features were to include articles on African American folklore, reports on the progress of race relations, profiles of black folk who passed themselves off as white and whites who passed for black, as well as formal, if simplified, academic studies, fictional extracts, and—most crucial for this essay—criminal case studies. Unable to rally enough moneyed interest in the project to finance its $16,000 start-up costs, Wright and his impressive coterie of supporting intellectuals, including Horace Cayton, St. Clair Drake, and Ralph Ellison, soon aborted their "American Pages" plans. Significantly, though, several of Wright's thematic concerns survived this project's aborted hopes. Among the most enduring was a deep-seated interest in criminality, criminal discipline, and youth delinquency. Indulging in what was to prove a lifelong intrigue, Wright went on to work out yet another culturally clarifying project one year later, one that seems to have been intent on realizing the concrete and metaphysical "framing" of black experience metaphorically invoked in the articulated objectives of "American Pages."

As if to link the mechanical and visual function of the photographic frame to the judicial lie of the "frame-up," Wright proposed in 1944 to organize a photographic exhibition of young black criminal delinquents in Harlem—a curious idea that suggested a complicitous kinship between the mechanical and social processes of publicly diffusing stereotypes of black criminality. While Wright's exhibition, like his "American Pages," never materialized, the idea alone is sufficient to explain why, to my mind, "Fate," book 3 of his 1940 *Native Son*, might have been better designated "Framed." Had Wright's objective to put up a showing of images of juvenile criminal delinquency in 1940s Harlem been realized, it would have not only extended the logic of the photographic realism of book 3 of *Native Son* to its farthest, mimetic end but highlighted fairly explicitly the ineluctable irony for the black writer: namely, that the problem of racial surveillance, of the spectatorship of looking on and over conspicuously colored bodies, "may be as deep a problem," as W. J. T. Mitchell has written, "as [the] various forms of reading (decipherment, decoding, interpretation, etc)" literary texts.[3] I argue, in fact, that it is precisely the deep problem of racial surveillance, of the gaze of Western racialism as an untoward menace to the "coherence and ideality of the [black masculine] corporeal ego"[4] that troubles the otherwise sluggish narrative waters of book 3 of *Native Son* and lends so much symbolic currency to the metaphor of enframement as the doubly signifying ur-trope of black masculine spectacularity, or what I have come to think of as the sociovisibility of black male subjects.

In the first part of this essay, then, I propose to look backward, from the unfulfilled criminographic ambitions of "American Pages" and the implicit panoptic critique of Wright's intended exhibition, upon the fictional designs of book 3 of *Native Son*, in order to look forward later at the specularizing exercises of the criminographic imagination upon the queer black body of James Baldwin.

Much has been made by Wright scholars of Bigger Thomas's incapability to articulate coherently the absurdity of his life in book 3 of *Native Son*. But what has escaped virtually all critical notice in the nearly six decades of critical thought about *Native Son* is the apprehension of Bigger's rhetorical failures in "Fate" as the corporeally arresting consequence of a kind of picture-taking racial gaze that "fixes" (in two senses) and "frames" him within a rigid and limited grid of representational possibilities. In other words, it is not simply that Bigger, once captured, "is deserted by [all] linguistic facility" before his accusers, to repeat a typical reading of book 3.[5] More than that, their looks are bodily "paralyzing,"[6] and in *Native Son* the tongue is simply another immobilized muscle. Aligned in book 3 with the implicitly male look of the still camera, which, as Kaja Silverman recently wrote, has "provided the gaze with its primary metaphor" (Silverman, 168) since the nineteenth century, the racial gaze in *Native Son* congeals Bigger's body into a Medusan rigidity that arrests representation, freezing, fixing, photographically framing the subject within a determinately racist symbolic schema of bestializing associations.[7] Accused of killing white Mary Dalton, Bigger is menaced unrelentingly in book 3 by the "compact array of [his accusers'] white faces and the constant flashing of bulbs for pictures" (Wright, *Native Son*, 318). Consistently in book 3, under the scopic threat of the look and the lens, Bigger "held very still" (324); "Bigger was paralyzed with shame" (348). He "stiffened" as Jan "stood facing him. . . . He lifted his eyes; Jan was looking straight at him and he looked away" (330), helpless to avert the ocular torment. Rendered wooden by the petrifying spell of white eyes, it is no wonder that words refuse him: "He tried to move his tongue and found it swollen," motionless in its place (320). Smaller wonder still—since any camera confrontation, mechanical or ophthalmic, is always "to experience a certain 'horror' or 'mortification'" (Silverman, 150)—that Bigger could not suffer long his specular fetishization at the arraignment for Mary Dalton's murder.

"Negro Rapist Faints at Inquest," the newspaper headlines announce. The story beneath the headlines, the sort of story Wright had hoped "American Pages" would counteract, discloses the ocular aspect of Bigger's representational arrest, the simultaneous enframement and frame-up of the black male as sexual beast:

> Overwhelmed by the sight of his accusers, Bigger Thomas, Negro sex-slayer, fainted dramatically this morning at the inquest of Mary Dalton, millionaire Chicago heiress.
>
> Emerging from a stupor for the first time since his capture last Monday night, the black killer sat cowed and fearful as hundreds sought to get a glimpse of him.
>
> "He looks exactly like an ape!" exclaimed a terrified young white girl who watched the black slayer being loaded onto a stretcher after he fainted.
>
> Though the Negro killer's body does not seem compactly built, he gives the impression of possessing abnormal physical strength. He is about five feet, nine inches tall and his skin is exceedingly black. (Wright, *Native*, 322)

Wright seems to want us to understand that literally Bigger could not bear "the *sight* of his accusers." He faints at the inquest not because he sees them but because they see him, their "eyes gazing at him with calm conviction" (318). If anyone in the mob of anxious, angry onlookers at the inquest missed catching the "glimpse of him" they were much too willing to be satisfied with, nothing is left wanting descriptively in this insinuated *Chicago Tribune* article to keep Bigger screened from the representational violation of reckless racial eye-balling. The article's anonymous author displaces the public (sexual) terror onto "a terrified young girl," photo-graphically reconstructing *her* primatal "picture" of Bigger with paternalistic precision.[8] Despite the obvious impotency of Bigger's languished, fainted body, the journalist's ocular imposition over-looks his distressed body, trusting rather in a familiarly filmic impression about Bigger, a pictorial imprint in the racialist imaginary of *King Kong* revisited. As the article goes on to sketch more of Bigger's physical features, his protruding lower jaw, his long "dangling" arms, and his "huge, muscular" shoulders, each outline, each apish appearance, is consistently attended by its enframed, overdetermined, cathected meaning in white eyes (322). Bigger's jaw, for example, "protrudes obnoxiously, *reminding one of a jungle beast*" (322; emphasis added). Seeing his arms "dangling . . . to his knees," the reporter writes that it "is easy to imagine how this man, in the grip of a brain-numbing sex passion, overpowered little

Mary Dalton" (323). His shoulders are kept "hunched, *as if about to spring upon you at any moment"* (323; emphasis added).

The effect of this brutish pictorialization of Bigger is at once ekphrastic (verbally representative of the visual) and taxonomic, inasmuch as it enframes Bigger visually within a primitivist discourse, even as it makes the black male body available—a naked specimen—for white public fantasies of wild, "brain-numbing sex" (Recall that "hundreds sought to get a glimpse of him.") Like King Kong kept at the safe remove of the movie screen,[9] Bigger, securely contained (i.e., framed) visually and criminally between the "two policemen to whom he was handcuffed" (Wright, *Native Son*, 386), is less the linguistically constituted subject of the article than the visual "figment of that black world which they," the real subjects, the white spectators, "feared and were anxious to keep under control" (318).

As ekphrastic text,[10] the newspaper now arrests representation as s(ec)urely as the racial gaze. Symbolically, after reading the *Tribune* article himself, Bigger "lowered the paper. . . . He held very still" (324). Mortified by the ekphrastic threat (if not much more) of "newspapermen ready with their bulbs" (388).[11] Bigger tries "to feel the texture of his own feelings . . . to tell what they meant" (404) but, "twice trapped" (422), in body and (potential) being, succumbs to the represented condition of objecthood—succumbs, in effect, to a deeper mortification:

> Listlessly, he talked. He traced his every action. He paused at each question [State's Attorney] Buckley asked him and wondered how he could link up his bare actions with what he had felt; but his words came flat and dull. White men were looking at him, waiting for his words, and all the feelings of his body vanished, just as they had when he was in the care between Jan and Mary. When he was through, he felt more lost and undone than when he was captured. Buckley stood up; the other white man rose and held out the papers for him to sign. He took the pen in hand. Well, why shouldn't he sign? He was guilty. He was lost. They were going to kill him. Nobody could help him. They were standing in front of him, bending over him, looking at him, waiting. His hand shook. He signed. (358)

Collapsing visual and verbal signs, the image and the word, Wright discloses in this scene "the social structure of representation as," in Mitchell's terms, "an activity and a relationship of power/knowledge/desire" (Mitchell, 180).

Although Max, Bigger's legal defender, hopes to "represent" (Wright, *Native Son,* 335) a hopelessly enframed man *as* a man before the court—"Just sit and say nothing," he counsels (336)—Bigger's representation is a *fait accompli*: "How can I," Max pleads with the court, "make the picture of what has happened to this boy show plain and powerful upon a screen of sober reason, when a thousand newspaper and magazine artists have already drawn it in lurid ink upon a million sheets of public print?" (446). Nowhere in all of African American literature, I submit, is the ekphrastic menace to black male subjecthood more plainly revealed. Even Max's desire to "make the picture . . . show . . . upon a screen," whatever good it aims to do, cannot help finally but deliver Bigger to peril. One might argue in this connection that it is precisely this representational crisis in public life and letters to which the particularity of black masculinist writing in the United States responds. From an altogether authorial, if not aesthetic, point of view, the black male writer, one discerns, shares Bigger Thomas's frustrations of self-expressivity: "He hated this; if anything could be done in his behalf, he himself wanted to do it; not others. The more he saw others exerting themselves, the emptier he felt" (338). Perhaps more explicitly, the black male writer is to be seen in the "brown-skinned Negro" professor, "turning and twisting in the white man's hands" as they manipulate him while he is "trying desperately to free himself" (396) from their assertive hold. Thrown in a cell with Bigger, he screams through the cell bars, "'Give me *my* papers'" (390; emphasis added), recalling those earlier papers—the newspaper, the signed confession—which were certainly *their* papers but not his. If Bigger is the Every (Black) Man of *Native Son,* the professor, who "was writing a book on how colored people live" (397), is the artist/scholar struggling, "turning and twisting," to convey black masculine life as it is, not as it is seen in the racialist's "illusionist" representational system (see Mitchell).

In *Native Son* bodily arrest and the paralyzing shock of the racial glare imitate the fetishistic enframement of black masculine being in white eyes. Bigger's capture by the Chicago police and the professor's restraint repeat, as Martin Heidegger outlines it, the pictorial and scopic function under modernity.

In his essay "The Age of the World Picture," Heidegger distinguishes the modern age from the premodern period by the former history's epistemological obeisance to the supremacy of the picture, the represented idea. According to Heidegger, whatever exists to the modern mind is cognitively comprehensible only "to the extent to which it lets itself be put at the disposal of representation." (Heidegger 126). As represented idea, then, "whatever is," is "set up" as an object of representation. And "only that which becomes object in this way" may be "considered to be in being" at all,[12] even only as an idea—since, as Derrida reminds us,[13] so much of the history and semantics of the European *idea*, in that term's Greek genealogy, equates seeing with knowing. (We have in the French, for example, the unmistakable kinship of *voir, percevoir,* and *savoir*—"to see," "to perceive," "to know.") Put another way, only that which is "imaginable" in the crudest sense (image + able) bears, in the present age of the world picture, the truth of being.

Heidegger, of course, is critical of this modern habit of ready submission to the image. For him the picture is always subject to reproducing ideational blind spots. Insofar as every picture and picturable idea is also delimited by the borders of meaning and sense that frame, localize, fix, and arrest its otherwise boundless transformations of signification, the supremacy of pictures may be said to account for the arrestive nature of the racial gaze. To gaze upon black male subjects such as Bigger Thomas and, as we shall see soon enough, James Baldwin, is hardly a different exercise from the undertaking to frame the art object, since, as the pervasiveness of visual and photographic tropes in book 3 of *Native Son* implies, the African American male appears to the white West *as a picture. Native Son* discloses nothing more profound than this. For if Bigger Thomas believed, in fleeing the basement scene of the discovery of Mary Dalton's charred body, that his physical absence was enough to dissociate him from his criminal demonization in the reactionary white mind, "a small picture" of him, "solemn and black" (Wright, *Native Son,* 258), captured on page 2 of the *Tribune,* promptly disabused him of that delusion. Above all else, what *Native Son* reveals in book 3 is a lived rather than a solely literary phenomenon of black masculine being. Concerning black men under the modern hegemony of vision, it is not their person so much as their image that incriminates them in the white mind. As an image—a soul-stealing visual projection of the fears and fixations of the white imaginary—Bigger becomes traceable, in a word; optically reproducible in the faces and, as I shall show shortly, the files of so many black men. Bigger realizes soon enough that "there would be a thousand white policeman on the South Side searching for him" or, as the pictorial frame-up is apt to do, "any black who looked like him" (258).

If *Native Son* is the *locus classicus* of the failure of vision in modern African American literature, it may have its rival in American letters (a distinction I borrow from Michael Warner's insistence on the formal pluralities of "literary" expression in his *Letters of the Republic*)[14] in the FBI files of James Baldwin. Although Baldwin's 1962 novel *Another Country* is in part a corrective rewrite of *Native Son*'s protest polemic, it also depicts the violence of the look in book 1, "Easy Riders." That effort (and Wright's), however, to expose the distorting machinations of the racial gaze is a mere fictional recapitulation of an ocular actuality documented in the more than seventeen hundred pages of the FBI's papers on Baldwin.[15] Wright, too, had been secretly followed by the FBI, from the time he worked on the Federal Writer's Project in Chicago in 1935 to his death in 1960, but never—as his comparatively meager 181-page file suggests—with such intense scrutiny as Baldwin. Though it was Wright who, in 1949, composed the unpublished satirical verse "FBEye Blues," it was Baldwin, much more than Wright, whose social spectacularity as gay black male in midtwentieth-century conservative America would actualize Bigger Thomas's fictional enframement.

Ironically, the first known mention of Baldwin in the FBI record was not the 1960 report that officially opened his file but an earlier, 1951 reference to him in a report on Richard Wright. An unknown source disclosed that Baldwin was "a young Negro writer . . . [and] a student in Paris" who had "attacked the hatred themes of Wright's writings" (quoted in Robins, 345). While Baldwin's very public denunciations of *Native Son* (in his essays "Everybody's Protest Novel" and "Many Thousand Gone") first captured the bureau's attention, it was the 1960 report that he was a "prominent member of the Fair Play for Cuba Committee" that began the federal government's twenty-year surveillance of him. FBI informants shadowed Baldwin and aided the agency in monitoring his nomadic changes of address, from New York to California to Istanbul to the south of France, where his and his lovers' worries about the increasing violence against homosexuals in America led him to take up permanent residence in 1970. The FBI also telephoned Baldwin under numerous pretexts and, not unexpectedly, they often photographed him. One compelling page of the file neatly juxtaposes an image of Baldwin to one of Wright, with not so much as a brief caption attending the photographs. To be sure, the photographic composition of the Baldwin file is crucial to comprehending Baldwin's vexed sociovisibility. But more critical to uncovering the visual complicities in black male misrepresentation are the ekphrastic features of the file, those textual descriptions of Baldwin that do not offer us a photograph at all (dozens of memos in the file introduce photos of Baldwin that are, in fact, absent from the declassified papers) but nevertheless frame him descriptively, as if to approximate, in the same overdetermined, picture-taking vein as in *Native Son*, a pictorial representation. Here, I offer two examples as complementing cases in point.

In the first example, a 1964 *New York Post* article entitled "James Baldwin: A *New York Post* Portrait," an article published in six serial installments between January 13 and January 19, appears clipped from the *Post* and pasted onto twenty-four pages of the Baldwin file. Despite its first gnomish impressions of him ("James Baldwin, a small, dark splinter of a man"), the profile sketches a remarkably embodied subject whose depiction not only belies the mininalism of the first glance but, like *Native Son*, reveals by virtue of its journalistic cast the public's culpability (or credulity) in the photo-graphic fetishization of black male subjects, which Baldwin's FBI papers merely formalize. In page after page of the records containing the *Post* profile (Papers #100-146553-87 through #100-146553-94), Baldwin is described in some variation of "huge-eyed [if] undersized," sometimes sitting "cross-legged," "pausing now and then to scratch his calf . . . [or] his elbow" or to rub his ankle. As he stabs out a cigarette, we are made to notice an ashtray that sits or stands somehow "near his knee." His knees, the reporter conveys, are propped up, as his arms are pictured "looping" around what are alternately depicted as "jack-knifed" and "rubber" legs. The corporeal preoccupations in the *Post*'s six-part profile on Baldwin—inevitably, now the bureau's too—dispute Baldwin's "frail person," "so thin it's hard to believe he casts a shadow." For cast a shadow he does—a shadow much more significant in the racist and homophobic imaginary than his small build could conceivably cast. For if it is indeed true, as Lauren Berlant has written, that "the white male body is the relay to [social and political] legitimation . . . [and] the power to suppress that body, to cover its tracks and its traces is the sign of real authority,"[16] then it is precisely the shadowy trace of blackness (to say nothing of the specter of homosexuality) that misrepresents Baldwin's smallness in prosimian terms (huge eyes, "looping" arms, "rubber" legs)—terms only once removed from those which, in *Native Son*, describe Bigger Thomas as an ape.

That the *New York Post*'s verbal picture of Baldwin is a fairly faithful reflection of the bureau's surveillance habits is supported by the text of the second document, reporting Baldwin's activities in Istanbul, where off and on he spent eight years between 1961 and 1969. One portion of the file reads:

> Baldwin's method of working is strange. There are times when he writes continuously for twenty-four hours without food or drink. Under such circumstances, he does not even notice if [someone] shout[s] at him. . . . Afterwards, he lies down and sleeps. Moreover, he is in a sound state of sleep for forty-eight hours. If [a man] is able to awaken him, how fortunate [he is].

This oddly clinical report is important for the familiarly colonial way in which it imagines Baldwin as "strange," picturing him within an anthropological (if not yet anthropoidal) frame of visual reference. Moreover, it links Baldwin's "strange" behavior to writing in such a way as to mystify that labor and bring it under scopic suspicion as well. Clearly, the bureau was just as interested in Baldwin's body of writings as it was his "strange" writing body.

When his novel *Another Country* and long essay *The Fire Next Time* were published, in 1962 and 1963 respectively, the bureau intensified its surveillance of Baldwin. Whereas the bureau's motives for redoubling its efforts after *The Fire Next Time* were plainly political, the most cursory review of the papers pertaining to *Another Country* discloses that political motives were often frequently confused by voyeuristic ones, prurient motives not unlike those of "that old FB eye" in Wright's "FBEye Blues." While it is certain, too, that Baldwin's private 1963 meeting with Attorney General Robert Kennedy, at the height of the civil rights crisis, was an additional catalyst for the FBI's interest in him (especially since he suggested to Kennedy that the attorney general fire FBI Director J. Edgar Hoover), the bureau was never so obviously fixated on Baldwin's sexual tastes as when it undertook to determine whether or not *Another Country*'s homoeroticism and scenes of interracial sex were sufficient to count as violations of federal obscenity laws.

Although the bureau's General Crimes Section concluded, curiously, that *Another Country* "contain[ed] literary merit and may be valuable to students of psychology and social behavior" (quoted in Robins, 347), this did not prevent FBI agents from keeping close watch on Baldwin's own sexual activities, as if the question of *Another Country*'s pornographic potential could be solved by knowing Baldwin's sexual practices ("Isn't Baldwin a well known pervert?" asked Hoover in one of his memos.) The question was followed by an intense, nearly obsessive scrutiny of Baldwin's sexual behaviors, starting with the observation that "although the theme of homosexuality figured in two of his three published novels . . . it is not possible to say that he is a pervert" (Robins, 348). Not much later, and after a spate of contradictory reports, the bureau came to another conclusion, one that hinged, tellingly, on what was not actually seen but rather overheard and inferred—an extrapolation, that is, of the visual from the auditory: "It has been heard that Baldwin may be a homosexual and *he appeared as if he may be one*" (emphasis added). Conflating empirical verbal evidence and ocular speculation, the FBI surveillance of Baldwin confirmed that the white pictorial reflex could be quickened as much through eavesdropping as through eyeballing. The aural allusion in Paper #100-146553-215 suggests further the possibility for racial specularity, as the file's missing photographs affirm, without even a trapped, objectified body to provoke it. The white racialist imagination does not always require a body, only the five senses and a racial or sexual context.[17] Given, too, what has now been proven about J. Edgar Hoover's personal obsessions with the sex lives of black men and women, with homosexuality, and, as historian David Garrow, author of *The FBI and Martin Luther King, Jr.*, put it, with "activities that were interracial,"[18] it is not surprising that Baldwin became an overwhelmingly captivating site of investigation for the bureau.

Despite the evidence of voyeuristic propensities in the FBI's relentless surveillance of a man who thought of himself, ironically enough, as a "witness" to the truth of American race matters, the bureau's tracking of Baldwin in the United States and abroad is hardly the exposé it appears it was intended to be. Nor are the FBI papers on Baldwin especially revealing of the more mundane curiosities that interest archivists and literary critics. Did Baldwin keep a journal? What literary periodicals did he read? Who were his turncoat friends and false lovers? Did he pray for inspiration? Of course, there may be something of a voyeuristic impulse in such curiosities, which Baldwin, for one, might be happy these files resist. The files remain provocative nonetheless, not for what secrets they reveal about Baldwin's comings and goings—indeed, they disclose little in that respect, owing to Baldwin's directness about his public and private activities—but for what they reveal about the spectacular conditions of historical black masculine identity and the chronic effort to "frame" the black male body, criminally and visually, for the visual pleasures of whites. The FBI's surveillance of Baldwin instantiates what philosopher Martin Jay calls "a scopic regime" in modern Western culture, a systematic visual violation of the body that tends first to criminalize, then to eroticize black (and of late, brown) men.[19] When FBI agents tracked Baldwin to a writer's colony in upstate New York in 1945, years before the bureau's official surveillance began,[20] their eyeballing interrogations left him feeling "humiliated" (Baldwin, 108). In search of an AWOL marine they were certain Baldwin knew, two agents "walked [Baldwin] out of [a] diner, and stood [him] against a wall":

> My color had already made me conspicuous enough in that town—this is putting it mildly indeed—and, from a distance, the townspeople stared. . . . I knew of nothing which I had done to have attracted their attention. *Much later in my life, I knew very well what I had done to attract their attention, and intended, simply, to keep on keeping on.* . . . I was terribly frightened, and I was desperately trying to keep one jump ahead of them—to guess what it was before they revealed it. If I could guess what it was, then I might know how to answer and know what to do. . . . They frightened me, and they humiliated me—it was like being spat upon, or pissed on, *or gang-raped.* (108; emphasis added)

In short, Baldwin's FBI papers tell a very real story about the social and symbolic consequences of the spectacular conditions of (gay) black male subjectivity, and their nearly impossible escape. Baldwin's desperation "to keep one jump ahead of them," however, to "know how to answer" and "what to do," represents nothing if not an indifferent will to defy with dancing words the criminal and sexual frame(-up), here vividly realized by the familiar enactment of a po-

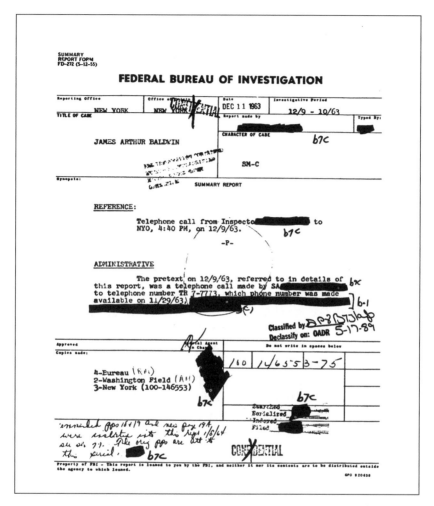

Fig. 11.1. Sample page from Baldwin FBI record, December 11, 1963.

lice line-up, as the eyes of a whole town study him poised against a wall.

Despite evidence of this early will to unmolested subjecthood, Baldwin grew ever more fearful of the bureau after the suspicious assassinations of his friends Malcolm X, Martin Luther King, Jr., and Medgar Evers. Fearing an attempt on his own life, Baldwin fled the United States, "made tracks," as it were, for France. Crucial though his expatriation may be to appreciating what was either his persistent will to elude the ubiquitous dis-ease of facial specularity in America or, conversely, the magnitude of his desperation, James Baldwin's FBI papers raise more interesting concerns about tracks of a different sort. Significantly, the FBI records of Baldwin's surveillance, like those of so many other actors in the conflict of civil rights and Black Power, are fraught with blacked out, expurgated text. The visible deletions are relevant not simply for the information they conceal but for the means by which the attempted "cover-up" of the bureau's suspiciously Orwellian (sometimes salaciously Orwellian) investigative pretexts is achieved—namely, for projecting the (un)known, often private details of Baldwin's life (his address, his friends, his lovers) as censorially "marked." Ironically, as Baldwin was making tracks to Europe, the bureau was making its own tracks on the pages of Baldwin's file, clearly blacking out text to cover its own traces after the 1966 Freedom of Information Act but "marking" Baldwin just the same.

Baldwin's announcement of a book he was preparing to publish on the FBI, called *The Blood Counters,* would seem to be his attempt to turn the tables, "marking" the bureau's activities as it marked his. Although there is no evidence Baldwin ever had a finished (or early) manuscript of *The Blood Counters*—his editor at Dial Press, James Silberman, said he "lied horribly" and "had a story for everybody" (Robins, p. 349)—the threat alone may have been Baldwin's revenge. Whatever the case, it seems clear that neither the FBI nor the *New York Post* writer, Fern Marja Eckman, whose portrait of Baldwin "marks" him by description rather than deletion, paid very close attention to Baldwin's own potentially subversive words in that *New York Post* article: "I'm small and I have big eyes, and I come on, you know, kind of dramatic. But there's something very misleading about my manner. I'm not entirely what I look like." Perhaps what the bureau might have seen in Baldwin's big eyes and dramatic manner, if it cared to look more closely, was a resistant look, a look (in both ocular and postural terms) aiming to "reanimate and open to change" (Silverman, p. 160) the representational potential the camera/gaze/ekphrastic text fixes and frames.

To the degree that the visual pleasures of racial fetishism in *Native Son* rely on the spellbinding power of white eyes to induce the very passivity they require for their exercise ("Overwhelmed by the sight of his accusers, Bigger Thomas . . . fainted dramatically this morning"), inversely, Baldwin's big eyes and dramatic manner stand to disrupt the fetishizing machinations of the racial gaze by an eye-balling disposition of his own, defying the hegemony of racial super-vision on its own terms. Baldwin's discreetly insinuated self-portrait, then, mocking the efforts of both the *New York Post* and, as it hap-pened, the FBI to verbally sketch a realistic picture of him ("there's something misleading about my manner"), may be the most illumi-nating material in the whole FBI record on him. For like Baldwin, black male subjects under white eyes are never entirely what they look like. If Wright's *Native Son* underscores the inevitable tragedy of phantasmic misrecognitions, Baldwin's theatrical mien promises a final transcendence of that tragedy. Where in *Native Son* "the ring of steel against steel" (502) symbolically seals Bigger Thomas's (mis)rep-resentational doom as an incorrigible villain, Baldwin's big eyes, on second glance, may well defy Bigger's doom symbolically and affirm the truth of the private life as Roland Barthes described it: "The 'pri-vate life' is nothing but that zone of space, of time, where [one is] not an image, an object. It is [one's] political right to be a subject which [one] must protect."[21] However invasive "the FBEye" may have been in Baldwin's private life, his big eyes and dramatic manner may well have screened him, in spite of the bureau, from the utter abjection of a more public racial and sexual visibility. For time made it perceptibly clear to Baldwin that the "infirmity" of "enormous eyes" "might not be [his] doom" but "might be forged into weapons" (Baldwin, p. 9) against "the devil" who lives far from hell, "in the eyes of the cop and the sheriff and the deputy, the landlord, the housewife, the football player: in the eyes of some junkies, the eyes of some preachers, the eyes of some governors, presidents, wardens, in the eyes of some or-phans, and in the eyes of my father, and [often enough] in my mirror" (146–47). Like beauty, one's wretchedness dwells in the eyes of the be-holder, and "he who has been treated *as* the devil recognizes the devil when they meet" (147). He who has been most menaced by him learns to resist him in the most spectacular ways.

NOTES

1. Richard Wright, quoted in Michel Fabre, *The Unfinished Quest of Richard Wright*, trans. Isabel Barzun (Urbana: University of Illinois Press, 1993), 258.

2. I have followed Fabre's convention of enclosing Wright's title in quotation marks.

3. W. J. T. Mitchell, *Picture Theory: Essays on Verbal and Visual Representation* (Chicago: University of Chicago Press, 1994), 16.

4. Kaja Silverman, *The Threshold of the Visible World* (New York: Routledge, 1996), 25.

5. Laura Tanner, "Uncovering the Magical Disguise of Language: The Narrative Presence in Richard Wright's *Native Son*," in *Richard Wright: Critical Perspectives Past and Present*, ed. Henry Louis Gates, Jr., and K. A. Appiah (New York: Amistad, 1993), 141.

6. Richard Wright, *Native Son* (1940; reprint, New York: HarperPerennial, 1983), 318. All subsequent citations are from this edition and are indicated parenthetically in the text.

7. We might note here how the frame—namely, the videographic freeze-frame—came to effectively "distort and dehistoricize the narrative logic of the 1992 Rodney King beating" before the eyes of white jurors in Simi Valley, California, barbarizing King in exactly the same bestial language as the gaze does Thomas. See Elizabeth Alexander, "'Can You Be BLACK and Look at This?': Reading the Rodney King Video(s)," in Thelma Golden, ed., *Black Male: Representations of Masculinity in Contemporary American Art* (New York: Whitney Museum of American Art, 1994).

8. I want to distinguish between the *photographic* and the *photo-graphic* here by stressing the latter term's graphic or textual element over and above its mechanical or even its chemical operations within photography. By the photo-graphic, I mean to evoke a writing that aspires toward picture taking. See, too, note 10, below.

9. For a discussion of Bigger Thomas as King Kong, see Harold Hellenbrand, "Bigger Thomas Reconsidered: *Native Son*, Film and *King Kong*," *Journal of American Culture* 6, 1 (1983): 84–95.

10. In the broadest sense, *ekphrasis* is "the verbal representation of visual representation" (Mitchell, 152). In the strictest sense, it denotes "a minor and rather obscure literary genre (poems which describe works of art)." I am appealing to the former sense in order to put a name on the impulse toward the hypervisualization of the racial subject in the foregrounded *Chicago Tribune* article. We might also take Mitchell's neologism *imagetext*, "composite, synthetic [written] works . . . that combine image and text" (89n.), as a suitable alternative. On ekphrasis, see Mitchell, 151–181; on imagetext, see 95.

11. Note the veiled phallicism and threat of penitentiary rape in the image of so many "newspapermen ready with their bulbs."

12. Martin Heidegger, "The Age of the World Picture," in *The Question*

Concerning Technology and Other Essays, trans. William Lovitt (New York: Harper Colophon Books, 1977), 126, 127.

13. See Jacques Derrida, *Memoirs of the Blind: The Self-Portrait and Other Ruins,* trans. Pascale-Anne Brault and Michael Naas (Chicago: University of Chicago Press, 1993), 12.

14. Michael Warner, *Letters of the Republic: Publication and the Public Sphere in Eighteenth-Century America* (Cambridge: Harvard University Press, 1990).

15. The contents of the FBI papers on Baldwin that I discuss in this chapter have been derived from two sources: Natalie Robins's book *Alien Ink: The FBI's War on Freedom of Expression* (New York: William Morrow, 1992), which devotes several pages to her research of the Baldwin papers, and copies of the more than seventeen-hundred-page file itself, obtained under the Freedom of Information Act, which, thanks to the generosity of Robins, I have in my possession. As Robins explains, "It is important to define what exactly a file *is.* At the point at which the documents reach anyone who has solicited them under the Freedom of Information Act, a dossier consists of separate pages of investigative reports, legal forms, interviews, memorandums, petitions, letters, articles, and news clippings that have been collected and clipped together in one [or more] folder[s] by the Federal Bureau of Investigations" (17). Any information in a file that the government deems important to the national defense or to foreign policy or that reveals the identities of "confidential sources" is consistently and thoroughly expurgated. A significant percentage of the Baldwin file has been deleted in this manner and remains, therefore, classified.

16. Lauren Beelant, "National Brand/National Bodies: *Imitation of Life* in ed. Hortense Spillers, *Comparative American Identities: Race, Sex and Nationality in the Modern Text* (New York: Routledge, 1991), 113.

17. For helping me think through the FBI's impulse to frame Baldwin sexually by a blind devotion to image-able hearsay, I am indebted to my brilliant student Nicholas Boggs.

18. David Garrow, *The FBI and Martin Luther King, Jr.: From "Solo" to Memphis* (New York: W. W. Norton, 1981), 165.

19. Martin Jay, "Sartre, Merleau-Ponty, and the Search for a New Ontology of Sight," in ed. David Levin, *Modernity and the Hegemony of Vision* (Berkeley: University of California Press, 1993), 159.

20. Robins states, "The first mention of . . . James Baldwin anywhere in the FBI files occurs in 1951—in Richard Wright's file." It must be insisted, however, that the appearance of Baldwin's name in Wright's file is only the first *known* mention of him, since it is likely he is also referenced in the (presumable) report made by those agents who accosted him in Woodstock, New York, in 1945. Two FBI agents, Baldwin writes in *The Devil Finds Work: An*

Essay (New York: Dial Press, 1976), led him out of a Woodstock diner and "stood [him] against the wall" (107). They were looking for a marine friend of Baldwin's who had deserted the military. Since Baldwin could scarcely remember the deserter's name, coming up only with "Teddy," it is doubtful Robins could have located, without great pains and inordinate time, the appropriate file to confirm or dispute her claim of the originality of the 1951 reference.

21. Roland Barthes, *S/Z*, trans. Richard Miller (New York: Hill and Wang, 1974), 15.

Chapter 12

Life According to the Beat
James Baldwin, Bessie Smith, and the Perilous Sounds of Love

Josh Kun

For Essex Hemphill, in loving memory

> When it rained five days and the sky turned dark as night
> When it rained five days and the sky turned dark as night
> Then trouble takin' place in the lowlands that night
>
> I woke up this mornin' can't even get outta my door
> I woke up this mornin' can't even get outta my door
> That's enough trouble to make a poor girl wonder where she wanna go
>
> Then they rowed a little boat up about five miles 'cross the pond
> Then they rowed a little boat up about five miles 'cross the pond
> I packed all my clothes, throwed 'em in, and they rowed me along
>
> When it thunders and lightnin' and the wind begins to blow
> When it thunders and lightnin' and the wind begins to blow
> There's thousands of people ain't got no place to go
>
> Then I went and stood up on some high old lonesome hill
> Then I went and stood up on some high old lonesome hill
> Then looked down on the house where I used to live
>
> Backwater blues done cause me to pack my things and go
> Backwater blues done cause me to pack my things and go
> Cause my house fell down and I can't live there no mo'
>
> Mmmmmm, I can't move no mo'
> Mmmmmm, I can't move no mo'
> There ain't no place for a poor old girl to go.
> —"Backwater Blues," Bessie Smith, vocals,
> and James P. Johnson, piano, 1927

In the winter of 1951, James Baldwin had a nervous breakdown. Baldwin had been living in self-imposed exile in Paris for two years, while struggling to write his first novel, when he became so deeply depressed that his Swiss lover, Lucien Happersberger, rushed him off to his family's chateau in Loèche-les-Bains, a small mountain town in Switzerland. The two lovers lived there for three months in what was, according to Baldwin's biographer David Leeming, the closest Baldwin ever came to "his dream domestic life with a lover."[1]

These months were of monumental significance for Baldwin and remain of extreme importance for any study of Baldwin's life and art. For it was here that Baldwin realized the racial and national significance of being the only black man in a European town of alabaster white and, in the type of revelatory moment that geographical displacement often brings, of being a black man living in America—double reflections that would provide the experiential content for two crucial early essays, "A Stranger in the Village" and "The Discovery of What It Means to Be an American."

But for me, it is of equal importance that these realizations were made possible by another relationship that Baldwin cemented in that chateau: his deeply and intensely personal lifelong relationship with the voice of renowned blues singer Bessie Smith. Indeed, during these months of gay domesticity and national and racial self-examination—twenty-eight years after Smith cut her first acoustically recorded sides for Columbia Records and fourteen years after her tragic death in a car crash—her voice was heard every day on the portable Victrola that Baldwin took with him to his mountain retreat. It was Bessie's blues that forced Baldwin to ask himself the questions he would later claim were at the root of all music: "Who am I? and what am I doing here?"[2]

We know of James Baldwin the writer, but what do we know of James Baldwin the listener? Indeed, it is crucial not to forget that in addition to his more famous typewriter, Baldwin brought a phonograph and a stack of Bessie Smith records with him to Switzerland. Yet the majority of scholarly work on Baldwin focuses only on his relationship to one of these objects, ignoring his relationship to the others: that talking machine that spoke so directly to the racial and sexual depths of his self-in-process and those invaluable black discs inscribed with endless volumes of replayable sonic information and coded personal confessions. This chapter intervenes here, in the technological gaps between typewriter and phonograph, in the unexplored and ineffable space between writing and sounding.

Baldwin said that music was his salvation; that he wanted to write the way jazz and blues musicians sound; that he wished he could be as free as Billie Holiday and Bessie Smith and as triumphant as Aretha Franklin; that music, not American literature, was his true language; and that it was only through music that the Negro in America has been able to tell his story.[3] Music was where Baldwin made his identifications, where he heard himself mirrored, where the performances of others became the phantasmic stage for performances of his own. My interest in Baldwin lies here, in Baldwin as an active listener in a world of black sounds, an active interpreter of sound and music who throughout his life—to borrow (and misuse) a notion from Theodor Adorno—thought with his ears.[4] For Baldwin, listening to and identifying with music—specifically, in the case I discuss here, the "classic blues" of Bessie Smith—was a way of confronting, voicing, and grappling with his sexual and racial identities: namely, the identificatory crossings of his queerness and his blackness.

As we know from Roland Barthes, "listening speaks."[5] And in the case of Baldwin, his listening speaks to an identificatory crossroads where, as the works of numerous writers and theorists have reiterated, being queer and being black are not mutually exclusive terms to be kept separate and policed but are instead sustaining modalities of existence, commonly experienced and lived through one other—contingent and overlapping coordinates in an always-shifting map of a self-in-the making. Indeed, as Houston Baker, Jr., has argued, the "polymorphous and multidirectional" juncture that is the blues crossroads, the x that maps the blues geography, produces not "a filled subject" but a subject of "ceaseless flux" that is, like the music it emerges from, a "scene of arrivals and departures," "betwixt and between" fixed positionalities.[6]

It is my claim that Baldwin's identification with both the persona and the voice of Bessie Smith reveals as much about his approach to race as it does about his belief in the possibilities of gay male desire. Thus, I highlight this particular moment of listening—Baldwin and Bessie Smith in the queerly charged and racially designated confines of Switzerland—as a double listening, a doubly interpretive act, that is instructive both as an indicator of Baldwin's struggle with "the obscenity of color"[7] central to the American racial nightmare and as a marker of Bessie Smith's role in the perilous sounding of gay love and gay sexuality.

By presenting a listener who actively interprets, deploys, and manipulates the music he chooses to allow into his life, I hope to complicate Theodor Adorno's view of commodity listening as producing a new breed of inattentive, deconcentrated, and hopelessly passive aural subjects who perpetuate what Adorno famously critiqued as a "regression of listening."[8] Baldwin—who in fact urges us in "Sonny's Blues" to "find a new way to listen"[9]—is more akin to the listener, outlined by composer Glenn Gould in 1966, who is "no longer passively analytical: he is an associate whose tastes, preferences, and inclinations even now alter peripherally the experiences to which he gives his attention."[10] Of course, it is only Baldwin's critics who have drastically overlooked the importance of listening—and the relationships he forged *through* listening—to the direction, development, and shape of his work. Baldwin understood it perfectly well and wrote about it with elegance, sophistication, and passion.

The Voice as Record: Hearing Yourself in the Sounds of Another

Baldwin made his restful and therapeutic rendezvous with Lucien and Bessie the compelling centerpiece of an essay he wrote for the *New York Times Book Review* in 1959, "The Discovery of What It Means to Be an American." The transcontinental road to this outernational discovery was paved with the sounds of Bessie Smith, specifically her 1927 collaboration with pianist James P. Johnson, "Backwater Blues," which constituted a large part of Baldwin's daily diet of sound while in Switzerland.

"It was Bessie Smith," Baldwin wrote, "through her tone and her cadence, who helped me to dig back to the way I myself must have spoke when I was a pickaninny, and to remember the things I had heard and seen and felt. I had buried them very deep. I had never listened to Bessie Smith in America (in the same way that for years I would not touch watermelon), but in Europe she helped to reconcile me to being a 'nigger.'"[11]

The only way Baldwin was able to come to terms with his status as a raced U.S. subject was by listening to these Bessie Smith records. In

Bessie's blues Baldwin literally heard a "record" of his past, an audible account of events and memories he had consciously and energetically repressed. Baldwin came to Paris to forget, and the records of Bessie Smith forced him to remember. In a moment of aural epiphany, two records saved Baldwin from forgetting himself. Two records restored something that he had lost. It was a truly remarkable moment of intersubjective listening: Baldwin listened to Bessie Smith, and he heard himself.

Indeed, as both Charles Grivel and Theodor Adorno have argued, this is precisely how the phonograph works, as an apparatus of what Grivel calls "mechanical memory"—a mirror device that offers up aural reflections of its listeners.[12] Because the listener hears herself in the music she chooses to play, the self becomes destabilized, split, if you will, between the self that is heard and the self that is hearing: the self as the object of listening versus the self as the agent of listening. Adorno explains it this way: "What the gramophone listener actually wants to hear is himself, and the artist merely offers him a substitute for the sounding image of his own person, which he would like to safeguard as a possession. . . . Most of the time records are virtual photographs of their owners, flattering photographs—ideologies."[13] This "mirror function" of the talking machine that talks back to its owner was precisely what one of the first phonograph companies had in mind. An early ad slogan from the Victor Company echoes Adorno's suggestion and Baldwin's attachment to his Bessie Smith records: "A mirror may reflect your face and what is written there; but the Victrola will reflect and reveal your soul to you—and what is hidden deep within it."[14]

In a 1973 interview, Baldwin similarly spoke of the vocal poetry of Billie Holiday—who, like Baldwin, also listened at length to Bessie Smith records—as enabling what he called a "re-creation of experience." A singer like Holiday "gave you back your experience. She refined it, and you recognized it for the first time because she was in and out of it and she made it possible for you to bear it. And if you could bear it, then you could begin to change it."[15] The voices of female singers, whether Holiday or Smith, Nina Simone or Aretha Franklin, operate for Baldwin as "effigies," both in the sense that they provided Baldwin with an image or likeness of himself and in the sense, as Joseph Roach has articulated it, of a performance that evokes the absence of a figure from the past and "fills by means of surrogation a vacancy created by the absence of the original."[16] Records like Smith's are "performed effigies," audio surrogates that sound forth distant absences and conjure up distant pasts. They allow Baldwin to construct aural countermemories and to chart—by putting the needle on the record—aural genealogies of musical performance.

The phonograph as audio effigy machine is especially fitting here when we consider that much of early phonographic discourse positioned the phonograph as a way of talking with the dead, a way of channeling silenced voices back into living sound. Thomas Mann thought of the phonograph as a "sarcophagus of music," while Wayne Koestenbaum has claimed that "playing a record is like playing the Ouija, speaking to the dead, asking questions of an immensity that only throws back the echo of one's futile question, a repeated 'myself, myself.'"[17] Thus, when used to sonically reimagine disembodied voices from the past, the act of listening to phonographic recordings continues to involve the search for the bifurcated self, a search that will always only be satisfied for the moment. In the relationship between a voice and its listener, there is always something that goes unheard.

In the bawdy demands and mournful wails of Smith's booming, aching voice—so full of queenly, bodied presence—was all that Baldwin was afraid of. For Baldwin, at that moment in his personal history of American race, Bessie Smith signified a version of American blackness he had yet to confront. She was the summation of all the stereotypes, all the prejudices, all the projected racial and sexual fantasies, all the watermelons and pickaninnies and dialect speech, and all the externally imposed self-hate. It was Bessie who, in her first studio test in 1922, was rejected for being "too rough"; it was Bessie whom both Okeh and Black Swan—the black label for which W. C. Handy and W. E. B. Du Bois sat on the board—turned down because her voice was too rough, too Negro, too black; it was Bessie who had been born into abject poverty in Chattanooga, Tennessee; and it was Bessie who was the most popular singer of "classic blues," which many educated, upwardly mobile blacks in the 1920s condemned as a crude art form and, ultimately, "a racial embarrassment."[18]

Contained in one voice within the memorial revolutions of spinning shellac was all that had motivated Baldwin to leave America. As he told Studs Terkel in a 1964 interview about his experience listening to Smith's "Backwater Blues": "I realized that I had acquired so many affectations, had told myself so many lies, that I really had buried myself beneath a whole fantastic image of myself which wasn't mine, but white people's image of me. . . . I had to find out what I had been like in the beginning. . . . I realized it was a cadence . . . a question of the *beat*. Bessie had the beat. . . . It's that *tone*, that sound, which is in me."[19]

What the Beat Confesses: Aural Identifications and Unusual Doors

But what does this "beat" in the music of Bessie Smith signify? In his essay "The Uses of the Blues," Baldwin writes extensively on the correlation between the beat of Bessie Smith's blues and the African American struggle to survive and transcend the burdens and trappings of American race. He even singles out "Backwater Blues" as a supreme example of how the blues are "used" to confront and transform realities imposed from above.[20] But it is my claim that Baldwin identified with the blues of Bessie Smith not only as "our witness, our ally" to a common racial history but as a witness and ally to the workings of male-to-male desire where discourses of race and sexuality converge.[21] The beat of Bessie's voice, the beat of her blues and the truths her tones and cadence tell, mark the emergent, audible site of identity as a matrix—a "blues matrix"—of racial and sexual intersectionality that maps out new and quite different "blues geographies."[22]

When asked in a 1984 interview what advice he would give to a gay man about to come out of the closet, Baldwin offered the following reply: "Best advice I ever got was an old friend of mine, a black friend, who said you have to go the way your blood *beats*. If you don't live the only life you have, you won't live some other life, you won't live any life at all."[23] Baldwin extends the domain of the beat into the domain of human sexuality and suggests a powerful relationship between the beat on the one hand and the articulation of love and the fulfillment of desire on the other. In his 1979 essay "Of the Sorrow Songs: The Cross of Redemption," he had already suggested that "the beat" is "the confession which recognizes, changes, and conquers time."[24] But what does the beat confess? If we listen with a Foucauldian ear, then it is through the musical confession of the beat that sex gets put into discourse, and "it is in the confession that truth and sex are joined, through the obligatory and exhaustive expression of an individual secret."[25] As Baldwin explained it in his 1951 essay "Many Thousands Gone," the beat—as cadence, as pulse, as rhythm, as blood, as desire—operates as an audible hieroglyph, a musical sign or symbol that tells its musical stories out of a "dangerous and reverberating silence." In short, Baldwin valued music's ability to articulate what he termed "things unsaid," sounding and negotiating silences through meanings and messages conveyed in sonic hieroglyphs that make audible what for too long has been swallowed up in an oppressive hush.[26]

While Baldwin had been immersed in the sounds of black music from a young age—he was a child preacher in love with the gospel music of the black church—it wasn't until he was sixteen and began to take shelter in the Greenwich Village apartment of black gay painter Beauford Delaney that, I argue, he made the first substantial conscious connection between blues and jazz, the construction of black identities, and the possibilities of a desire that transcends the limits and traps of heteronormative identifications. Also a minister's son, also an artist, and also queer, Delaney became a surrogate father for Baldwin and, in some sense, a role model. It was while living in his apartment that Baldwin received his first extended exposure to the secular black sounds of blues and jazz.

In a rarely commented on passage in his landmark essay "The Price of the Ticket," which has been endlessly discussed for its contributions to debates around American race, Baldwin makes it clear that the price of the ticket also involves sexuality, a crucial link that appears in a description of his days with Delaney and Delaney's singing of a queer self. "Lord, I was to hear Beauford sing," Baldwin wrote, "and for many years, *open the unusual door*." Baldwin walked though that "unusual door" that the gay painter sang of, as he "walked into music" playing from Delaney's phonograph. "I had grown up with music," he continued, "but now on Beauford's small black record player, I began to hear what I had never dared or been able to hear. . . . In his studio and because of his presence, I really began to hear Ella Fitzgerald, Ma Rainey, Louis Armstrong, Bessie Smith, Ethel Waters, Paul Robeson, Lena Horne, and Fats Waller. . . . And these people were not meant to be looked on by me as celebrities, but as a part of

Beauford's life and as part of my inheritance."[27] With "the unusual door" now opened, new sounds encoded with new sets of meanings began to pour forth, sounds that from those days forward belonged to him and became a part of his life. By listening anew, by really listening to the music reproduced through a record player in a small Greenwich Village apartment, Baldwin heard a part of himself being given back to him.[28]

LeRoi Jones has remarked that by the 1930s, when the heyday of the classic blues came to a close with the death of Smith and the end of Ma Rainey's career, the phonograph had become a "vital artifact" of "the America they sang of and the black consciousness that had reacted to that America."[29] Decades later, in Beauford Delaney's apartment, the phonograph was still a vital artifact of black life in America, and it was still playing the records of Bessie and Ma Rainey. Only now it was being listened to with a difference—as an artifact of black gay America, an artifact of the open, unusual door. Such artifacts and the identifications they made possible were crucial to Baldwin's survival. "I grew up with music, you know, much more than with any other language," he declared in a 1980 interview. "In a way, the music I grew up with saved my life."[30]

Baldwin attached himself to these recordings partly because their indeterminate meanings allowed him to reshape them to fit the demands and contours of his own life. In her important essay "Queer and Now," Eve Sedgwick has shown how queer children "cross-identify" with cultural objects in order to survive, searching for "sites where the meanings didn't line up tidily with each other," which they would then learn "to invest . . . with fascination and love." Sedgwick writes of books, not records, and how those books produce "perverse readers" whose "near identifications" with the texts allow them to read against the grain of the texts' institutionalized meanings.[31]

Sedgwick's books are Baldwin's records, the cultural objects to which he was intensely attached, the sites that he invested with fascination and love and that were, in the end, necessary to his survival. He became, instead, a perverse listener, listening against the accepted grain of blues and jazz recordings. Baldwin held onto his music because it was all he had, because it contained the songs of his self-in-process. They were sounds, black sounds, of triumphant survival where mourning bred transcendence and suffering produced a song that made it possible to continue living. It is in this sense that

Baldwin's relationship to Bessie can be considered, in Lawrence Grossberg's phrase, "an affective alliance" that not only reshaped Baldwin's emotional life but provided him with a safe space for the realization and expression of oppositional desires and pleasures.[32]

Wayne Koestenbaum has similarly documented how gay male opera queens "cross-identify" with opera divas through active identificatory listening. Koestenbaum emphasizes how divas become identificatory sites crucial to the fans' formation and enactment of self. Through a process of what he names "sonic drag," opera queens transform the mechanically reproduced voice of the opera diva into something they can wear and use, something that fits the dimensions of their own lives.[33] A parallel survival strategy is at work in Baldwin's acoustic relationship with Smith, with Baldwin becoming a blues queen who turns the voice and persona of a blues diva into an identificatory site, a mirror, a fantasy space of self-transformation and literal self refashioning. According to Leeming:

> The female within the male had long fascinated Baldwin . . . by the 1980s he had long since given in to a love of silk, of the recklessly thrown scarf, the overcoat draped stole-like over the shoulders, the large and exotic ring, bracelet, or neckpiece. Even his movements assumed a more feminine character. . . . He dreamed of novels he could write about women who would convert the Jimmy Baldwin he still sadly thought of as an ugly little man into someone tall, confident, beautiful, and to use a favorite word of his, "impeccably" dressed in silks and satins and bold colors.[34]

In an essay written later in his life, "Here Be Dragons," Baldwin elaborated on his displeasure with the limits and boundaries of normative gender binaries. "We are all androgynous," he proclaimed, "born of a woman, impregnated by a man. Each of us, helplessly and forever, contains the other."[35]

It makes sense, then, that Bessie Smith, the extravagant "empress of the blues," would hold a special place in Baldwin's phantasmic musical pantheon. Smith was as famous for her elaborate headdresses and feathers, sequined gowns, costumes of red and blue satin, pearl necklaces and fake rubies as she was for her "mannish ways" and bisexual desires; not to mention her insistence on traveling from performance to performance in a private, seventy-eight-foot-long, two-story-high, yellow railroad car, complete with seven rooms. As jazzman Zutty Singleton put it: "Stately, just like a queen."[36] From the age of sixteen to his nervous breakdown in Switzerland and up until the final weeks of his life, Baldwin consistently listened to Bessie Smith and continually identified with her fierceness, her toughness, her celebration of her body, her open bisexuality, her pain, her triumph over poverty, and ultimately, as he declared in his 1959 review of *Porgy and Bess*, her freedom—her ability to escape the world's definitions and be that rare, unattainable thing: herself.

Out of Silence, a Secret: Listening to Another Country

Nowhere is Baldwin's identification with the voice of Smith more revealing than in his 1962 novel, *Another Country*, where Baldwin employs Smith's voice as the soundtrack to a mapping of queer desire across an amorous, interracial geography of silences, secrets, and impenetrable mysteries.[37] In a series of different musically saturated scenes, Baldwin depicts his three principal male characters, Eric, Rufus, and Vivaldo, as all listening to and, in different ways, identifying with the voice and words of Bessie Smith. In each scene, Baldwin casts their individual and collective acts of listening as a means of "decoding what is obscure, blurred, or mute, in order to make available to consciousness the 'underside of meaning.'"[38] I focus principally here on the scenes involving the tumultuous relationship between two bisexual friends: Rufus Scott, a black jazz drummer, and Vivaldo Moore, an Irish American writer.

By listening to the blues of Bessie Smith and to "the grain" of her voice, Rufus and Vivaldo are able to confront their gendered incarceration in what Baldwin called "the male prison"[39] and to decipher racial codes and confront sexual secrets that alter the course of their lives. As Koestenbaum argues, "Every playing of a record is a liberation of a shut-in meaning—a movement, across the groove's boundary, from silence into sound, from code into clarity. A record carries a secret message, but no one can plan the nature of that secret, and no one can silence that secret once it has been sung."[40] Like Baldwin, Alberta Hunter—another classic blues queen of the 1920s, who wrote the lyrics to the first song Smith recorded in 1923 for Columbia, "Down Hearted Blues" (which sold 780,000 copies in six months)—also recognized the liberatory power of the shut-in meanings, secrets, and silences in Bessie's blues. "Even though she was raucous and loud," Hunter attested, "she had a sort of tear—no not a tear, but there was a misery in what she did. It was as though there was something she had to get out, something she just had to bring to the fore."[41]

In an early scene in *Another Country*, Rufus and Vivaldo face their inarticulated love for each other while both sides of a Bessie Smith record play, "Backwater Blues" and "Empty Bed Blues." The change of side signals a change in content and tone in each scene, with each song supplying its own stories and its own set of identificatory moments. After "peddling his ass" (48) along Forty-second Street after a violent breakup with his lover Leona, Rufus resurfaces at Vivaldo's apartment, following a month of absence as "one of the fallen." To break the silence that hangs heavily in the room, Vivaldo puts Bessie Smith and James Pete Johnson's "Backwater Blues" on the phonograph. It is in Rufus's identification with the lyrics of the song that his emotions and sentiments become articulated, explained, and understood. Through Bessie's voice, we learn that he, too, is one of the "thousands of people, ain't got no place to go." Not unlike Baldwin himself, Rufus hears "in the severely understated monotony of this blues, something which spoke to his troubled mind."

Baldwin uses "Backwater Blues" and its tale of one woman surviving the devastation of a flood to "bear witness" to the pain and struggle of Rufus, to give Rufus the space and the freedom to wonder "how others had moved beyond the emptiness and horror which faced him now" (49). In the story of "Backwater Blues" and in the voice of Bessie Smith, Baldwin hears Rufus and Rufus hears himself. Faced with the stormy events of his own life of darkness—his troubled relationship with Vivaldo, his sexual and racial violence against Leona, his bar fights with anonymous white men—Rufus also finds himself without a home, searching for at least one place for a "po' ol' girl" to go.

As the song ends, Vivaldo turns the Bessie Smith record over to play "Empty Bed Blues." In the midst of a sexually charged and heavy silence, Smith sings, "When my bed get empty, make me feel awful mean and blue / My springs is getting rusty, sleeping single like I do," as Vivaldo urges, "Sing it Bessie." Rufus then tells Vivaldo that when it came to problems with him and Leona, "there was lots of other things, too." These "other things" become loaded with suggestion as Baldwin combines silences and music to construct a moment of intense erotic and sexual tension, as the "Empty Bed Blues" continue to play:

> Then there was a long silence. They listened to Bessie.
> "Have you ever wished you were queer?" Rufus asked suddenly.
> Vivaldo smiled, looking into his glass. "I used to think maybe I was. Hell, I think even wished I was." He laughed. "But I'm not. So I'm stuck."
> Rufus walked to Vivaldo's window. "So you been all up and down that street, too," he said.
> "We've all been up the same streets. There aren't a hell of a lot of streets. Only, we've been taught to lie so much about so many things, that we hardly ever know where we are." (51–52)

The song continues to play as Vivaldo suggests they make a toast "to all things we don't know" (52). The music of "Backwater Blues" and "Empty Bed Blues" becomes one space where the unknowable and the inexpressible—those inaudible sexual silences and secrets that live between the beats and sustain the play of desire—can, if not actually be heard, at least be imagined.

Baldwin depicts Rufus "pressing darkness against his eyes, listening to the music." The combination of darkness, music, and memory makes Rufus aware of the bounds and confines of his individual male body, causing the "air through which he rushed" to become "his prison and he could not even summon the breath to call for help." And all the while, "the music went on, far from him, terribly loud" (53). With the help of Vivaldo's comfort, Rufus accepts his pain as his destiny; "this was himself." He resolves to accept the fact that

> his body was controlled by laws he did not understand. Nor did he understand what force within this body had driven him into such a desolate place. The most impenetrable of mysteries moved in this darkness for less than a second, hinting of reconciliation. And still the music continued, Bessie was saying that she wouldn't mind being in jail but she had to stay there so long. (54)

Baldwin uses the continual presence of the music of Bessie Smith to reinforce and link the ways in which Rufus is imprisoned within himself, the ways in which he is imprisoned by the impenetrable darkness and mystery of all the things he doesn't know.

Toward the novel's end, at the very beginning of book 3, Baldwin once again reaches for his copy of "Backwater Blues," this time

replaying it in a dream sequence through overt evocation and allusion. Vivaldo dreams that he is running against time in the midst of a
torrential downpour. As he approaches a high wall covered in glass
splinters, Vivaldo, whom Baldwin describes as "both fleeing and
seeking," hears a music that makes him certain he has forgotten
something, "some secret, some duty, that would save him." Like the
singer of "Backwater Blues," Vivaldo is looking desperately for somewhere to go, struggling to survive a flood and to climb up a wall to
save himself from the ensuing destruction below. Fittingly, Vivaldo
hears a blues song marked by a "steady, enraged beating on the
drums," but it is a blues he has never heard before, one that fills "the
earth with a sound so dreadful that he could not bear it." The steady,
enraged drumbeat of this unfamiliar music pulses through a nightmarish dreamscape that includes a reenactment of Rufus's suicidal
leap to death from the George Washington Bridge, which ended the
novel's first chapter.

Toward the end of Vivaldo's blues-soaked dream, he and Rufus
end up next to each other, both impaled on shards of glass. Vivaldo's
renewed ability to tell Rufus how much he loves him invites a "sweet
and overwhelming embrace" from Rufus, to which Vivaldo "surren-
ders," causing the dream to shatter (381–82). Music, both seen and
heard, sounds its way through Vivaldo's attempt to transcend the
"Backwater Blues," to find the truth about the secrets within himself
and give love to Rufus in an eternal embrace that would, at least in
the space of a dream, save him from an impending death through the
fulfillment of love.

Vivaldo wakes up from his dream in the arms of Eric, a white
Southerner who had also been involved with Rufus, and the two pro-
ceed to make love, in an act of overdue consummation that Baldwin
portrays as "strangely and insistently double-edged, it was like making love in the midst of mirrors. . .. But it was also like music, the
highest, sweetest, loneliest reeds, and it was like the rain" (385). For
Vivaldo, the music of gay male sex contains seductive mysteries of its
own, with the desirous and desirable male body becoming "the most
impenetrable of mysteries." The music composed and performed by
Eric and Vivaldo out of the silences of inarticulated desires and out of
the sonic dreamscape of "Backwater Blues" leads Vivaldo to turn his
meditative lens inward and wonder about the limits and boundaries
of his own flesh, of his body's "possibilities and its imminent and ab-

solute decay, in a way that he had never thought about of it before."
Yet, like any double-edged or double-voiced music, it also causes him
to reflect outward and wonder about Eric's body, about "what moved
in Eric's body which drove him, like a bird or a leaf in a storm,
against the wall of Vivaldo's flesh."

Ultimately, Vivaldo recognizes the dialectical possibilities of this
double movement of music and love and returns inward only to wonder about the synthesis produced by the coming together of two male
bodies, asking himself, "What moved in his own body: what virtue
were they seeking, now, to share?" Caught in the double play of
music and mirrors, Eric and Vivaldo are two separate bodies moved
by similar storms into mysteries as impenetrable as the sounds of
their own love. As it did for Baldwin, music acts as their salvation,
providing the beats and impulses that bring love and desire out of secrecy, into truth, and ultimately, into life.

"Call Me a Freakish Man": Blues Desires and Looking for Langston[42]

The connections Baldwin draws between listening to the blues of
Bessie Smith and the realization (or confession) of sexual secrets and
silences cannot be heard outside of a blues tradition that explicitly
links musical performance to the articulation of love, the enunciation
of desire, and particularly, in the case of the "classic blues" singers of
the 1920s, the play of sexuality. Blues and jazz pioneer Jelly Roll Morton is one of many performers and critics who have located the origins of blues genealogies in the experience of slavery. But for Morton,
the blues' position within the traumatic transatlantic histories of slavery also involves the production and channeling of desire. "The blues
came from nothingness, from want, from desire," Morton once argued, "And when a man sang or played the blues, a small part of the
want was satisfied from the music. The blues go back to slavery, to
longing."[43]

In the case of the classic blues of the 1920s—a period dominated
not by desirous men but by desirous women such as Smith, Ma
Rainey, Victoria Spivey, Gladys Bentley, and Alberta Hunter—the use
of music to work through sexual desire of all forms played a uniquely
central role. Albert Murray similarly argues that for all the political

and social emphasis put on the content of blues lyrics by critics and scholars, the majority of blues songs deal with love and affairs of the heart. As his central example, Murray notes that of the 160 recordings made by Bessie Smith, only a few do not address the "careless love of aggravating papas, sweet mistreaters, dirty nogooders, and spider men."[44]

But what Murray fails to consider are the aggravating *mamas* and spider *women* in Smith's life and music, a history of queer blues desire that has principally been told by Smith's biographer Chris Albertson. Albertson's work on his 1972 biography of Smith, *Bessie*, led to his compiling the two-volume series *AC/DC Blues: Gay Jazz Reissues*, a collection of blues recordings culled predominantly from the 1920s and 1930s (including Smith's 1927 recording of "Foolish Man Blues") that all, in various ways, address gay and lesbian sex and sexuality. Gathering such queer blues classics as George Hannah's "Freakish Man Blues," Ma Rainey's "Prove It on Me Blues," and George Noble's "Sissy Man Blues" together in one place, *AC/DC Blues* directly challenges any heteronormative assumptions of desire and identification that might otherwise mistakenly be ascribed to the blues and celebrates a vision of sexuality without gender borders that was characteristic of "the life" that singers like Smith and Rainey openly participated in.[45]

AC/DC Blues also contains Albertson's recorded interviews with Bessie Smith's niece Ruby Smith, who, in lurid, graphic, and often hilarious detail, explains exactly what went on behind "the unusual doors" of the notoriously promiscuous and illicit "buffet flat" parties of the 1920s, which Bessie frequented and even sang about in her "Soft Pedal Blues." In the following excerpt from their interview, Ruby Smith tells Albertson of a particularly memorable party in Detroit:

> The fags used to dress like women there. It wasn't against the law. That was a real open house for everybody there in that town. . . . Bessie and all of us went to the party . . . at some house, some friend of Bessie's . . . had a house there, a buffet flat. A buffet flat is nothin' but faggots and bulldaggers, an open house. Everything goes on in that house. A very gay place. Everything that was in the life. Everybody that was in the life. Buffet means everything, everything goes on. They had a faggot there that was so great that people used to come there just to watch him

make love to another man. He was real great. He'd give him a tongue bath and everything and by the time he got to the front of that guy he was shaking like a leaf. . . . Every room was different. Two women go into together. A man and a man go into together. Anything that you want to see is in that place. And if you interested, they do the same thing to you. I wanted to get in with that one cat, but he said it wasn't fish day! So I was out!

Tales of Smith's defiant, demanding, and aggressive attitudes toward sex and the open secret of her bisexuality are by now legion. Her affairs and relationships with the chorus women in her traveling show are documented in detail in Albertson's biography and are recounted by Ruby in her interviews with Albertson.[46] With her frequent collaborations with gay piano player and songwriter Porter Grainger, the sexual allusions of her lyrics ("Empty Bed Blues" is one famous example), and her penchant for wearing elaborate headdresses and sequined gowns and men's tuxedos, Smith was the dame of an era of transvestitism, sexual exploration, and rampant gender-bending; one that was populated by stage after stage and rent party after rent party of, as "Foolish Man Blues" puts it, "mannish-acting women" and "skipping, twistin' woman acting men."

Baldwin's racial and sexual investment in the blues of Bessie Smith and his strategic use of her voice in *Another Country* are particularly fitting when we consider that, as Hazel Carby has argued, the songs of women's blues singers reveal black women eager to actively represent themselves as desiring agents of sexuality. Carby understands singers such as Smith as musical agents who use song to craft a self of her own design and explore "the various possibilities of a sexual existence."[47]

Though they dominated the black recording industry of the 1920s—the first commercially released and commercially successful blues recordings to reach wide, national audiences were all written by and performed by women—women blues singers still operated as "liminal figures" who were forced to make their own rules about sexual agency and to map new alternatives inherited definitions of gender. By taking their desire out of the private, domestic sphere of the home and recording it onto ten-inch discs, women blues singers enacted the public voicing of private, marginal desire, making it available for consumption by an audience of listeners (which would grow to include Baldwin) who would then privatize and reenact those discourses of sexuality and gender through acts of domestic listening.

This cross-identificatory relationship between Bessie Smith the performer and James Baldwin the listener—and all of the sexual codes, secrets, and silences embedded in it—is well understood by black British filmmaker Isaac Julien, who references it in *Looking for Langston*, his 1989 filmic meditation on the life, work, and homosexuality of African American writer Langston Hughes. *Looking for Langston* poses a direct connection between the many queer writers of the Harlem Renaissance and those involved with the so-called black gay renaissance of the 1980s (a movement for which Baldwin was a major inspiration). While Hughes—his words, his voice, his image, his memory—occupies the film's central frame of visual and conceptual reference, *Looking for Langston* is dedicated to the memory of Baldwin, begins with a reading of his essay "The Price of the Ticket," and contains numerous audiovisual echoes of Bessie Smith—including the ten-inch album cover of her recording of "Tain't Nobody's Business" and an image of her from the short film *St. Louis Blues*, in which she sings the blues classic to the accompaniment of the Fletcher Henderson Orchestra while drowning her sorrows at the bar.

Julien includes these direct references to Smith in a compelling collage of image and sound. Beginning with a shot of a spinning phonograph record, Julien's montage of a revisited and sexually charged "dream deferred" fades the voice of Langston Hughes into "Blues for Langston," a song by contemporary black gay singer-songwriter Blackberri. In the middle of Blackberri's song we see and hear a brief excerpt of Bessie's performance in *St. Louis Blues*, which readies us for the arrival of Baldwin's close-up portrait cradled in the arms of a heavenly queer black angel. History will surely have many forgotten angels, but as we hear in Blackberri's song, neither Bessie nor Baldwin will be one of them.

By including them in his film—through acts of dedication, memorial, and evocative audiovisual homage—Julien positions Baldwin and Smith as two figures crucial to his century-spanning filmic mapping of black gay life. Baldwin and Smith join the ranks of the black gay men and women whom Manthia Diawara collects into the figure of "the Absent One," and their pronounced presence in Julien's film helps link the queerness of the Harlem Renaissance to Baldwin and, ultimately, to the 1980s renaissance of black gay writing.[48] Lastly, Smith's voice and Baldwin's name perform a re-gaying of Houston Baker, Jr.'s notion of "renaissancism," in that the film itself enacts a queering of renaissancism's transmission and repeated rebirth of black cultural forms across generations.[49]

But Julien's use of the blues in *Looking for Langston*—particularly the blues of Smith and George Hannah's previously mentioned "Freakish Man Blues"—has unfortunately been overlooked by numerous critics, who choose to focus on the visual work the film does at the expense of what it accomplishes through its artful and strategic deployment of sound. In an interview with Essex Hemphill, Julien emphasized the importance of the blues to the articulation of black gay identity, insisting that "blues songs were some of the first spaces where one could actually *hear* black gay desire" (emphasis added).[50] In *Looking for Langston*, as in the songs of Bessie Smith heard by James Baldwin and replayed in *Another Country*, black gay sexuality is, as Julien suggests, heard as much as it is seen.

Coda: And the Beat Goes On

During the final months of his life, James Baldwin was once again living abroad, this time in the French hilltop town of St. Paul de Vence. With his fragile health rapidly fading, Baldwin was visited by friends who would come to sit with him around his kitchen table to reminisce over the past. One frequent guest at Baldwin's legendary "welcome table" was his old lover, Lucien Happersberger, with whom this narrative of sound and desire began.

One day, the reunited pair were watching television and happened to come across a documentary on the life of Bessie Smith. Together, in another small hideaway in another part of Europe, they watched and listened to Smith sing the very songs they had once lived with in Switzerland. Two days later, James Baldwin died, with the voice of Bessie Smith ringing in his ears and the beat of her music leaving its final sonic impressions on the beat of his blood.

NOTES

This essay would not have been possible without the support, encouragement, and close readings of Catherine Gallagher, Glenda Carpio, José Muñoz, Stephen Best, Waldo Martin, Rhacel Parrenas, and Viet Nguyen.

1. David Leeming, *James Baldwin: A Biography* (New York: Henry Holt & Co., 1994), 78–79.

2. James Baldwin, "Of the Sorrow Songs: The Cross of Redemption," in *New Edinburgh Review Anthology*, ed. James Campbell (Edinburgh: Polygon Books, 1982), 90.

3. These declarations can be found, separately, in the following essays: Quincy Troupe, "The Last Interview," in *James Baldwin: The Legacy*, ed. Quincy Troupe (New York: Simon & Schuster, 1989), 207; Leeming, *James Baldwin*, 206; James Baldwin, "On Catfish Row," in *The Price of the Ticket: Collected Nonfiction, 1948–1985* (New York: St Martin's/Marek, 1985), 181; Jewell Handy Gresham, "James Baldwin Comes Home," in *Conversations with James Baldwin*, ed. Fred L. Standley and Louis H. Pratt (Jackson: University of Mississippi Press, 1989), 163; James Baldwin, "Many Thousands Gone," in *Notes of a Native Son* (Boston: Beacon Press, 1955), 24.

4. Theodor Adorno, "Cultural Criticism and Society," in *Prisms* (Cambridge: MIT Press, 1967), 19.

5. Roland Barthes, "Listening," in *The Responsibility of Forms: Critical Essays on Music, Art, and Representation* (Berkeley: University of California Press, 1985), 249.

6. Houston Baker, Jr., *Blues, Ideology and Afro-American Literature: A Vernacular Theory* (Chicago: University of Chicago Press, 1984), 7.

7. James Baldwin, "Here Be Dragons," in *Price of the Ticket*, 687.

8. Theodor Adorno, "On the Fetish Character in Music and the Regression of Listening," in *The Essential Frankfurt School Reader*, ed. Andrew Arato and Eike Gebhardt (New York: Urizen Books, 1978).

9. James Baldwin, "Sonny's Blues," in *Going to Meet the Man* (1965; reprint, New York: Vintage Books, 1993), 133.

10. Glenn Gould, "The Prospects of Recording," in *The Glenn Gould Reader*, ed. Tim Page (New York: Alfred A. Knopf, 1984), 347.

11. James Baldwin, "The Discovery of What It Means to Be an American," in *Nobody Knows My Name* (1961; reprint, New York: Vintage Books, 1989), 5.

12. Charles Grivel, "The Phonograph's Horned Mouth," in *Wireless Imagination: Sound, Radio, and the Avant-Garde*, ed. Douglas Kahn and Gregory Whitehead (Cambridge: MIT Press, 1992), 37.

13. Theodor Adorno, "The Curves of the Needle," *October* 55 (winter 1990): 54.

14. Cited in Wayne Kostenbaum, *The Queen's Throat: Opera, Homosexuality, and the Mystery of Desire* (New York: Vintage Books, 1993), 55.

15. The Black Scholar, "The Black Scholar Interviews James Baldwin," in *Conversations with James Baldwin*, ed. Standley and Pratt, 155.

16. Joseph Roach, *Cities of the Dead: Circum-Atlantic Performance* (New York: Columbia University Press, 1996), 36.

17. Thomas Mann, cited in Michael Chanan, *Repeated Takes: A Brief History of Recording and Its Effects on Music* (London: Verso, 1995), 42; Kostenbaum, *Queen's Throat*, 54.

18. Ann Douglas, *Terrible Honesty: Mongrel Manhattan in the 1920s* (New York: Farrar, Straus & Giroux, 1995), 391–95.

19. Studs Terkel, "An Interview with James Baldwin," in *Conversations with James Baldwin*, ed. Standley and Pratt, 4–5.

20. James Baldwin, "The Uses of the Blues," *Playboy*, no. 11 (January 1964): 164.

21. Baldwin, "Of the Sorrow Songs," 92.

22. On "blues geographies," see Houston Baker, Jr., *Modernism and the Harlem Renaissance* (Chicago: University of Chicago Press, 1987), 106.

23. Richard Goldstein, "Go the Way Your Blood Beats: An Interview with James Baldwin," in *James Baldwin*, ed. Troupe, 185.

24. Baldwin, "Of the Sorrow Songs," 92.

25. Michel Foucault, *The History of Sexuality: An Introduction*, Vol. 1 (New York: Vintage Books, 1990), 61.

26. Baldwin, "Many Thousands Gone," 24.

27. James Baldwin, "Introduction: The Price of the Ticket," in *Price of the Ticket*, x.

28. The figure of the unusual door reappears in Baldwin's 1979 novel *Just above My Head*. To gain access to the room where the black gay characters Arthur and Crunch secretly make love, you must first knock on "the unusual door." See James Baldwin, *Just above My Head* (New York: Dell, 1979), 263.

29. LeRoi Jones, *Blues People: Negro Music in White America* (New York: Morrow Quill Paperbacks, 1963), 120–21.

30. Wolfgang Binder, "An Interview with James Baldwin," in *Conversations with James Baldwin*, ed. Standley and Pratt, 190.

31. Eve Kosofsky Sedgwick, *Tendencies* (Durham: Duke University Press, 1993), 3–4.

32. See Lawrence Grossberg, "Postmodernity and Affect: All Dressed Up with No Place to Go," in *Dancing in Spite of Myself: Essays on Popular Culture* (Durham: Duke University Press, 1997).

33. Kostenbaum, *Queen's Throat*, 49.

34. Leeming, *James Baldwin*, 377.

35. Ibid., 379.

36. Zutty Singleton, in *Hear Me Talkin' to Ya: The Story of Jazz by the Men Who Made It*, ed. Nat Shapiro and Nat Hentoff (New York: Rinehart & Co., Inc, 1955), 244.

37. All references to the novel are from James Baldwin, *Another Country* (1962; reprint, New York: Vintage Books, 1993).

38. Barthes, "Listening," 249.

39. See James Baldwin, "The Male Prison" in *Nobody Knows My Name*.

40. Kostenbaum, *Queen's Throat*, 51.

41. Alberta Hunter, in *Hear Me Talkin' to Ya*, ed. Shapiro and Hentoff, 247.

42. "Call me a freakish man" is the opening line of George Hannah's "Freakish Man Blues," which is featured in Isaac Julien's film *Looking for Langston* (1989). It can also be found on *AC/DC Blues: Gay Jazz Reissues* (Stash Records, 1977).

43. Jelly Roll Morton, in *Hear Me Talkin' to Ya*, ed. Shapiro and Hentoff, 252.

44. Albert Murray, *Stomping the Blues* (New York: Da Capo, 1976), 66.

45. *AC/DC Blues: Gay Jazz Reissues* (Stash Records, 1977). These issues are also discussed, with significantly less success, in John Gill's *Queer Noises: Male and Female Homosexuality in Twentieth-Century Music* (Minneapolis: University of Minnesota Press, 1995).

46. See Chris Albertson, *Bessie* (New York: Stein & Day, 1972). Albertson's complete interviews with Ruby Smith are now available as part of volume 5 of Columbia Records' Bessie Smith box set collection, *Bessie Smith: The Final Chapter* (Columbia Records, 1996).

47. Hazel Carby, "'It Jus Be's Dat Way Sometime': The Sexual Politics of Women's Blues," in *Unequal Sisters: A Multi-Cultural Reader in U.S. Women's History*, ed. Vicki L. Ruiz and Ellen Carol DuBois (New York: Routledge, 1994), 330–41.

48. Manthia Diawara, "The Absent One: The Avant-Garde and the Black Imaginary in *Looking for Langston*," in *Representing Black Men*, ed. Marcellus Blount and George P. Cunningham (New York: Routledge, 1996), 216–22.

49. Baker, *Modernism and the Harlem Renaissance*, 8.

50. Essex Hemphill, "Looking for Langston: An Interview with Isaac Julien," in *Brother to Brother: New Writings by Black Gay Men*, ed. Essex Hemphill (Boston: Alyson Publications, 1991), 178–79.

Part V

Baldwin and the Literary

Chapter 13

The Discovery of What It Means to Be a Witness

James Baldwin's Dialectics of Difference

Joshua L. Miller

A witness to whence I came, where I am. Witness to
what I've seen and the possibilities that I think I see
. . . it was an obligation that was impossible to fulfill.
—James Baldwin (CJB 225)[1]

At a critical moment of his life and literary career, James Baldwin rejects the term *exile* as a description of his position as an African American writer living predominantly in Europe.[2] Baldwin distinguishes himself from previous American and African American authors in Europe by arguing pointedly that exile and expatriation are, at some deeply personal level, not even an option for him. He is quoted in Karen Thorsen's 1989 documentary, *The Price of the Ticket,* remarking that one of his first insights after arriving in Paris is that "you don't ever leave home. You take home with you. You better. Otherwise you're homeless" (JBPT). This sense of the inevitability and (even more important) the inescapability of home runs throughout Baldwin's career, but in the late 1950s and early 1960s he explicitly outlines his critique of exilic writing and formulates his own role as what he calls a "witness."

I want to place Baldwin's choice of the term *witness* in the dynamic context of the cold war culture in which his literary presence began

Fig. 13.1. Photomat self-portrait with James Baldwin. Photograph by Richard Avedon, September 17, 1964, New York City. © 1964 by Richard Avedon. All rights reserved.

and of the death (in 1960) of Richard Wright, Baldwin's artistic mentor. After Wright's death Baldwin articulates, with a clarity he could not previously summon, his searing criticism of exile as a simplified "way out" of complex conflicts of nationality and sexuality. Whether or not one accepts his critique of Wright's political and artistic exile, this formulation of his mentor's nationality gives Baldwin a basis from which to come to terms with his own notion of cultural citizenship and American national identity. Baldwin thus clarifies his status as a vocal American simultaneously claiming and challenging his ambiguous heritage through an active witnessing of U.S. culture and society. I will work through Baldwin's crucial refiguring of this remarkably overdetermined word and examine the metaphorics of sight and *in*sight in his work from the period after Wright's death. I am not interested in determining whether or not this is the most "successful" period in Baldwin's career; however, it is undeniably a moment of intense creativity, and clearly, he confronts the issue of exile in a way that will organize much of his later thinking on the subject. Visual imagery suffuses all of Baldwin's work, but *Nothing Personal* in 1964 allows him to literalize his poetics through a dynamic contrast with the photographs of artist (and high school friend) Richard Avedon.

Drawing on a rich tradition of religious imagery (as is well known, his first career was as a child preacher), Baldwin transforms the already deeply ingrained cold war notion of the witness, testifying for or against the West in its absolute struggle with the Soviet Union, into that of a truth seeker observing his own society. Baldwin rejects the absolute terms of expatriation (largely because this involves some form of *re*patriation elsewhere) and instead creates a dialectic of distance through the figure of the active witness, a mobile observer and commentator on the workings of U.S. society. Only as a viewer constantly moving closer to and further from the United States could Baldwin express his own sense of being both internal and external to "American" life.

Religion, the Law, and Cold War Culture: A (Very) Brief Genealogy of Witnessing

One cannot speak of the term *witness* in this time frame without taking into account the fact that the word is a meeting point for a number of vocabularies, among which it slides uneasily. Baldwin glories in the seemingly anomalous conjunction of political, religious, and legal discourses that this role makes possible.

In the Hebrew Bible, the witness confirms the evidence of God's unseen presence. For example, Isaiah 43:10 pronounces: "You are my witnesses, says the Lord . . . that you may know and believe me, and understand that I am he: before me there was no God formed, neither shall there be after me."[3] In U.S. literature the witness has played a new role, confirming otherwise invisible principles of justice. For example, Frederick Douglass makes use of both the religious and the legal aspects of witnessing in contesting the Fugitive Slave Act of 1850. In his 1852 address "What to the Slave Is the Fourth of July?" Douglass accuses the nation of withholding the role of witness from African Americans:

> For black men there are neither law, justice, humanity, nor religion. The Fugitive Slave *Law* makes MERCY TO THEM, A CRIME. . . . His own testimony is nothing. He can bring no witnesses for himself. The minister of American justice is bound by the law to hear but *one* side; and *that* side, is the side of the oppressor. Let this damning fact be perpetually told.[4]

James Baldwin undoubtedly participates in the perpetual retelling of African American history from the active vantage point of the witness for whom Douglass called a century earlier.

By the 1950s, however, Baldwin's invocation of a witness has overtly political resonances as well as legal and religious ones. Like others of his generation, Baldwin is well aware of Whittaker Chambers's role in the Alger Hiss affair. Although he rarely refers to Chambers by name, in his 1976 *The Devil Finds Work*, Baldwin associates the "obscenely fomented hysteria" of the 1950s with the "self-important paranoia of Whittaker Chambers" (PT 612). Even as he discounts Chambers's claim to the mantle of witness, Baldwin utilizes the meanings that the cold war warrior attaches to the term.

Whittaker Chambers's politically charged autobiography, *Witness*, was published in 1952. Chambers quickly points out that for the U.S. public, the term signified the act of testifying either for or against something in a court of law. Chambers makes use of the theological connotations of the role, but essentially, he neatly conflates the religious with the legal when he sums up his life in Manichaean terms:

I was a witness. . . . A man is not primarily a witness *against* something. That is only incidental to the fact that he is a witness *for* something. A witness, in the way I am using the word, is a man whose life and faith are *so completely one* that when the challenge comes to step out *and testify for his faith*, he does so, disregarding all risks, accepting all consequences.[5]

In Chambers's telling, he is a witness not simply in the perjury case of Alger Hiss but in the titanic struggle between the United States and the Soviet Union for world supremacy. Although he begins as a legal witness in the Hiss trial, as the stakes of the conflict become clear to him, he says, he "became a witness in a deeper sense" (Chambers 699). According to his narrative, Chambers becomes a triple agent (a U.S. government worker recruited to be a Soviet spy, who then turns in Hiss and identifies him as the leader of the spy network) whose own surveillance (obtaining hidden documents from the Soviets) yields secret information that can alter the course of the entire nation. In the term *witness*, Chambers merges U.S. national interests with religious "faith" and "testifies" against Soviet espionage for the safety of the U.S. nation (which, of course, he allies with Christianity, against the atheistic Soviet Union).

While retrospection allows the contemporary reader to discount Chambers's overblown rhetoric, one cannot forget that in the context of the Hiss hearings, the Rosenbergs' execution, and the activities of the House Un-American Affairs Committee, Chambers's narrative eerily confirms the worst nightmares of the cold war. Philip Rahv, in his review of this "authentic expression of historical crisis and . . . presentation of crucial facts" in *Partisan Review*, points to the inner/outer dichotomy that pervades U.S. cold war culture.[6] In reading the work, Rahv suggests that "we communicate almost exclusively with the externalized Chambers . . . [who is] incapable of projecting himself on any level but that of objectified meaning" (Rahv 475). At the same time that he lampoons Chambers's "Dostoevskyean" tone of "apocalyptic prophecy," Rahv is nonetheless caught up in Chambers's many layers of identity and finds that readers cannot peel away the author's multiple ideologies to a sense of the non-externalized Chambers (Rahv 474). Whittaker Chambers's version of the witness ultimately depends on his observation of events and his inner "faith" in his testimony on behalf of an absolute good over the darkest evil.

A slightly more nuanced description of the insider/outsider observatory role that the witness plays in the cold war culture comes from George Kennan. Kennan is most readily identified as the architect of the "containment" stance that the United States took toward the Soviet Union, but he has written extensively over the past decades to argue that his cold war role was that of the master actor-observer diplomat rather than (inter)national foreign policy controller. In his memoirs Kennan paints himself as a "good observer" who can submerge himself entirely in another culture, so seamlessly that the "ordinary" citizens accept him as one of their own.[7] Fully aware of his "usefulness" as a performer, he describes how he was able to "assume a personality" to gain access to the countries in which he was a diplomat, without ever losing his identity as an agent of the U.S. government (Kennan 10–11). As easily as the practiced "actor on the stage," Kennan learns German to the point of thinking and dreaming in it (a point he makes repeatedly) and finds what he calls a "second home" with his in-laws in Norway—although he spends so few words on this home that the country is not even mentioned in his book's index (Kennan 11, 39).

The Kennanian witness/observer strives to blend invisibly into another culture, watching and taking notes in order to report back to his home country with his insider's perspective and cultural-political analysis. This role emerges from Kennan's anecdotes, most notably of a three-day trip he took from Siberia to Moscow, during which he allows the NKVD (precursor to the KGB) to "lose track" of him (Kennan 274). "For once," he relates, out of the firm grasp of his Soviet handlers, he has "the feeling of not being a stranger, of belonging to a company of ordinary Soviet people." Testing out his skills, Kennan quickly reports that his "companions . . . did not seem to recognize me as anything out of the ordinary." He relishes his success and writes lyrically of a stopover during which he read to them a history of Peter the Great while "sitting in the grass under the shade of the wing of the plane in the heat of the day." During these days of travel, Kennan says he felt "as though I were a common citizen" and entirely "at home" with the Moscovites.

Even as he cultivated his status as an insider-observer within a foreign nation, Kennan differed sharply with some of the actions taken (based in no small part on his own reports) by his superiors in Washington, D.C. His consternation is apparent in his memoir when he suggests that his telegraphed observations (especially the famous "X article") were misread in the United States as a containment strategy. In his most recent set of "reflections" on his career, Kennan describes his attitude toward what became the doctrine of containment through a parable: he was "like one who has inadvertently loosened a large boulder from the top of a cliff and now helplessly witnesses its path of destruction in the valley below, shuddering and wincing at each successive glimpse of disaster."[8] This description of the witness as passive and impotent observer provokes Fareed Zakaria to suggest, in a review, that "Today's America is *a foreign country* to George Kennan. It is aggressively modern, ceaselessly moving and changing, constantly uprooting the past."[9] To the extent that Kennan's role of the "good observer" dovetails with Chambers's "witness," he, too, sets up a dichotomy between inner and outer that only he can penetrate. In Kennan's account, his skill with languages and ability as a natural performer allow him insight into a complex, foreign society. But Zakaria offers yet another aspect to Kennan's observatory role: the risk that the witness, once engaged in another society, will forget or develop myopia with regard to his or her own country. This critique, in one form or another, haunts American witnesses (notably, but not exclusively, Baldwin and Richard Wright), from the first manifestations of U.S. literature to the present day.[10]

If Kennan is the actor-observer extraordinaire (performing the role of a Russian in order to gain access to knowledge of the society), then James Baldwin's formulation of the witness is almost exactly the opposite: a truth teller whose insight into his *own* society's contradictions force him to leave it. Baldwin's reversal of Kennan's mission is particularly acute given that his first departure from the United States coincides with Armistice Day, 1948. The celebration of national military might provides the backdrop for Baldwin's pronounced claustrophobia within the American rhetoric of freedom, which the war victory was supposed to confirm. Kennan dons his "mask" and takes on the useful personae of both internal (of the Soviet Union) and detached (of U.S. foreign policy) observers. By contrast, Baldwin's uncompromisingly engaged witness scorns detachment in favor of the vision of proximity and intimacy—even when such intimacy requires an ocean between the viewer and his subject.

"You Drag Your Past with You Everywhere, or It Drags You":
Formulating the Dialectics of Distance

At almost the same time that participants such as Chambers and Kennan were drawing the rhetorical lines of the cold war, the young James Baldwin was formulating his politics and poetics. The cold war rhetoric of discrete difference forms the baseline against which Baldwin consistently struggles, arguing for a complicated sense of U.S. nationality and individuality. In everything he wrote, Baldwin denied the viability of simple polarities, such as white/black, gay/straight, patriot/expatriate, American/exile, masculine/feminine. As he wrote in 1951, "Life was just not that simple" (PT 43). Baldwin rejected the inherited vocabulary of cold war dichotomies and was (and is) often misread as a result. In his essays and fiction, he turned on its head the cold war notion of a witness as one testifying for good over evil with secret, dangerous knowledge of the enemy. Baldwin was a witness both for and against his own homeland, the United States, in what he viewed as a struggle of truth. Although Chambers's and Kennan's versions of the witness depend on firm internal-external distinctions (ideological in the former and national or cultural in the latter), the Baldwinian witness necessitates an ongoing, dialectical relationship with the distance between himself and the United States. The ceaseless mobility of the Baldwinian witness's prospect subverts the passage from inner to outer that Chambers, Kennan, and many other cold war thinkers sought to inscribe.[11] The dialectic of distance is driven in part by idealism and pessimism but most importantly by the inevitability of return: "America is my country," Baldwin told Henry Louis Gates, Jr., in a 1973 interview. "Not only am I fond of it, I love it. America would change itself if it could, if that change didn't hurt, but people rarely change" (JBL 167). In 1987, Baldwin reaffirmed this always present necessity of return when he told the poet Quincy Troupe that "because my family's in America I will always go back" (JBL 191). Sadly, this was too true; his funeral was three weeks later, in New York City's Cathedral of St. John the Divine.

As a witness dedicated to blurring the distinction between patriotism and expatriatism, citizenship and exile (he was uncomfortable with all of these absolutes), Baldwin made identity his ever-present theme and, as such, linked it inextricably to his notion of the witness. Ironically, during the Chambers-Hiss hearings, then Senator

Fig. 13.2. Paula and James Baldwin in their mother's home. Photograph by Richard Avedon, October 15, 1946, Harlem, New York. © 1946 by Richard Avedon. All rights reserved.

Richard Nixon made the same connection when he informed Alger Hiss that "this case [between Hiss and Chambers] is dependent upon the question of identity" (Chambers 604). Identity for Baldwin (unlike Nixon) is always a case of interpretive vision and of distance from one's subject. Baldwin's initial characterization of leaving the United States in 1948 as an "escape" quickly became a critical presumption that he would use as a stepping-stone toward a more complexly accurate notion of national identity. In his 1959 essay "The Discovery of What It Means to Be an American," he wrote that to find his personal, interior life as an American, he had to leave the United States. In other words, living in Paris "I proved, to my own astonishment, to be as American as any Texas GI" (PT 172). This discovery, in turn, allowed him to be reconciled to "my role—as distinguished, I must say, from my 'place'—in the extraordinary drama which is America" (PT 172). Baldwin's sense of his *place* as opposed to his *role*, and the agency (or lack thereof) implied by each of these terms, is precisely his point.

In "Alas, Poor Richard," a series of three essays collected and published together in *Nobody Knows My Name* (1961), Baldwin eulogizes the dead Richard Wright unsentimentally as a father figure but not a friend. Baldwin's critique of Wright settles decidedly on the subject of exile. Both writers lived long periods of their lives in France, but Baldwin suggests, with both vehemence and clarity, that Wright genuinely saw himself as an exile, as one who was irrevocably divorced from his past. He remembers that Wright "was fond of referring to Paris as the 'city of refuge,'" as if refuge were possible (and he was later even more forceful on this point).[12] Baldwin responds to this idea of Parisian safety with a reminder that if he and Wright were American (he is thinking, presumably, of the Algerians and other North Africans and Arabs facing persecution in France), they would not experience France as safe. Acidly, Baldwin observes that "it did not seem worthwhile to me to have fled the native fantasy to embrace a foreign one" (NKN 185).

Undoubtedly, both Baldwin and Wright distort aspects of their relationship in their accounts. Even Chester Himes, the observer of their celebrated feud in the Café Deux Magots, refuses to validate one story over the other. Himes recalls Wright urging him to meet Baldwin, and Himes presciently thought that "he sounded as though he wanted a witness."[13] Ultimately, we are able to say with certainty only that Baldwin's version tells us primarily about Baldwin himself, just as Wright's does about Wright. If one focuses too intently on the details of the Wright-Baldwin encounter, one can easily overlook the fact that by aligning Wright with an exilic perspective, Baldwin effectively rules out the status of exile for himself. Even Michel Fabre, Wright's biographer, implicitly alludes to Baldwin's critique ("the 'city of refuge'") when he concludes that, for Wright, "Paris was *his* *refuge* from the growing hysteria of anti-communism in America and practically a second home."[14] Wright himself, in an unpublished essay, called France, "above all, a land of refuge" for displaced and oppressed Americans.[15]

Wright describes his physical and intellectual life outside U.S. borders in a number of significant formulations. His exilic position (as he articulates it after 1946) as an international spokesperson for oppressed peoples made him a threatening figure for both the U.S. government and the literary-critical establishment.[16] Even though all his writings from this time period take up the viability (or perhaps, the necessity) of exile, two make this theme explicit: "I Choose Exile" and *The Outsider*. These two texts, one an essay that publishers refused to print and the other a novel that reviewers (now as then) considered a failure,[17] define an exilic consciousness that informs Wright's enormously important later work, such as *The Color Curtain* (1956), *Pagan Spain* (1957), and *White Man, Listen* (1957). In "I Choose Exile," Wright argues that the view from afar of U.S. politics and history is liberating as well as enlightening: "Living in exile made me realize that we Americans are not only 'isolationists', but that we are *isolated*."[18] He contrasts American isolation with European (chiefly French) openness and mixture ("Paris is racially a free city") of various peoples (Wright, "I Choose," 15). "But can you write in Paris, so far from your subject matter?" is the question that Wright says he's asked "with frequent unctiousness [*sic*]" (13). Wright's answer is that "I took my subject matter with me in the baggage of my memory when I left America, and I'm distressingly confident that American race relations will not alter" (13). These notions of an author mobilizing his subject matter (as "baggage") and considering his "native" heritage from another continent James Baldwin would utilize; however, they would lead the younger writer to another conclusion. The France that Wright describes in "I Choose Exile" is precisely the kind of refuge from racism that Baldwin critiques. Wright writes that he does not think of France as "a paradise," but even if it doesn't offer a perfect form of "justice . . . at least there's some logic in it" (13).

Wright dedicates his third novel, *The Outsider*, to Rachel—"my daughter who was born on alien soil"—and makes alienation the central theme of the novel, with an epigraph from Søren Kierkegaard that defines "dread" as "an alien power which lays hold of an individual" irrepressibly, "for one fears what one desires."[19] The dedication describes Wright's own exile as a presence on "alien soil," which through the epigraph he links to the internal, psychological exile in his protagonist (an "alien power"). This confluence of fear, desire, and alienation sets up the plot of *The Outsider*, in which Cross Damon sheds his identity and personality to escape a vicious crime. This "burden of non-identity," as Wright names it, quickly becomes the central "preoccupation" of the novel (490). Damon engages his adversary, the New York City district attorney, in an ongoing philosophical debate over the status of African Americans and other "outsiders" in society. Houston, a hunchback and therefore an outsider as well, hypothesizes that the historical role of a people formerly enslaved (and currently oppressed) would lend "a *dread*ful objectivity," in the Kierkegaardian sense, to their perspective on society (500).[20] This is, of course, exactly what Damon has found out, through his attempted escape into nonidentity.

In New York, Damon finds that he is an outcast from all communities that he might be inclined to join: African American, communist, white, law-abiding, criminal. As a result of his internal exile, his status as an outsider within U.S. society, Damon can view the empty abstractions of each form of society. He thinks to himself, while talking to one of the communists, "I've got just as many fronts as he's got" (558). Ultimately, Wright's notion of exile and of national belonging depends on precisely this overdetermined metaphor of personal "fronts." The exile is always the one who has enough "distance" to distinguish a "front" in a personal form of warfare from an artificial dilemma ("front" as artifice). In other writings, Wright suggests that *distance* is a loaded term; it implies a form of cultural imperialism that takes many shapes. Wright's consideration of colonialism in the Third World during the 1950s leads him to what he calls "the problem of distance, a psychological distance, a feeling that one must retain something lost."[21] But the proximity or "physical nearness" of African Americans to their oppressors does not lessen this perceptual distance that "the reality of whiteness" instills in "the interior of colored life" (Wright, *White Man, Listen*, 7-8). Whiteness as a tradition of hierarchy and oppression only makes the "psychological" distance greater between those who live side by side in the same society. Ultimately, then, Wright's point in *White Man, Listen* and in many of his later writings is akin to the position of Cross Damon in *The Outsider*: the devastating effects of "distance" can be physical, temporal, or even psychological. The result is the nonidentity of an outsider within society.

Baldwin clearly learned from and incorporated many of the concepts that Wright used in his later writings. But Baldwin marks a sharp contrast between himself and his predecessor on this subject of distance. He perceives that Wright's sense of distance and of belonging is absolute: once an exile renounces the ideals of the nation of origin, the exile can view only them from afar. Baldwin responds to this with a mobile model of distance, one that engages ideals both from a distance and from within. His writings on Americans in France (as well as all over Europe, the Middle East, and Africa) carefully emphasize the paradoxical nature of national belonging. Proximity for James Baldwin does not solve the "problem of distance," but the various forms of distance allow one constantly to reenvision the source of the problem itself: cultural forms of oppression.

Michel Fabre notes Baldwin's unusual relationship with France by examining the writer's descriptions of Paris in both fiction and essays.[22] Fabre contends that he "made a point of shunning romantic stereotypes about Paris which others had willingly accepted" (Fabre, "Paris," 130).[23] Later, Baldwin would restate his sense of exile as a misguided attempt to sever oneself from one's cultural and historical lineages in temporal terms: he perceived the effect of the past on the present as inescapable and the attempt to separate the two (as he saw exile) as dangerously tempting. In 1965 he wrote:

> History, as nearly no one seems to know, is not merely something to be read. And it does not refer merely, or even principally, to the past. On the contrary, the great force of history comes from the fact that we carry it within us, are unconsciously controlled by it . . . and history is literally *present* in all that we do. (PT 410)

Twelve years later, in an abrupt formulation that takes for granted the earlier point, he stated firmly that "you drag your past around with you everywhere, or it drags you" (PT 641). While the later Baldwin continued to elaborate the ways in which temporal distance is always bridged by the fact that "history is literally *present*," in 1961 he made this crucial differentiation in terms of physical geography. To state the matter in crudely parallel form (and ruin the temporal metaphor): the United States is present in everything Baldwin does while in Europe. Thus he definitively marked his own ever-changing distance from the United States as something other than expatriation.

"It's Up to You": Turning Readers into Witnesses

Perhaps most important to Baldwin's notion of the witness in the 1964 text *Nothing Personal* is its contrast with the role of a passive observer. In the Baldwinian language of fiery Protestant sermons, the witness records and reminds his country, acting as his country's conscience. In Karen Thorsen's documentary, Baldwin states this distinction between activity and passivity in absolute terms: "I have never been in despair about the world. . . . I'm *enraged* by it . . . [but] I can't afford despair" (JBPT). Turning the language of cold war surveillance[24] into the tools of a visionary of his own society, in *Nothing Personal*, Baldwin juxtaposes symbols of passive sight (television, film, other visual media) with his own active observations and Avedon's startling photographs. This fascinating collaboration between the writer and the photographer is summed up in a self-portrait that Avedon made, in which half of his own face is covered by a mask of Baldwin's striking features.[25] The identities of the authors of this work are similarly blurred through their interconnected eloquence and wit.

Nothing Personal is divided into four sections of Baldwin's text surrounded by Avedon's photo sequences. In this hybrid collaboration between image and text, both the construction and the destruction of verbal and visual illusions anchor the work's central themes. Avedon's style of portraiture, which shows his subjects in the harshest light and at their most vulnerable, impels Baldwin to a prose style that similarly digs below the surface of the naïveté they set out to expose.[26] David Leeming quotes Avedon's summary of their collaboration as being that of exploring "despair, dishonesty, the . . . things that keep people from knowing each other" (Leeming 227). The two determined to use a coffee-table-sized book to bring their audiences together; Avedon's fashion and artistic following could be introduced to the civil rights struggles through both images and words.[27] Although both Baldwin and Avedon had been planning a collaborative work since high school, turbulent events in the early 1960s made their work even more pressing. The killing of Medgar Evers (whom Baldwin had met and been deeply impressed by that January) in 1963 spurred Baldwin to portray the conflict between U.S. ideals and realities with great urgency and immediacy.[28] Although this is Baldwin's only published image-text work, he was well aware of the tradition (both American and African American) of this multidisciplinary genre.

In 1941, on the heels of the unprecedented success of *Native Son*, Richard Wright was asked to write a short essay to accompany a collection of photographs that photographer Edwin Rosskam had culled from the Farm Security Administration archives. Wright's 20-page essay quickly grew into a 150-page manuscript, which he edited down to approximately 50 pages (four chapters) for the final form of *Twelve Million Black Voices* (1941). Wright drew on sociological and historical works to describe African American migration from the rural South to the urban North.[29] His text stands apart from the included photographs, rarely referring to them explicitly yet engaging the situations that the photos depict: poverty, the sharecropping system, overcrowding, religious institutions, urban tenements, dance and musical expression, hopes and fears for the future. Reviewers hailed *Twelve Million Black Voices* as a major success for Wright.[30] On viewing the published book, Ralph Ellison told Wright in a moving letter that reading it was "a deeply emotional experience."[31] Ellison wrote that he found criticism of the work "impossible": "I felt so intensely the fire of our common experience when reading *12 Million Black Voices* that I felt the solder of my discipline melt and found myself opened up and crying over the painful pattern of remembered things." Baldwin, too, was influenced by the Wright-Rosskam book, but he left fewer traces of admiration than Ellison. Perhaps the most powerful evidence of the impact of Wright's photo-text collaborative work is a project that Baldwin planned as early as 1946. He and a friend, Theodore Pelatowski (whom Baldwin later called his "first real love," although their relationship was apparently not sexual), planned a book that would join a long essay by Baldwin with photographs of Harlem storefront churches by Pelatowski. Although the two began the work, tentatively titled *Unto the Dying Lamb*, they did not complete it.[32] One can only speculate that the similarity of this project's form owes something to Wright's earlier text, though the later appearance of *Nothing Personal* suggests that Baldwin's version would have been anything but a carbon copy of *Twelve Million Black Voices*.

Almost a decade and a half after the publication of *Twelve Million Black Voices*, Langston Hughes pored through sets of Harlem photographs by Roy DeCarava. Hughes wrote a fictional monologue to accompany (and possibly to interrogate as well) the images; the two artists published *The Sweet Flypaper of Life* in 1955.[33] Unlike Wright's first-person plural narrative of African American history and sociology, Hughes assumes the voice of a single woman in one of DeCarava's photographs and creates a narrative that refers directly to the pictures on the page. Hughes's narrator, Sister Mary Bradley, uses the photos to illustrate the lives of Harlem residents. While similar in form (photos interspersed with text) to the Wright-Rosskam work, the Hughes-DeCarava collaboration welds the images with the texts to the degree that one could not easily publish Hughes's text apart from DeCarava's photographs. In direct contrast to these precursors,[34] Baldwin and Avedon's book is neither sociological nor personal. Baldwin's text does not refer to Avedon's photographs individually; however, he evokes the emotional and political ambiguities that the silver-toned portraits capture. In fact, Baldwin and Avedon worked entirely apart on the project. Baldwin wrote the text without seeing Avedon's photographs and vice versa. The only exception came in the final section of the book. After Avedon read Baldwin's redemptive conclusion, he took the last sequence of photographs. "I was much more sour than Jimmy was," Avedon recently recalled.[35]

Roland Barthes calls photography "a certain but fugitive testimony" in his meditations on the medium, *Camera Lucida*.[36] If one expects evidence from this "fugitive testimony," Baldwin plays on the notion of images that transfer the status of the witness from the individual observer present at the original event to anyone who views the photograph. Repeatedly, Baldwin and Avedon test what Barthes calls the "arrest of interpretation [in which] the Photograph's certainty lies" (Barthes 107). The interrelatedness of image and text ensure that the faculty of interpretation will not be allowed to rest in this collaboration.[37]

Nothing Personal opens with stark photographs of wealthy, well-dressed, fur-draped denizens kissing each other; these bejeweled figures quickly give way to more modest ceremonies and less-manicured subjects. The weddings represented were all ceremonies at New York's City Hall; the participants agreed to let Avedon photograph them in the moments after their ceremonies.[38] Setting the stage for the rest of the work, these wedding scenes freeze illusions and hold them up for reexamination. The text of *Nothing Personal* begins with the "distraction" of television—the black and white ("my screen was colorless") window into the world of smiling, surgery-corrected, artificially improved, utterly plastic and sterile life (PT 381).[39] Pointedly, Baldwin refers to the television fantasies of vacant sexuality as "poor, betrayed exiles," nicely turning the tables on the society that has strayed so far from its stated aims that it is the exile, not he, the writer in France (382). Further, Baldwin describes pityingly the willed ignorance of U.S. life on the part of "those homeless Europeans who now call themselves Americans" (382). These photo-negative reversals suggest that whiteness and "white people" are at issue, not the so-called Negro problem. A characteristically trenchant Baldwin comment from the Thorsen documentary makes a similar point regarding the artificiality of constructed whiteness: "It's up to you. As long as you think you're white, there's no hope for you. 'Cause as long as you think you're white, I'm going to be forced to think I'm black!" (JBPT).

American masculinity and hypersexuality, as envisioned and constructed by the "remote control gadget" culture, is castrated by constant images of "the virile male [and] . . . the aluminum-and-cellophane girl" who are desperately "trying to discover if, behind . . . all those barriers, either of them has a tongue" (PT 381–82). Masculinity, at least, "certainly doesn't seem to have a tongue" and when Baldwin equates it with the nation ("the lives of men—and, therefore, of nations"), he condemns a culture that enforces transfixed, passive, mute acceptance to its myths (384). Baldwin's use of verbs of vision (*discover, examine, reveal, look,* etc.) reinforces the divide between the passive viewer described by and the active witness describing the scene. When he writes that it is both "easier" and seemingly "safer" to "give a name to the evil without than to locate the terror within," Baldwin states simply both the need for and the purpose of the Baldwinian witness. Yet again, his explanation of the role of a witness requires a mobile prospect, with a view of society that can slide closer to and farther from its subject, searching for the correct frame from which to observe and record. One hardly has to point out that Avedon is engaged in precisely the same process in his portraits—sometimes closing in on his subjects to focus on every wrinkle (see the strikingly bloated and exhausted-looking Dorothy Parker, figure 13.3) and other times stepping back to examine their telling body language (for example, Allen Ginsberg and the Everly Brothers, figures 13.4 and 13.5).

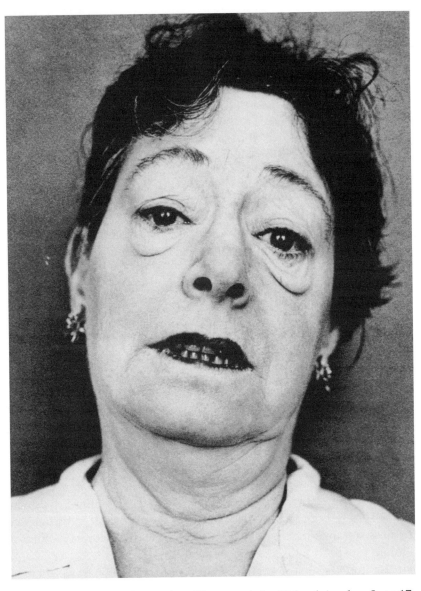

Fig. 13.3. Dorothy Parker, writer. Photograph by Richard Avedon, June 17, 1958, New York City. © 1958 by Richard Avedon. All rights reserved.

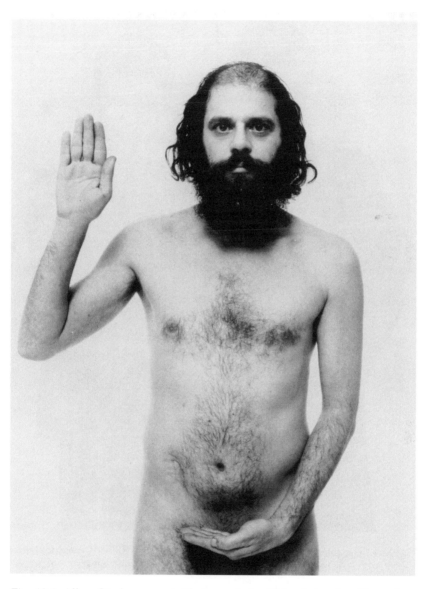

Fig. 13.4. Allen Ginsberg, poet. Photograph by Richard Avedon, December 30, 1963, New York City. © 1963 by Richard Avedon. All rights reserved.

Fig. 13.5. The Everly Brothers, singers. Photograph by Richard Avedon, January 17, 1961, Las Vegas, Nevada. © 1961 by Richard Avedon. All rights reserved.

Both Avedon and Baldwin consider framing to be of the utmost concern, and so Baldwin responds to Avedon's portraits with one of his own. In the second text passage, he tells of hosting a Swiss friend in New York, who experiences "the warmth of his reception in the land of the free" when the two are arrested for having "looked" like criminals (385). The frame of this anecdote begins to shift when its teller reveals that the police were blind enough to have mistaken the Swiss friend for a Puerto Rican. Rather than being a story about a foreign visitor to New York (as it briefly appears in the beginning), it is very much about "the eye of the beholder," in this case, the police (386). This fusion of the religious and the legal (the police actually detain the two and later release them with embarrassment) brings the surveillance of the cold war to the streets of New York. Baldwin describes the plainclothed, disguised police as appearing "suddenly, down from heaven, or up through the sidewalk" (385). Fortunately, or unfortunately, the story shows how poorly the legal system *sees* its citizens, how myopic U.S. internal surveillance is. In language that internalizes and reorients (toward the United States rather than its outer "enemies") the cold war rhetoric into a kind of domestic domino theory, Baldwin states darkly that "if a society permits one portion of its citizenry to be menaced or destroyed, then, very soon, no one in that society is safe" (387).[40] That the media of communication—print and television (both of which are visual at some level)—participate in this process is clear from the parenthetical comment that magazines and such are "communications whose role is not to communicate, but simply to reassure" (387). Needless to say, Avedon's photographs and Baldwin's text studiously avoid reassuring subjects.

If Baldwin is concerned about witnessing the effect of the past on the present ("to be locked in the past means, in effect, that one has no past, since one can never access it, or use it . . . so one can never be free" [383]), he is equally distressed at the risk of falsified, "nostalgic" history (388). The third text section, foreshadowing Avedon's painful series of photographs of patients in a psychiatric hospital, is a meditation on the "inertia" of liminality (391). Beginning with "four a.m." as the moment at which "the day, no matter what kind of day it was, is indisputably over [and] . . . a new day begins" (388), this moment of division between past, present, and future is also the moment at which renewal is possible, if one survives. Baldwin's repetition of the role of the "witness" (388, 389) in the context of redemption alludes to the original biblical witness, who also plays a liminal role in "a miracle of coherence and release" (389). Moses, who travels to the top of Mt. Sinai to speak to God and receive his laws, is not allowed to reach (or even to see) the Promised Land itself. Although Baldwin certainly does not posit himself as the Mosaic savior, he does open up the role of the witness as ultimately redemptive and states unequivocally, "I do not for an instant doubt, and I will go to my grave believing that we can build Jerusalem, if we will" (392).[41] In keeping with the stubborn attempt to combat the "striking addiction to irreality," this third section is also suffused with metaphors of vision; words such as *look* (388, 389, 390), *eyes* (388, 390), *peeks* (390), and *discover* (390) appear with regularity in the text.

In the final section of interspersed text and photographs, hope resurfaces in its visual manifestations: mobility and light. "The light in the eyes" of hope is made problematic by the fact that "this life is . . . dependent, entirely, on things unseen" (392). But the movement between light and dark, between seen and unseen, is precisely the dialectic that Baldwin and Avedon have organized throughout this text. "One can never remain where one is" (392) because "nothing is fixed" (393), not language, not photographic images; and so the observer has to move with his subject. The constant mobility that this realization demands is exhausting, but it also makes possible a clarity and "coherence" that are as powerful as they are contingent (389). As generations are born, "it is not fixed; the earth is always shifting, the light is always changing"; and these changes provide the vantage point of that most important of roles: "We are the only witnesses they have" (393).

What Evidence Can the Witness Leave Behind? What Is the Witness's Legacy?

Nothing Personal is an engagement of U.S. political and social ideology from the mobile perspective of the witness as opposed to the fixed, external perspective of the exile. In this work, as nowhere else, Baldwin darts in and out of his subject with both optimism and rage, in a sustained effort to perform as narrator what he accomplished personally: to remain defiantly liminal and yet relevant to U.S. society. As he told David Leeming in an interview, Baldwin felt that the painful process of facing up to national ideals was akin to an individual's attempt to do the same. It would be as difficult for Baldwin to renounce his country through expatriation as it would be for him to give up a part of his own self:

In principle I could stay here [in Europe] and never go back to Harlem and New York City again. . . . But . . . I can't do it because if I were to avoid the journey back to America I'd be avoiding everything—the people who have produced me (both black and white), the central reality of my life. And once you do that I don't know what you can write about or what you can write out of. (Leeming 256)

In a review of recent biographies of Baldwin, Ekwueme Michael Thelwell points out one of the unique facets of Baldwin's literary career.[42] Although he does not explicitly link this point to Baldwin's idea of the witness, it provides evidence for the depth of Baldwin's engagement with Americanism while living outside U.S. borders. "Baldwin's role," explains Thelwell, emerged from "the urgency and power of an uncommon communion between writer and the common reader" (Thelwell 100). Baldwin was able to forge this "communion" through a tone that was as intimate as the traditional religious confessional and yet maintained the accusatory indictment of the society that had alienated him to the point of leaving it. This fusion of intimacy and rage is possible for Baldwin only through the tone of the witness as he is able to transform it from legal, religious, and cold war cultural modes into a singular, inimitable voice.

While I share Thelwell's concern regarding the efforts of many critics to argue that Baldwin experienced some sort of "artistic collapse" after 1963–1964, one can maintain with certainty that his productivity level was high during the late 1950s and early 1960s, and it is true he never again reached that pace of creation and thought.[43] Given the significance that Baldwin attributed to the role of the witness, and the historical fact that this term reemerged in U.S. discourses during the cold war 1950s, one has to wonder if the freedom of the witness was constraining as well as liberating. In the final decades of his life, the *witness* became a much more univocally religious term, rather than the point of contact between several vocabularies it was in and around 1964. One has to wonder to what extent Baldwin felt like more of an exile and less of a witness in his later years. In his final interview, with the poet Quincy Troupe, Baldwin provides a bittersweet assessment of his own work: "I was right . . . I was right about what was happening in the country. . . . And the choices people would have to make. And watching people make them and denying them at the same time. I began to feel more and more homeless" (JBL 190). In the same interview he is more tentative about his cherished role than he had been at any time before, using the past tense to describe his career: "I was a witness, I thought. I was a very despairing witness, though too" (190). This seems a striking comment on his own legacy when one considers the fact that he—as an engaged witness—actively scorned despair throughout his life. As Baldwin put it earlier in his career, "I have never been in despair about the world. . . . I'm *enraged* by it . . . [but] I can't afford despair" (JBPT). His own statement that he "can't afford" despair makes his later admission of being "a very despairing witness" all the more tragic when one considers the critical (non)response to Baldwin's oeuvre.

Regardless, Baldwin's admonition for the enduring need of witnesses not tied to one vantage point or one ideology but rather free to document (from a distance that only increases the possibility of intimacy) the incompatibility of American ideals and historical U.S. realities still stands: "Black people need witnesses in this hostile world in which everything is white" (JBPT).

NOTES

1. For purposes of convenience, I hereafter cite Karen Thorsen's 1989 documentary *The Price of the Ticket* as JBPT. I cite Baldwin's works accordingly: *Nobody Knows My Name* (1961; reprint, New York: Vintage Books, 1993) as NKN; *The Price of the Ticket: Collected Nonfiction, 1948–1985* (New York: St. Martin's/Marek, 1985) as PT; *Nothing Personal* (New York: Atheneum, 1964) as NP; *Conversations with James Baldwin* (Jackson: University of Mississippi Press, 1989) as CJB; and *James Baldwin: The Legacy* (New York: Simon & Schuster, 1989) as JBL.

2. For detailed readings and sage counsel, I am indebted to Ann Douglas, Robert G. O'Meally, Dwight A. McBride, Deborah M. Levy, and Martin and Ylana Miller. I am also deeply grateful to Richard Avedon for allowing his photographs to accompany this chapter and for sharing his observations of Baldwin and *Nothing Personal*. Elizabeth Alexander and Lauren Berlant provided early encouragement for my readings of Baldwin. This essay is dedicated to a witness in my own family, Alfred W. Feiler, for setting an impressive life example and for urging me to seek out the visionaries in every society.

3. *The Jerusalem Bible* (Jerusalem: Koren Publishers, 1992), p. 518.

4. Frederick Douglass, "What to the Slave Is the Fourth of July?" in *The Heath Anthology of American Literature*, vol. 1, 2d ed., ed. Paul Lauter (New York: Heath, 1994), p. 1743. See also Douglass's *Narrative of the Life of Frederick*

Douglass (Boston: Bedford Books, 1993), in which he refers to himself as "a witness and a participant" in the violence of slavery (p. 42).

5. Whittaker Chambers, *Witness* (Washington, D.C.: Regnery Gateway, 1952), p. 5; emphasis added.

6. Philip Rahv, "The Sense and Nonsense of Whittaker Chambers," *Partisan Review*, July–August 1952, p. 477.

7. George Kennan, *Memoirs: 1925-1950.* (New York: Pantheon Books, 1967), pp. 8, 274.

8. George Kennan quoted in Fareed Zakaria, "Divining Russia," *New York Times Book Review,* April 7, 1996, p.6.

9. Fareed Zakaria, "Divining Russia," p. 6 (emphasis added).

10. Paul Gilroy's work on Richard Wright in *The Black Atlantic* (Cambridge, Mass.: Harvard University Press, 1993) provides an excellent corrective to the long-standing critical fallacy that Wright's later work suffered as a result of his presence in Europe and Africa. This chapter is motivated by some of the same questions that Gilroy raises, but my focus is on the context of Baldwin's life and work rather than on Wright's.

11. Examples of the ways in which Baldwin sought to make cold war distinctions more complexly attuned to issues of race and nationality abound throughout everything he wrote. Baldwin delighted in the irony that having been a Trotskyite during the 1940s, he was in the "interesting" position of being "an anti-Stalinist when America and Russia were allies" (PT xii).

12. Herbert Hill suggests that Wright also considered himself within the tradition of American (and other) writers in exile:

I saw [Wright] in the summer of 1959 in Paris and then again in the summer of 1960. . . . He said . . . 'so many other writers, white writers, have come to Paris—William Faulkner, James Joyce, Hemmingway, Djuna Barnes, Morley Callaghan—they all came here for a time. They all worked here and studied. This enriched them. Why am I different? Is it because I'm a black writer? Am I not to be given the same opportunity as other writers to come to Paris, to come to Europe, to have the experience? Why is this denied me?' (in Herbert Hill, ed., *Anger and Beyond: The Negro Writer in the United States* [New York: Harper & Row, 1966], p. 206)

13. Chester Himes, *The Quality of Hurt: The Autobiography of Chester Himes,* vol. 1 (New York: Thunder's Mouth Press, 1971), p. 200.

14. Michel Fabre, *The Unfinished Quest of Richard Wright* (Urbana: University of Illinois Press, 1993), p. 354; emphasis added. For an invaluable chronology of the Wright-Baldwin relationship and a survey of some of the critical interpretations, see Fred L. Standley's "'. . . . Farther and Farther Apart': Richard Wright and James Baldwin," in *Critical Essays on Richard Wright,* ed. Yoshinobu Hakutani (Boston: G. K. Hall & Co., 1982). Albert Mur-

ray provides an original view in his essay "Something Different, Something More" (Hill 112–37).

15. Richard Wright, "Greetings from American Artists Who Live in France!" Richard Wright Collection, Beinecke Rare Book and Manuscripts Library, Yale University (JWJ MSS 3, Box 5, Folder 89), p. 2.

16. Again, see Gilroy, *Black Atlantic* (pp. 146–86), on the critical reception of Wright's later works. For more on the FBI surveillance of Wright (as well as Baldwin, Chester Himes, and other African American writers), see Fabre, *Unfinished Quest*; and James Campbell, *Exile in Paris* (New York: Scribner's, 1995), pp. 85–103, 120–21.

17. As just one example, Arna Bontemps remarks that *"The Outsider* was not quite up to Wright's earlier books. Something was missing. Perhaps it was anger. His new French friends had made the suffering, alienated author feel at home" (Hill 203).

18. Richard Wright, "I Choose Exile," Richard Wright Collection, Beinecke Rare Book and Manuscripts Library, Yale University (JWJ MSS 3, Box 6, Folder 110), p. 12.

19. Richard Wright, *Later Works: Black Boy (American Hunger), The Outsider* (New York: Library of America, 1991), p. 369. John M. Reilly provides a useful contextualization of Wright's interest in African decolonization and the Third World in "Richard Wright and the Art of Non-Fiction: Stepping Out on the Stage of the World," *Callaloo* 9, 3 (Summer 1986): 507–20.

20. Wright's white district attorney's main point is worth quoting at length: "Negroes, as they enter our culture, are going to inherit the problems we have, but with a difference. They are outsiders and they are going to *know* that they have these problems. They are going to be self-conscious; they are going to be gifted with a double vision, for, being Negroes, they are going to be both inside and outside of our culture at the same time. . . . Negroes will develop unique and specially defined psychological types. They will become psychological men, like the Jews. . . . They will not only be Americans or Negroes; they will be centers of *knowing*" (Wright, *Outsider*, 499–500).

21. Richard Wright, *White Man, Listen! Lectures in Europe, 1950–1956* (New York: HarperCollins, 1995), p. 7.

22. Michel Fabre, "Paris as a Moment in African American Consciousness," *The Black Columbiad: Defining Moments in African American Literature and Culture,* ed. Werner Sollors and Maria Diedrich (Cambridge, Mass.: Harvard University Press, 1993). Tyler Stovall captures an important aspect of this when he suggests in *Paris Noir* that for African American writers such as Wright, Baldwin, and Chester Himes, "Paris was not radically different but rather an intensification of an expatriate experience that had already begun at home" (*Paris Noir* [New York: Houghton Mifflin, 1996], p. 212).

23. A notable example of such stereotypes comes from Baldwin's former

teacher Countee Cullen. Fabre cites Cullen to the effect that he has "found across a continent of foam / What was denied my hungry heart at home" (Fabre, "Paris," 135).

24. He was thinking about surveillance on another level as well. Around this time (after his meeting with Attorney General Robert Kennedy, according to David Leeming), Baldwin became aware that the FBI was following him and listening to his phone conversations. See David Leeming, *James Baldwin: A Biography* (New York: Alfred A. Knopf, 1994), pp. 225–26; and W. J. Weatherby, *James Baldwin: Artist on Fire* (New York: Donald I. Fine, 1989), pp. 225–29. See also chapter 11 by Maurice Wallace in this book.

25. Richard Avedon, *Evidence: 1944–1994* (New York: Random House, 1994), p. 147. See also Avedon's 1946 photograph of Baldwin in his mother's apartment (Avedon 126).

26. W. J. T. Mitchell's account in *Picture Theory: Essays on Verbal and Visual Representation* (Chicago: University of Chicago Press, 1994) of what he calls "image-text combinations" and "collaborations" has sharpened my sense of this dynamic (p. 91). Mitchell differentiates between a photo that accompanies text simply to illustrate what the text has described and one that produces creative tension between the textual and the photographic. His chapter on "the photographic essay" highlights the dissonance between, for example, Walker Evans's photos and James Agee's text in *Let Us Now Praise Famous Men* (Mitchell 281–322). As I indicate below, the Baldwin-Avedon collaboration similarly contains a complex interrelatedness between image and text that conceals some aspects of this exchange between the two artists from readers/viewers.

27. Richard Avedon, interview with author, 16 April 1998.

28. Elizabeth Alexander considers the relationship between African American history and visual representations of bodily violence in her essay "'Can You Be BLACK and Look at This?': Reading the Rodney King Video(s)," in *Black Male: Representations of Masculinity in Contemporary Art* (New York: Whitney Museum of American Art, 1994). She asks, "What do the scenes of communally witnessed violence in slave narratives tell us about the way that 'text' is carried in African American flesh?" (95). With regard to Frederick Douglass, Harriet Jacobs, Emmett Till, and Rodney King, Alexander suggests that visual imprints of violence done to African American male bodies are etched in the history of U.S. literature in a continuing struggle over viewership and ownership. In particular, Alexander's discussion of Emmett Till's open-casket funeral (at the request of his mother) and of the photograph of the mutilated body in the black news magazine *Jet* has been enormously helpful to me as I attempt to make sense of the complex relationship between visual culture and African American history. Another engaging set of personal meditations on visual representations is Deborah Willis's collec-

tion of essays *Picturing Us: African American Identity in Photography* (New York: New Press, 1994).

29. Nor was this Wright's only photo-text collaboration. In 1951 he wrote an article for *Ebony* magazine titled "The Shame of Chicago" that accompanied photographs by Wayne Miller of Chicago's South Side (*Ebony*, December 1951, pp. 24–31). Michel Fabre also describes a planned 1944 photo-text piece that never came to fruition, "a photographic documentary about the children of Harlem," for which Wright contacted Helen Levitt (Fabre, *Unfinished Quest*, 267).

30. For more on the publication history of *Twelve Million Black Voices*, see Fabre, *Unfinished Quest*, pp. 232–35. Houston Baker is one of the few literary critics who has considered the work within the context of Wright's career. See Baker on gender and "place" in *Twelve Million Black Voices* in his *Workings of the Spirit* (Chicago: University of Chicago Press, 1991), pp. 105–33. See also John M. Reilly's essay "Richard Wright Preaches the Nation: *12 Million Black Voices*," *Black American Literature Forum* 16, 3 (Fall 1982); pp. 116–19. Reilly calls Wright's voice in *Twelve Million Black Voices* a "secularization of the sacred moral voice of the folk," a "simulated sermon," and a way of "preaching the national text" (117). For a general survey of reviews of Wright's work, see *The Critical Response to Richard Wright*, ed. Robert J. Butler (Westport, Conn.: Greenwood Press, 1995), which includes some excellent essays but, unfortunately, reinforces the critical silence on *Twelve Million Black Voices*.

31. Ralph Ellison, letter to Richard Wright, 3 November 1941, Richard Wright Collection, Beinecke Rare Book and Manuscripts Library, Yale University (JWJ MSS 3, Series II, Box 97, Folder 1314).

32. David Leeming relates this story in the context of Baldwin's young adulthood and formative friendships with Pelatowski and Richard Avedon, among others (Leeming 54–55). In his biography of Baldwin, *Talking at the Gates: A Life of James Baldwin* (London: Faber & Faber, 1991), James Campbell writes of the similarity of this proposed book to Wright's and considers the "possible" links between them (p. 37).

33. Roy DeCarava and Langston Hughes, *The Sweet Flypaper of Life* (1955; reprint, Washington, D.C.: Howard University Press, 1984).

34. Another crucial precursor to consider is Ralph Ellison, who was a studio photographer of some renown before writing a novel that is predicated on metaphors (and technologies) of vision and visibility, *Invisible Man* (New York: Random House, 1952).

35. Avedon, interview with author.

36. Roland Barthes, *Camera Lucida: Reflections on Photography* (New York: Hill & Wang, 1991), p. 93.

37. When considering Barthes in this context, it may also be worthwhile to keep in mind where he differs from Baldwin and Avedon in significant

ways: "History is hysterical: it is constituted only if we consider it, only if we look at it—and in order to look at it, we must be excluded from it . . . impossible for me to believe in 'witnesses'; impossible, at least, to be one" (Barthes 65).

38. Avedon, interview with author.

39. Since *Nothing Personal* does not include page numbers, I cite text from *The Price of the Ticket* collection and refer to the photographs according to the five groups (i.e., wedding set, portrait sets 1 and 2, hospital set, and final set).

40. This also obliquely hints at the other event of this century for which "witnesses" have played a major role: the Holocaust. This sentence brings to mind the famous parable: "They came for the Gypsies, but I was not a Gypsy so I didn't speak; they came for the Jews. . . . And in the end there was no one left to speak for me."

41. In this context, it may be worth remembering Richard Wright's comment in his "Why and Wherefore" introduction to *White Man, Listen*: "I'm much more the diagnostician than the scribbler of prescriptions. I'm no Moses" (xxviii). Baldwin, in contrast, was willing to take on the prophetic mantle from time to time. He began a speech in 1965 by declaring: "I feel myself, not for the first time, in the position of a Jeremiah" (PT 403).

42. Ekwueme Michael Thelwell, "A Prophet Is Not without Honor," *Transition* 58 (1992): 90–113.

43. See Leeming's "Chronological Bibliography of Printed Works" for evidence (Leeming 405–17). Quantity never equals quality or substance, however, and one cannot draw particularly firm conclusions from a statistical compilation.

Chapter 14

Selfhood and Strategy in
Notes of a Native Son

Lauren Rusk

Notes of a Native Son,[1] James Baldwin's first collection of essays, portrays his personal experience of the ill-fitting, anonymous role inflicted on African Americans by white society. This work of rhetorical life writing addresses an audience riven in two by racial difference. In it Baldwin pulls out all the stops to demonstrate, especially to white readers, the pathological relations between and essential kinship of black and white Americans.

The Divided Audience

One of Baldwin's eminent forebears, James Weldon Johnson, in his essay "The Dilemma of the Negro Author" observes that the African American writer faces a "double audience . . . made up of two elements with differing and often opposite and antagonistic points of view . . . always both white America and black America."[2] Of these two readerships, Baldwin speaks primarily to white readers. One reason for this emphasis is that African Americans did not constitute a large market; Sidonie Smith's remark that a female writer realizes the male audience holds "the power of her reputation in its hands"[3] pertains in even greater measure to the position of minority writers with regard to majority readers. Or as Johnson observes, "It is impossible for an American Negro to write with total disregard for nine-tenths of the people of the United States. Situated as his own race is amidst and amongst them, their influence is irresistible" (481). However, it's not just that Baldwin *has* to speak to white people; he is driven to confront and inform them, to sway their power.[4] Indeed, Johnson, in the 1920s, believes every black writer is partly "impelled by the desire to make his work have some effect on the white world for the good of his race" (481). Baldwin's essays of 1940s and 1950s display the same sort of urgency.

Like Johnson, Baldwin does not identify himself or his secondary audience with oppressed people other than those of African descent.[5] In general, he confines his thoughts on otherness to black-white relations and directs those thoughts to a dual audience, primarily white and secondarily black. We can identify white readers as his primary addressees because most of his rhetorical strategies target them. The later sections of this chapter examine several of those strategies.

In Johnson's experience, however, it is hard for a writer to keep one audience "in the orchestra chairs" and the other "in the gallery . . . he is likely at any moment to find his audience[s] shifting places" (481). In *Notes*, although the primary audience is white, the title essay in particular, as we shall see, speaks to readers in both groups. Further, it is important to realize that the primary target of Baldwin's rhetoric is no more important than the secondary audience, those meant to overhear.[6] The latter group's crucial role becomes apparent if we consider the text, with its often preacherly cadences, as a performance. The African American reader hears Baldwin speak to white Americans as a trenchant observer, a critic, and at times a self-critic; as a man willing to confront and articulate the ways in which "people are trapped in history" together, "and history is trapped in them" (163).

Correspondences with Du Bois

Johnson's description of the black writer's double audience clearly echoes W. E. B. Du Bois's renowned portrayal, in *The Souls of Black Folk*, of the African American's "double-consciousness": "One ever feels his twoness,—an American, a Negro . . . two unreconciled strivings . . . in one dark body."[7] In fact, Arnold Rampersad suggests that all subsequent African American literature stems from this work, which Johnson revered.[8]

Certainly, *Notes* has features that recall *Souls*.[9] Both take issue with the state of otherness forced on African Americans. Both books are compilations of earlier articles in magazines with a mainly white audience. Both also contain new material; the pieces Du Bois added include the most personal one, which concerns his son's death, and the new essay in *Notes* is also Baldwin's most intimate, centering on the death of his father. Moreover, both writers display tonal virtuosity. Du Bois's variety of tone, Rampersad writes, serves as one of the many ways in which he "shows himself a man of learning and feeling" (88). Similarly, Baldwin's tone ranges from meditative to ironic to sermonic, offering a glimpse of one African American man's multifarious humanity. In addition, the two share a preference for formal diction; Richard Wright would undoubtedly class Du Bois and Baldwin among those artists who "put forth their claims in a language that their nation had given them," because they "hoped and felt that they would ultimately be accepted in their native land as free men," instead of escaping by "sensualiz[ing] their sufferings" in "folk utterance."[10] Robert B. Stepto, among others, calls Du Bois's voice "prophetic,"[11] a quality that *Notes* achieves in its last essay, which alludes to *Souls* and ends by proclaiming, "This world is white no longer, and it will never be white again" (163, 175).

Beyond formal and tonal similarities, Baldwin's life writing, like Du Bois's, as Gordon O. Taylor observes, "identif[ies] the personal with the race's general condition" and insists "that while this condition persists it will be America's national condition as well."[12] Further, each author maintains that suffering has given African Americans insight that the rest of the nation needs to mature spiritually.[13]

Notes *as Life Writing*

Generally, the life writing of otherness, in my view, represents the self in three ways: as a singular personality, as a human being like everyone else, and as a subject shaped by the opposing forces of society, those forces that designate the less powerful as "others." I call these three views of the textual self, in order of increasing breadth, *unique*, *collective*, and *inclusive* selves. Both *Souls* and *Notes* emphasize the hallmark of such works, the collective self. For both Du Bois and Baldwin, the unique and collective aspects of self merge, and the inclusive aspect is one's Americanness in the nation as a whole. However, this wholeness and participation are as yet only ideals, blocked by the otherness enforced on African Americans. Though each life writer speaks collectively, he wishes he did not need to. Each writes to clear the way for a culture that will not make race a stumbling block.

In the introduction to the 1984 edition, Baldwin attempts to account for his aims thirty years earlier in creating the collection as a work of life writing. Beyond his ambivalence about trying to discover who he was, there stood

> between that self and me, the accumulated rock of ages. This rock scarred the hand, and all tools broke against it. Yet, there was a *me,* somewhere: I could feel it, stirring within and against captivity. The hope of salvation—identity—depended on whether or not one would be able to decipher and describe the rock. (xi)[14]

The movement from *I* to *one* is telling; Baldwin is talking about his own motives in terms that apply to other African Americans as well. In doing so, he informs white readers about a collective state of mind and also seems to propose that black readers adopt his strategy of facing and analyzing what holds him back. The rock, the burden of collective oppression and its effects on black people's lives and psyches, Baldwin says, is "part of my inheritance . . . but, in order to claim my birthright, of which my inheritance was but a shadow, it was necessary to challenge and claim the rock." Baldwin's birthright is that of an American native son, and more—of a human being: "My birthright was vast, connecting me to all that lives, and to everyone, forever." Baldwin writes that in *Notes* he "was trying to locate myself within a specific inheritance and to use that inheritance, precisely, to claim the birthright from which that inheritance had so brutally and specifically excluded me" (xi–xii).

The historical burden that hampers self-realization influences how Baldwin represents the self in all its aspects. Expressing the collective self is crucial because African Americans have been set apart as "other." Yet the deeper self, he insists, is one with those who call him "other." It is inclusive and, like each of them, unique. "I am what time, circumstance, history have made of me, certainly, but I am, also, much more than that. So are we all" (xii). Nevertheless, the cultural divide that defines the collective self gives Baldwin his subject matter.

Otherness also dictates how he represents the inclusive self—as one that demands to be acknowledged. The wall that separates black and white Americans incites him to reveal their underlying connectedness. Finally, the wall blocks full expression of the unique self. Baldwin images this barrier as an extension of slavery, with such phrases as "scarred the hand . . . tools broke against it . . . within and against captivity" and with snatches of song such as *"the rock cried out, no hiding place!"* (xi).

Baldwin's life writing is not so much *of* as *from* his life. We don't get much of a portrait of him, but he is ever present in the uncompromising character of his voice and his outlook.[15] The collective experience of continuing bondage looms larger and clamors louder for revelation than his personal self; it echoes inside and becomes himself, and becomes what he must reveal to the reader as the reader's self—the common problem, the shared burden of cultural imbalance.

Hiding in the Rock: Dodges and Masks

To show what's wrong with European American culture, Baldwin recounts highly charged events in his personal history. But only parsimoniously, except in the title essay, does the text re-create how he felt at those times. The narrative skims the surface of his emotional turbulence, touching a crest of feeling or a telling incident and then quickly moving away. Baldwin sometimes alludes to painful feelings or humiliating consequences, but he always goes on to generalize from the incident. In one example, Baldwin tells of his stay in a remote Swiss village whose people had never seen a black person, where

> the children shout *'Neger! Neger!'* as I walk along the streets. . . . I reacted by trying to be pleasant. . . . . This smile-and-the-world-smiles-with-you routine worked about as well in this situation as it had in the situation for which it was designed, which is to say that it did not work at all. No one, after all, can be liked whose human weight and complexity cannot be, or has not been, admitted. (161)

At such moments in the text, I have the sense that Baldwin is jumping out of the range of danger—away from readers whom he can't trust to hear more and away from the strength of his own feelings. Looking back in 1984 at the process of writing *Notes*, Baldwin admits that the idea that "I was trying to discover myself" is "on the whole, when examined, a somewhat dubious notion, since I was also trying to avoid myself." The obscuring of Baldwin the individual by the collective "Negro in America"—"*hide me in the rock!*"—is partly a matter of self-protection (xi).

Self-masking is one way in which Baldwin dodges the problem of revealing too much;[16] refuting stereotypes is another. Both have value as defenses against racism. However, as textual strategies they also allow Baldwin to represent what he is *not,* while what he *is* remains, in great part, absent.

The notion of a mask hiding black from white (and vice versa) recalls Du Bois's image of the "veil," the white world's socially constructed blindness to African Americans in all their human intricacy. Baldwin refers to the same sort of defective vision in describing white people's moments of vague realization "when, beneath the black mask, a human being begins to make himself felt" (167). This blindness, in turn, makes it hard for African Americans to know themselves, reflected as they are by blank stares. In part, Du Bois writes to "raise" the veil that hides the black world from white people, "that [they] may view faintly its deeper recesses" (xii).

The act of *self*-masking, in contrast, is a venerable survival tactic by which African Americans have made use of the veil between white and black. It began during their enslavement, when, as Sidonie Smith writes,

> self-assertion was self-defeating. It more than likely meant mutilation; it often meant death. . . . The alternative to self-assertion was the fabrication of a mask, prerequisite for a less onerous existence, even for sheer survival itself. The slave learned to perfect the game of "puttin' on ole Massa!." Deceit, cunning, fawning ingratiation, stupidity—these were only some of the many faces of his mask, a subtle psychological device to prevent the master from knowing what was really happening in the mind and heart of the "darky." (*Where I'm Bound,* 14–15)

The practice still has its uses; Baldwin suggests how it works in the narrative essay "Equal in Paris." Arrested by the French for being in possession of a bedsheet stolen by an acquaintance, he finds:

> None of my old weapons could serve me here. I did not know what [the French] saw when they looked at me. I knew very well what Americans saw when they looked at me and this allowed me to play endless and

sinister variations on the role which they had assigned me; since I knew
that it was, for them, of the utmost importance that they never be confronted with what, in their own personalities, made this role so necessary
and gratifying to them, I knew that they could never call my hand. (145)

(As usual in Baldwin's writing, the indignities that the tactic has cost
him remain veiled, at least to those readers who have not experienced
them.) However, such self-protective subterfuge is also self-distort-
ing, Baldwin realizes. "In the game I was playing," he writes, "I did
myself a violence of which the world, at its most ferocious, would
scarcely have been capable" (145).

Baldwin not only tells us about self-masking but demonstrates it,
with the fluidity of his personal pronouns, taking on various personae—a strategy I examine near the end of this chapter.

Another way in which Baldwin hides in the text is by constructing,
and then demolishing, portraits of who he is not. Much of the time,
rather than conceiving himself as a being-in-the-text, he appears as
the *non*being of others' misconceptions of his collective self. Indeed,
particularly in the first two essays, Baldwin argues that the "white
world" projects onto African Americans whatever it wants to deny in
itself, portraying them as "benighted, brutal," and irredeemable (37).
Baldwin, then, is much occupied with reacting to and negating these
negative images.[17] (In doing so, he also refutes the way in which the
white world represents itself.)[18] Thus, as life writing, this collection
might well be considered notes *toward* a native son.

Baldwin's admission that even while putting together these "memoirs" (ix) he was avoiding self-scrutiny is itself yet another personal
issue that he raises but does not pursue. The word *avoid* connotes—
fear, but of what? Perhaps he is afraid of finding untapped veins of
"intolerable bitterness of spirit," ungovernable rage, or despair, over
the hypocrisy, meanness, and exploitation that African Americans
still undergo (88–89, 71, 95–98, 165, 114). Maybe he even fears that his
detractors are onto something, that their accounts of his otherness
have some validity. Baldwin says that he "can conceive of no Negro
native to this country who has not, by the age of puberty, been ir-
reparably scarred by the conditions of his life. All over Harlem,
Negro boys and girls are growing into stunted maturity, trying desperately to find a place to stand"; he adds, "The American image of
the Negro lives also in the Negro's heart" (71, 38). (Though Baldwin

claims his birthright as an American native, he often uses the term *American* to mean white, reflecting the fact that many white people see themselves exclusively as American.) From the perspective of a white reader, I can only speculate about Baldwin's reasons for stopping short of fuller self-revelation.

The attempt "to avoid [him]self" in life writing concerns the perils not only of confronting painful details and feelings but also of disclosing them to his readers, particularly white readers.[19] Stepto writes, "Once we consider distrust of the American reader and of American acts of reading to be a primary and pervasive motivation for Afro-American writing, we are equipped to read the autobiographies of Douglass, Wright, and many other writers in fresh and useful ways" (198). Baldwin's fluid personal reference, including the white *we*, is a way of eluding definition by readers in the dominant group of society, the group that makes the meanings the rest of society must make do with.[20] By donning masks and avoiding the "What happened next?" and "How did you feel?" queries of those who have not experienced the predicaments and emotions of black otherness, Baldwin evades capture.

Additionally, Baldwin's personal reserve takes control, in a sense, of the invisibility conferred on black people by the white majority. That white people do not really see African Americans has been a common theme in black literature, for example, in Arna Bontemps's historical novel *Black Thunder*,[21] which refers to black slaves among white people as shadows, and notably in Ralph Ellison's *Invisible Man*,[22] as well as in Du Bois's *Souls*. Baldwin's elusiveness, in effect, throws this invisibility back at white readers, as if he were saying, "You've refused to see me; now I decline to reveal myself. You'll have to do your best to interpret my shadow where it falls." In doing so, Baldwin also fulfills his contention that African Americans understand much more about white people, by observing the obsessive stereotypes they construct, than white folks perceive about them (28, 166, 167).

The Personal Fervor of the Collective Self

While Baldwin's expression of the unique self is guarded, a personal urgency drives his sociological commentary. In particular, his assertions about the collective African American *he* often seems fervently to reveal Baldwin the individual,[23] in their intensity and in the ways in which they correspond to his own circumstances. Certain passages in the concluding essay, such as the following, implicitly speak to Baldwin's aims and desires as a writer:[24]

> [S]ince white men represent in the black man's world so heavy a weight, white men have for black men a reality which is far from being reciprocal; and hence all black men have toward all white men an attitude which is designed, really, either to rob the white man of the jewel of his naïveté, or else to make it cost him dear. The black man insists, by whatever means he finds at his disposal, that the white man cease to regard him as an exotic rarity and recognize him as a human being. (166)

The impassioned phrase "rob the white man of the jewel of his naïveté" is an apt figure for Baldwin's confrontational stance in this book. And of course, the "exotic rarity" clause refers in part to his experience as the black stranger in a Swiss village. Near the end of the same essay, another generalization resonates with feeling about Baldwin's quest as a writer:

> [The African American's] survival depended, and his development depends, on his ability to turn his peculiar status in the Western world to his own advantage and, it may be, to the very great advantage of that world. It remains for him to fashion out of his experience that which will give him sustenance, and a voice. (173)

Reading such passages as projections of the writer's own experience is not to deny their collective reality but rather to observe that through most of the book Baldwin expresses his feelings most intimately when he speaks not as himself alone but as an African American, his collective self.

Yet Baldwin deplores being compelled always to keep race in mind. As David Levin observes, "his predicament as an American Negro" and his consequent "didactic purpose . . . force him to ignore his conviction that color does not matter."[25] Baldwin finds the fact that the collective is defined *as against* others a burden. Though his is a voice that seldom speaks without acknowledging his collective identity, Baldwin maintains that one's uniqueness and humanity are paramount. The human being, he says,

is not, after all, merely a member of a Society or a Group. . . . He is—
and how old-fashioned the words sound!—something more than that,
something resolutely indefinable, unpredictable. In overlooking, denying, evading his complexity . . . we are diminished and we perish. (15)

The contrast of *more* with *merely* and *diminished* gives precedence to
the inclusive and unique aspects of self. Hence, "the failure of the
protest novel," Baldwin believes, "lies in . . . its insistence that it is [a
person's] categorization alone which is real and which cannot be
transcended" (23). In the narrative essay "Notes," Baldwin again proclaims that he values uniqueness and humanity over racial identity:
"The dead man [his one-of-a-kind father] mattered, the new life [de-
scribed in universal terms] mattered; blackness and whiteness did
not matter; to believe that they did was to acquiesce in one's own destruction" (113).[26]

"Equal in Paris," a Kafkaesque tale of Baldwin's victimization by
the bureaucracy of the French justice system, is one narrative that
does not focus on race. It eventuates in court, where Baldwin's case is
finally dismissed, amid "great merriment. . . . the laughter of those
who consider themselves to be at a safe remove from all the
wretched." The last sentence starts by making a point of Baldwin's individuality: "In some deep, black, stony, and liberating way, *my life, in
my own eyes,* began during that first year in Paris" (emphasis added).
However, when the sentence ends, "it was borne in on me that this
laughter is universal and never can be stilled," it divides the world
once again into two opposed groups—in this case, those who are vulnerable to being thrown into jail and those who are not (158). The collective self has changed its complexion but prevails in the end.
Throughout, the story concerns the need for compassion, common
feeling, among various strata of society. Were it widespread, the ideal
of the inclusive self could be realized.

The overall structure of *Notes* also reveals Baldwin's view that,
like it or not, the social is the ground from which the individual
grows. Although only three of the ten essays, excluding the original
and new introductions,[27] are explicitly autobiographical, the speaker
emerges as a person more and more throughout the course of the
book. As his portrayal of the society develops, Baldwin himself takes
shape. The body of the book is divided into three parts, each a

roughly contemporaneous collection of essays from the period 1948 to 1955. Each part is arranged chronologically, except for the essay with which the book concludes, "Stranger in the Village."

Part 1 comprises cultural reviews of two American books and a film. The reviews of Harriet Beecher Stowe's *Uncle Tom's Cabin*[28] and Richard Wright's *Native Son*[29] do not try to do justice to the merits of the works they critique;[30] rather, they take the books as jumping-off points from which to explore the thoughts these works spark in the critic. Each review serves as an occasion for Baldwin to expand on his philosophy of race relations. Overall, part 1 concerns the typology of blackness as damnable that permeates American society and is reflected in reputedly pro-black works. In this first part, Baldwin himself appears only as a point of view.

Part 2 consists of three essays on black experience in America, moving from an impersonal analysis to a secondhand account and then to the story of a crucial period in Baldwin's own life. The first essay surveys general forces and conditions in "The Harlem Ghetto." The second recounts the off-handed scorn and political exploitation faced by a singing group that includes Baldwin's brothers, on a "Journey to Atlanta." The third, title essay is the only explicitly personal one, but it is longer than the other two put together. It takes place during Baldwin's eighteenth year, which ends with his father's death, the birth of his youngest sibling, and a race riot,[31] and it treats Baldwin's discovery of how anger over racism can affect his spirit.

Part 3 meditates on what American experience in Europe can teach us. The first two essays are phrased in general terms; the last two are explicitly autobiographical. The first piece concerns what black Americans learn about themselves by encountering French Africans, white French people, and white Americans in France. The second, without mentioning race, addresses what American students in France discover about their identity. Together, this pair represents the "double-consciousness" Du Bois describes: "an American, a Negro" (45). Finally, Baldwin's decision to end part 3 with the pair of essays "Equal in Paris" and "Stranger" once again reflects the view that the personal emerges out of the societal.

In terms of emphasis, the book as a whole, and parts 2 and 3 within it, moves from journalistic descriptions of Baldwin's social contexts to personal accounts of how living in these contexts has affected him. The collection also moves from experiences of the United States to observations concerning Europe that have helped him better understand America.[32] In the essay he chose to conclude with, however, these directions are reversed. "Stranger in the Village" begins with Baldwin's particular experience in Switzerland and then widens out to treat the general situation of America in regard to race. These counterposed motions—from the cultural to the personal overall, and from the personal to the cultural in the last piece—demonstrate the inextricability of the two realms of being. Moreover, these two realms are interwoven all through the 1984 introduction. Finally, the fact that the body of the work begins and ends with analyses of racial division in American society reflects Baldwin's focus, as a life writer, on the collective aspect of the self.

Diagnosing Hatred

In a sense, though Baldwin disdains psychiatry,[33] his book diagnoses American society, especially white society, as sick with repressed knowledge and feelings about its racial relations. Earlier, Du Bois derived his notion of "double-consciousness" from the work of contemporary psychologists such as William James (Rampersad, 74). Similarly, Baldwin's psychodynamic model of his culture's pathology reflects the ideas popular at mid-century. The cure he envisions is a kind of self-administered psychoanalysis. He wants members of societal factions to scrutinize their feelings and actions toward others, denying nothing. Baldwin believes that only by acknowledging our destructive impulses and acts can we outgrow them. Sigmund Freud defines repression as "rejecting and keeping something out of consciousness" because one "finds it unbearable."[34] Baldwin, talking of social psychology but like a Freudian, says, "I think that the past is all that makes the present coherent, and further, that the past will remain horrible for exactly as long as we refuse to assess it honestly" (6, xii). We must face our history—personal and collective—and own up to it.

This imperative applies particularly to white Americans, who continue to reap the benefits of economic ascendance over African Americans. "Many Thousands Gone," which takes off from a review of Wright's *Native Son*, mulls over the social pathology of dominance. In this essay, Baldwin adopts a white *we*, prompting white readers to try on the diagnosis for size:

> The ways in which the Negro has affected the American psychology are betrayed in our popular culture and in our morality; in our estrangement from him is the depth of our estrangement from ourselves. We cannot ask: what do we *really* feel about him—such a question merely opens the gates on chaos. . . .
>
> In our image of the Negro breathes the past we deny, not dead but living yet and powerful. . . . It is this which . . . lends to interracial cocktail parties their rattling, genteel, nervously smiling air. . . . Wherever the Negro face appears a tension is created, the tension of a silence filled with things unutterable. (24, 28–29)

The paragraph ends with an analogy to the effects of history that clearly reveals the influence of psychodynamics on Baldwin's account of social dynamics: "The man does not remember the hand that struck him, the darkness that frightened him, as a child; nevertheless, the hand and the darkness remain with him, indivisible from himself forever, part of the passion that drives him wherever he thinks to take flight" (29).

"Autobiographical Notes," the 1955 introduction, mentions Baldwin's own therapeutic, social self-analysis. In the context of the essays that follow, this disclosure serves as an example to his readers:

> I was forced to admit something I had always hidden from myself, which the American Negro has had to hide from himself as the price of his public progress; that I hated and feared white people. This did not mean that I loved black people; on the contrary, I despised them, possibly because they failed to produce Rembrandt. (7)

Eldridge Cleaver, in his critique of Baldwin's early work, misreads this passage, using it as evidence of what he considers the older writer's hatred of his own race,[35] when Baldwin is, it seems to me, owning up to an earlier state of mind that he has moved beyond.[36]

What he has moved on to is the acknowledgment of a more emotionally complex relation to white people. In "Many Thousands Gone," Baldwin critiques Wright for ignoring this complexity. He uses the global *we* at this point in the essay, linguistically enacting the connectedness of which he speaks:

> It is not simply the relationship of oppressed to oppressor, of master to slave, nor is it motivated merely by hatred; it is also, literally and morally, a *blood* relationship, perhaps the most profound reality of the American experience, and we cannot begin to unlock it until we accept

how very much it contains of the force and anguish and terror of love.(42)

The double sense of the phrase "blood relationship" suggests that so-called black and white people are bound together by a shared history of consanguinity and violence.

Later, in "Encounter on the Seine," Baldwin describes a revelation of kinship with white Americans, which black Americans experience, he says, in talking to Africans and realizing how different their own position is:

> Dimly . . . there begins to fall into perspective the nature of the roles they [black and white Americans] have played in the lives and history of each other. Now he [the African American] is bone of their bone, flesh of their flesh; they have loved and hated and obsessed and feared each other and his blood is in their soil. Therefore he cannot deny them, nor can they ever be divorced. (123)

Black and white Americans have long been bound up in each other's lives, in mostly dysfunctional but nonetheless intimate relations with lasting effects that they cannot simply cast off.

The title essay amplifies the problematics of hate, with an account of a pivotal year in Baldwin's life. The mainly narrative essays, "Notes" and "Equal," describe personal experiences of interest, I believe, to both black and white readers. These pieces seem less to address a hierarchically separated audience, which is fitting, to my mind, since "Notes" implies the need for love and "Equal" for compassion, both leveling emotions. Moreover, "Notes" in particular reaches conclusions that are germane to each audience. The ending announces Baldwin's aims with regard to white people: to speak out and fight on behalf of the African American collective for equal power but also to overcome his feelings of hostility toward whites (113–14). It also offers practical spiritual counsel to black readers, by sharing Baldwin's revelation that "hatred, which could destroy so much, never failed to destroy the man who hated and this was an immutable law" (113).

Baldwin's earlier stress on the genetic kinship of black and white Americans suggests an analogy in "Notes" between, on the one hand, the intermingled hate and love he feels toward his father and, on the other, black people's similar emotions toward white people.[37] This parallel cannot be taken too far, because Baldwin's father, though harsh and aloof, is attempting to act in his children's interest, which cannot be said generally of whites with regard to their black kindred. The point, however, is that both relationships are familial ones in which love is entangled with feelings of fear, repulsion, and anger, and with acts of violence.[38] Baldwin writes, "This was [my father's] legacy: nothing is ever escaped" (113). His father cannot escape the yoke of blackness in a racist country; Baldwin cannot escape it either, nor the hurt his father inflicts on him, nor distant memories of his father's love, nor his own impulse to love others who are likely to hurt him.

In "Notes," Baldwin focuses on the absence of love and, most of all, the self-destructiveness of hatred, bitterness, and rage. In the narrative, the teenage Baldwin has lived in New Jersey and worked for a year in defense plants during World War II, with white and black Southerners. He was confronted there with Jim Crow discrimination—refusals to serve or rent to him—and continual insults. Baldwin describes the rage that grew in him as "a kind of blind fever, a pounding in the skull and fire in the bowels" that "can recur at any moment," and he asserts, "There is not a Negro alive who does not have this rage in his blood—one has the choice, merely of living with it consciously or surrendering to it" (94). In "Many Thousands Gone" he refers to this fury as the Bigger Thomas within (Bigger being the protagonist who becomes a murderer in Wright's *Native Son*).

On the young Baldwin's last night in New Jersey after he has been fired, rage overcomes him, triggered in part by his being denied service at the "American Diner." Furious, he strides through the streets, wanting "to crush these white faces, which were crushing me." Eventually, Baldwin barges into a glamorous restaurant he knows won't serve him and loses his temper, with a waitress as his target:

> I hated her for her white face, and for her great, astounded, frightened eyes. I felt that if she found a black man so frightening I would make her fright worth-while. . . . "We don't serve Negroes here." She did not say it with the blunt, derisive hostility to which I had grown so accustomed, but, rather, with a note of apology in her voice, and fear. This made me colder and more murderous than ever. . . . I wanted her to come close enough for me to get her neck between my hands. (96)

Seeing that she won't move nearer, he "hurl[s]" a water mug "with all my strength at her" and escapes. Baldwin hates the waitress because she is white but also because she shows fear and weakness; because she represents the powers that be but also because he sees his own powerlessness mirrored in her. In response, he flings back the hatred with which African Americans have been served—the desire to frighten, hurt, and obliterate her—the kinds of feelings to which Bigger Thomas is driven. After the event, Baldwin realizes that he might have been killed by the customers "rising as one man," and that he himself had been about to kill someone (97). He concludes that "my life, my real life"—his integrity of spirit—"was in danger, and not for anything other people might do but for the hatred I carried in my own heart" (98).

This account shows the way in which unrelenting racism can distort its victim,[39] even a thoughtful, open-minded, nonviolent person. However, as a female reader, I find that Baldwin's self-examination stops short. Gender dynamics are also at work in the encounter, but Baldwin does not acknowledge them. Viewed from another angle, the exchange between a white waitress and a black man is one that takes place between a woman and an enraged man. Baldwin, though, does not consider the ways in which woman is to man as black is to white. Similarly, in "Many Thousands Gone," he writes that "there is, I should think, no Negro living in America who has not . . . wanted to smash any white face he may encounter in a day, to violate, out of motives of the cruelest vengeance, their women" (38). The assumption of woman as property to be destroyed, by one who also says, "At some point in history I became Baldwin's nigger,"[40] remains unexamined.

Baldwin's language in the passage from "Many Thousands Gone" also assumes somehow that all African Americans are male, as does his use of the generic *he*, sometimes to the point of absurdity: "One wonders what on earth the first slave found to say to the first dark child he bore" (169). In "Autobiographical Notes," Baldwin says that "part of the business of the writer—as I see it—[is] to examine attitudes, to go beneath the surface" (5-6), and *Notes of a Native Son* urges white people to discover how they really regard African Americans. This self-scrutiny is what I find lacking in the book, regarding Baldwin's attitudes about women. Its primary and secondary audiences are white and black by design, male by default. Nevertheless, despite this blind spot (even as late as the 1970s in *No Name in the Street*),[41] Baldwin's work proposes ways of thinking—about, for example, the problematics of mingled love and outrage, of relations among those alienated from each other, and of the special knowledge the oppressed has of the oppressor—that apply as well to relations between women and men.

Schooling the White Reader

I now examine in more detail how Baldwin's rhetorical strategies guide his audiences as he has defined them, but especially white readers, whom he sets out to reeducate, or to "rob . . . of the jewel of [their] naïveté" (166). In doing so, Baldwin also implicitly offers himself to black readers as an example of toughmindedness—the willingness to face racial complexities, to accept the existence of mixed emotions and motives, and to confront white readers with what he finds, incisively and contentiously yet without hostility.

As a white reader seeking a sense of the life of this particular African American, I am generally left wanting more. Baldwin's withholding of facts and feelings seems to demonstrate the limited ability of white people to put themselves in his place. By giving only glimpses of his life, the text underscores white Americans' need to listen to and find avenues of discourse with African Americans.

From the autobiographical scenes he does depict, Baldwin goes on to draw conclusions, not trusting white readers in particular to arrive at them on their own. For instance, he writes of his stay in the racially isolated Swiss village:

> My smile was simply another unheard-of phenomenon which allowed them to see my teeth . . . I began to think that, should I take to snarling, no one would notice any difference. . . . It was jocularly suggested that I might let [my hair] all grow long and make myself a winter coat. If I sat in the sun for more than five minutes some daring creature was certain to come along and gingerly put his fingers on my hair, as though he were afraid of an electric shock, or put his hand on my hand, astonished that the color did not rub off. (161–62)

After characterizing the villagers' view of him with images of animals and of objects, Baldwin then interprets the images, telling the reader outright that the Swiss folk did not see him as human.

Baldwin provides interpretations, but only to a degree. The discourse slips rapidly along, moving associatively, each topic gliding away into the next. Though Baldwin uses the language of logic to create transitions that sound smooth, he often skips the logical connections, making me think, "Wait a minute—what did I miss?" For example, while indicting *Uncle Tom's Cabin*, Baldwin writes, "Sentimentality . . . is the mark of dishonesty, the inability to feel; the wet eyes of the sentimentalist betray his aversion to experience, his fear of life, his arid heart; and it is always, therefore, the signal of secret and violent inhumanity" (14). Each piece of the sentence seems a logical extension of the preceding one, until the last clause, which takes a logical leap. The word *therefore* is a logical connective, but, in fact, violence does not necessarily or obviously follow from the inability to feel. Baldwin's diction, however, asserts that the connection is obvious to *him*; it prompts careful readers whose experiential perspective is not his to ask, "How could this be?" and to construct the link themselves. There are numerous ways to forge the missing connection, depending on the reader's acquaintance, for instance, with the attacks of those who are trying to cover their own weakness, with people's urge to avoid the responsibility that comes with empathy, and so on. We are taught to fill the gaps by thinking in ways analogous to those demonstrated in other parts of the book.

Baldwin shows us how to think, feelingly, about racial otherness and the humanity of the other. He does not dwell on the particulars of the occasion for thought; each segment of an essay is only a starter, an example of how to begin thinking about such problems, from which one is to continue on one's own. Hence my sense of being told, by turns, too much and too little, being overcontrolled and then left. An analogy that occurs to me is that of having someone teach you how to ride a bike: first they're holding onto the bicycle so tightly that you're not able to do it yourself at all—then they just let go. The analogy suggests that Baldwin's strategies are those of someone aiming to teach white readers something entirely new, a kind of exercise he feels they have not done before.

Thus, *Notes* is both didactic and writerly, two strategic modes that the reader-response theorist Wolfgang Iser views as largely incompatible. Writerliness (to use Richard Miller's well-known translation of Roland Barthes's term) aims to make reading work intensive, thereby affording the reader the intimate knowledge and enjoyment of the text that comes from creating it anew.[42] Iser describes didactic texts, in contrast, as those that limit what we can make of them by offering fewer cognitive gaps for us to fill and fewer ways in which to do so,[43] as when Baldwin interprets his imagery for us. Yet Baldwin also employs the literary technique of confronting us with striking juxtapositions that we must resolve on our own. Another way in which literary texts make readers work, according to Iser, is by placing social (and other) norms in new contexts, so that the reader can construe them in a new light, as unfamiliar, rather than taking them for granted. "If the literary work arises out of the reader[s'] own social . . . background," they are "in a position from which [they] can take a fresh look at the forces which guide and orient" them and become aware of "the projective nature of [their] mental images." This process, which Iser calls *negation,* serves to reveal "a deficiency in familiar knowledge" (212, 74, 224, 227). Baldwin often sets up such a situation for the reader— but "negates" the old notions himself. For instance, speaking of playgrounds and boys' clubs that do-gooders build in Harlem without addressing the nature of a ghetto, he remarks that these measures are "about as helpful as make-up to a leper" (58). Such didacticism does not give the reader less work to do; it simply locates more of that work in the world outside the text.

This point corresponds to Iser's useful distinction between the reader's creation of *meaning* and of *significance,* which is the incorporation of the meaning into one's life (151). *Notes* frequently offers its readers strenuous work to do in construing its meaning but even more in realizing its significance. In the case of Baldwin's work, to use Iser's terms, the "unformulated double" of the text that we map out by negotiating its gaps and negations, or the vision of "what is not given" that we conceive (Iser, 225–26), is an image of what society, beyond the text, does not offer.

Preacherly Persuasion

Baldwin's urgings that we go into the world with the scales fallen from our eyes and act accordingly recall his background as a teenage preacher in Harlem. Indeed, the fact that Iser's opposition between the didactic and the literary does not seem to comprehend Baldwin's art has partly to do with the influence on Baldwin's work of the traditional African American sermon. This improvisational form clearly uses literary techniques for didactic effect. And as numerous critics have observed, Baldwin's prose manifests a variety of stylistic features that derive from the kinds of sermons he heard and delivered.

William H. Pipes, who has documented old-time black preaching, makes a point about these sermons much like one I have made about Baldwin's discourse: he observes that "the discussion, although having the appearance of logical order, is not always logical."[44] Similarly, Henry H. Mitchell seems to describe the style of argument in *Notes* when he writes, "The force of the message does not hinge so much on logical persuasion . . . a Black preacher . . . is likely to seem more to probe the depths than to argue."[45] Or, as Mel Watkins puts it, "Baldwin's intent," like the preacher's, "is not to explicate but to dramatize."[46] One way in which Baldwin does this is by using personal anecdotes to exemplify a message of broad import. He also uses repetition with variation, for emphasis. Moreover, Baldwin's prose, as Pipes remarks about the old-time sermon, "gains effect by the change from conversational to rhythmical speaking" (158).[47]

It is partly Baldwin's sermonic cadences that breathe life into long sentences, formal diction, and what might otherwise seem an overdose of repetition, as in the following passage.

> The cathedral at Chartres, I have said, says something to the people of this village which it cannot say to me; but it is important to understand that this cathedral says something to me which it cannot say to them. Perhaps they are struck by the power of the spires, the glory of the windows; but they have known God, after all, longer than I have known him, and in a different way, and I am terrified by the slippery bottomless well to be found in the crypt, down which heretics were hurled to death, and by the obscene, inescapable gargoyles jutting out of the stone and seeming to say that God and the devil can never be divorced. (174)

Baldwin mentions "the King James Bible [and] the rhetoric of the store-front church" among the influences on his work (5), and clearly their subject matter, as well as their style, is entwined with his. However, while traditional African American sermons assume an audience that shares the preacher's position in society, Baldwin writes largely to work a change in an audience that does not share his viewpoint. Nevertheless, he may hope the white audience comes to the text seeking conversion.

Writerly Persuasion

Though Baldwin displays certain preacherly desires and devices, he identifies himself instead as a writer and as a participant in literary life. Indeed, in "Notes," Baldwin recalls "the one time in all our life together when [he and his father] had really spoken to each other" as the time when his father, himself a pastor, asks his teenage son, "You'd rather write than preach, wouldn't you?" and James agrees (108). Baldwin's writing is more impersonal, restrained, formal, and abstract than the tradition of preaching he comes from.[48] Writing enables him to articulate feelings different from those characteristic of that preaching tradition—feelings such as ambivalence, uncertainty, humanistic hope rather than religious faith, and disillusionment.

With regard to style, I do not mean to counterpose the oral and the literary; though often Baldwin does not sound like a preacher, I always have the sense of listening to him speak.[49] In his greatly varied modes of address I hear diverse tones and volumes. Intense, highly colored, musically phrased, and hyperbolic passages sound louder; personal stories, conversational rhythms, and understatement, softer. An aural influence other than preaching that Baldwin cites is "something ironic and violent and perpetually understated in Negro speech" (5).[50] Writing, in contrast to preaching, allows him to use techniques that require the reader to stop and think, rather than be swept along. These strategies include irony,[51] understatement, and shifts in the reference of pronouns.

Irony

Several of Baldwin's titles are laden with ironic import. For example, "Everybody's Protest Novel," which pretends to sound positive, seems ironic initially because, since protest is opposition, a statement congenial to everyone would hardly be a radical critique. Then, after I have read further, I find that the title reflects Baldwin's notion that protest novels don't tell the truth about the complexity of anyone's inner life. Either way, everybody's protest novel is really nobody's.

Similarly, the apparent felicity of the title "Equal in Paris" is undermined by the story that follows. In Paris, unlike New York, Baldwin is deemed equal to most. The story describes a two-tier society of the secure and the poor. The civil authorities, agents of those in the upper tier, don't discriminate against Baldwin for occupying the larger and lower tier, much less for being black. On the contrary, they are tolerant, often polite. They simply don't care. For example, the officer who arrests Baldwin and his friend neglects to remind the court that they are American and will need interpreters, which delays their trial until after Christmas. Tolerance, which results in the kind of equality Baldwin finds in Paris, would improve the lives of many African Americans at home: they would be left, blessedly, alone. Baldwin's story, however, shows that being tolerated is not enough. More energy and warmth are needed in the world, actually caring for one another—as when a prisoner being released urges the depressed, incarcerated Baldwin to name someone on the outside who might help get him out too and then actually contacts Baldwin's friend.

The title "Stranger in the Village" also gathers ironic resonance for me as the piece progresses. The essay concerns how white people conceive of black people as strangers even though they are essentially alike. On the part of white Americans, as opposed to the isolated Swiss villagers, the estrangement is willed, Baldwin feels. The Americans are unwilling to face their own sordid history and stop projecting their destructive impulses on "others." A stranger is someone whom the namer identifies as "not I," simultaneously defining the self as not the stranger. Thus both parties are negated. Moreover, the fact that *stranger* applies to Baldwin's situation in both Switzerland and America suggests that the word *village* does too. If so, the remote part of Switzerland—in summer, a haven for "cripples"—corresponds in its provinciality to the United States, except, again, that the Americans have willfully cut themselves off, crippling themselves morally.

Pervading the essays are passages of dense ironic language and imagery, some of which refer to how easily Christianity can be twisted to empower white supremacy. Images of economic exploitation in two such passages—one in the first piece in *Notes*, the other in the last—mirror each other's warnings. In the first, Baldwin argues that what fuels Stowe's writing is not concern for the lives or souls of others but rather fear of being damned herself. Thus, in *Uncle Tom's*

Cabin, he finds that Stowe "embraces this merciless doctrine [of eternal punishment] with all her heart, bargaining shamelessly before the throne of grace: God and salvation becoming her personal property, purchased with the coin of her virtue" (17). The words *merciless, bargaining, personal property, purchased,* and *coin* imply that although Stowe condemns the slave trade, her own writing has the character of a crass, exploitive transaction. A deeper irony, I find, lies in the suggestion that in her exercise of virtue, black folk become irrelevant—on a symbolic level, they once again become a medium of exchange, a means to a profitable end. In this essay Baldwin also makes the widely accepted argument that Stowe equates blackness with evil and, in constructing her African American characters, finds ways to purify, or whiten, them. Elsewhere in the book these two arguments resurface as one idea, which is that seeing black people as pagans allows white Christians to rationalize dominating and using them.

The last essay meditates on this danger, depicting the efforts of the village Catholics in

> "buying" African natives for the purpose of converting them to Christianity. . . . During the *carnival* which precedes Lent, two village children have their faces blackened—out of which bloodless darkness their blue eyes shine like ice—and fantastic horsehair wigs are placed on their blond heads . . . they solicit among the villagers for money for the missionaries in Africa. . . . The village "bought" last year six or eight African natives. This was reported to me with pride by the wife of one of the *bistro* owners and I was careful to express astonishment and pleasure at the solicitude shown by the village for the souls of black folk. (163)

Despite the villagers' good intentions, Baldwin views their efforts as related to slave-taking in Africa. The common attitude that the natural condition of black people is sinful supports both conversion and conquering. While the next paragraph makes the point explicitly, the imagery of this one has already revealed the irony, by the emphasis on *bought* and *buying*—which in turn may remind the reader who is learning to think like Baldwin that the implied terms *saving* and *redeeming* carry economic import that is at odds with their spiritual meaning. Moreover, the words *bloodless* and *ice* suggest the dangers of unfeelingness in such missionary endeavors, and the horsehair wig implies that the villagers associate Africans with animals. Further, when I envision the children out collecting, I also see the adults laughing at the grotesque sight of their own little "Africans." Thus the passage evokes a sense of the turbulence masked by Baldwin's careful response. It also, of course, echoes the title of Du Bois's revelation of the actual lives and feelings of black people, the kind of enlightenment the Swiss provincials, like their American counterparts, sorely need.

Emotional Understatement

Beyond irony, Baldwin's literary techniques include subtle ways of gradually leading readers to his point of view. One of his strategies is simply to chronicle disturbing events, leaving the emotional response to the reader, as in "Journey to Atlanta" and "Equal in Paris."

The narrative in "Journey" demonstrates the opening assertion that political groups which seem to offer hope to African Americans in fact just use them to get votes and don't change much of anything. The spare, factual narrative concerns a Harlem quartet the Melodeers, which includes two of Baldwin's brothers, that is invited to sing on a campaign tour in Georgia with the Progressive Party. The agreement is that the Melodeers are to sing in churches, with time free to make money on other gigs. In fact, church performances are not arranged; the group is ill housed and fed and is pressed to canvass black neighborhoods for votes and sing on a sound truck for free. The Melodeers begin to make their own engagements, but the party crashes the performances and turns them into meetings. Finally, when the Melodeers refuse to sing a fifth song at a political gathering, they are vilified as uppity blacks and kicked out by Southern party leaders.

The low-key, step-by-step narrative gives white readers a chance to feel the frustration of such treatment for themselves. Although the threat of physical harm lurks in the background, the actual events constitute a relatively subtle example of racist treatment. Anyone can imagine undergoing such inconveniences, discomfort, rudeness, and broken promises. The white reader's mind is unlikely simply to shut down, as it might on encountering a description of a beating. And since Baldwin does not wax eloquent about the young men's feelings or his own, readers are left to generate a sense of outrage themselves. The essay may also raise a question for the reader. The aristocratic, white regional leader of the party demands: Has the group's black agent "forgotten that he was in Georgia? Didn't he know better than sit in a white woman's office?" And just who did "those black boys" think they were? (83, 82). Whereas the Northerners' promises have turned out to be lies, in the South making promises to black people seems an unknown form of discourse, a nonsensical idea. Is the Southern attitude significantly worse or just clearer? Is a journey from Harlem to Atlanta essentially going nowhere new? The story and its title seem to suggest that we ponder the question.

"Equal in Paris," another understated chronicle, likewise takes its readers through a distressing series of events, more detailed than in "Journey," so we can see how the predicament would feel to us. Baldwin distantly comments on and describes his feelings but does not recreate them (as in "Notes"). Much of the time the piece simply faces us with what he has faced: filth, claustrophobia, uncertainty about what will happen next. A great part of the essay's impact comes from bald statements of fact:

> The next day, Christmas, unable to endure my cell . . . I asked to be allowed to go to Mass, hoping to hear some music. But I found myself, for a freezing hour and a half, locked in exactly the same kind of cubicle as in the wagon which had first brought me to prison, peering through a slot placed at the level of the eye at an old Frenchman, hatted, overcoated, muffled, and gloved, preaching in this language which I did not understand, to this row of wooden boxes, the story of Jesus Christ's love for men. (158)

Again without comment, we are left—with an image of formulaic, incomprehensible Christianity, administered as if to isolated units rather than people, by one who remains snug as they shiver—to contemplate what is missing.

Fluctuating Pronoun Reference

Baldwin also uses shifting pronoun reference to guide his readers, the white audience in particular. He often refers to white people in the first person, to deliver his insights into their fear, fascination, and guilt regarding African Americans. In doing so, Baldwin positions himself to turn them inside out. For example, he writes that to the white *we*, "the 'protest' novel, so far from being disturbing, is . . .

comforting. . . . Whatever unsettling questions are raised are evanescent, titillating; remote, for this has nothing to do with us . . . so that finally we receive a very definite thrill of virtue from the fact that we are reading such a book at all" (19). Baldwin's use of the white *we, I,* and *one* give a tone of authority and even fellow feeling to his visions of European Americans' attitudes toward African Americans. The strategy urges white readers to acknowledge these feelings and the ways in which they degrade both white and black.

In the last essay, the emotionally charged conclusion of the book's argument, the pronouns are especially chameleon-like. "Stranger" builds to an expansion of the point that African Americans are an inextricable part of what defines Americanness, that the black-white struggle has given the country and its people the character they have today. The pronoun shifts in the final two paragraphs support this contention. The next-to-last paragraph again adopts the rhetorically white first-person pronoun, to argue that "we" are coming to see the notion of separate races as "dangerously inaccurate, and perfectly useless." Then, in the last paragraph, Baldwin uses the collective black *I* to hasten this realization by linguistically enacting a face-to-face confrontation with the white reader, insisting that "I am not, really, a stranger anymore for any American alive." Finally, the races merge into the inclusive *us:* "It is precisely this black-white experience which may prove of indispensable value to us in the world we face today" (174–75).

The Challenge to White Readers

I would like to consider one more way that *Notes* prompts its white readers to change, colloquially called "reverse psychology."[52] "Equal in Paris" aims to stimulate the comfortable reader's capacity and will to imagine what someone else's trouble feels like. It ends with the mirth of those who have not done so. However, the last clause, "it was borne in on me that this laughter is universal and never can be stilled" (158), challenges the reader to belie its conclusion.

Another argument that incites us to prove it false appears in the essay that introduces the 1984 edition. After looking at how *Notes* began and what sort of memoir it has become, Baldwin goes on to express disillusionment at how little the lot of the African American has improved in the thirty years since he first published *Notes,* and at how, "morally, there has been no change at all." The piece touches on outrages and betrayals he has endured. In Greenwich Village, for instance, "the bulk of the populace, egged on by the cops, thought it was great fun to bounce tables and chairs off my head," until "I soon stopped talking about my 'constitutional' rights." He also chastises "friends like these," a twice-repeated phrase referring to those who betrayed their friends to the McCarthyites during the 1950s and those who urge African Americans to better themselves by joining the army or becoming mail carriers. He dubs white people "in all but actual fact: obsolete." Thirty years earlier, Baldwin's white friends assured him, "*It takes time, Jimmy.* . . . I was being told it will take time before a Black person can be treated as a human being here, but it will happen. We will help to make it happen. We promise you." In the penultimate paragraph, Baldwin writes bitterly, "No promise was kept with [my ancestors], no promise was kept with me, nor can I counsel those coming after me, nor my global kinsmen, to believe a word uttered by my morally bankrupt and desperately dishonest countrymen" (xiii–xvii). His disillusionment is profound; I would not minimize its depth and passion. Yet one thread of the declaration seems to dare its white readers: "Prove me wrong."

My sense that Baldwin holds out a shred of hope is reinforced by his choice to end the essay with the following quotation from Doris Lessing's *African Stories:*[53] "While the cruelties of the white man toward the black man are among the heaviest counts in the indictment against humanity, colour prejudice is not our original fault, but only one aspect of the atrophy of the imagination that prevents us from seeing ourselves in every creature that breathes under the sun." Baldwin's use of the quotation (xvii) seems to say, "If you're a white reader trying to stretch your imagination to encompass my experience, maybe you can follow Lessing's example and move toward becoming fully human." It also, of course, brings the ideal of the inclusive self to the fore.

The last words of the introduction are Baldwin's: "Amen. *En avant* [Forward]." Despite James Baldwin's literariness and his proclaiming that he would "rather write than preach," his aims are those of the traditional black preacher: to arouse, persuade, and instruct (Pipes, 77); to spark the expansion of the human spirit; to urge us forward, as one.

NOTES

1. James Baldwin, *Notes of a Native Son* (1955; reprint, Boston: Beacon, 1984).

2. James Weldon Johnson, "The Dilemma of the Negro Author," *American Mercury* 15 (1928): 477.

3. Sidonie Smith, *A Poetics of Women's Autobiography: Marginality and the Fictions of Self-Representation* (Bloomington: Indiana University Press, 1987), 49.

4. See Stephen Butterfield, *Black Autobiography in America* (Amherst: University of Massachusetts Press, 1974) 3, for a discussion of these aims in black autobiography generally.

5. An exception occurs in "The Harlem Ghetto," in *Notes of a Native Son*, where he talks about the relations between black residents and Jews (67–72). However, even in this piece Baldwin does not attempt to portray Jewish consciousness, as he does the black and white points of view, except to claim that since Jews are in a socially vulnerable position, they must try to act as much like white Gentiles as possible, which includes going along with the notion of black inferiority. Otherwise the essay considers Jewishness, in a sense, as an overlapping of white and black. On the one hand, Baldwin writes, African Americans view Jews as white people who "should 'know better'" than to exploit black people financially, having "suffered enough," in ancient and modern times, "to know what suffering means." On the other hand, Baldwin acknowledges that Jews are convenient scapegoats—"Georgia has the Negro and Harlem has the Jew"—when the real source of inequity is the dominant majority (69, 72). There is, however, a paragraph in the essay "Many Thousands Gone" that treats Jews empathetically (35–36).

It is also worth noting that Baldwin does not address homosexuality at all in *Notes of a Native Son*. Even the 1984 introduction refers only obliquely to the publishers' refusal of *Giovanni's Room* and to Baldwin's lover in the 1950s, without specifying either the novel's subject matter or his lover's sex. (James Campbell, in *Talking at the Gates: A Life of James Baldwin* [New York: Penguin, 1991], 33, writes that "Baldwin declared his homosexuality more or less immediately to new acquaintants," and in 1954 he published the essay "Gide as Husband and Homosexual," which was reprinted as "The Male Prison," in *The Price of the Ticket: Collected Nonfiction, 1948–1985* [New York: St. Martin's/Marek, 1985], 101–5. However, throughout Baldwin's career his work focused primarily on race.) Thus readers who would view his gayness as compromising his authority to speak for the black man can overlook Baldwin's sexuality. Neither does Baldwin link the oppression of African Americans with that of women, a subject I discuss further on in this chapter.

6. For one thing, as Leigh Gilmore writes in *Autobiographics: A Feminist Theory of Women's Self-Representation* (Ithaca: Cornell University Press, 1994),

"for many readers the possibility of seeing not only some aspect of their lives but a member of their community represented in print may decisively alter their notions of what counts culturally, of what is possible" (24).

7. W. E. B. Du Bois, *The Souls of Black Folk* (New York: New American Library, 1982), 45.

8. Arnold Rampersad, *The Art and Imagination of W. E. B. Du Bois* (Cambridge: Harvard University Press, 1976), 89. On assessments of the importance of *Souls* by Johnson and others, see Rampersad, 68.

9. Du Bois is not one of the writers whom Baldwin talks a lot about, like Henry James. (Regarding James's influence on Baldwin, see Horace A. Porter, *Stealing the Fire: The Art and Protest of James Baldwin* [Middletown, Conn.: Wesleyan University Press, 1989].) Nor does Baldwin, in the 1955 introduction to *Notes of a Native Son*, identify Du Bois's work as an influence, as he does Harriet Beecher Stowe's *Uncle Tom's Cabin* and the works of Charles Dickens (both of which he also mentions in his book-length conversation with Margaret Mead, *A Rap on Race* [New York: Laurel-Dell, 1971], 36), along with the King James Bible (*Notes*, 3). However, it is not unusual for writers not to acknowledge the influence of a contemporary or a recent predecessor whose work their own resembles. Baldwin does occasionally make an intertextual reference to Du Bois, as in *Notes*, 163; and in a later essay entitled "Of the Sorrow Songs: The Cross of Redemption" (cited in Campbell, 259, 296).

10. Quoted by Geneva Smitherman in *Talkin and Testifyin: The Language of Black America* (Detroit: Wayne State University Press, 1977), 102–3. Apropos of assimilationist diction, Butterfield writes that "the burden of *Notes of a Native Son* . . . is to resolve the problems of being a black American without rebelling against the mainstream culture. The object is not to resist it as a system, but to change it through moral persuasion" (187), which is Du Bois's object at the beginning of the century.

11. Robert B. Stepto, *From behind the Veil: A Study of Afro-American Narrative* (Urbana: University of Illinois Press, 1979), 85.

12. Gordon O. Taylor, "Voices from the Veil: Black American Autobiography," *Georgia Review* 35 (1981): 342. Taylor similarly discusses Richard Wright's *Black Boy*, Ralph Ellison's *Invisible Man*, and *The Autobiography of Malcolm X* as descendants of *Souls*.

13. Butterfield identifies further similarities between Baldwin's first two collections and Du Bois's *Souls* (185).

14. Of later African American life writers such as Eldridge Cleaver, George Jackson, and Imamu Amiri Baraka, Sidonie Smith observes with relevance to Baldwin that "in society where blackness is met with implicit and explicit forms of racism, the understanding of that very racism, its motivations, its effects upon the self and the society at large, is tantamount to the understanding of one's identity" (*Where I'm Bound: Patterns of Slavery and Free-*

dom in Black American Autobiography [Westport, Conn.: Greenwood, 1974], 120).

15. Albert E. Stone remarks on "the current willingness of African-American [autobiographers] . . . to ground personal experience in historical and social circumstances common to other black lives, but to do so increasingly in an unmistakable, individual voice" ("After Black Boy and Dusk of Dawn: Patterns in Recent Black Autobiography," *African American Autobiography: A Collection of Critical Essays*, ed. William L. Andrews [Englewood Cliffs, N.J.: Prentice-Hall, 1993], 187). And Butterfield observes the individualistic character of Baldwin's insistence on finding "one's own moral center" (Butterfield, 191; *Notes*, 9).

16. Smith, in *Where I'm Bound*, makes this point in relation to Ralph Ellison and more recent African American writers.

17. For a different slant on the absent black subject, see Phillip Brian Harper, *Framing the Margins: The Social Logic of Postmodern Culture* (New York: Oxford University Press, 1994), 116.

18. Robert F. Sayre, "Autobiography and the Making of America," in *Autobiography: Essays Theoretical and Critical*, ed. James Olney (Princeton: Princeton University Press, 1980), 165.

19. For a discussion of the threat of censure that African American authors face with respect to African American readers, see Johnson, 480.

20. Shirley Ardener, "Introduction," in *Perceiving Women*, ed. Shirley Ardener (New York: Wiley, 1975), xii; Edwin Ardener, "The 'Problem' Revisited," in *Perceiving Women*, ed. Shirley Ardener, 22.

21. Arna Bontemps, *Black Thunder* (Boston: Beacon, 1968).

22. Ralph Ellison, *Invisible Man* (New York: Vintage, 1995).

23. Porter makes such an observation about "Everybody's Protest Novel" and "Many Thousands Gone" (33).

24. Jocelyn Whitehead Jackson comments on the implicit personal content of the first two essays, which concern protest novels—in particular, Harriet Beecher Stowe's *Uncle Tom's Cabin* and Richard Wright's *Native Son*. She finds that in these essays Baldwin considers his successors and his aims as an African American writer ("The Problem of Identity in Selected Early Essays of James Baldwin," in *Critical Essays on James Baldwin*, ed. Fred L. Standley and Nancy V. Burt [Boston: Hall, 1988], 255). Taylor, discussing the first of these pieces, writes that "one senses the degree to which Baldwin is the unresolved subject of his ostensibly objective analysis" (351).

25. David Levin, "Baldwin's Autobiographical Essays: The Problem of Negro Identity," *Black and White in American Culture*, ed. Jules Chametzky and Sidney Kaplan (Amherst: University of Massachusetts Press, 1969), 377.

26. See Porter, *Stealing the Fire*, 37.

27. I have chosen not to focus on the 1955 introduction, "Autobiographical

Notes," because it seems to me less than integral to the book. This is not surprising, since it was written for Baldwin's first novel and then reprinted in *Notes* (see W. J. Weatherby, *James Baldwin: Artist on Fire* [New York: Laurel-Dell, 1989], 117).

28. Harriet Beecher Stowe, *Uncle Tom's Cabin* (New York: Penguin, 1981).

29. Richard Wright, *Native Son* (New York: Harper, 1966).

30. Baldwin doesn't give the books their due as documents of significant social impact. Moreover, his discussion of *Native Son* seems occasionally to confuse Bigger Thomas's viewpoint with Wright's. Regarding *Uncle Tom's Cabin*, Baldwin's critique of Stowe's portrayal of her black characters as unrealistic and antiblack is certainly justified and important. But if he wanted to give Stowe a fair shake, he would also have talked about her exacting, critical portrayals of certain major white characters. The best example is her anatomizing of St. Clare's ineffectual conscience, that is, his understanding of the motives and hypocrisy of those who support slavery, which does not move him enough to undermine the institution or even to hurry up and free his own slaves. Stowe also incisively develops the righteous Yankee cousin's failing: Miss Ophelia wants slaves freed and educated, but she feels aversion rather than affection for Topsy and can offer the girl no joy until she learns how to love her.In the 1955 introduction to *Notes*, Baldwin writes that he read *Uncle Tom's Cabin* "over and over and over again" (3), and in *Rap on Race* he says it "meant a lot to me" (36).

31. See Porter for a chapter-length examination of this essay, beginning with a discussion of the significance of its (and the book's) title (21–37).

32. Smith discusses the theme of flight from an oppressive environment to one that offers a hope of freedom as a "prototypal pattern" in African American life writing, established in the slave narrative (*Where I'm Bound*, ix); and Sayre specifically cites moving to Europe as part of this pattern (165).

33. Weatherby, *James Baldwin*, 7.

34. Sigmund Freud, *A General Selection from the Works of Sigmund Freud*, ed. John Rickman (Garden City, N.Y.: Anchor-Doubleday, 1957), 89, 38.

35. Eldridge Cleaver, *Soul on Ice* (New York: Ramparts-Dell, 1968), 98–99.

36. Baldwin's biographers Campbell (218) and Weatherby (331) take attitudes similar to mine regarding Cleaver's attack. Cleaver's explicit motivations for Soul's harsh criticism of Baldwin's writing and of his homosexuality are an essay by Norman Mailer titled "The White Negro" and anger at Baldwin's unfavorable reviews of Wright's *Native Son*.

37. Campbell offers an interesting biographical source for Baldwin's emphasis throughout the book on the blood kinship of black and white Americans:

David Baldwin senior [actually James Baldwin's stepfather; Baldwin never found out the identity of his biological father] . . . had a half-brother who was, in effect, "white", conceived by Barbara and her white master: "Daddy's distant eyes, the same tension in the mouth. . . . Strange, to see your father in whiteface." The implications of this aspect of miscegenation meant a great deal to Baldwin and came to occupy a place at the centre of his philosophy: American racism was a sin against the blood. (5)

38. Alfred Kazin writes that he admires Baldwin for "want[ing] to describe the exact place where private chaos and social outrage meet" (*Contemporaries* [Boston: Atlantic-Little, 1962], 1257).

39. Similarly, the race riot later in the essay is, Porter writes, "Harlem's collective black rage monstrously personified" (34).

40. Campbell, *Talking at the Gates,* 1.

41. James Baldwin, *No Name in the Street* (New York: Laurel-Dell, 1972).

42. Roland Barthes, *S/Z: An Essay,* trans. Richard Miller (New York: Hill & Wang, 1974), 4.

43. Wolfgang Iser, *The Act of Reading: A Theory of Aesthetic Response* (Baltimore: Johns Hopkins University Press, 1980), 189–90. Iser is talking about fiction, but his ideas are useful when thinking about life writing as well.

44. William H. Pipes, *Say Amen, Brother! Old-Time Negro Preaching: A Study in American Frustration* (Detroit: Wayne State University Press, 1992), 147.

45. Henry H. Mitchell, *Black Preaching* (Philadelphia: Lippincott, 1970), 179.

46. Mel Watkins, "The Fire Next Time This Time," in *Critical Essays on James Baldwin,* ed. Standley and Burt, 238.

47. For other remarks about Baldwin's use of the techniques of traditional black preaching, see Watkins, 237–38. His article focuses mainly on the collection *No Name in the Street.*

48. Concerning the style of traditional African American sermons, see Mitchell, 162–77; and Pipes, 72, 136, 141.

49. Malini Johar Schueller writes, "Because [personal-political narratives] are, in the largest sense, polemical, the writers emphasize their speaking voices" (*The Politics of Voice: Liberalism and Social Criticism from Franklin to Kingston* [Albany: State University of New York Press, 1992], 5).

50. Walter J. Ong observes that literate people can be more or less oral, in heritage and habits. Specifically, he writes that "in contrast to the dominant culture around them, many if not most of the minority cultures in the United States are decidedly oral," and he cites African American culture, among others ("Oral Culture and the Literate Mind," in *Minority Language and Literature,* ed. Dexter Fisher [New York: MLA, 1977], 134).

51. Writing about Frederick Douglass's autobiography in particular and the life writing of African American slaves in general, Henry Louis Gates, Jr., argues that

to attempt to employ a Western language to posit a black self is inherently to use language ironically. The relation of the speaking black subject to the self figured in these languages must by definition be an ironical relation, since that self exists only in the "non-place of language," and since these languages encoded figuratively the idea that blackness itself is a negative essence, an absence. (*Figures in Black: Words, Signs and the "Racial" Self* [New York: Oxford University Press, 1989], 117)

52. For a discussion of a similar technique used in the slave narratives of the 1840s, see William L. Andrews, *To Tell a Free Story: The First Century of Afro-American Autobiography, 1760–1865* (Urbana: University of Illinois Press, 1986), 29.

53. Doris May Lessing, *African Stories* (New York: Simon & Schuster, 1965).

Chapter 15

Select Bibliography of Works by and on James Baldwin

Jeffrey W. Hole

Introduction

When James Baldwin died in 1987, what would be the critical legacy of cultural studies was relatively new to the North American scene. Although criticism pertaining to issues of race, sexuality, gender, and class had been present much earlier, the milieu of cultural theory brought with it a shift in the discursive practices that addressed these issues. This edited volume, including the bibliography, considers the notion of what it means to study James Baldwin and his work in the sphere of poststructuralism and cultural studies. It is for this reason that the following select bibliography lists only secondary sources from 1985 to the present, thereby functioning as a continuation of where previous bibliographic work on Baldwin has left off.

The first portion of the bibliography lists the entire slate of books by Baldwin, including his work from the 1960s, 1970s, 1980s, and the double volume of collected essays, novels, and stories recently published in 1998 by the Library of America and edited by Toni Morrison. This is the only section of the bibliography that lists works prior to 1985, and although many readers will be familiar with the titles, I thought it important to include all of Baldwin's books for the sake of informing a diverse and extensive readership. Next is a section that lists other works by Baldwin published since 1985, including interviews, introductions, forewords, and other articles. Though it would be informative to attend to all of Baldwin's titles from his entire career, this perhaps would not be pertinent to the spirit of this selective bibliographical project. I also note that others have already done much of this work. I think specifically of David Leeming's *James Baldwin: A Biography*, which includes an exhaustive bibliography of Baldwin's work from 1947 to 1989.

While I did not list the dozens of anthologies that have included Baldwin's texts, as I am afraid the list would seem as unending as the number of published anthologies themselves, the various themes around which these anthologies have been compiled tacitly inform and highlight the ways in which Baldwin is being read today. To mention but a few: Bennet L. Singer has included in his anthology *Growing Up Gay/Growing Up Lesbian: A Literary Anthology* (New York: New Press, 1994) an excerpt of Baldwin's *Giovanni's Room*; Marc Robinson's *Altogether Elsewhere: Writers on Exile* (Boston: Faber and Faber, 1994) includes Baldwin's "The New Lost Generation"; and Paul Berman's *Blacks and Jews: Alliances and Arguments* (New York: Delacorte Press, 1994) includes "Negroes Are Anti-Semitic Because They're Anti-Black."

I further note that when one studies these numerous and often disparate themes, one also glimpses the categories in which James Baldwin the person has been constructed: black, homosexual, exile, and famous writer. There is a subtle irony in all this, for Baldwin's writing implicitly and explicitly undermines and makes slippery the very categories to which he has been relegated. For instance, it is not that he denies the color of his skin but rather that he questions socially constructed categories such as "race" and therefore posits that the notion of "blackness" overdetermines societal positions for him and other African Americans. This becomes no more apparent than when he leaves America to live in France, where the categories of "race" and "sexuality" shift and take on new meanings. That fresh, recent anthologies are addressing these issues is no coincidence, for they contribute to and reflect on the discursive work being done in cultural and critical theory. Importantly, a number of these anthologies, viewed individually, delineate the black Baldwin, the homosexual Baldwin, the expatriate Baldwin, and the famous writer Baldwin. Viewed collectively, however, in the sum of these bibliographical references remains the idea that James Baldwin is representative of not just one of these categories; rather, his is a voice that contributes to all these diverse conversations, a fact that hence further problematizes the essentialist positions these categories can sometimes elicit. As the anthologies—like the books, articles, and dissertations written on Baldwin since 1985—well illustrate, these discourses become part of the central project of the cultural and critical work being done on Baldwin today. And unlike the projects of fifteen to twenty years ago, these projects and the inroads that cultural studies has made are better able to complicate notions of race, sexuality, gender, and class.

While compiling this bibliography, it also became evident to me that the scholarship on Baldwin is not limited to North American academia and society but that James Baldwin's influence has over-reaching consequences in academic endeavors outside the United States and outside predominantly English-speaking countries. Japanese, Spanish, French, and German are but few of the many languages in which Baldwin has gained international attention. I think specifically of the article by Federico Equiluz Ortiz de Latierro, "El 'Otro Pais' de James Baldwin" (1989), and the dissertation written by Franciscus Josef Hirs from the Universiteit van Amsterdam, entitled "De prediking van James Baldwin." Although this bibliographical project does not include all the titles of non-English texts, what seems most important is that interest in Baldwin continues to develop.

In the last portion of this bibliography I have included books written for juvenile readers, pertaining to the life and work of Baldwin. Like many of the texts written for academic and "adult" audiences, these books share interests in the issues of race and sexuality. Randall Kenan's *James Baldwin* (Lives of Notable Gay Men and Lesbians) series addresses itself to secondary school students, grades nine through twelve. That a text such as Kenan's would be available to students (though I note that many school libraries may yet be hesitant to display a text that openly admits homosexual topics) speaks to the changing discourses and attitudes present in secondary education. Though juvenile texts may not delineate the full range of complexities relating to issues of race and sexuality, they may introduce students to the practice of critical thinking and inquiry.

Even as this bibliography goes to press, I realize that new thoughts and ideas are being written, that the list of articles and books grows longer, and that even Baldwin himself has yet more work to contribute. As Hilton Als notes in his February 16, 1998, article in the *New Yorker*, "The Enemy Within: The Making and Unmaking of James Baldwin": "There is one great Baldwin masterpiece waiting to be published—one that was composed in an atmosphere of focused intimacy—and this is a volume of his letters." Though Baldwin's family has yet to allow publication of these letters, it becomes evident, from Als's article and from biographies of Baldwin, that further study of his work will open up, question, and possibly alter the future trajectory of discourse on James Baldwin. In this, it becomes difficult, if not impossible, for us to answer Baldwin's rhetorical question, "How much time do you want for your progress?" Our humble answer comes in the critical works we produce. Even though this list of works is long and the progress is seemingly evident, we still need more time.

Books by James Baldwin

The Amen Corner. New York: Dial Press, 1968.

Another Country. New York: Dial Press, 1962.

Blues for Mister Charlie. New York: Dial Press, 1964.

The Devil Finds Work: An Essay. New York: Dial Press, 1976.

A Dialogue. With Nikki Giovanni. Philadelphia: J. B. Lippincott, 1973.

The Evidence of Things Not Seen. New York: Holt, Rinehart, & Winston, 1985.

The Fire Next Time. New York: Dial Press, 1963.

Giovanni's Room. New York: Dial Press, 1956.

Going to Meet the Man. New York: Dial Press, 1965.

Go Tell It on the Mountain. New York: Alfred A. Knopf, 1953.

Gypsies and Other Poems. Edition limited to 325 copies. Leeds, Mass.: Gehenna Press/Eremite Press, 1989.

If Beale Street Could Talk. New York: Dial Press, 1974.

James Baldwin: Collected Essays. Edited by Toni Morrison. New York: Library of America, 1998.

James Baldwin: Early Novels and Stories. Edited by Toni Morrison. New York: Library of America, 1998.

Jimmy's Blues. New York: St. Martin's Press, 1985.

Just above My Head. New York: Dial Press, 1979.

Little Man Little Man: A Story of Childhood. Illustrations by Yoran Cazac. New York: Dial Press, 1976.

Nobody Knows My Name: More Notes of a Native Son. New York: Dial Press, 1961.

No Name in the Street. New York: Dial Press, 1972.

Notes of a Native Son. Boston: Beacon Press, 1955.

Nothing Personal. With photographs by Richard Avedon. New York: Atheneum, 1964.

One Day When I Was Lost: A Scenario Based on Alex Haley's The Autobiography of Malcolm X. London: Michael Joseph, 1972.

The Price of the Ticket: Collected Nonfiction, 1948–1985. New York: St. Martin's Press/Marek, 1985.

A Rap on Race. With Margaret Mead. Philadelphia: J. B. Lippincott, 1971.

Tell Me How Long the Train's Been Gone. New York: Dial Press, 1968.

Works by James Baldwin since 1985: Articles, Interviews, Introductions, and Other Writings

"Architectural Digest Visits: James Baldwin." Photographs by Daniel H. Minassian. Text by James Baldwin. *Architectural Digest,* August 1987.

"Blacks and Jews." Lecture delivered at University of Massachusetts–Amherst, 28 February 1984. *Black Scholar* 19 (November–December 1988): 3–15.

"Blues for Mr. Baldwin." Report of a conversation by Angela Cobbina. *Concord Weekly,* 28 January 1985, 31ff.

Foreword. *Daddy Was a Number Runner.* By Louise Meriwether. New York: Feminist Press, 1986. Pages 5–7.

Introduction. *Duties, Pleasures, and Conflicts: Essays in Struggle.* By Michael Thlema. Amherst: University of Massachusetts Press, 1987. Page xxii.

"The Fire This Time." *New Statesman* 110 (23 August 1985): 8–9. Partially reprinted as "Whites' Freedom Depends on Blacks.'" *Los Angeles Times,* 21 January 1986, part 2, page 5.

"Freaks and the American Ideal of Manhood." *Playboy* (Jan 1985) Represented as "Here Be Dragons" in *The Price of the Ticket.*

"Going to Meet the Man: An Interview with James Baldwin." Interviewed by James A. Baggett. *New York Native,* 21 December 1987, 20–23.

"Go Tell It on the Mountain: Belatedly, the Fear Turned to Love for His Father." *TV Guide,* 12 January 1985, 26–29.

"An Interview with James Baldwin on Henry James." Interview by David Adams Leeming. *Henry James Review* 8, 1 (1986): 47–56.

"An Interview with James Baldwin." Interview by David C. Estes. *New Orleans Review* 13, 3 (1986): 59–64.

"An Interview with Josephine Baker and James Baldwin." Interview by Henry Louis Gates, Jr. *Southern Review* 21, 3 (1985): 594–602.

"The Last Interview." Interview by Quincy Troupe. In "James Baldwin, 1924–1987: A Tribute." *Essence* 18 (March 1988): 53, 114ff. Reprinted in Fred L. Standley and Louis H. Pratt, eds., *Conversations with James Baldwin.*

"Last Testament: An Interview with James Baldwin." Interview by Quincy Troupe. *Village Voice*, 12 January 1988, 36. Reprinted in Fred L. Standley and Louis H. Pratt, eds., *Conversations with James Baldwin.*

Interview with Michael John Weber. In Perspectives: Angles on African Art. James Baldwin et al. New York: Center for African Art, 1987. Pages 113–27.

"Removing Barriers; To James Baldwin, the Goal Is 'To Sail Through Life on at Least One Smooth Tide of Unity.'" Interview by George Hadley-Garcia. *New York Native*, 14 October 1985: 28.

"To Crush the Serpent." *Playboy*, June 1987, 66ff.

"When a Pariah Becomes a Celebrity: An Interview with James Baldwin." Interviewed by Clayton G. Holloway. *Xavier Review*. 7, 1 (1987): 1–10.

Essays on the Work of James Baldwin since 1985

Achebe, Chinua. "Postscript: James Baldwin." In *Critical Fictions: The Politics of Imagination*, 278–81. Edited by Philomena Mariani. Seattle: Bay Press, 1991.

Alexis, Florence. "A Tribute/Hommage." *Présence africaine: Revue culturelle du monde noir*, 145 (1988): 182–87.

Als, Hilton. "The Enemy Within: The Making and Unmaking of James Baldwin." *New Yorker*, 16 February 1998, 72–80.

Amper, Susan. "Love and Death Reconstructed: The Union of Lovers in Another Country." *Journal of the Association for the Interdisciplinary Study of the Arts* 1, 1 (1995): 103–11.

Baraka, Amiri. "We Carry Him as Us." *Présence africaine: Revue culturelle du monde noir,* 145 (1988): 188–90.

Bawer, Bruce. "Race and Art: The Career of James Baldwin." *New Criterion* 10, 3 (1991): 16–26.

———. "Race and Art: James Baldwin." In *The Aspect of Eternity,* 17–35. Saint Paul: Graywolf Press, 1993.

Bieganowski, Ronald. "James Baldwin's Vision of Otherness in 'Sonny's Blues' and *Giovanni's Room.*" *College Language Association Journal* 32, 1 (1988): 69–80.

Bobia, Rosa. "L'Orniere de James Baldwin en France." *Temps modernes,* 485 (1986): 207–13.

Brown, Joseph A. "I, John, Saw the Holy Number: Apocalyptic Visions in *Go Tell It on the Mountain* and *Native Son.*" *Religion and Literature* 27, 1 (1995): 53–74.

Bruck, Peter. "Dungeon and Salvation: Biblical Rhetoric in James Baldwin's *Just above My Head.*" In *History and Tradition in Afro-American Culture,* 130–46. Edited by Gunter H. Lenz. Frankfurt: Campus, 1984.

Callahan, John F. "'A Long Way from Home': The Art and Protest of Claude McKay and James Baldwin." *Contemporary Literature* 34, 4 (1993): 767–76.

Clark, Michael. "James Baldwin's 'Sonny's Blues': Childhood Light and Art." *College Language Association Journal* 29, 2 (1985): 197–205.

Cohen, William A. "Liberalism, Libido, Liberation: Baldwin's *Another Country.*" *Genders* 12 (1991): 1–21.

Collier, Eugenia. "Baldwin's Plays: A Criticism of the Critics." *MAWA Review* 5, 2 (1990): 29–34.

Colombo, Furio. "E per James Baldwin silenzio e imbarazzo." *La stampa* 14, 459 (1988): 3.

Conger, Lesley. "Jimmy on the East Side." *African American Review* 29, 4 (1995): 557–66.

Cooper, Grace C. "Baldwin's Language: Reflection of African Roots." *MAWA Review* 5, 2 (1990): 40–45.

Courage, Richard A. "James Baldwin's *Go Tell It on the Mountain*: Voices of People." *College Language Association Journal* 32, 4 (1989): 410–25.

Cunningham, James. "Public and Private Rhetorical Modes in the Essays of James Baldwin." In *Essays on the Essay: Redefining the Genre,* 192–204. Athens: University of Georgia Press, 1989.

DeGout, Yasmin Y. "Dividing the Mind: Contradictory Portraits of Homoerotic Love in *Giovanni's Room.*" *African American Review* 26, 3 (1992): 425–35.

Dixon, Melvin. "Rocks Gonna Cry Out: James Baldwin." In *Ride Out the Wilderness: Geography and Identity in Afro-American Literature*, 123–40. Urbana: University of Illinois Press, 1987.

Ezenwa, Ohaeto. "Notions and Nuances: Africa in the Works of James Baldwin." In *Of Dreams Deferred, Dead or Alive: African Perspectives on African-American Writers*, 107–14. Edited by Ade Femi Ojo. Westport, Conn.: Greenwood Press, 1996.

Florence, Alexis. "A Tribute/Hommage." *Présence africaine: Revue culturelle du monde noir*, 145 (1988): 182–87.

Frontain, Raymond Jean. "James Baldwin's *Giovanni's Room* and the Biblical Myth of David." *CEA-Critic* 57, 2 (1995): 41–87.

Fryer, Sarah Beebe. "Retreat from Experience: Despair and Suicide in James Baldwin's Novels." *Journal of the Midwest Modern Language Association* 19, 1 (1986): 21–28.

Gates, Henry Louis, Jr. "The Welcome Table: Essays from the Fiftieth Anniversary of the English Institute." In *English Inside and Out: The Places of Literary Criticism*, 47–60. Edited by Susan Gubar and Jonathan Kamholtz. New York: Routledge, 1993.

Hakutani, Yoshinobu. "If the Street Could Talk: James Baldwin's Search for Love and Understanding." In *The City in African-American Literature*, 150–67. Edited by Yoshinobu Hakutani and Robert Butler. Madison, N.J.: Fairleigh Dickinson University Press, 1995.

Halasz, Laszlo. "Affective Structural Effect and the Characters' Perception in Reception of Short Stories: An American-Hungarian Cross-Cultural Study." *Poetics: International Review for the Theory of Literature* 17, 4–5 (1988): 417–38.

Henderson, Carol. "Knee Bent, Body Bowed: Re-Memory's Prayer of Spiritual Re(new)al in Baldwin's *Go Tell It on the Mountain.*" *Religion and Literature* 27, 1 (1995): 75–88.

Hernton, Calvin C. "James Baldwin: Dialogue and Vision." In *American Writing Today*, 245–53. Edited by Richard Kostelanetz. Troy, N.Y.: Whitston, 1991.

Holmes, Carolyn L. "Reassessing African American Literature through an Afrocentric Paradigm: Zora N. Hurston and James Baldwin." In

Language and Literature in the African American Imagination, 36–51. Edited by Carol Aisha Backshire-Belay. Westport, Conn.: Greenwood Press, 1992.

Kubitschek, Missy Dehn. "Subjugated Knowledge: Toward a Feminist Exploration of Rape in Afro-American Fiction." In *Black Feminist Criticism and Critical Theory*, 43–56. Edited by Houston A. Baker, Jr., and Joe Weixlmann. Greenwood, Fl.: Penkevill, 1988.

Kunda, Tony. "Tributes to James Baldwin." *Présence africaine: Revue culturelle du monde noir*, 145 (1988): 181–95.

Lee, Robert A."Self-Inscriptions: James Baldwin, Tomás Rivera, Gerald Vizenor, and Amy Tan and the Writing-in of America's Non-European Ethnicities." In *A Permanent Etcetera: Cross-Cultural Perspectives on Post-War America*, 20–42. Edited by Robert A. Lee. London: Pluto, 1993.

Lynch, Michael F. "Beyond Guilt and Innocence: Redemptive Suffering and Love in Baldwin's *Another Country.*" *Obsidian II* 7, 1–2 (1992): 1–18.

———. "The Everlasting Father: Mythic Quest and Rebellion in Baldwin's *Go Tell It on the Mountain.*" *College Language Association Journal* 37, 2 (1993): 156–75.

Marquez, Roberto. "One Boricua's Baldwin: A Personal Remembrance." *American Quarterly* 42, 3 (1990): 456–77.

McCarthy, Mary. "A Memory of James Baldwin." *New York Review of Books* 36, 7 (1989): 48–49.

Mengay, Donald H. "The Failed Copy: *Giovanni's Room* and the (Re)Contextualization of Difference." *Genders* 17 (1993): 59–70.

Menke, Pamela Glenn. "'Hard Glass Mirrors' and Soul Memory: Vision Imagery and Gender in Ellison, Baldwin, Morrison, and Walker." *West Virginia University Philological Paper* 38 (1992): 163–70.

Mooty, Maria K. "Baldwin's *Go Tell It on the Mountain.*" *Explicator* 43, 2 (1985): 50–52.

Murphy, Geraldine. "Subversive Anti-Stalinism: Race and Sexuality in the Early Essays of James Baldwin." *ELH* 63, 4 (1996): 1021–46.

Nagpal, B. R. "Baldwin's Black Vision: The Beyond." *Panjab University Research Bulletin (Arts).* 20, 1 (1989): 75–79.

Nash, Julie. "'A Terrifying Sacrament': James Baldwin's Use of Music in *Just above My Head.*" *MAWA Review* 7, 2 (1992): 107–11.

402 JEFFREY W. HOLE

Nelson, Emmanuel S. "Continents of Desire: James Baldwin and the Pleasures of Homosexual Exile." *James White Review* 13, 4 (1996): 8, 16.

———. "Critical Deviance: Homophobia and the Reception of James Baldwin's Fiction." *Journal of American Culture* 14, 3 (1991): 91–96.

———. "James Baldwin (1924–1987)." In *Contemporary Gay American Novelists: A Bio-Bibliographical Critical Sourcebook*, 6–24. Edited by Emmanuel Nelson. Westport, Conn.: Greenwood Press, 1993.

———. "The Novels of James Baldwin: Struggles of Self-Acceptance." *Journal of American Culture* 8, 4 (1985): 11–16.

Nichols, Lee. "In Memoriam: James Baldwin: Achebe and Baldwin: The 1980 ALA Dialogue." *African Literature Association Bulletin* 14, 1 (1988): 2–6.

Ogbaa, Kalu. "Protest and the Individual Talents of Three Black Novelists." *College Language Association Journal* 35, 2 (1991): 159–84.

Onyeberechi, Sydney. "Satiric Candor in *The Fire Next Time*." *MAWA Review* 5, 2 (1990): 46–50.

Pemberton, Gayle. "A Sentimental Journey: James Baldwin and the Thomas-Hill Hearings." In *Racing Justice, Engendering Power: Essays on Anita Hill, Clarence Thomas, and the Construction of Social Reality*, 172–99. Edited by Toni Morrison. New York: Pantheon, 1992.

Phillips, Carly. "A Good Man and an Honest Writer." *Presence Africaine: Revue culturelle du monde noir*, 145 (1988): 191–92.

Reid-Pharr, Robert F. "Tearing the Goat's Flesh: Homosexuality, Abjection and the Production of a Late Twentieth-Century Black Masculinity." *Studies in the Novel* 28, 3 (1996): 372–94.

Robbins, Susan. "Anguish and Anger." *Virginia English Bulletin* 36, 2 (1986): 59–61.

Robertson, Patricia. "Baldwin's 'Sonny's Blues': The Scapegoat Metaphor." *University of Mississippi Studies in English* 9 (1991): 189–98.

Rohy, Valerie. "Displacing Desire: Passing, Nostalgia, and 'Giovanni's Room.'" In *Passing and Fictions of Identity*, 218–33. Edited by Elaine Ginsberg. Durham: Duke University Press, 1996.

Rosenshield, Gary. "Music and Melancholy: Chekhov's 'Rothschild's Fiddle' and Baldwin's 'Sonny's Blues.'" In *Madness, Melancholy, and the Limits of the Self: Studies in Culture, Law, and the Sacred*, 122–34. Edited by Andrew D. Weiner and Leonard V. Kaplan. Madison: University of Wisconsin Law School, 1996.

Rowden, Terry. "A Play of Abstractions: Race, Sexuality, and Community in James Baldwin's *Another Country.*" *Southern Review* 29, 1 (1993): 41–50.

Savery, Pancho. "Baldwin, Bebop, and 'Sonny's Blues.'" In *Understanding Others: Cultural and Cross-Cultural Studies and the Teaching of Literature,* 165–76. Edited by Joseph Trimmer and Tilly Warnock. Urbana, Ill.: National Council of Teachers of English, 1992.

Savoy, Eric. "Other(ed) Americans in Paris: Henry James, James Baldwin, and the Subversion of Identity." *English Studies in Canada* 18, 3 (1992): 335–46.

Scott, Linda Jo. "James Baldwin and the Moveable Feast." *Michigan Academician* 24, 2 (1992): 401–8.

Searles, George J. "An Authorial Miscue in James Baldwin's *Tell Me How Long the Train's Been Gone.*" *ANQ* 6, 1 (1993): 27–28.

Spurlin, William J. "Rhetorical Hermeneutics and Gay Identity Politics: Rethinking American Cultural Studies." In *Reconceptualizing American Literary/Cultural Studies: Rhetoric, History, and Politics in the Humanities,* 169–83. Edited by William E. Cain. New York: Garland, 1996.

Standley, Fred L. "'But the City Was Real': James Baldwin's Literary Milieu." In *The City in African-American Literature,* 138–49. Edited by Yoshinobu Hakutani and Robert Butler. Madison, N.J.: Fairleigh Dickinson University Press, 1995.

Thelwell, Ekwueme Michael. "A Prophet Is Not Without Honor." *Transition: An International Review* 58 (1992): 90–113.

Thompson, Thelma B. "Romantic Idealists and Conforming Materialists: Expression of the American National Character." *MAWA Review* 3, 1 (1988): 6–9.

Tsomondo, Thorell. "No Other Tale to Tell: 'Sonny's Blues' and *Waiting for the Rain.*" *Critique: Studies in Contemporary Fiction* 36, 3 (1995): 195–209.

Urban, Isabel. "James Baldwin in Switzerland: 'Stranger in the Village.'" In *Images of Central Europe in Travelogues and Fiction by North American Writers,* 242–48. Edited by Waldemar Zacharasiewicz. Tübingen: Stauffenburg, 1995.

Waldrep, Shelton. "'Being Bridges': Cleaver/Baldwin/Lorde and African-American Sexism and Sexuality." In *Critical Essays: Gay and Lesbian Writers of Color,* 167–80. Edited by Emmanuel Nelson. New York: Haworth, 1993.

Warren, Nagueyalti. "The Substance of Things Hoped For: Faith in *Go Tell It on the Mountain* and *Just above My Head*. *Obsidian II* 7, 1–2 (1992): 19–32.

Wood, Joe. "Witness for the Persecution: James Baldwin in Black and White." *Village Voice Literature Supplement* 76 (1989): 14–16.

Wyler, Siegfried. "An Essay on Colour and James Baldwin's Novel *Another Country*." *Der gesunde Gelehrte: Literatur, Sprach und Rezeptionzanalysen*, 243–58. Edited by Armin Arnold and Stephen Jaeger. Herisau: Schlapfer, 1987.

Dissertations on the Works of James Baldwin Since 1985

Applegate, Nancy Paula. "Significant Others: Images of Whites and Whiteness in the Works of African American Writers." Florida State University, 1994.

Auger, Philip George. "ReWrighting Afro-American Manhood: Negotiations of Discursive Space in the Fiction of James Baldwin, Alice Walker, John Edgar Wideman, and Ernest Gaines." University of Rhode Island, 1995.

Balfour, Katharine Lawrence. "Political Theory." Princeton University, 1996.

Baylor, Cherry Revona. "James Baldwin and the Fall of Man." Columbia University Teachers College, 1985.

Carroll, Michael Charles. "Music as Medium for Maturation in Three Afro-American Novels." University of Nebraska, Lincoln, 1991.

Cataliotti, Robert Henry. "The Words to the Song: Representing Music in African American Fiction." State University of New York at Stony Brook, 1993.

Clark, Keith Spencer. "Reforming the Black Male Self: A Study of Subject Formation in Selected Works by James Baldwin, Ernest Gaines, and August Wilson." University of North Carolina at Chapel Hill, 1993.

Dievler, James Anthony. "Sexual Exiles: Edith Wharton, Henry Miller, James Baldwin and the Culture of Sex and Sexuality in New York City." New York University, 1997.

Dudley, David Lewis. "'The Trouble I've Seen': Visions and Revisions of Bondage, Flight, and Freedom in Black American Autobiography." Louisiana State University and Agricultural and Mechanical College, 1988.

Eisner, Douglass J. "The Homophile Difference: Pathological Discourse and Communal Identity in Early Gay Novels." University of California, Riverside, 1996.

Ferebee, Floyd Clifton. "The Relationship between Violence and Christianity in the Novels of James Baldwin." University of Cincinnati, 1995.

Henderson, Carol E. "The Body of Evidence—Reading the Scar as Text: Williams, Morrison, Baldwin, and Petrys." University of California, Riverside, 1995.

Hendrickson, Roberta Makashay. "The Civil Rights Movement in American Fiction: A Feminist Reading." Brandeis University, 1990.

Henson, Leslie June. "From Abjection to Coalition: Sexual Subjectivities and Identity Politics in Twentieth-Century Lesbian and Gay Novels." University of Florida, 1996.

Hill, Daniel A. "On Display: The Celebrity Self in Contemporary American Nonfiction." Rutgers University, New Brunswick, 1991.

Hollis, Christopher Wayne. "Artist to Spokesperson: The Rise and Fall of James Baldwin as Essayist." University of Louisville, 1995.

Hubbard, Dolan. "Preaching the Lord's Word in a Strange Land: The Influence of the Black Preaching Style on Black American Prose Fiction." University of Illinois at Urbana–Champaign, 1986.

Hurd, Myles Raymond. "Rhetoric versus Eloquence in the Afro-American Double Narrative: Perspectives on Audience, and Ambiguity." City University of New York, 1985.

Jennings, La Vinia Delois. "Sexual Violence in the Works of Richard Wright, James Baldwin, and Toni Morrison." University of North Carolina at Chapel Hill, 1989.

Johnson, Cyraine E. "The Writing of Exile: Configurations of Romantic Value in the Modern Novel." State University of New York, Buffalo, 1993.

Johnson, Gerald Byron. "Baldwin's Androgynous Blues: African American Music, Androgyny, and the Novels of James Baldwin." Cornell University, 1993.

Jones, Jacqueline Carlissa. "His Tale to Tale: James Baldwin and the Artist as a Hero in Fiction." City University of New York, 1996.

Manglitz, Lawrence William. "The Homosexual Narrative as Opposition to Hegemonic Inscription: Reinscription of the Homosexual Body in Edmund White's 'A Boy's Own Story,' James Baldwin's 'Giovanni's Room,' and Melvin Dixon's 'Vanishing Room.'" Michigan State University, 1994.

Mayne, Heather Joy. "Biblical Paradigms in Four Twentieth Century African-American Novels." Stanford University, 1991.

Moon, Sahng Young. "The Dilemma of a Black Writer: James Baldwin's Quest for Racial Justice in the 1960s." University of California, San Diego, 1994.

Muñoz, José E. "Disidentifications." Duke University, 1995.

Panish, Jon Seebart. "The Color of Jazz: Race Representation in American Culture, 1945–1966." University of California, Irvine, 1994.

Ramm, Hans-Christoph. "Model für eine literarische Amerikakunde: Zugange zum modernen Schwarz-Amerikanischen Roman am Beispiel von Ann Petry's *The Street*, James Baldwin's *Go Tell It on the Mountain* und Ralph Ellison's *Invisible Man*." Universität Frankfurt am Main, 1988.

Rusk, Lauren. "Three-Way Mirrors: The Life Writing of Otherness." Stanford University, 1995.

Schnapp, Patricia Lorine. "The Liberation Theology of James Baldwin." Bowling Green State University, 1987.

Schwartz, Gregory A. "*Comedy Night* and Contextual Essay: What Is the Impact of a Political Novel upon the Reader?" The Union Institute, 1995.

Simawe, Saadi A. "Music and the Politics of Culture in James Baldwin's and Alice Walker's Fiction." University of Iowa, 1994.

Smith, Kenneth Alan. "Contesting Discourses in the Essays of Virginia Woolf, James Baldwin, Joan Didion, and E. B. White." University of Iowa, 1992.

Sohn, Hongeal. "Literature and Society: African-American Drama and American Race Relations." University of Iowa, 1993.

Taylor, Charles Lavalle, III. "Figurations of the Family in Fiction by Toni Morrison, John Updike, James Baldwin, and Philip Roth." University of Michigan, 1996.

Timberlake, Jean. "'Examined, Cracked, Changed, Made New': Conversations, Themes and Structures in American Short Fiction." University of Cincinnati, 1995.

West, James Stevens. "Bessie Smith: A Study of Her Influence on Selected Works of Langston Hughes, Edward Albee, Sherley Anne Williams, and James Baldwin." University of Southern Mississippi, 1995.

Young, Brenda Joyce. "Baldwin and Hansberry as 'Privileged Speakers': Two Black Writers and the Civil Rights Movement, 1955–1965." Emory University, 1996.

Books on James Baldwin and His Work Since 1985

Bloom, Harold, ed. *James Baldwin*. New York: Chelsea House, 1986.

Bobia, Rosa. *The Critical Reception of James Baldwin in France*. New York: Peter Lang, 1997.

Campbell, James. *Exiled in Paris: Richard Wright, James Baldwin, Samuel Beckett and Others on the Left Bank*. New York: Simon & Schuster, 1995.

———. *Talking at the Gates: A Life of James Baldwin*. New York: Viking, 1992.

Chametzky, Jules, ed. *Black Writers Redefine the Struggle: A Tribute to James Baldwin*. Amherst: Institute for Advanced Studies, 1989.

———, ed. *A Tribute to James Baldwin: Black Writers Redefine the Struggle: Proceedings of a Conference at the University of Massachusetts at Amherst, April 22–23, 1988*. Amherst: Institute for Advanced Study in the Humanities: University of Massachusetts Press, 1989.

Champion, Ernest A. *Mr. Baldwin, I Presume: James Baldwin–Chinua Achebe, a Meeting of the Minds*. Lanham, Md.: University Press of America, 1995.

Clark, Kenneth B. *King, Malcolm, Baldwin: Three Interviews*. Middletown, Conn.: Wesleyan University Press, 1985.

Davis, Ursula Broschke. *Paris without Regret: James Baldwin, Kenny Clarke, Chester Himes, and Donald Byrd*. Iowa City: University of Iowa Press, 1986.

Gounard, Jean-François. *The Racial Problem in the Works of Richard Wright and James Baldwin*. Translated by Joseph J. Rodgers, Jr. Westport, Conn.: Greenwood Press, 1992.

Harris, Trudier. *Black Women in the Fiction of James Baldwin*. Knoxville: University of Tennessee Press, 1985.

———, ed. *New Essays on* Go Tell It on the Mountain. Cambridge: Cambridge University Press, 1996.

Jothiprakash, R. *Commitment as a Theme in African American Literature: A Study of James Baldwin and Ralph Ellison*. Bristol: Wyndam, 1994.

Kollhofer, Jakob, ed. *James Baldwin: His Place in American Literary History and His Reception in Europe*. Frankfurt: Peter Lang, 1991.

Lee, Robert A. *James Baldwin: Climbing to the Light*. New York: St. Martin's Press, 1991.

Leeming, David Adams. *James Baldwin: A Biography*. New York: Alfred A. Knopf, 1994.

Middle Atlantic Writers' Association. *James Baldwin, in Memoriam: Proceedings of the Annual Conference of the Middle Atlantic Writers' Association, 1989*. Edited by Ralph Reckley. Baltimore: Middle Atlantic Writers' Association Press, 1992.

Porter, Horace. *Stealing the Fire: The Art and Protest of James Baldwin*. Middletown, Conn.: Wesleyan University Press, 1989.

Standley, Fred L., and Nancy V. Burt, eds. *Critical Essays on James Baldwin*. Boston: Hall, 1988.

Standley, Fred L., and Louis H. Pratt, eds. *Conversations with James Baldwin*. Jackson: University Press of Mississippi, 1989.

Troupe, Quincy. *James Baldwin: The Legacy*. New York: Simon & Schuster, 1989.

Washington, Bryan R. *The Politics of Exile: Ideology in Henry James, F. Scott Fitzgerald, and James Baldwin*. Boston: Northeastern University Press, 1995.

Weatherby, William J. *James Baldwin: Artist on Fire*. New York: D. I. Fine, 1989.

Film on James Baldwin Since 1985

Go Tell It on the Mountain. Monterey Movie Company, 1985.

James Baldwin: The Price of the Ticket. Directed by Karen Thorsen. Nobody Knows Productions, 1989.

Juvenile Literature on the Life and Works of James Baldwin Since 1985

Gottfried, Ted. *James Baldwin: Voice from Harlem*. New York: F. Watts, 1997.

Green, Richard L., ed. *A Salute to Historic Blacks in the Arts*. Chicago: Empak, 1989.

Kenan, Randall. *James Baldwin*. Lives of Notable Gay Men and Lesbians. New York: Chelsea House, 1994.

Rosset, Lisa. *James Baldwin*. New York: Chelsea House, 1989.

Tachach, James. *James Baldwin*. San Diego: Lucent Books, 1997.

Contributors

Rebecca Aanerud is acting instructor in English at the University of Washington where she completed her dissertation entitled "Maintaining Comfort, Sustaining Power: Narratives of American White Liberalism." She is also the author of the recently published essay "Fictions of Whiteness: Speaking the Names of Whiteness in U.S. Literature," in *Displacing Whiteness: Essays in Social and Cultural Criticism*, ed. Ruth Frankenberg (Durham: Duke University Press, 1997).

Lawrie Balfour was formerly a fellow in the Center for the Study of Values in Public Life at Harvard Divinity School. She is assistant professor of politics at Babson College and is currently completing a book manuscript titled *The Evidence of Things Not Said: James Baldwin, Race Consciousness, and the Promise of American Democracy*. She received her Ph.D. in politics from Princeton University. Her interests include political theory, Afro-American studies, moral philosophy, and international relations.

Nicholas Boggs is a graduate student in the Department of English and Comparative Literature at Columbia University. A recent graduate of Yale University, his essay in this book is taken from his award-winning senior thesis and treats a little-known children's book by James Baldwin. Boggs was formerly a writer for the *Washington Blade* in Washington, D.C.

James Darsey is associate professor of Communication at Georgia State University. He did his graduate work at Purdue and the University of Chicago and received his Ph.D. from the University of Wisconsin. His book *The Prophetic Tradition and Radical Rhetoric in America* (New York: New York University Press, 1997) was the

1998 recipient of the National Communication Association's Diamond Anniversary Book Award, and his essays have appeared in *Quarterly Journal of Speech, Communication Monographs, Communication Studies,* and the *Western Journal of Communication.* His interests include gay and lesbian studies and radical rhetoric.

James A. Dievler received his Ph.D. in American Studies at New York University. His interests include late-nineteenth- and twentieth-century American literature and post–World War II American culture. His dissertation, which he completed in 1997, is titled "Sexual Exiles: Edith Wharton, Henry Miller, James Baldwin and the Culture of Sex and Sexuality in New York City."

Roderick A. Ferguson is a doctoral candidate in the Department of Sociology at the University of California, San Diego, and is currently working on his dissertation, titled "Call Me by My Name: Race, Sociological Discourse, and the Conflict over Cultural Representation."

Jeffrey W. Hole is a graduate student in the Department of English at the University of Pittsburgh.

Sharon Patricia Holland is assistant professor of English at Stanford University. She is the author of the forthcoming book *Raising the Dead: Death and (Black) Subjectivity in Twentieth Century Literature and Culture* (Durham: Duke University Press). She has also authored numerous essays on race, black lesbian identity, and African American literature in a variety of edited collections and journals, including *Callaloo, Cultural Matrix,* and *LIT.*

Josh Kun is assistant professor of English at the University of California, Riverside. He completed his doctoral work in Ethnic Studies at the University of California, Berkeley, where his dissertation was titled "Strangers among Sounds: Listening, Difference, and the Unmaking of Americans." He has written widely on contemporary music and popular culture and is a freelance journalist whose work has appeared in numerous venues, including *Rolling Stone, Village Voice, Details, Boston Phoenix,* and the *San Francisco Bay Guardian.*

Dwight A. McBride is assistant professor of English at the University of Illinois at Chicago. The recipient of a University of California President's postdoctoral fellowship and of a Mellon research fellowship, he completed his A.B. in English and Afro-American Studies at Princeton University in 1990 and his M.A. and Ph.D. in English at the University of California, Los Angeles, in 1993 and 1996, respectively. He has published essays in the areas of race theory and black cultural studies and is the author of the forthcoming *Impossible Witnesses: Truth, Abolitionism, and Slave Testimony*, also from New York University Press, and is the co-editor of the literature anthology *Black Like Us: A Century of Queer African American Literature*, forthcoming from Clies Press.

Joshua L. Miller is a doctoral candidate in the Department of English and Comparative Literature at Columbia University. His dissertation, "Lingual Politics: The Nationalization of U.S. English, 1919–1948," examines the monolingualization of U.S. cultural citizenship and several multilingual responses.

Marlon B. Ross is associate professor of English and Afro-American and African Studies at the University of Michigan. He is the author of *The Contours of Masculine Desire: Romanticism and the Rise of Women's Poetry* (New York: Oxford University Press, 1989). He is also the author of numerous essays, including "Some Glances at the Black Fag: Same-Sex Desire and the Culture of Belonging," published in 1994 in the *Canadian Review of Comparative Literature*. He is currently at work on a book-length study titled *The Color of Manhood: Racial Imagining and Sexual Politics in the Civil Rights Era*.

Lauren Rusk is a lecturer in the Continuing Studies Program at Stanford University, where she received her doctorate in English. She teaches courses on modern life writing, fiction, and poetry, with emphasis on women's and ethnic literatures. She has published various essays on Maxine Hong Kingston, Virginia Woolf, and Wallace Stevens, as well as her own poems.

William J. Spurlin is a visiting scholar at Columbia University. He has co-edited two books, *The New Criticism and Contemporary Literary Theory: Connections and Continuities*, with Michael Fischer (Garland, 1995), and *Reclaiming the Heartland: Lesbian and Gay Voices from the Midwest*, with Karen Lee Osborne (Minneapolis: University of Minnesota Press, 1996). He is also the author of several articles on critical theory, gay and lesbian studies, and queer theory.

His most recent essay, "Sissies and Sisters: Gender, Sexuality, and the Possibilities of Coalition," appears in *Lesbian and Gay Studies: Coming Out of Feminism?* ed. Elizabeth Wright et al. (Oxford: Blackwell, 1998).

Maurice Wallace is assistant professor of English and African American Studies at Duke University. His book *Constructing the Black Masculine: Identity and Ideality in African American Men's Literature and Culture,* is forthcoming from Duke University Press. His current work is a book-length project titled *Hostile Witness: James Baldwin as Artist and Outlaw.*

Michelle M. Wright is the Estella Loomis McCandless Chair and assistant professor of English at Carnegie Mellon University. She received her Ph.D. in Comparative Literature from the University of Michigan in 1997. Her interests are in postcolonial literature and theory and African diasporic literatures. She has published essays on African American and Afro-German cultural identity and is at work on a book manuscript titled *Missing Persons: The Search for the Postcolonial Subject in the African Atlantic.*

Index